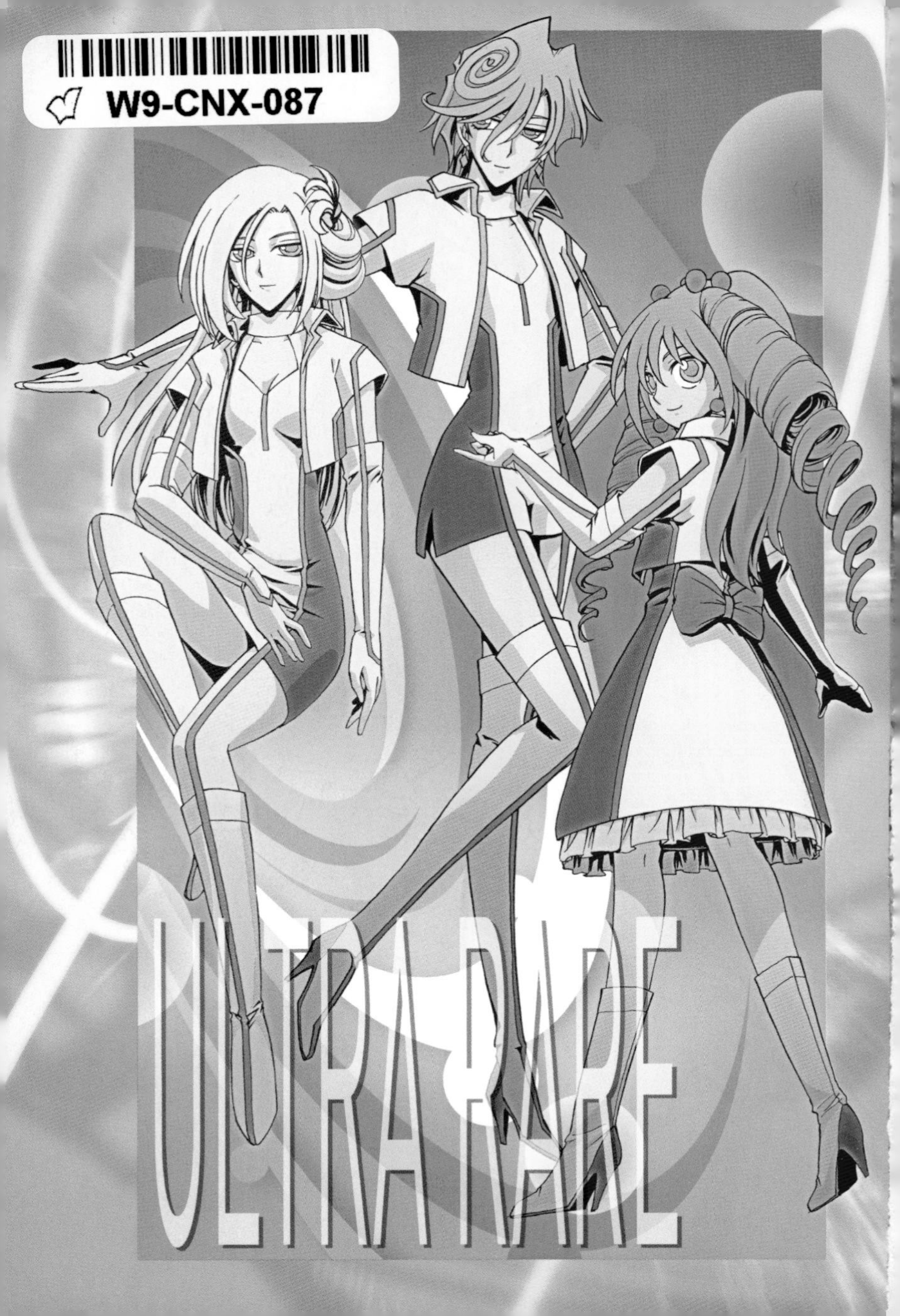
ULTRA RARE

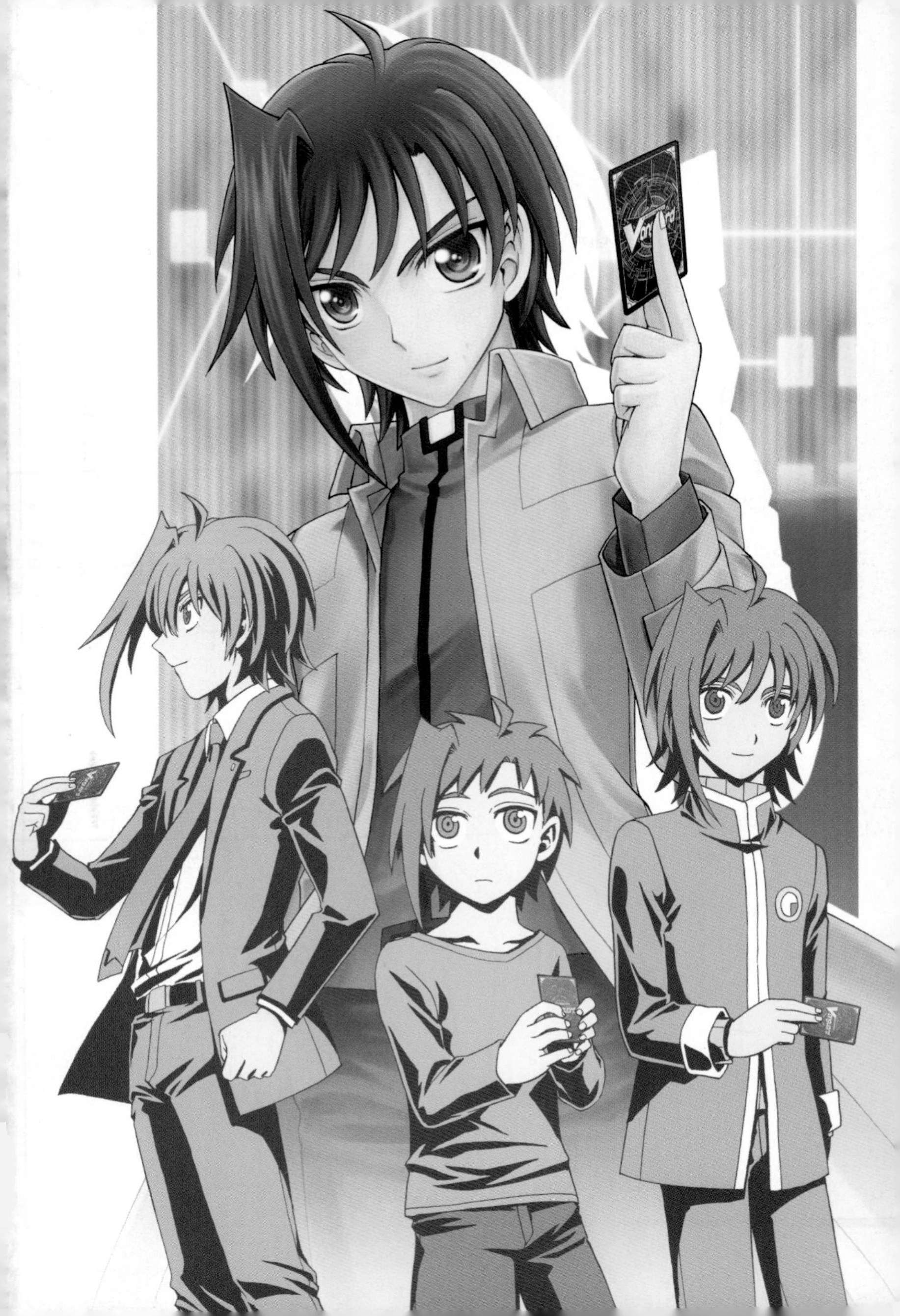

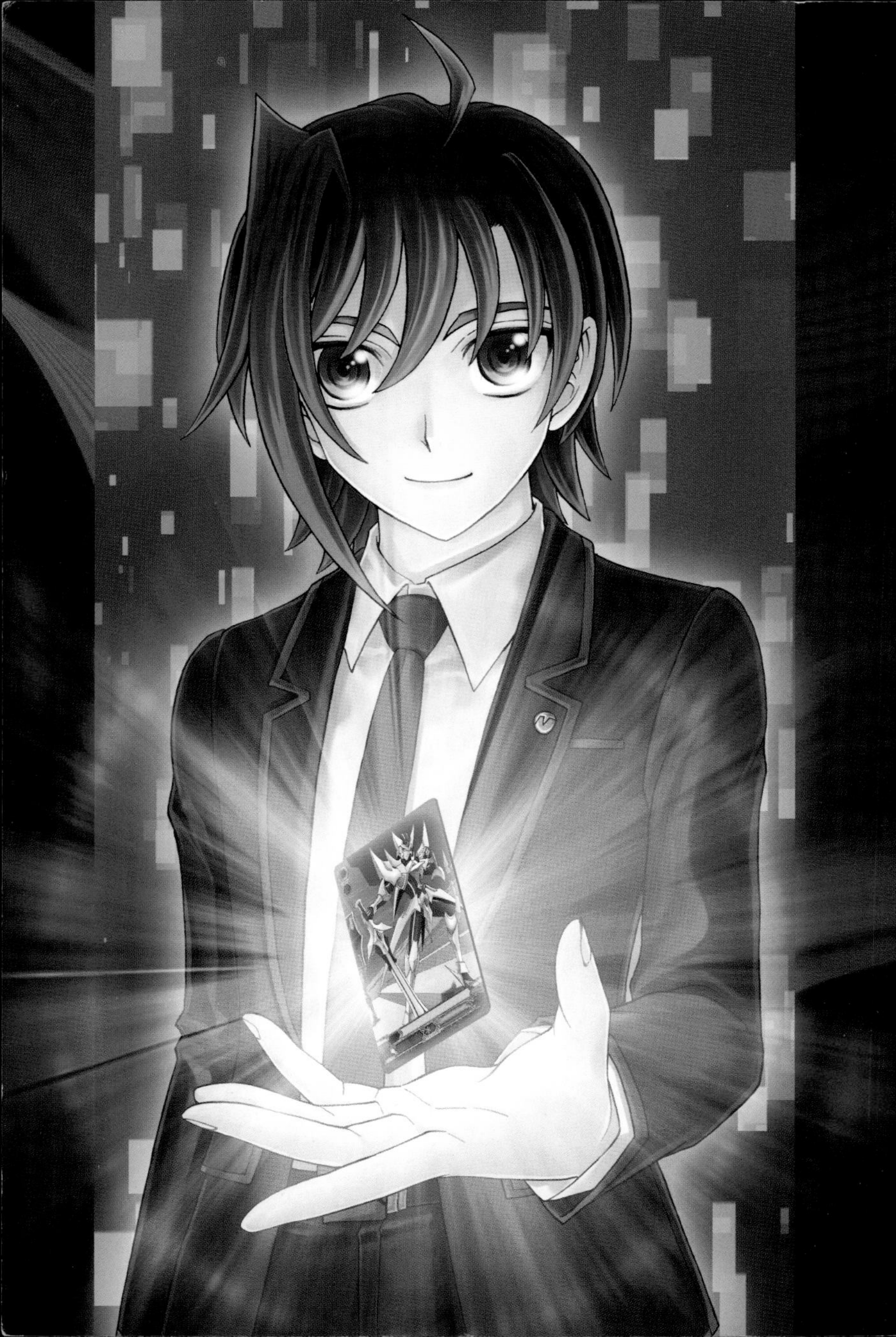

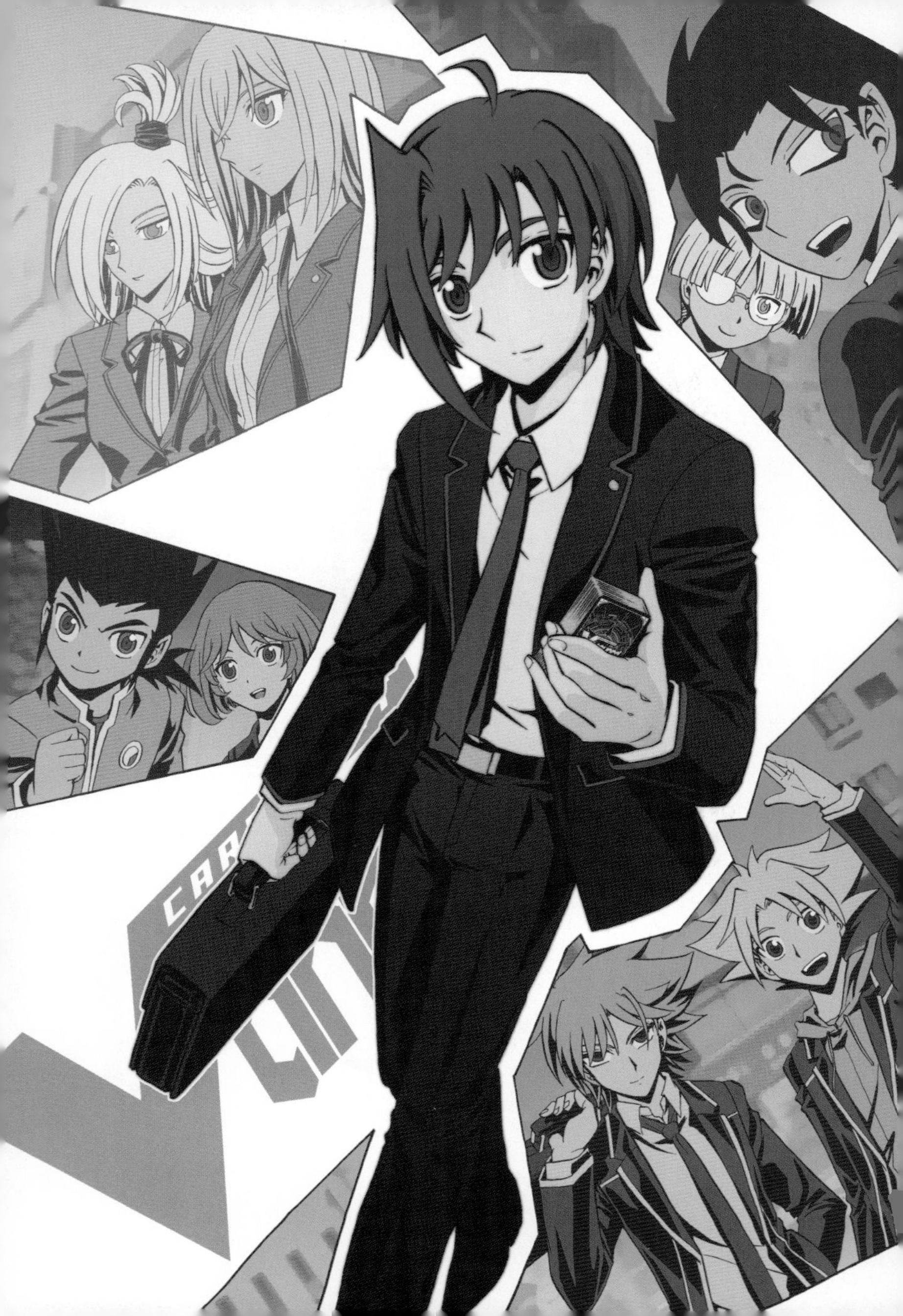

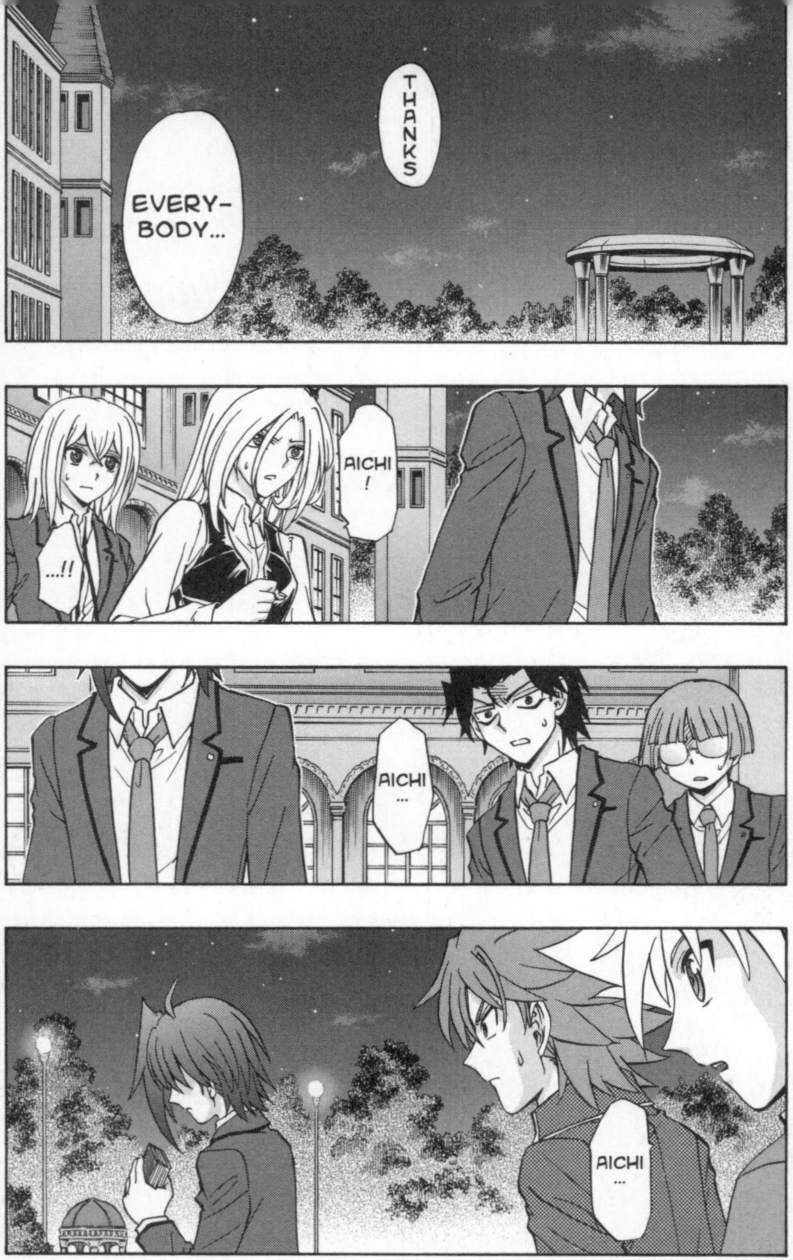
THANKS
EVERY-BODY...
AICHI!
...!!
AICHI...
AICHI...

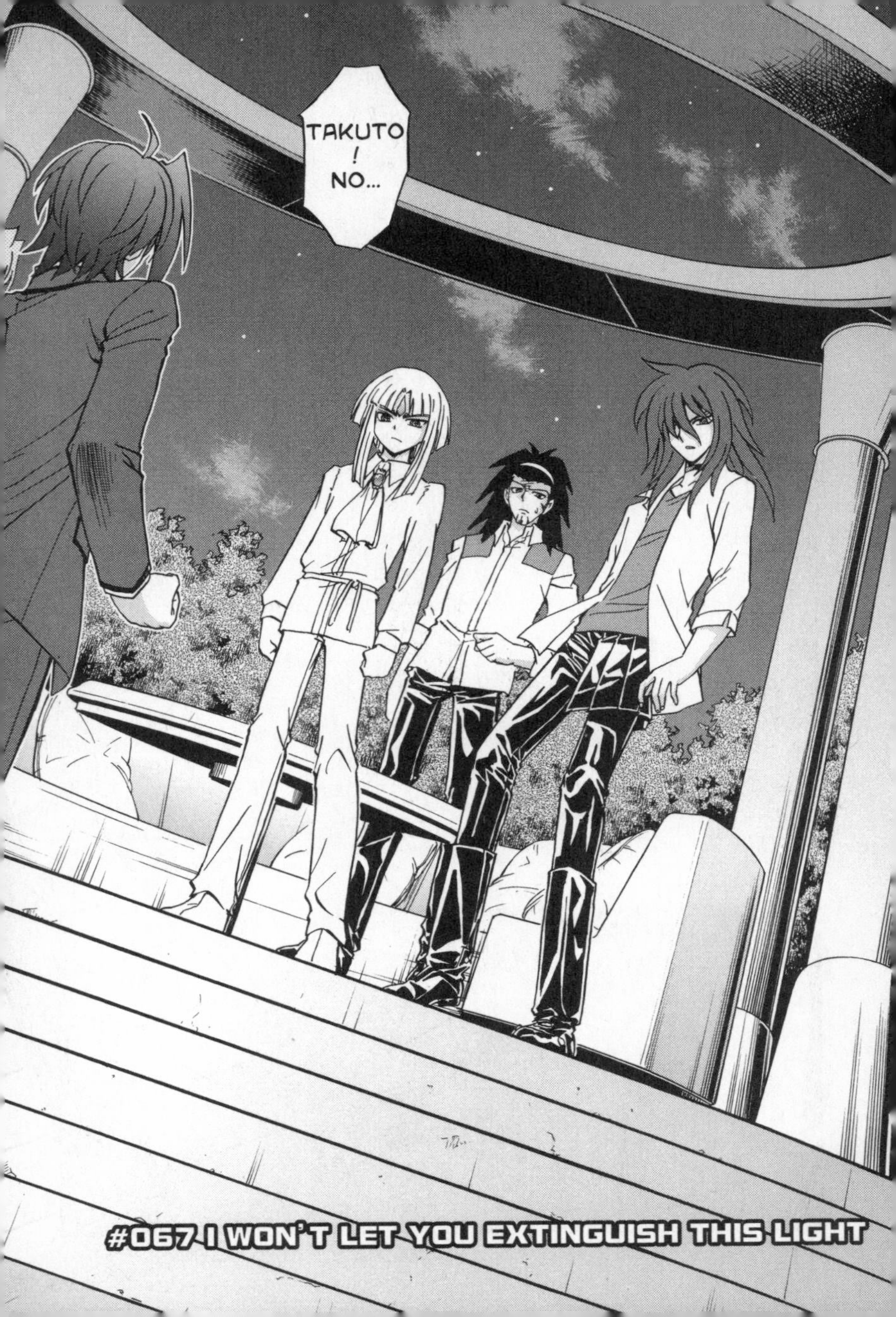
TAKUTO! NO...

#067 I WON'T LET YOU EXTINGUISH THIS LIGHT

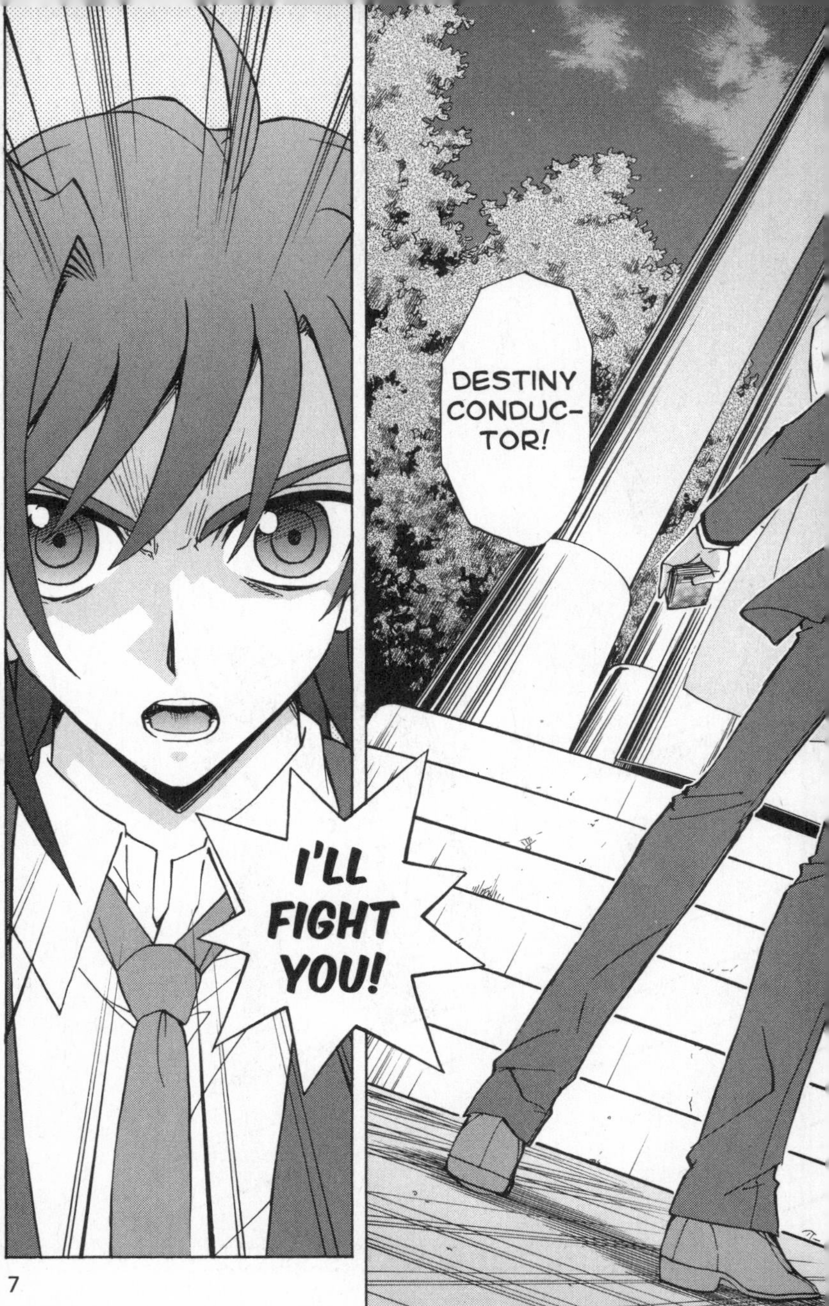
DESTINY CONDUC-TOR!
I'LL FIGHT YOU!

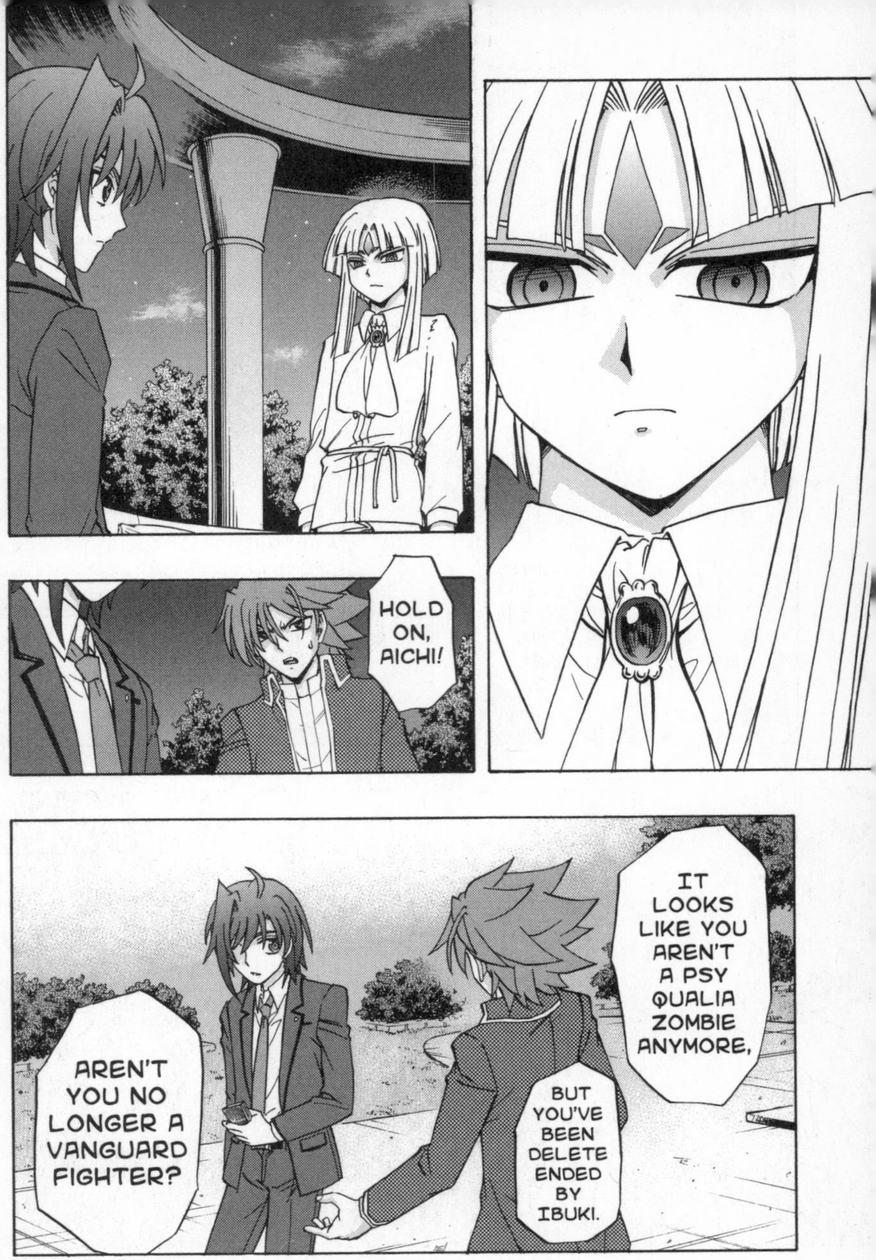
HOLD ON, AICHI!
IT LOOKS LIKE YOU AREN'T A PSY QUALIA ZOMBIE ANYMORE,
BUT YOU'VE BEEN DELETE ENDED BY IBUKI.
AREN'T YOU NO LONGER A VANGUARD FIGHTER?

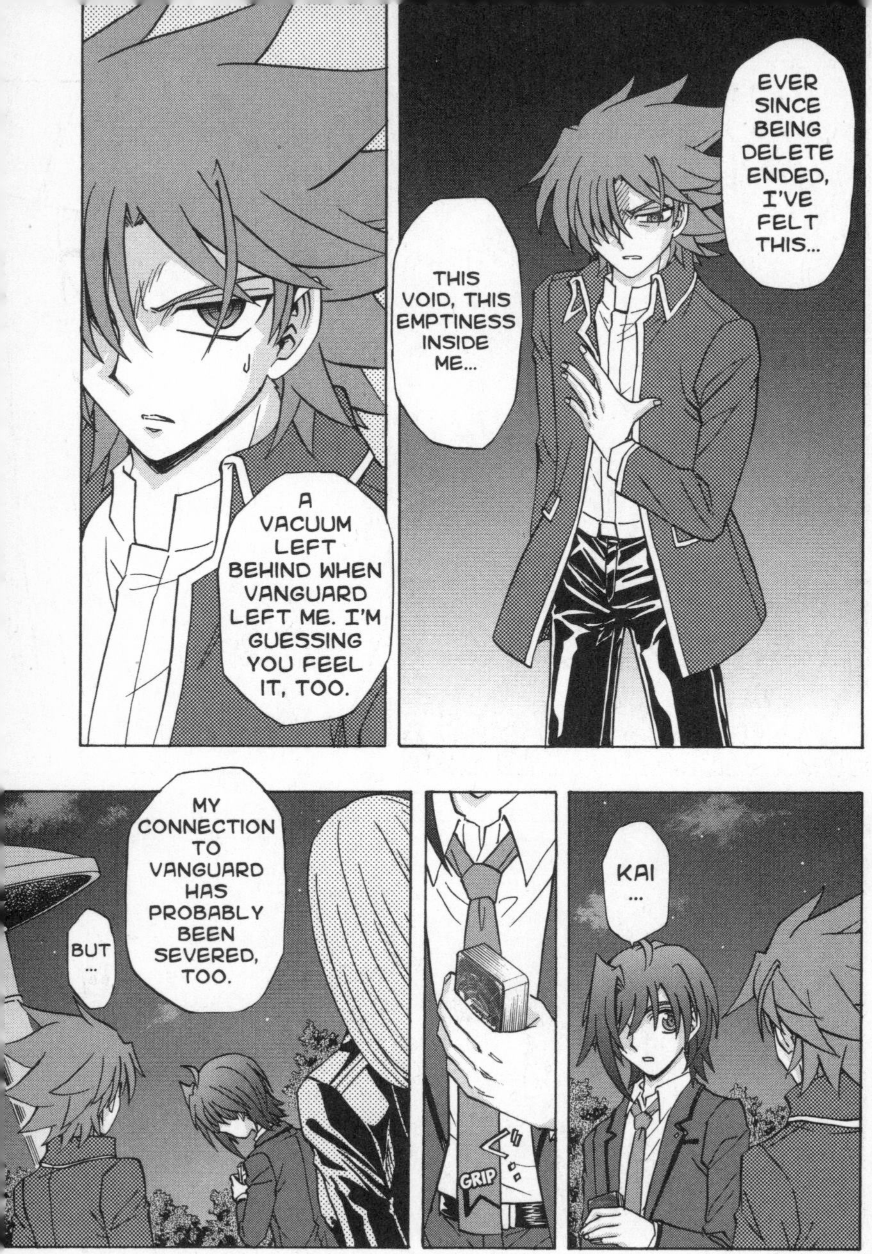
EVER SINCE BEING DELETE ENDED, I'VE FELT THIS...
THIS VOID, THIS EMPTINESS INSIDE ME...
A VACUUM LEFT BEHIND WHEN VANGUARD LEFT ME. I'M GUESSING YOU FEEL IT, TOO.
KAI ...
GRIP
MY CONNECTION TO VANGUARD HAS PROBABLY BEEN SEVERED, TOO.
BUT ...

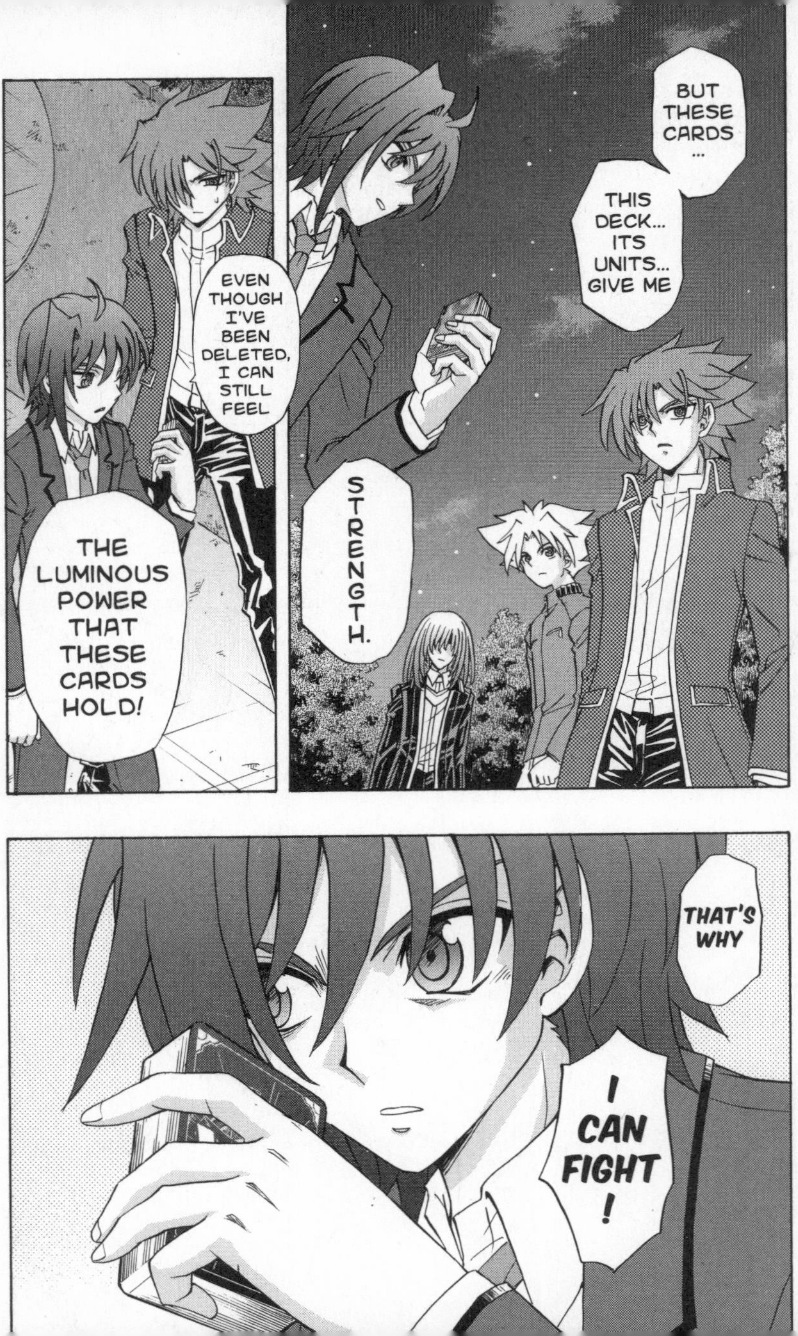
BUT THESE CARDS ...
THIS DECK... ITS UNITS... GIVE ME
STRENGTH.
EVEN THOUGH I'VE BEEN DELETED, I CAN STILL FEEL
THE LUMINOUS POWER THAT THESE CARDS HOLD!
THAT'S WHY
I CAN FIGHT!

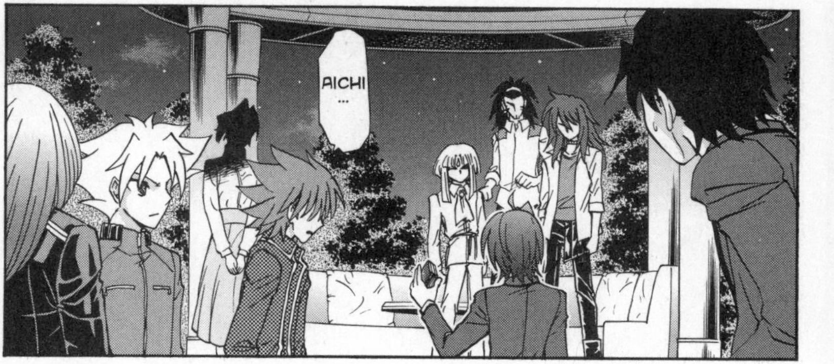
AICHI ...

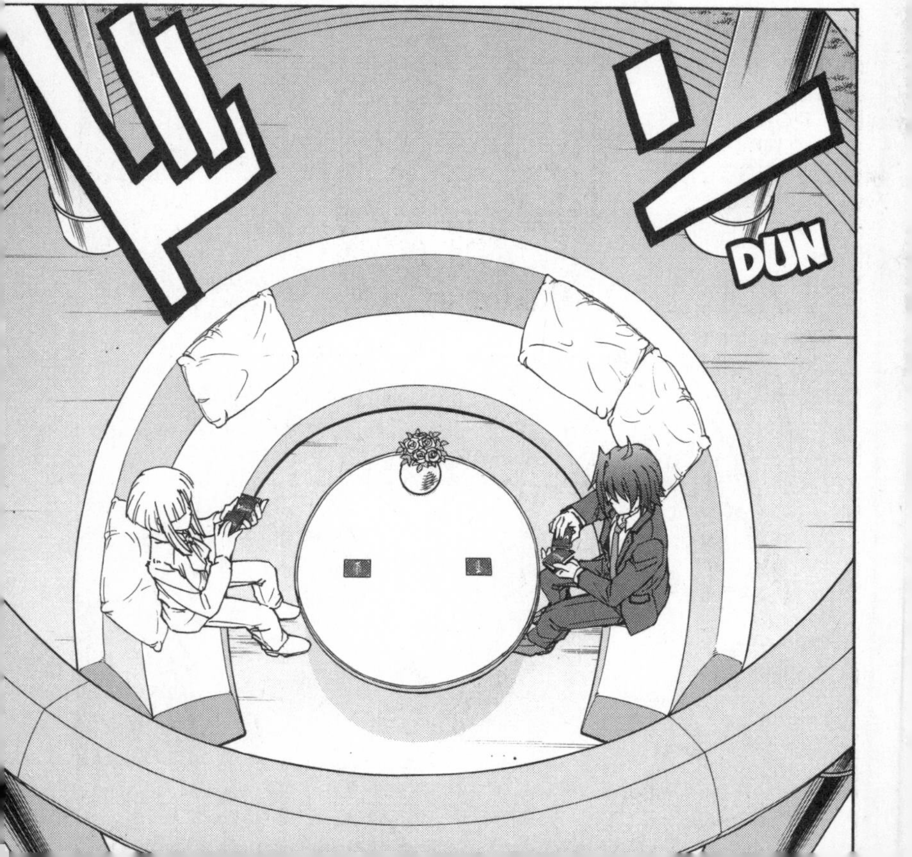
DUN

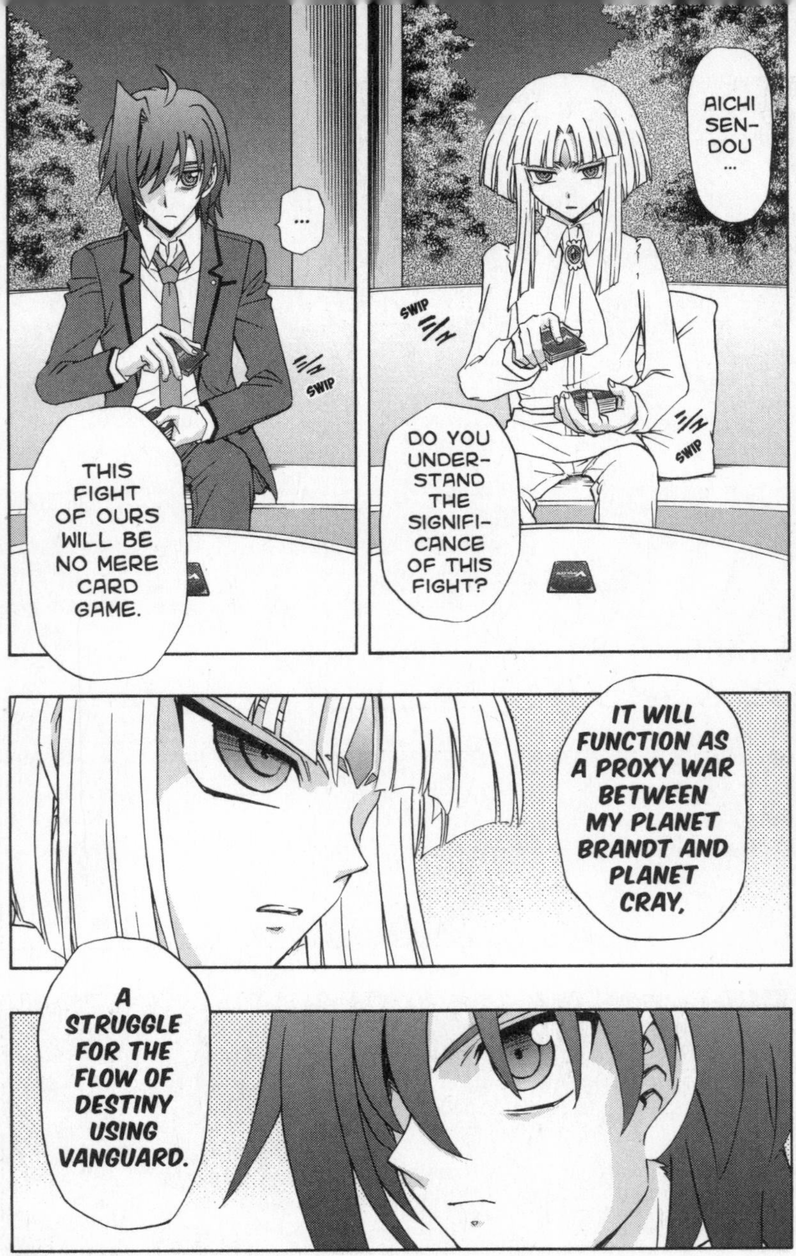
AICHI SEN-DOU ...
SWIP
SWIP
DO YOU UNDER-STAND THE SIGNIFI-CANCE OF THIS FIGHT?
...
SWIP
THIS FIGHT OF OURS WILL BE NO MERE CARD GAME.
IT WILL FUNCTION AS A PROXY WAR BETWEEN MY PLANET BRANDT AND PLANET CRAY,
A STRUGGLE FOR THE FLOW OF DESTINY USING VANGUARD.

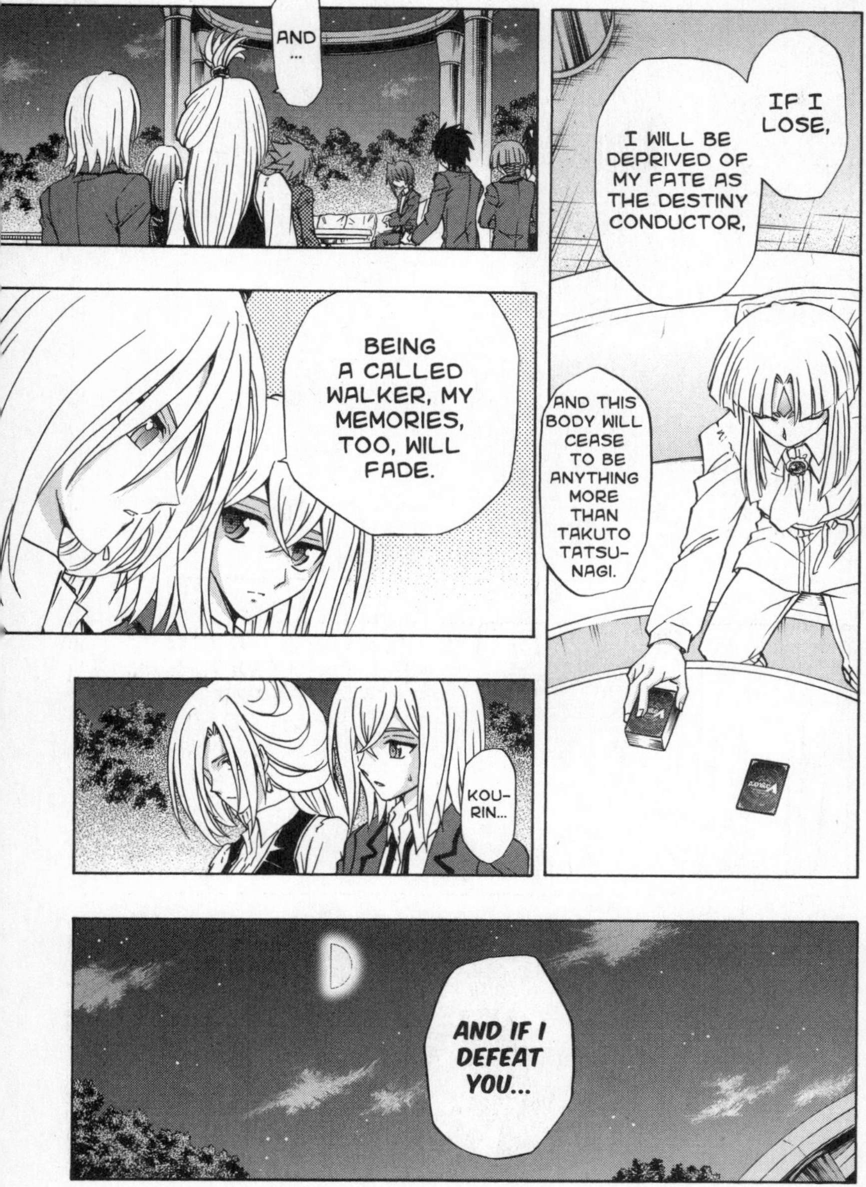

IF I LOSE, I WILL BE DEPRIVED OF MY FATE AS THE DESTINY CONDUCTOR,
AND THIS BODY WILL CEASE TO BE ANYTHING MORE THAN TAKUTO TATSU-NAGI.
AND ...
BEING A CALLED WALKER, MY MEMORIES, TOO, WILL FADE.
KOU-RIN...
AND IF I DEFEAT YOU...

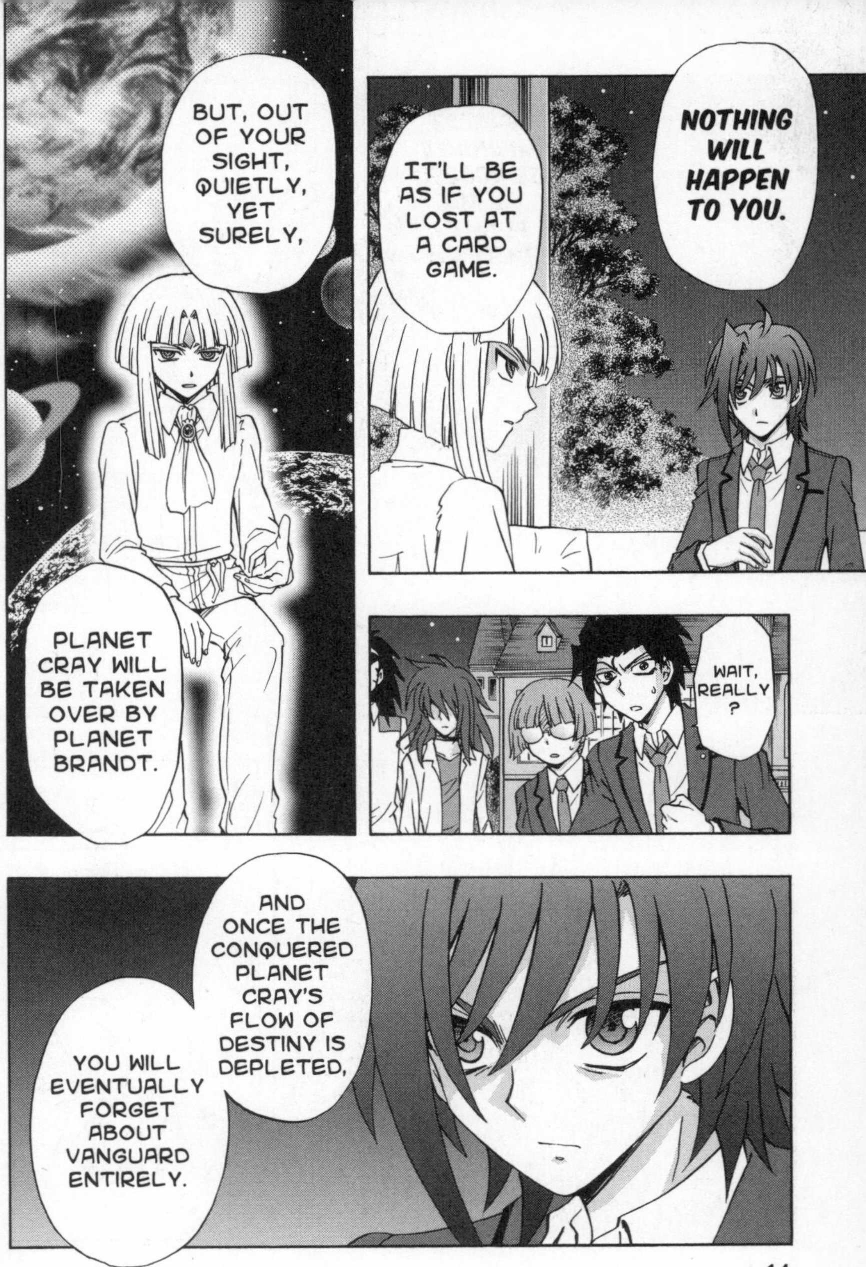
NOTHING WILL HAPPEN TO YOU.
IT'LL BE AS IF YOU LOST AT A CARD GAME.
WAIT, REALLY?
BUT, OUT OF YOUR SIGHT, QUIETLY, YET SURELY,
PLANET CRAY WILL BE TAKEN OVER BY PLANET BRANDT.
AND ONCE THE CONQUERED PLANET CRAY'S FLOW OF DESTINY IS DEPLETED,
YOU WILL EVENTUALLY FORGET ABOUT VANGUARD ENTIRELY.

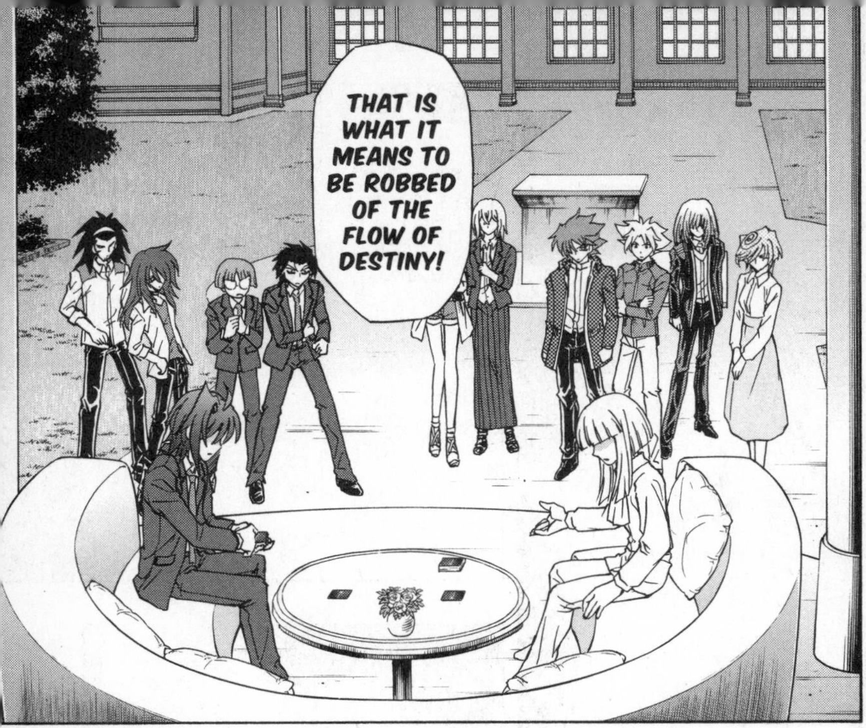
THAT IS WHAT IT MEANS TO BE ROBBED OF THE FLOW OF DESTINY!

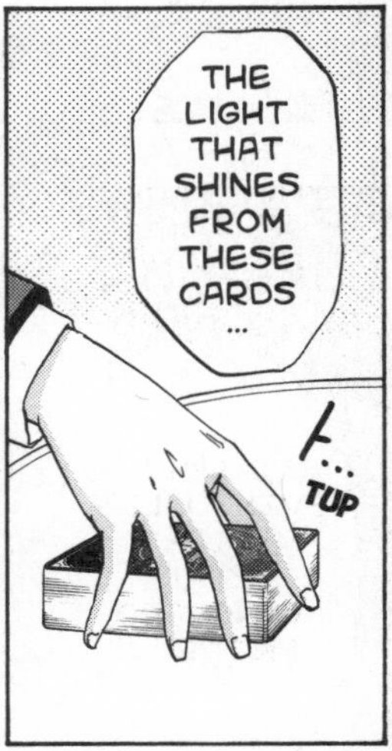
THE LIGHT THAT SHINES FROM THESE CARDS ...
T...
TUP

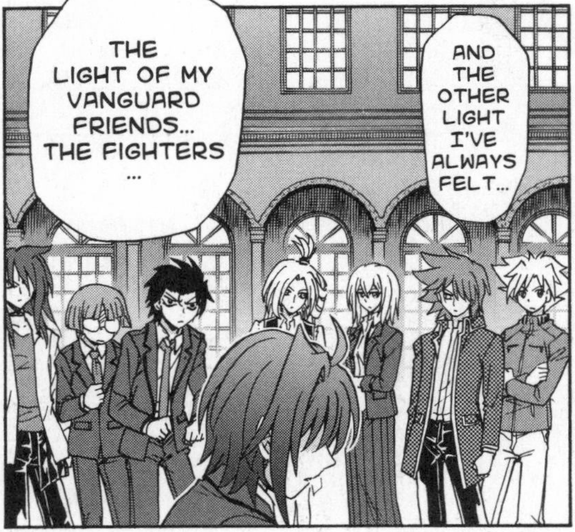
AND THE OTHER LIGHT I'VE ALWAYS FELT...
THE LIGHT OF MY VANGUARD FRIENDS... THE FIGHTERS ...

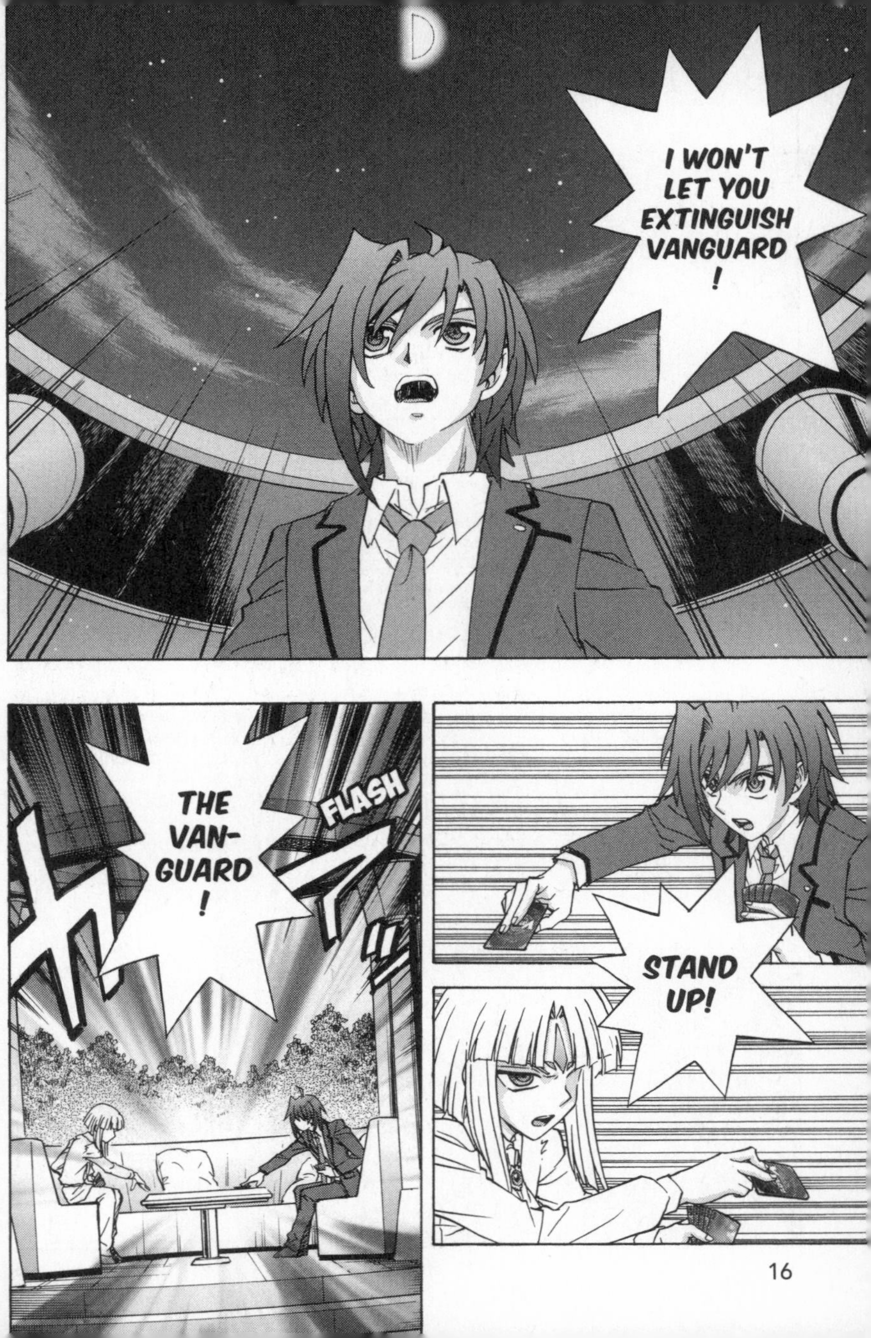
I WON'T LET YOU EXTINGUISH VANGUARD !
STAND UP!
THE VAN-GUARD !
FLASH

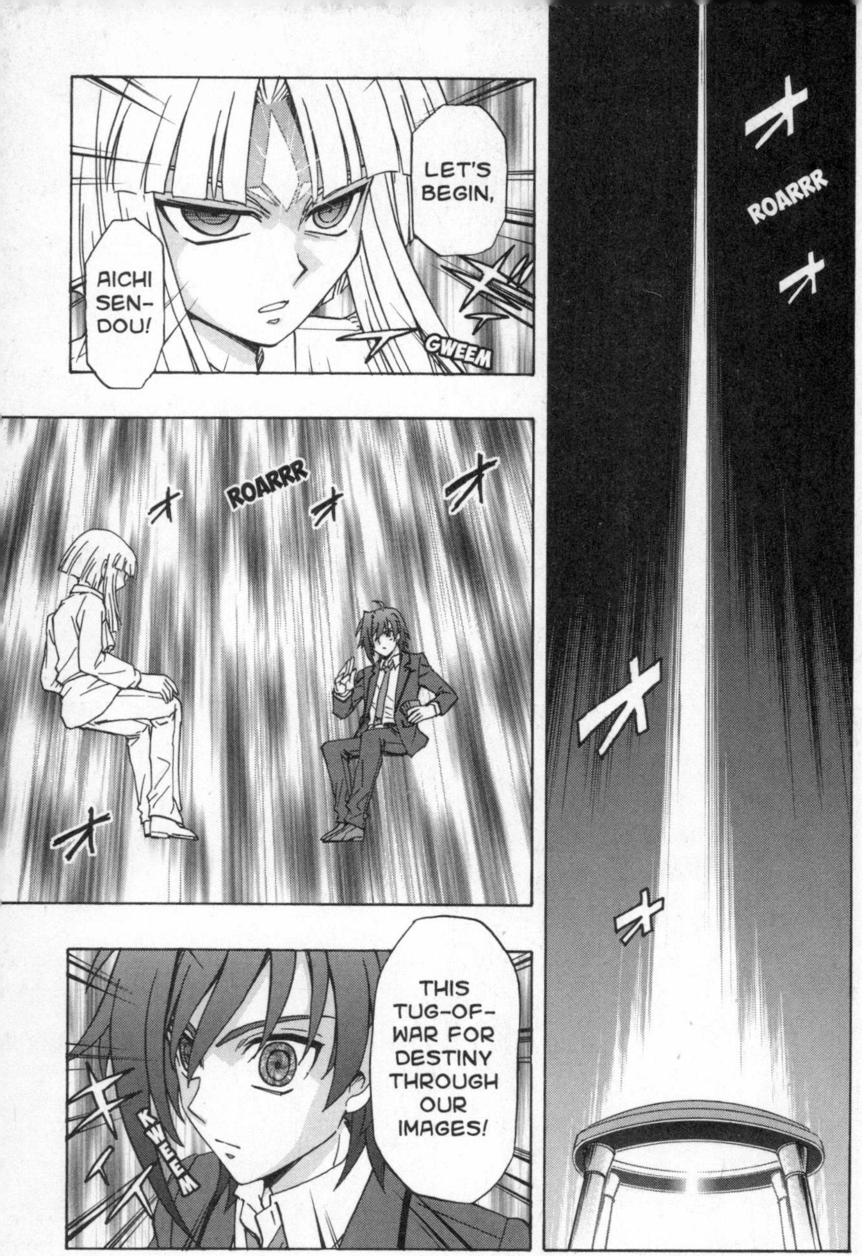

ROARRR
LET'S BEGIN,
AICHI SEN-DOU!
GWEEM
ROARRR
THIS TUG-OF-WAR FOR DESTINY THROUGH OUR IMAGES!
KWEEEM

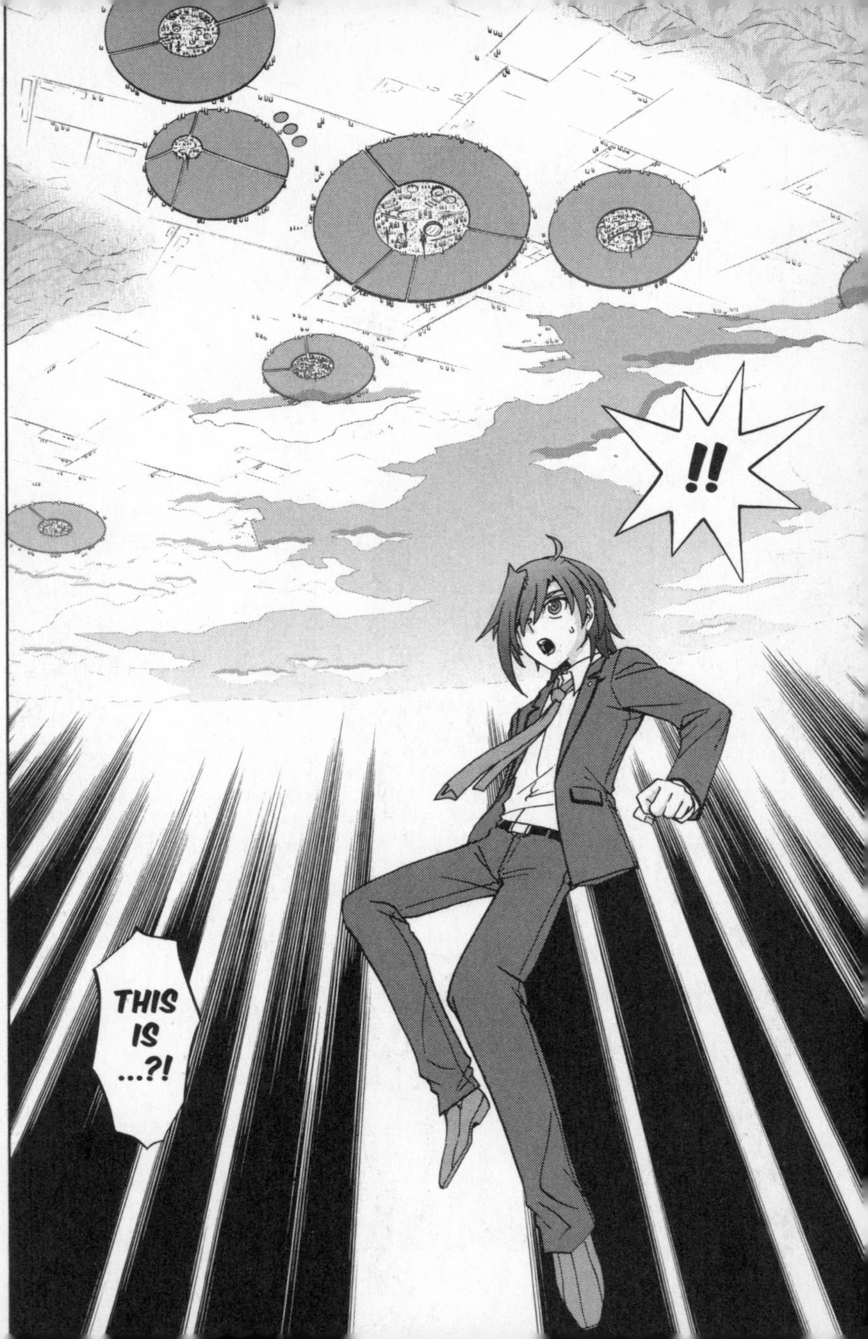
!!
THIS IS ...?!

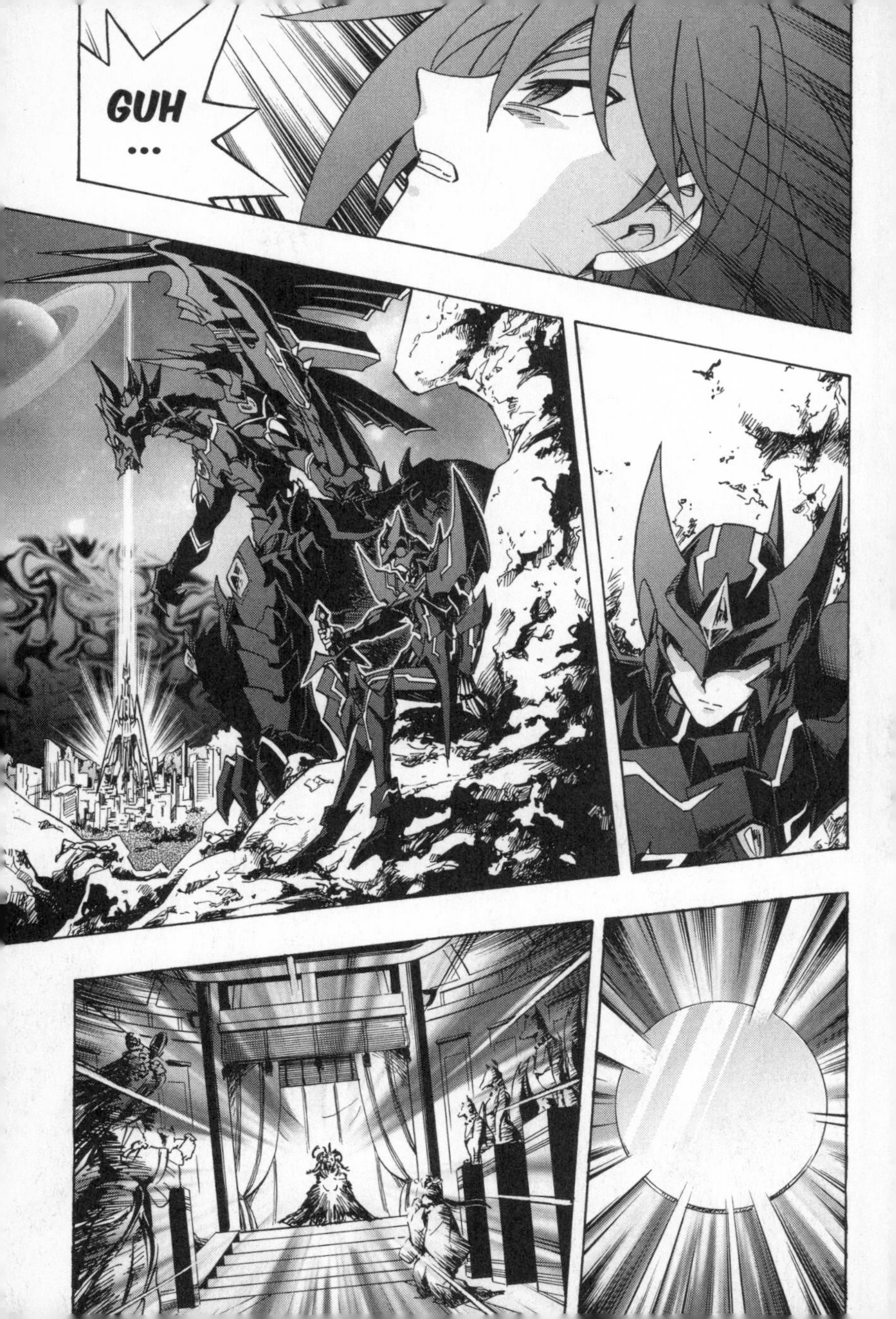
GUH
...

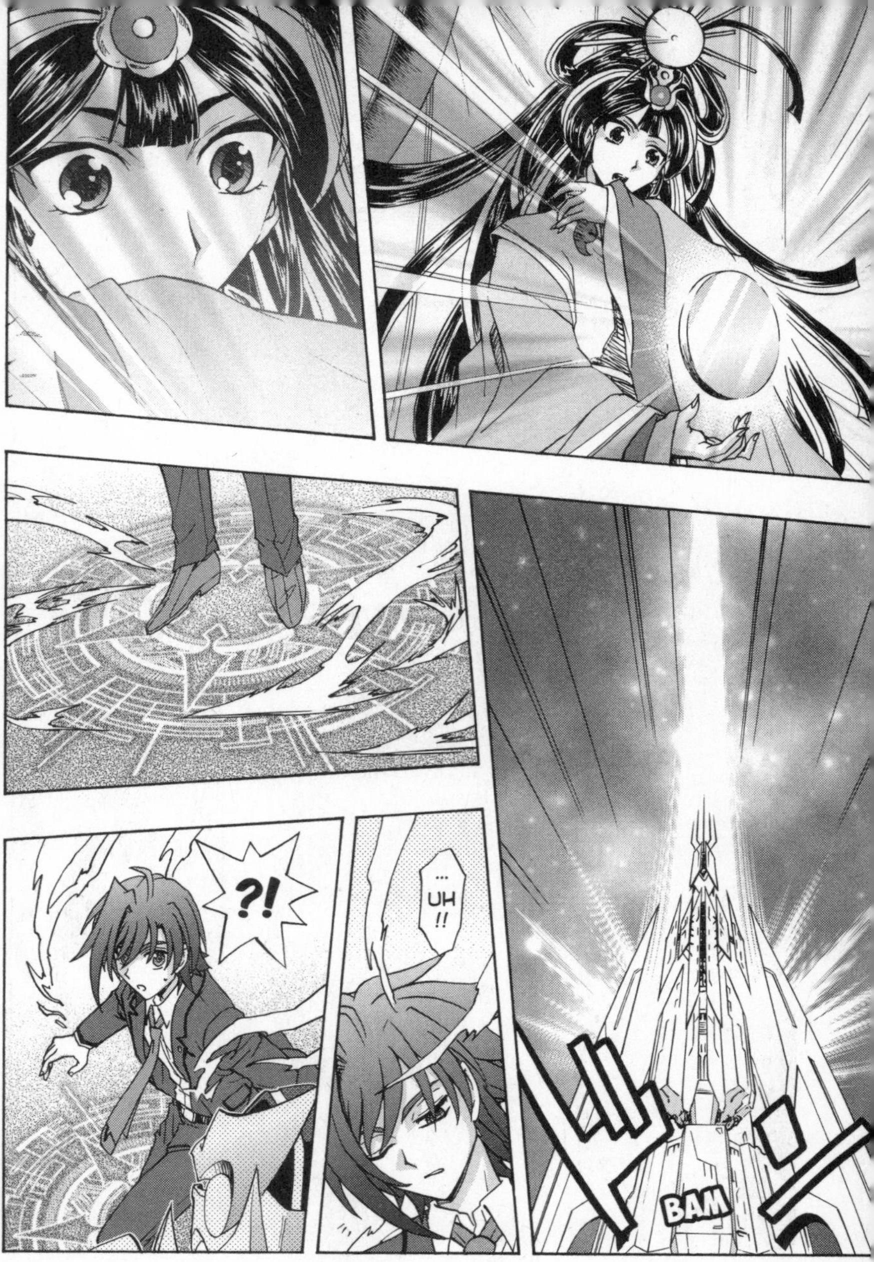

... UH !!
?!
BAM

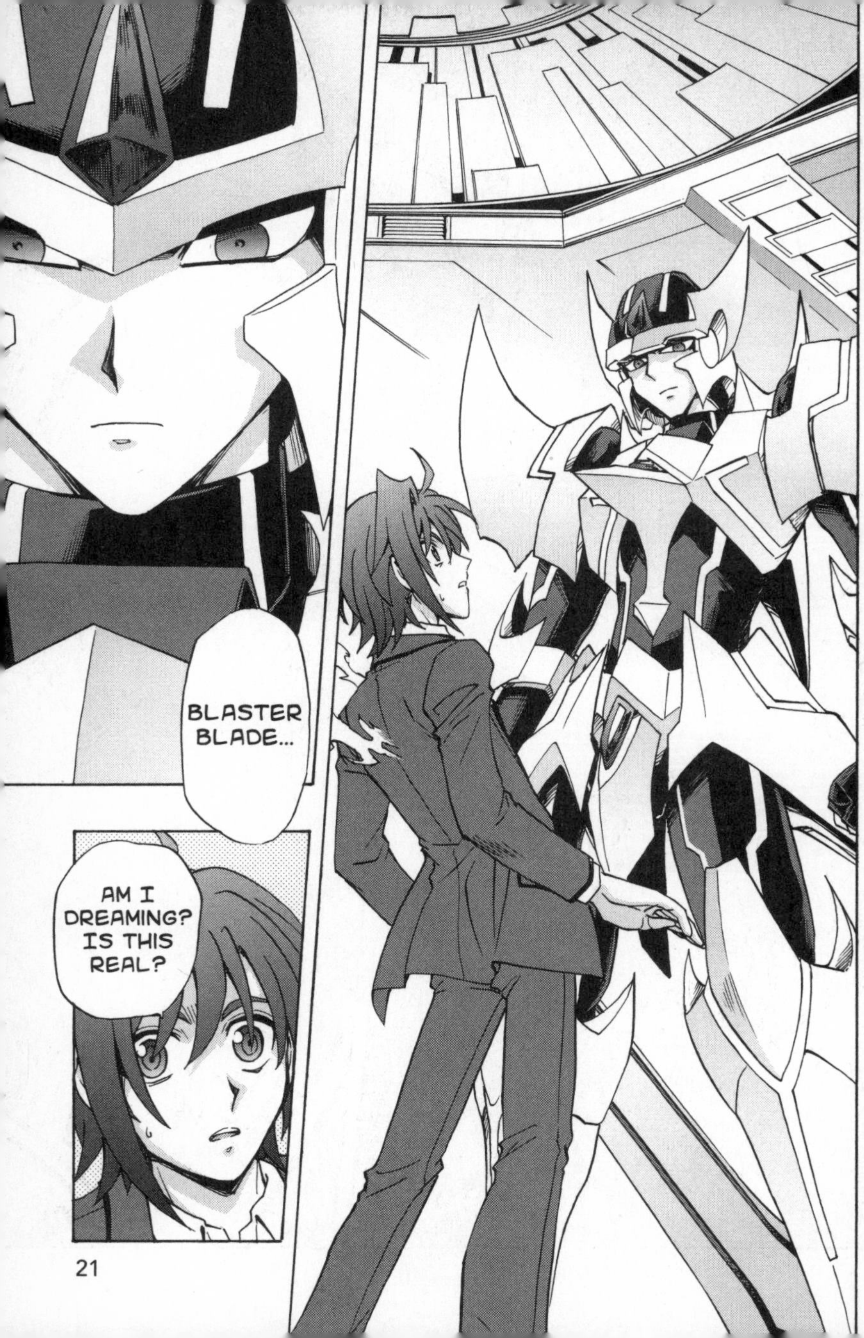
BLASTER BLADE...
AM I DREAMING? IS THIS REAL?

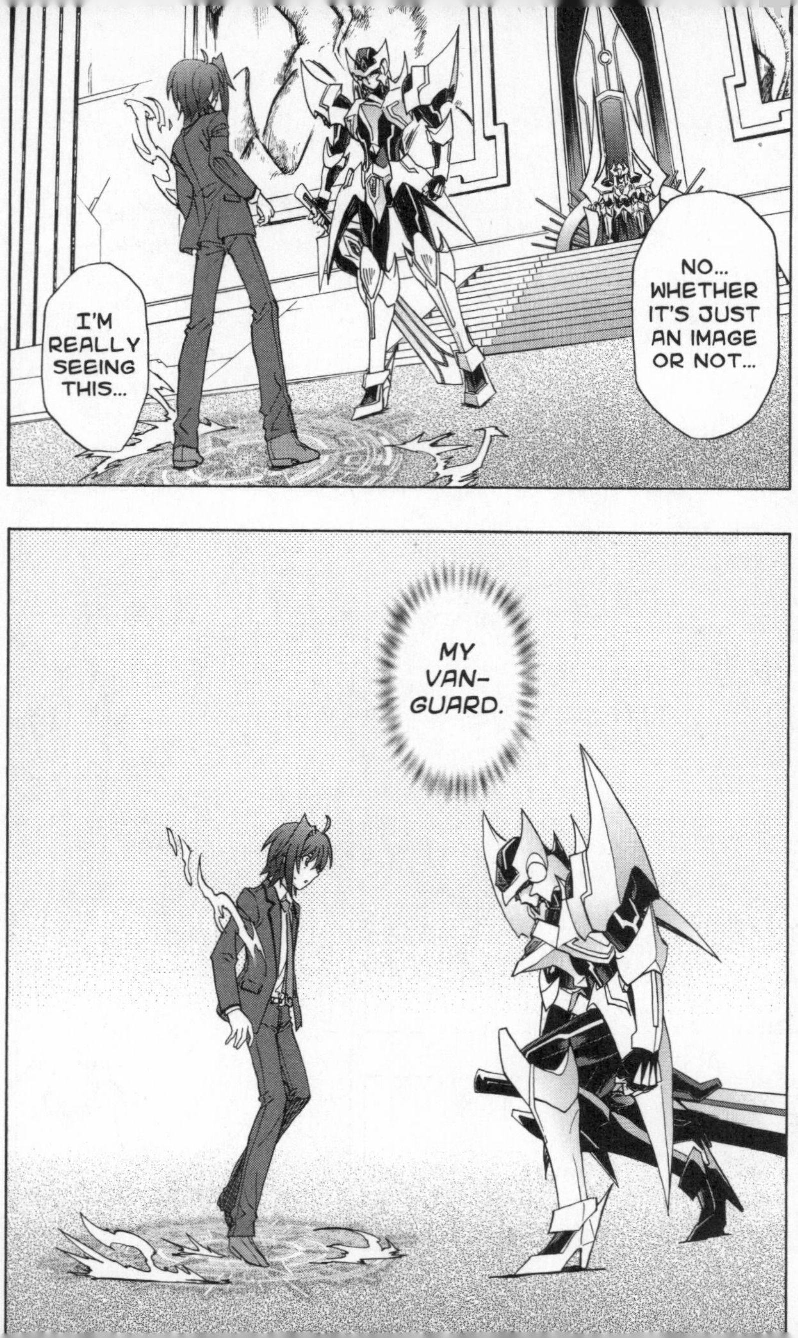
NO... WHETHER IT'S JUST AN IMAGE OR NOT...
I'M REALLY SEEING THIS...
MY VAN-GUARD.

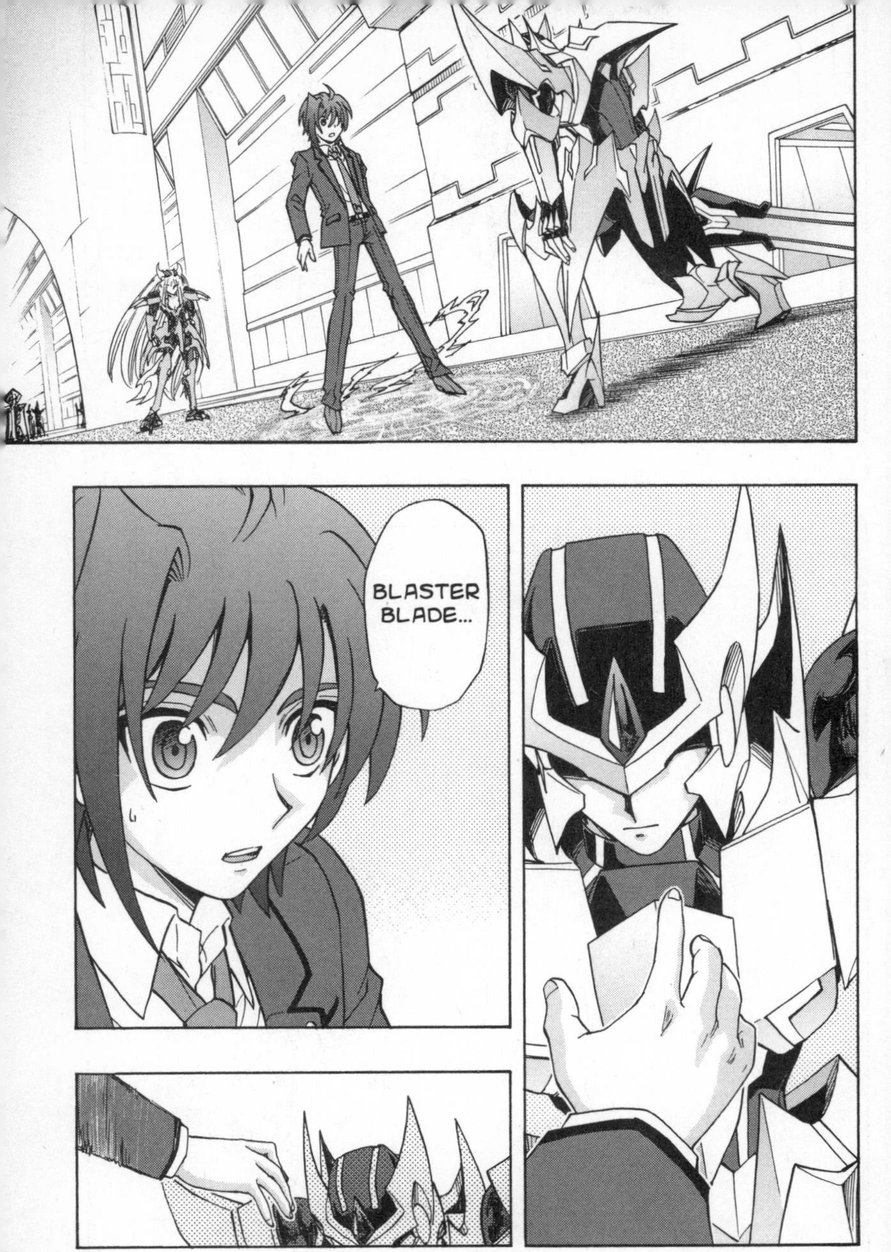
BLASTER BLADE...

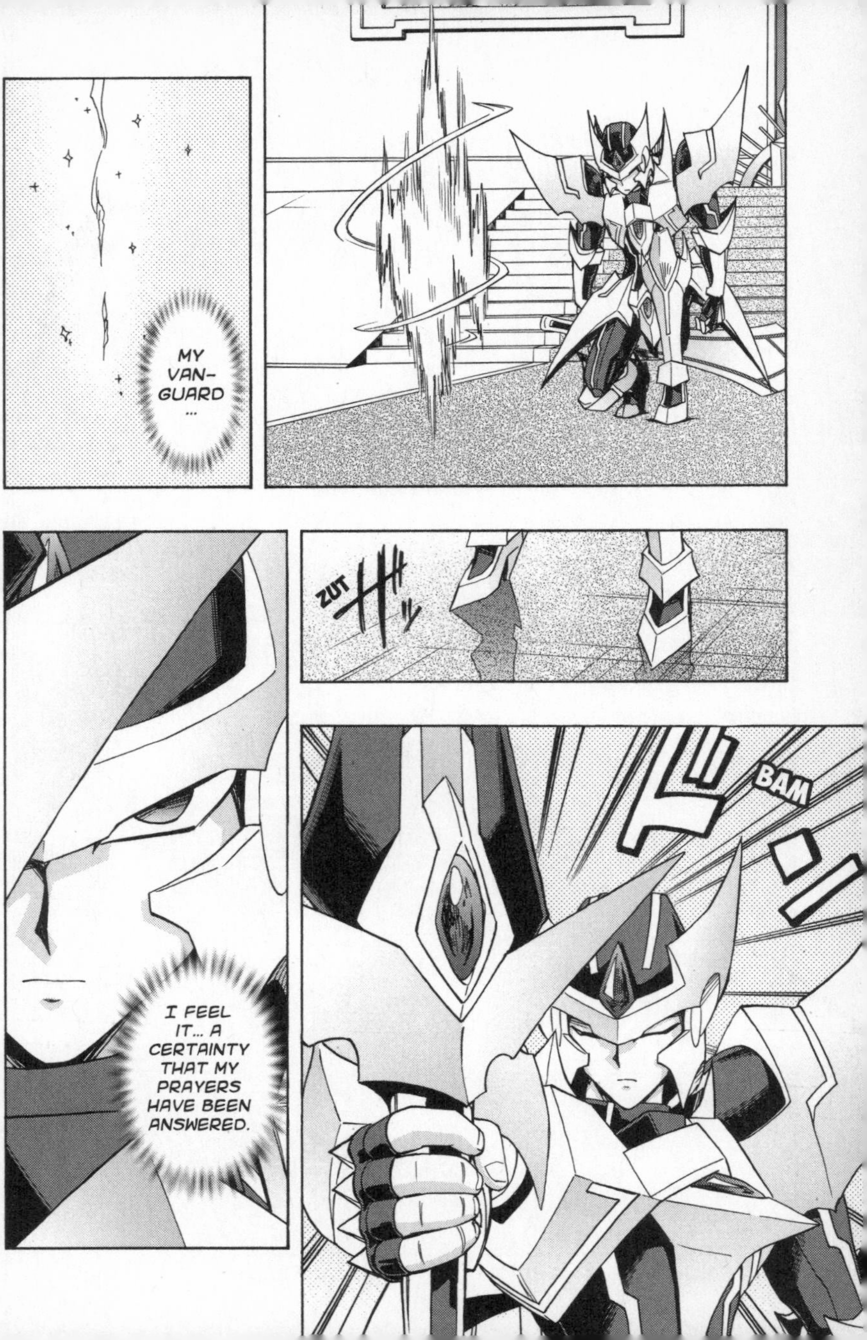
MY VAN-GUARD ...
ZUT
BAM
I FEEL IT... A CERTAINTY THAT MY PRAYERS HAVE BEEN ANSWERED.

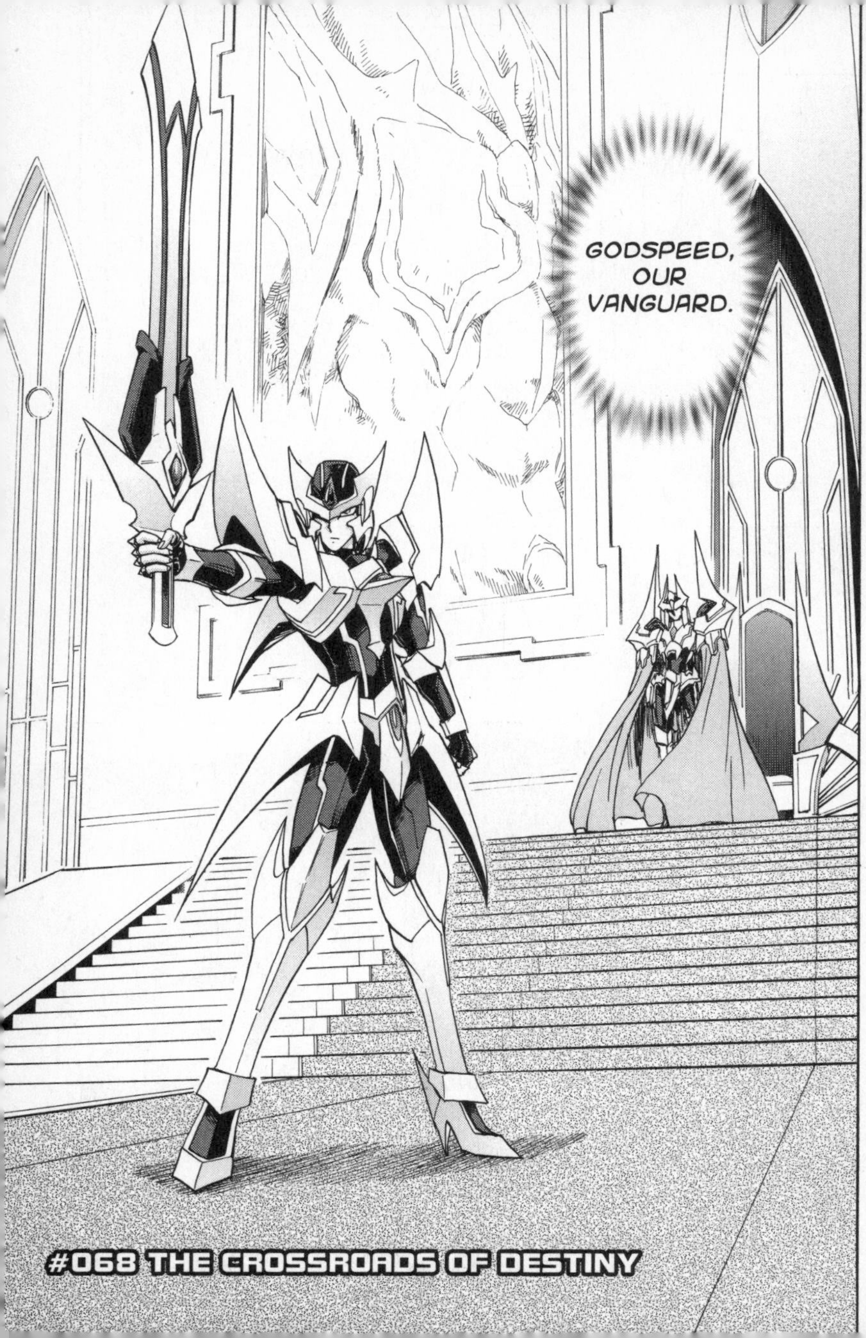
GODSPEED, OUR VANGUARD.
#068 THE CROSSROADS OF DESTINY

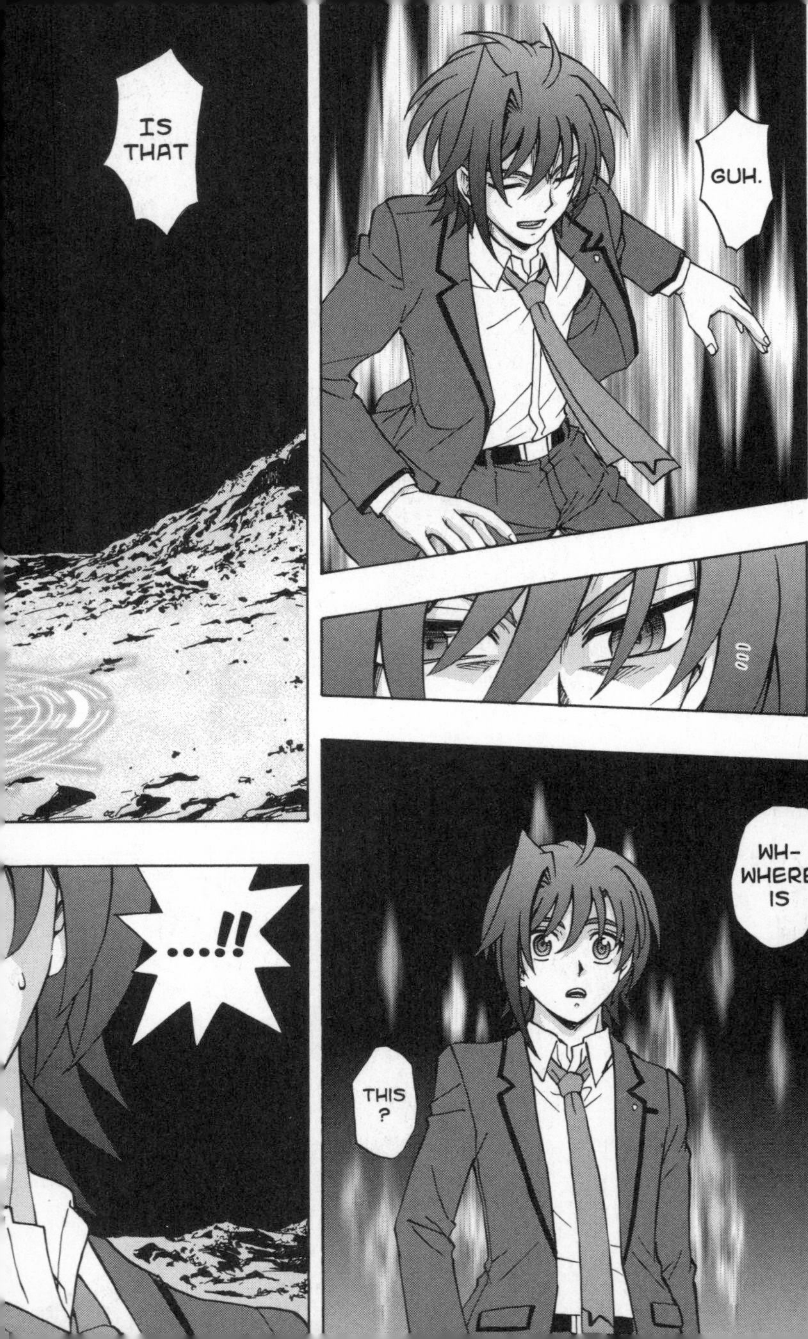
GUH.
IS THAT
WH- WHERE IS
THIS ?
...!!

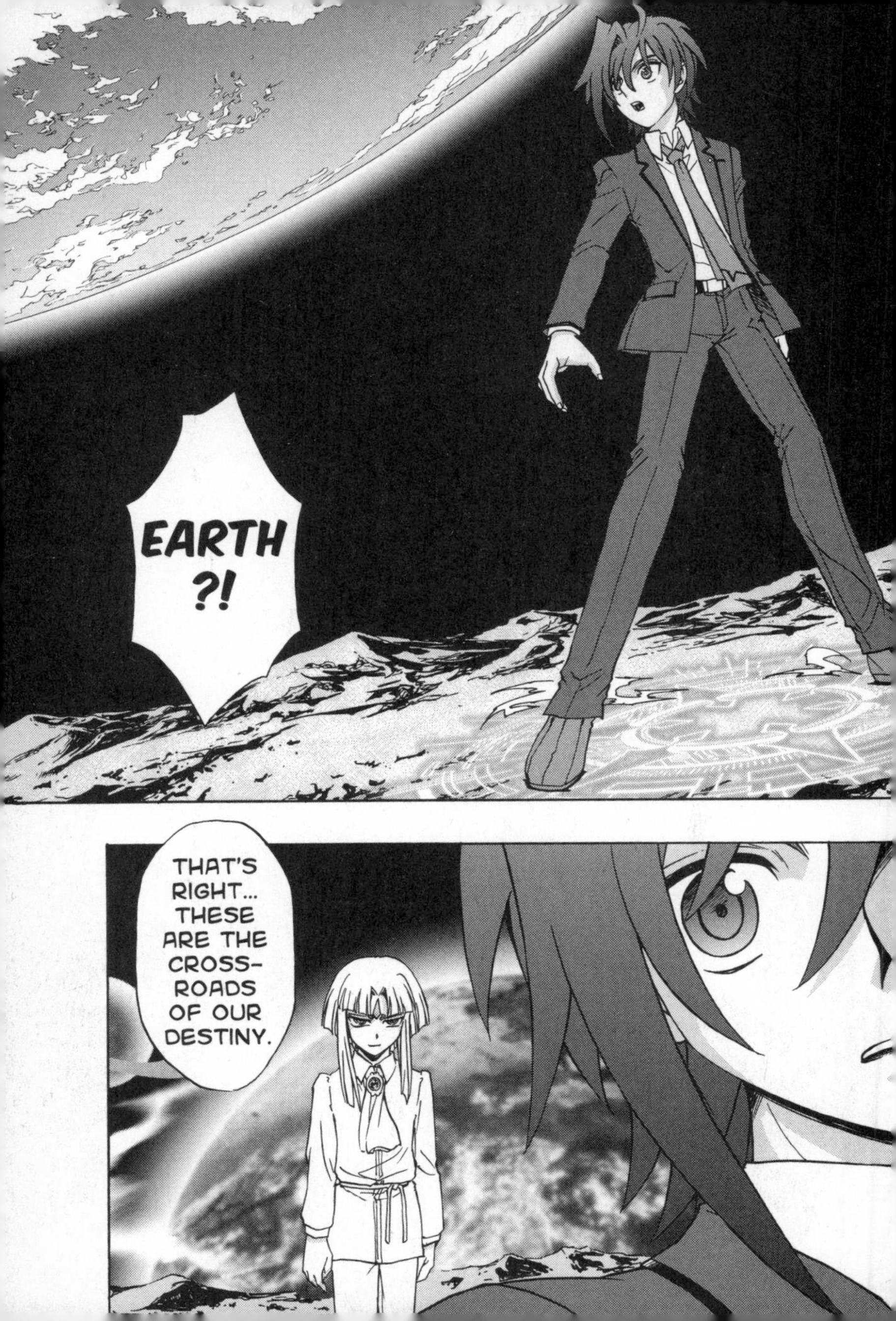
EARTH ?!
THAT'S RIGHT... THESE ARE THE CROSS-ROADS OF OUR DESTINY.

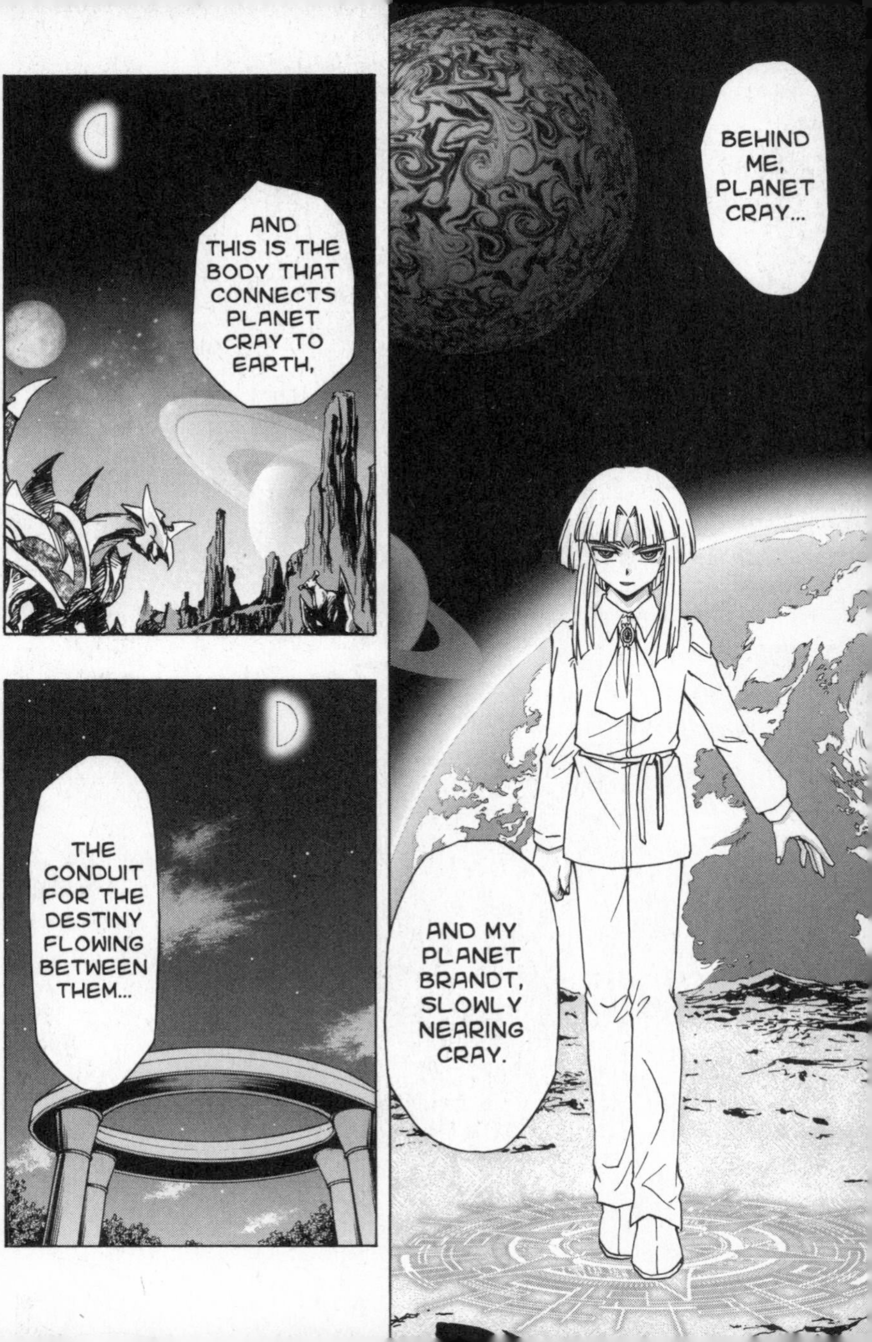
BEHIND ME, PLANET CRAY...
AND MY PLANET BRANDT, SLOWLY NEARING CRAY.
AND THIS IS THE BODY THAT CONNECTS PLANET CRAY TO EARTH,
THE CONDUIT FOR THE DESTINY FLOWING BETWEEN THEM...

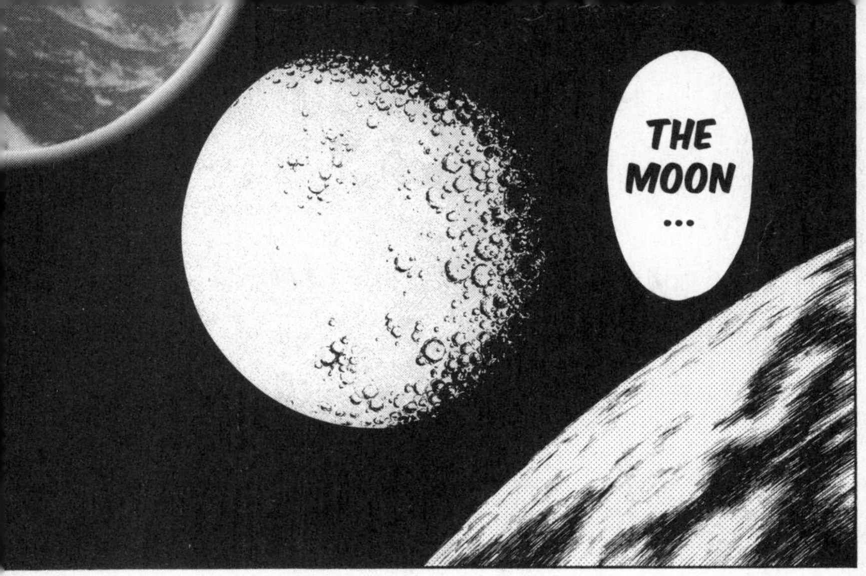
THE MOON ...
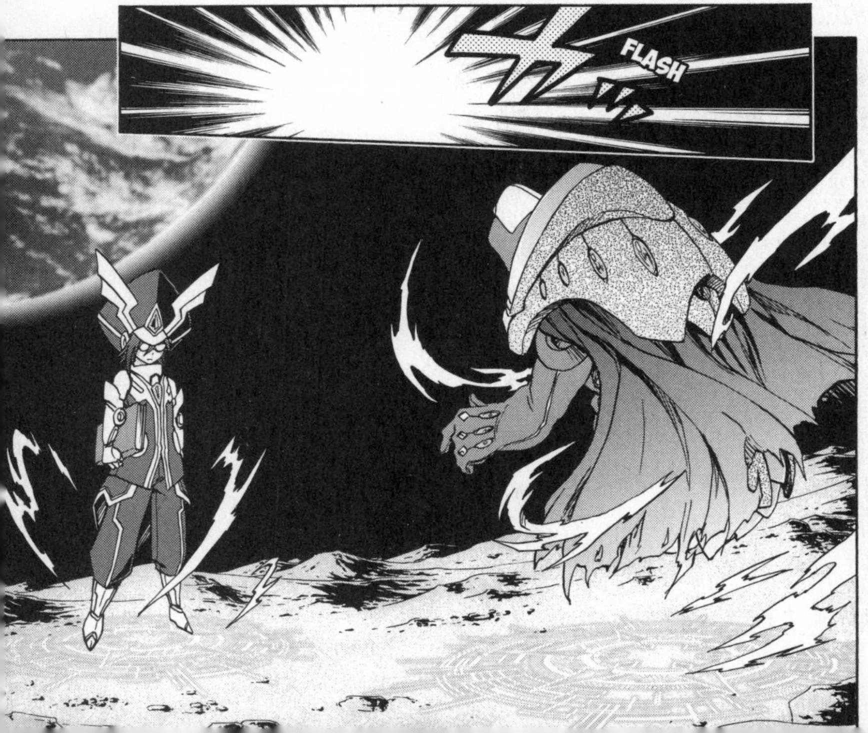
FLASH

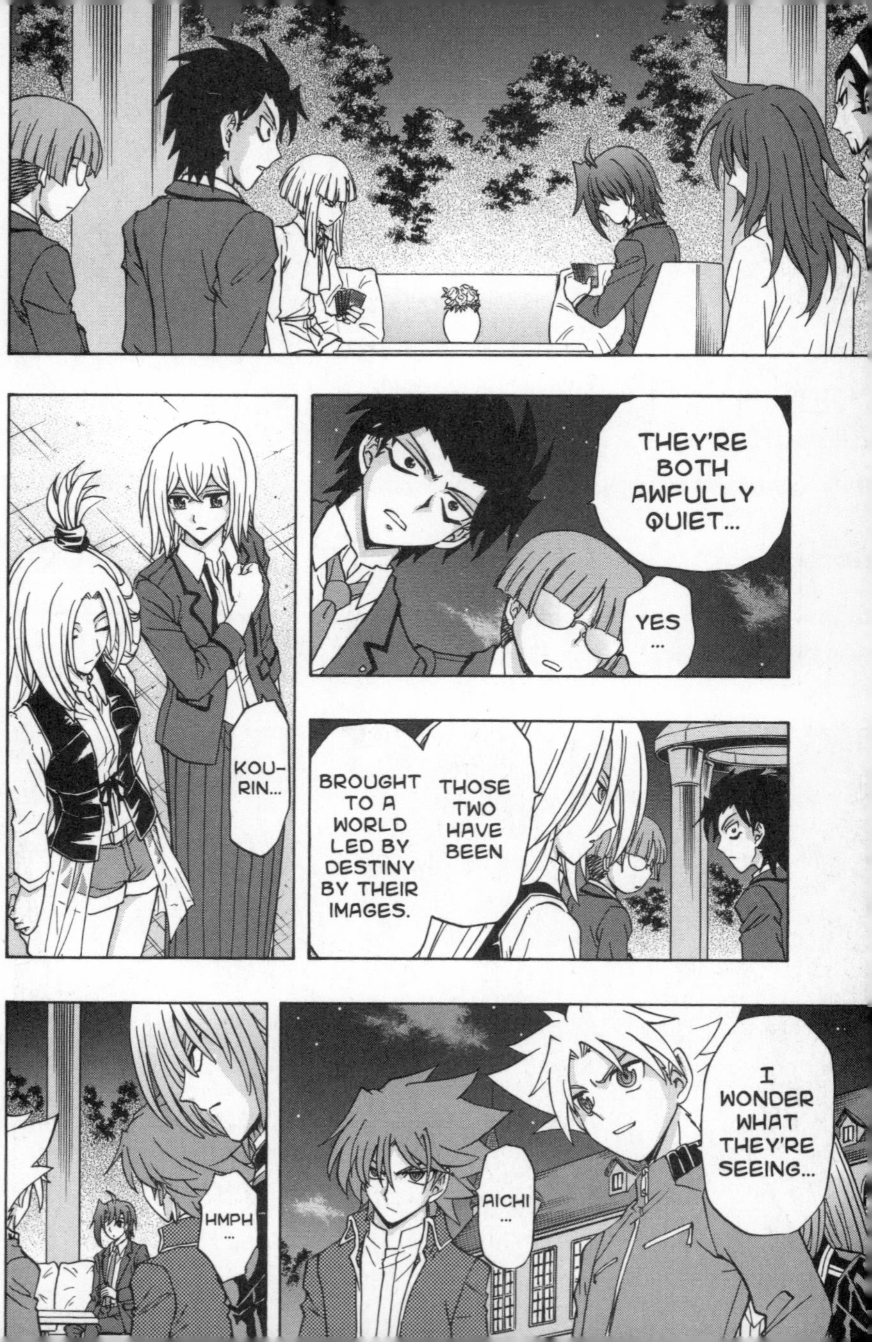
THEY'RE BOTH AWFULLY QUIET...
YES ...
THOSE TWO HAVE BEEN
BROUGHT TO A WORLD LED BY DESTINY BY THEIR IMAGES.
KOU-RIN...
I WONDER WHAT THEY'RE SEEING...
AICHI ...
HMPH ...

MY TURN ...

DRAW.

HE'S MOVING !!

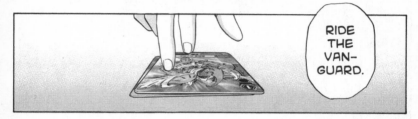

RIDE THE VAN- GUARD.

ENVOY OF PLANET BRANDT,

STAR CORPSE MAN, KAIRAL.

GWOOO

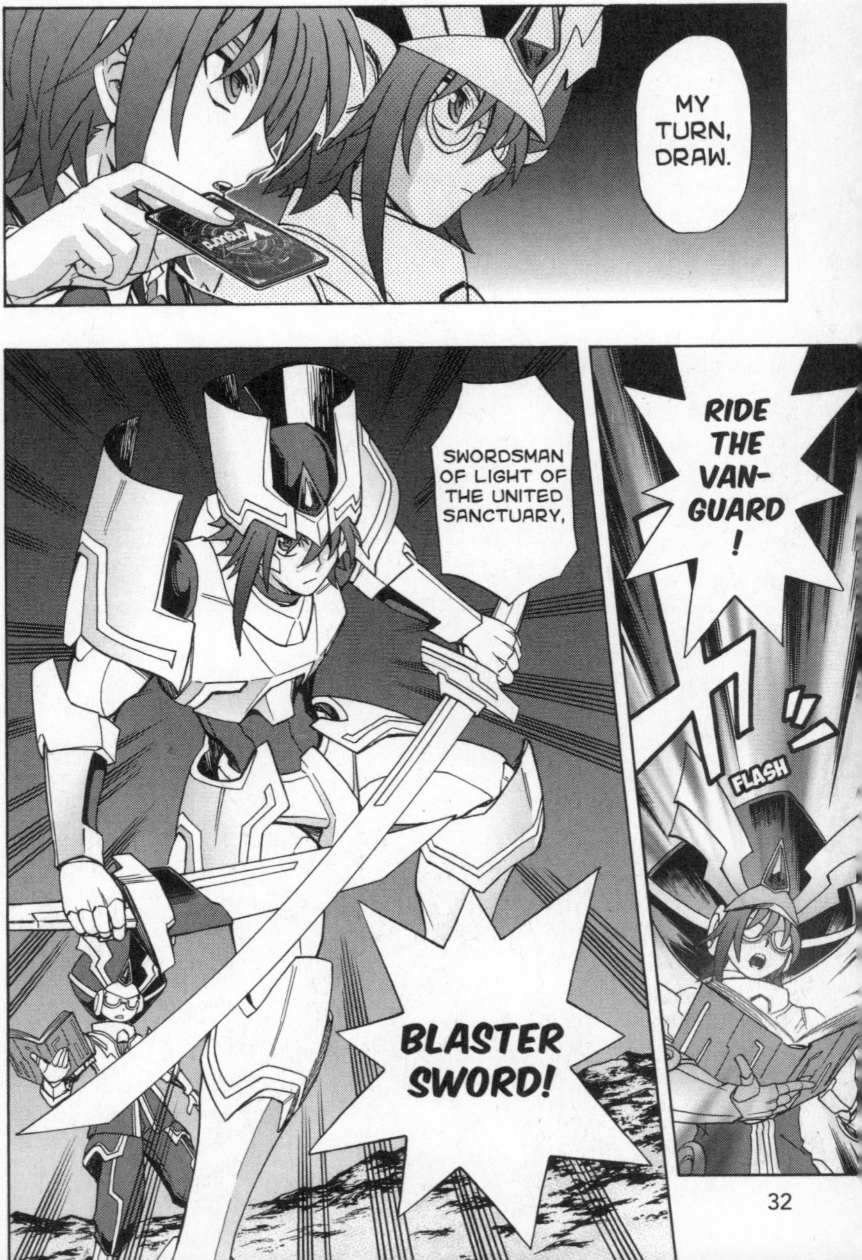
MY TURN, DRAW.
RIDE THE VAN-GUARD!
FLASH
SWORDSMAN OF LIGHT OF THE UNITED SANCTUARY,
BLASTER SWORD!

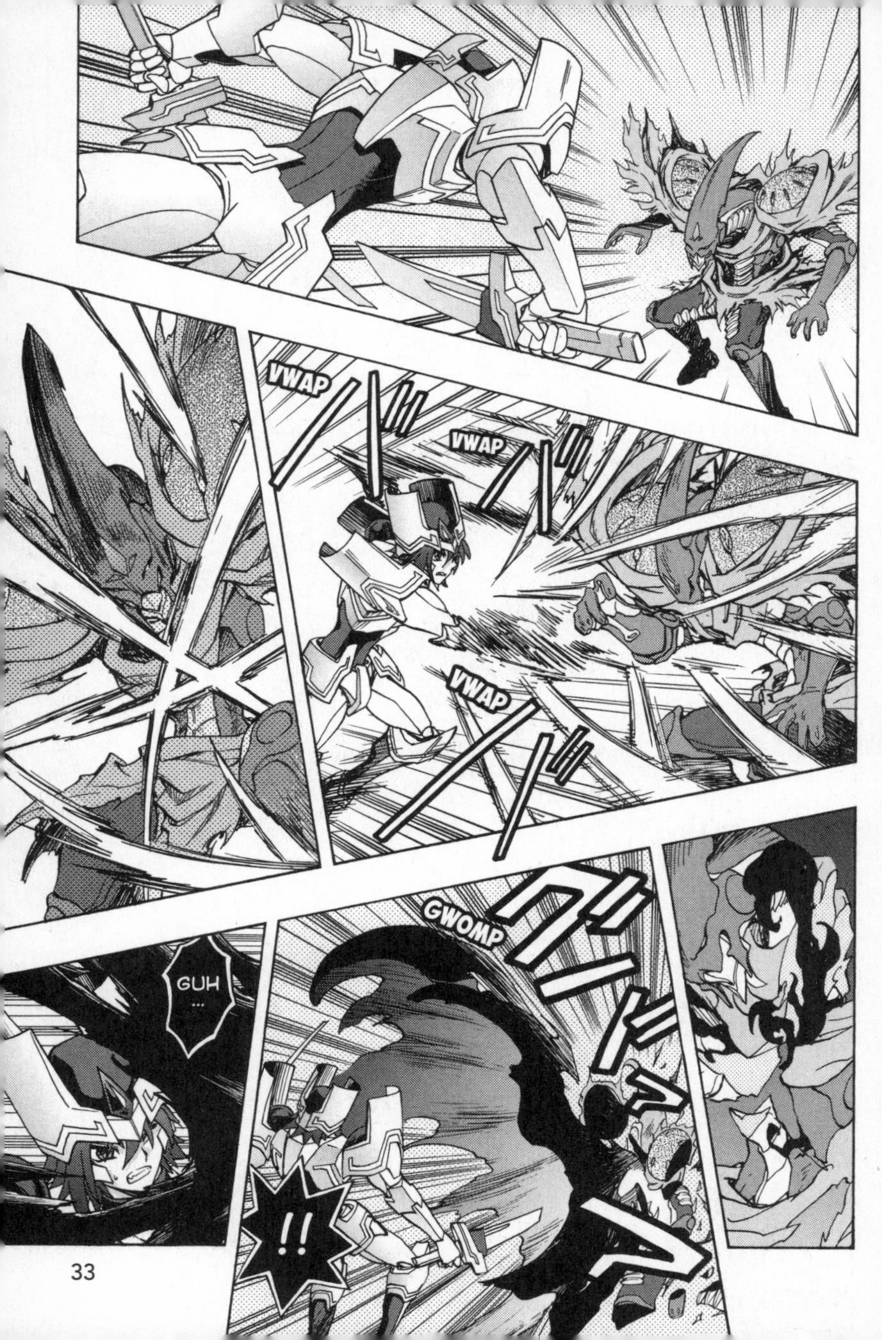
VWAP
VWAP
VWAP
GWOMP
!!
GUH ...

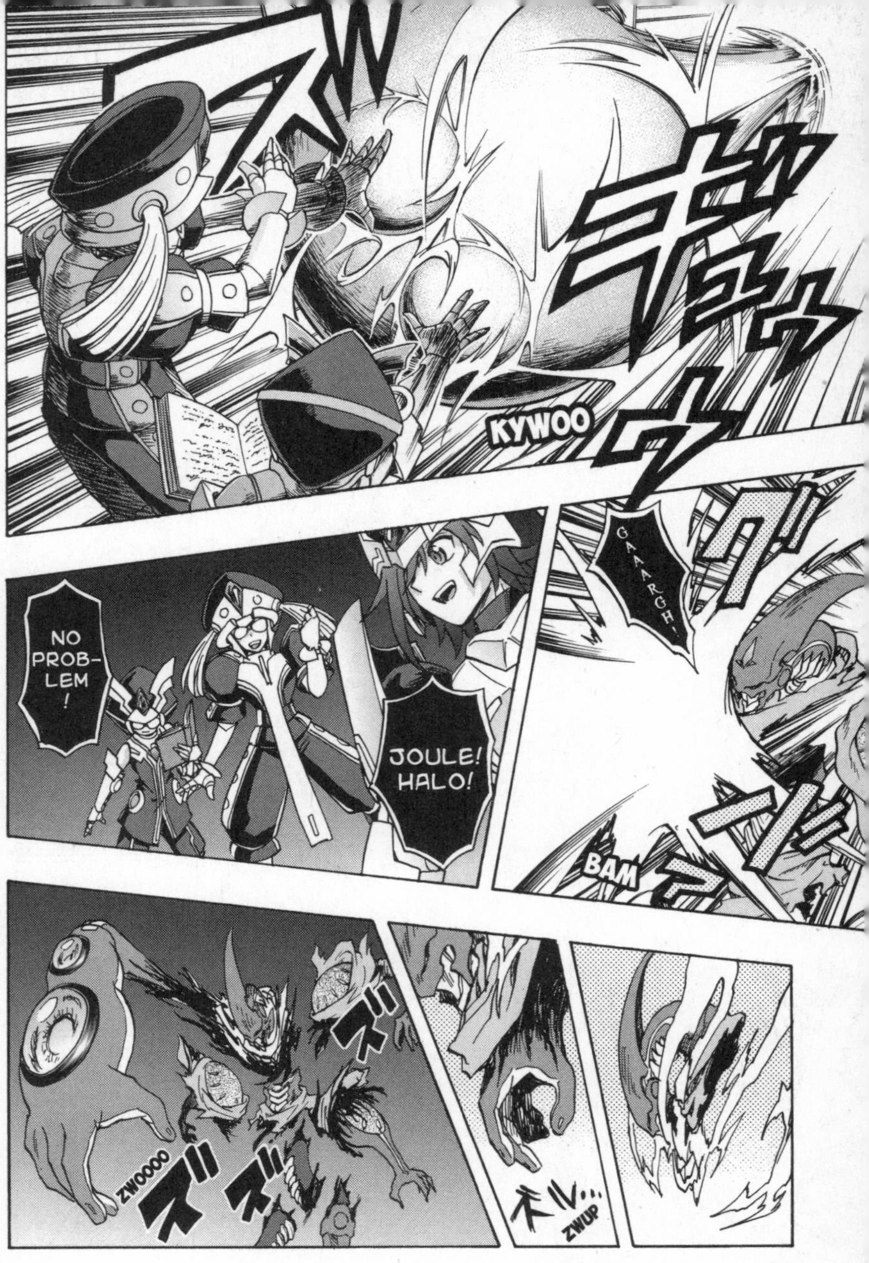
KYWOO
GAAARGH!
BAM
JOULE! HALO!
NO PROB-LEM!
ZWUP
ZWOOOO

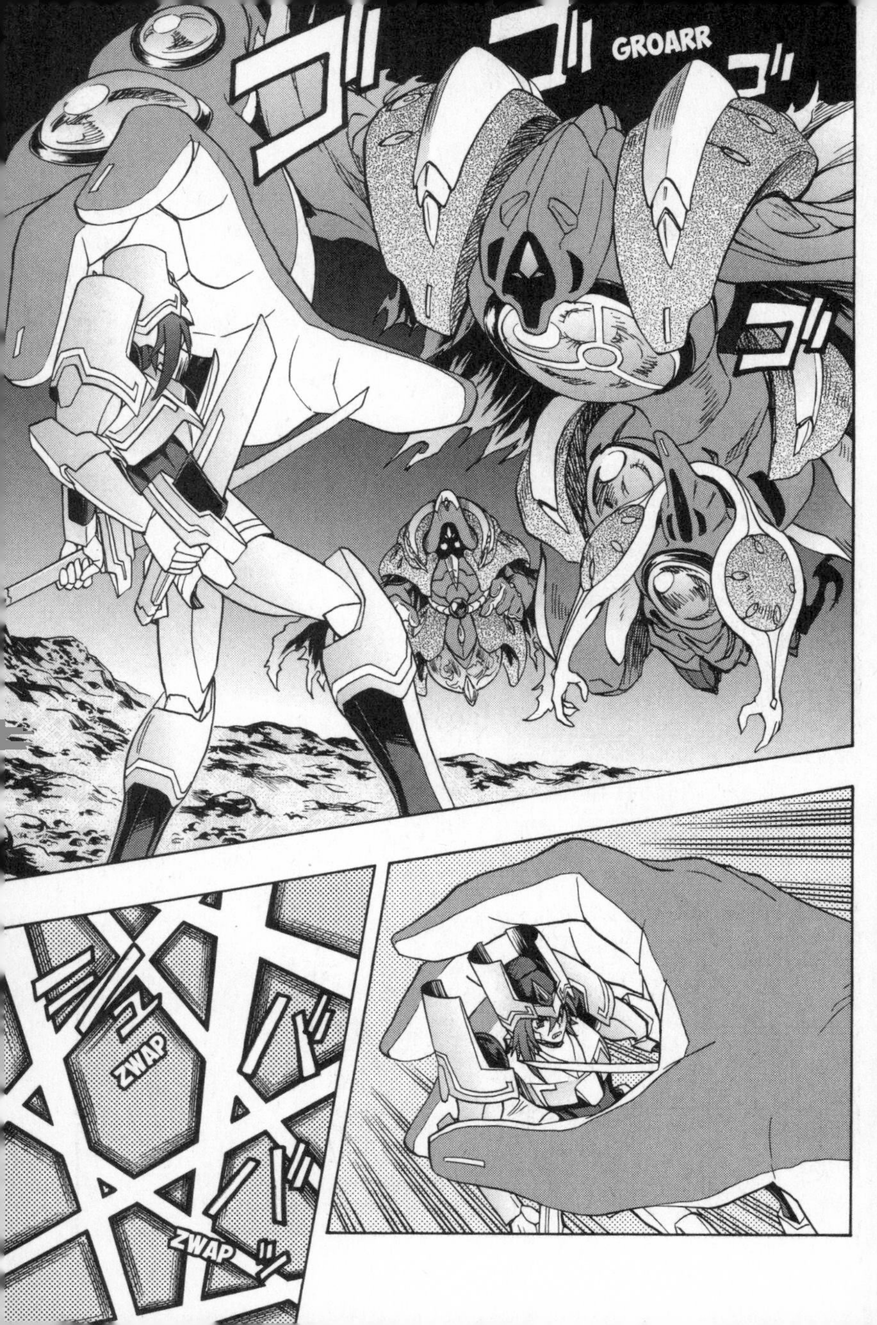
GROARR
ZWAP
ZWAP

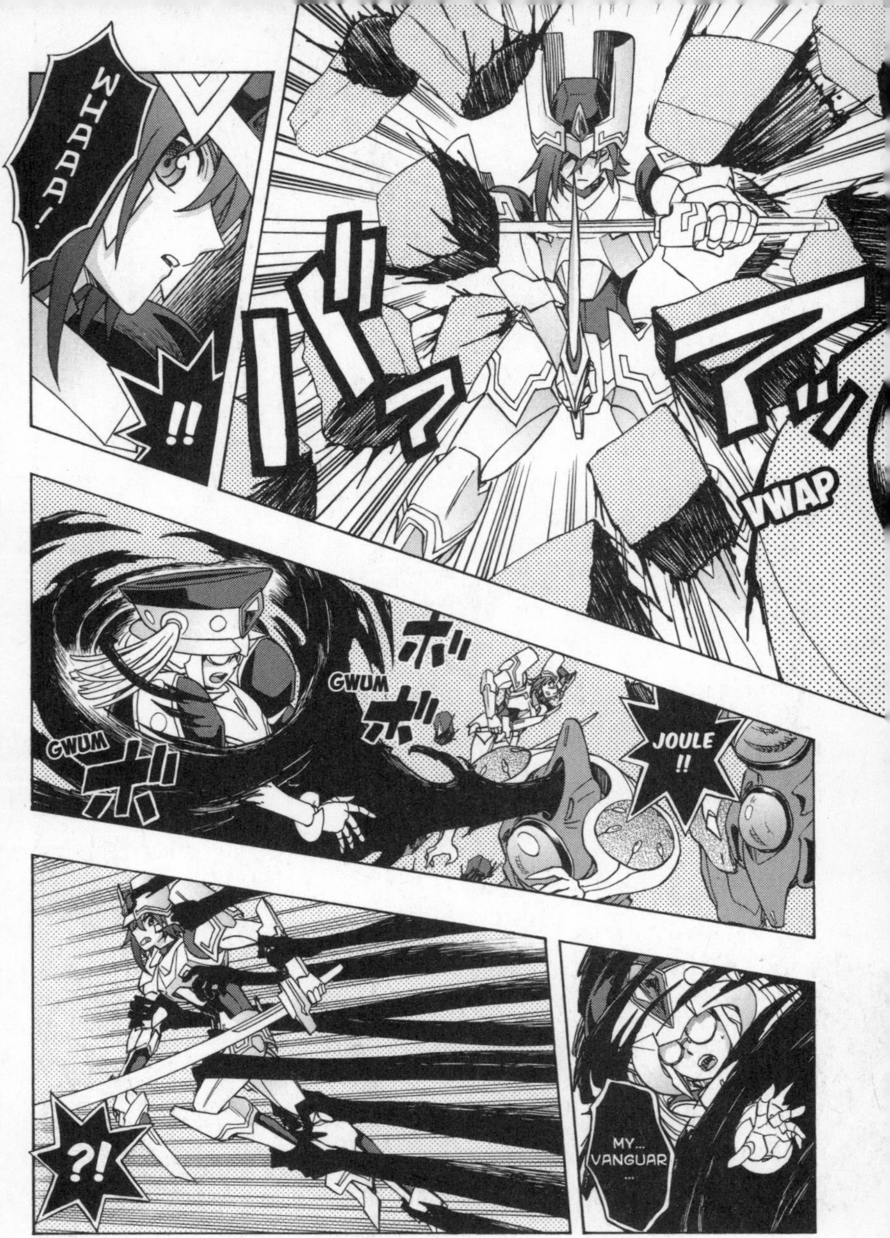
VWAP
WHAAAA!
!!
JOULE !!
GWUM
GWUM
MY... VANGUAR ...
?!

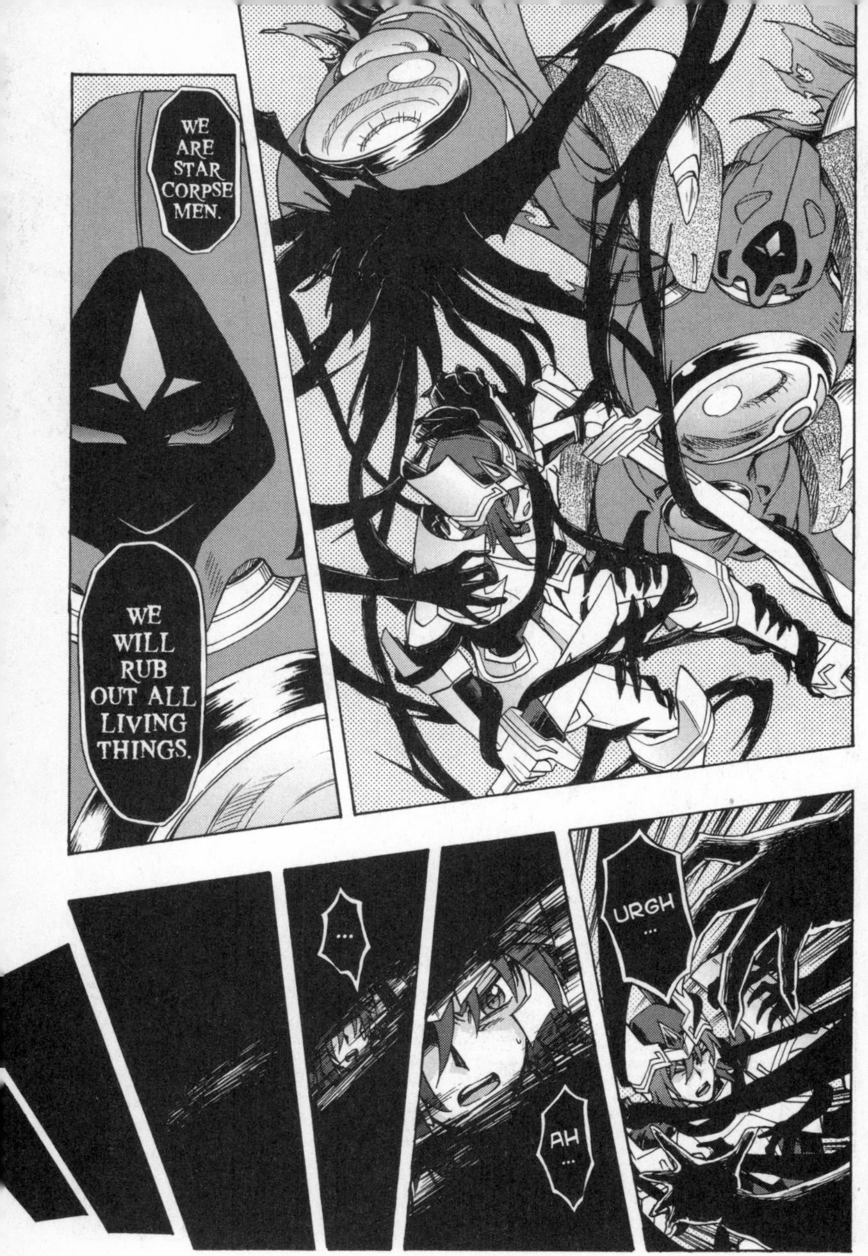
WE ARE STAR CORPSE MEN.
WE WILL RUB OUT ALL LIVING THINGS.
URGH ...
AH ...
...

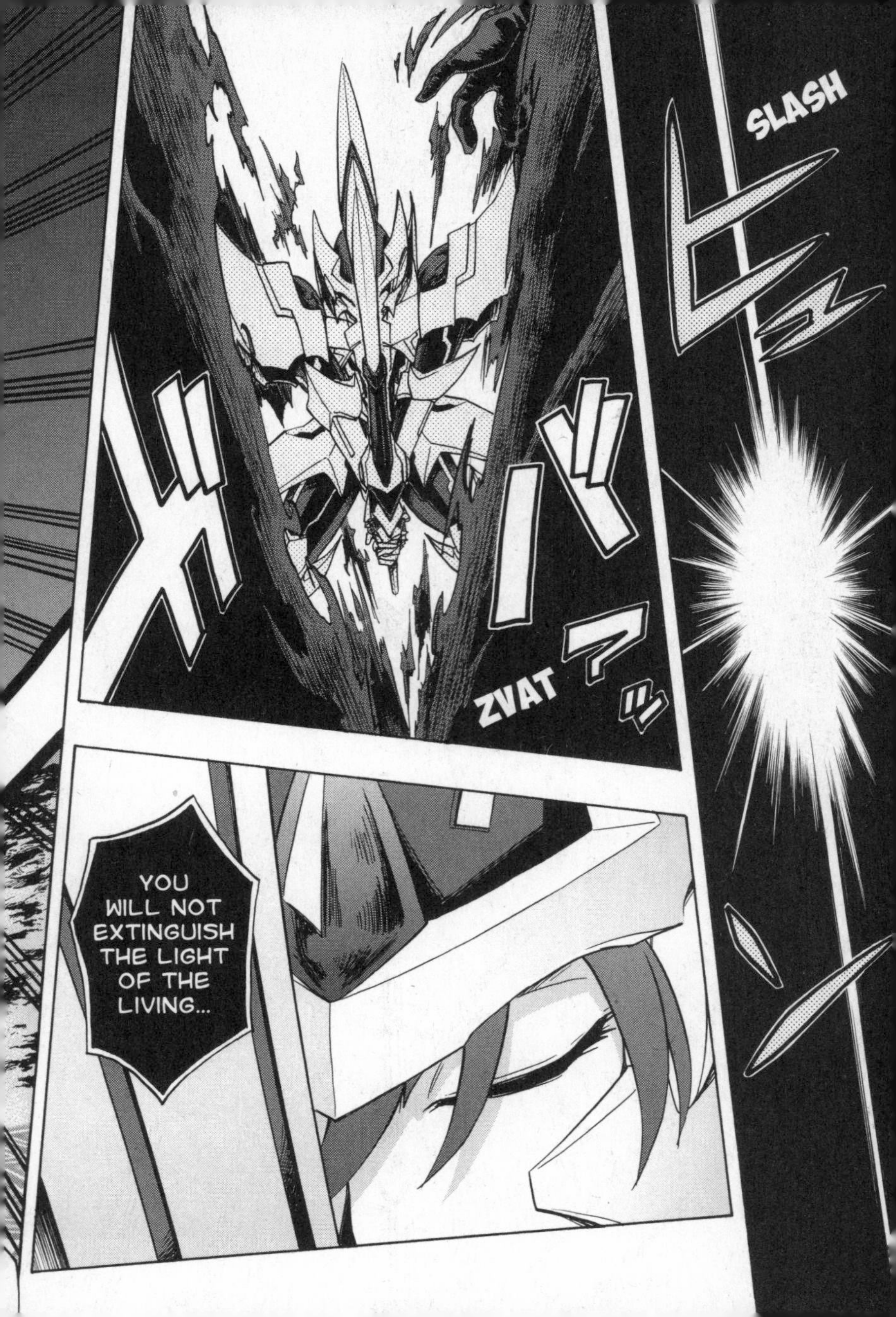
SLASH
ZVAT
YOU WILL NOT EXTINGUISH THE LIGHT OF THE LIVING...

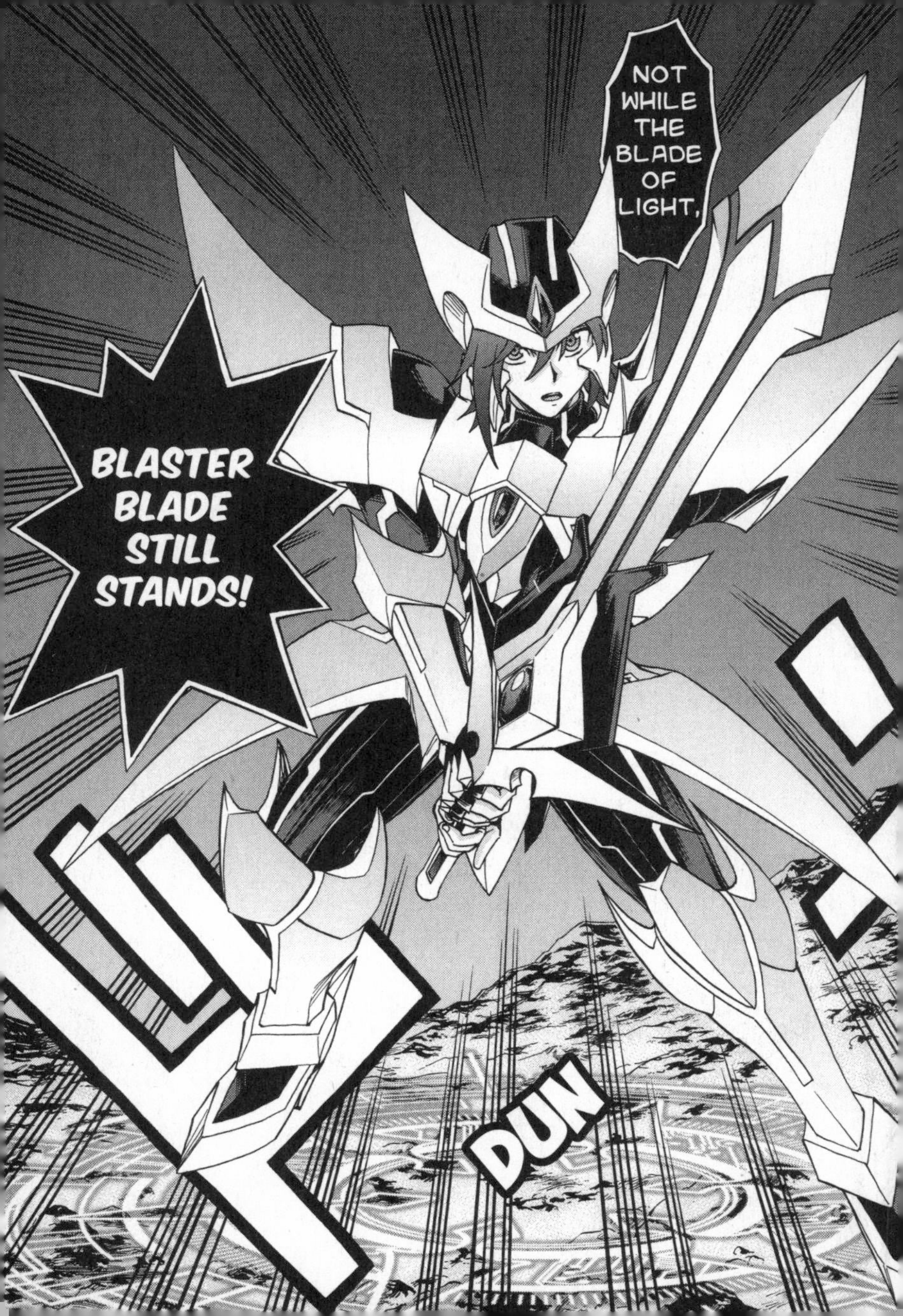
NOT WHILE THE BLADE OF LIGHT,
BLASTER BLADE STILL STANDS!
DUN

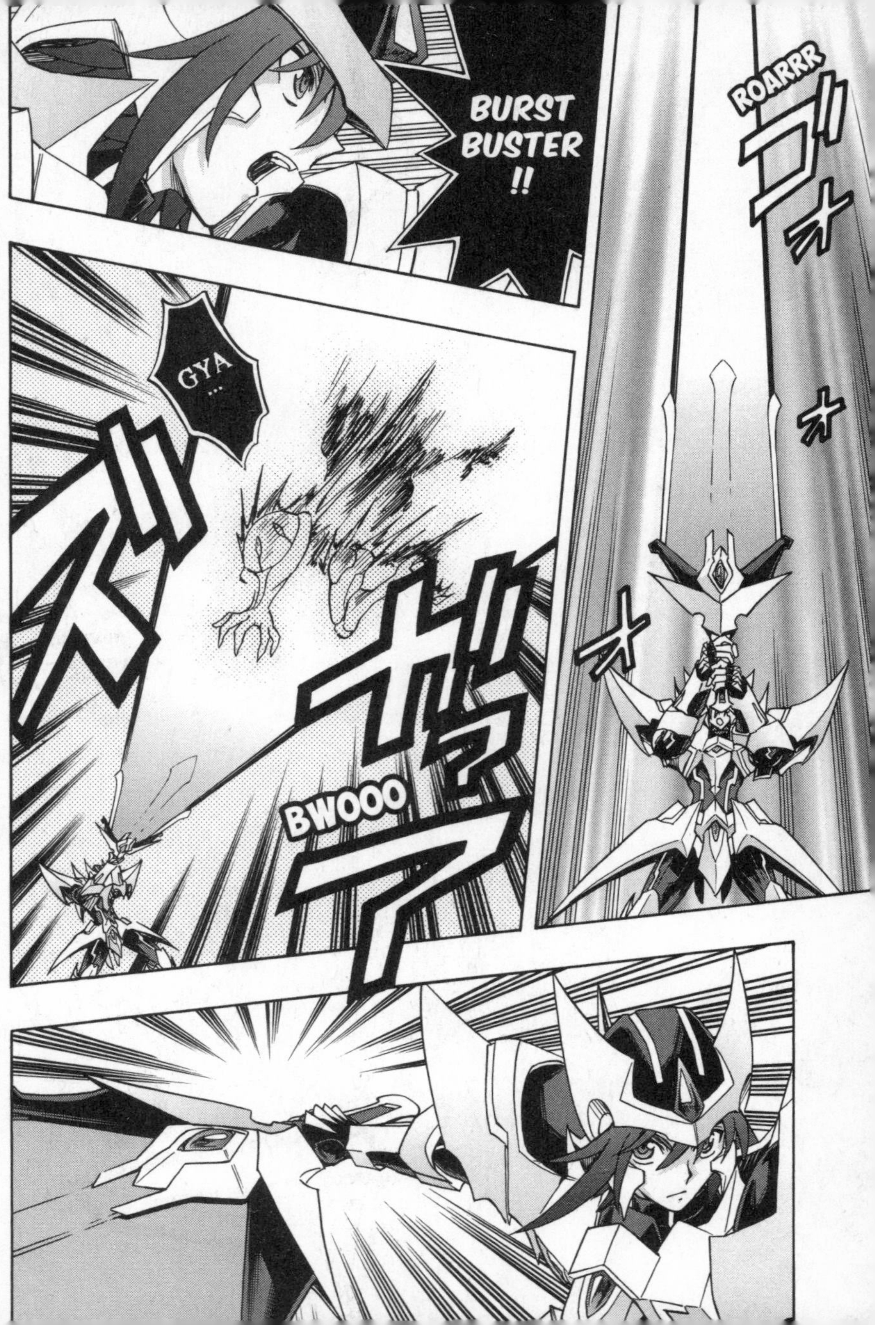
ROARRR
BURST BUSTER !!
GYA ...
BWOOO

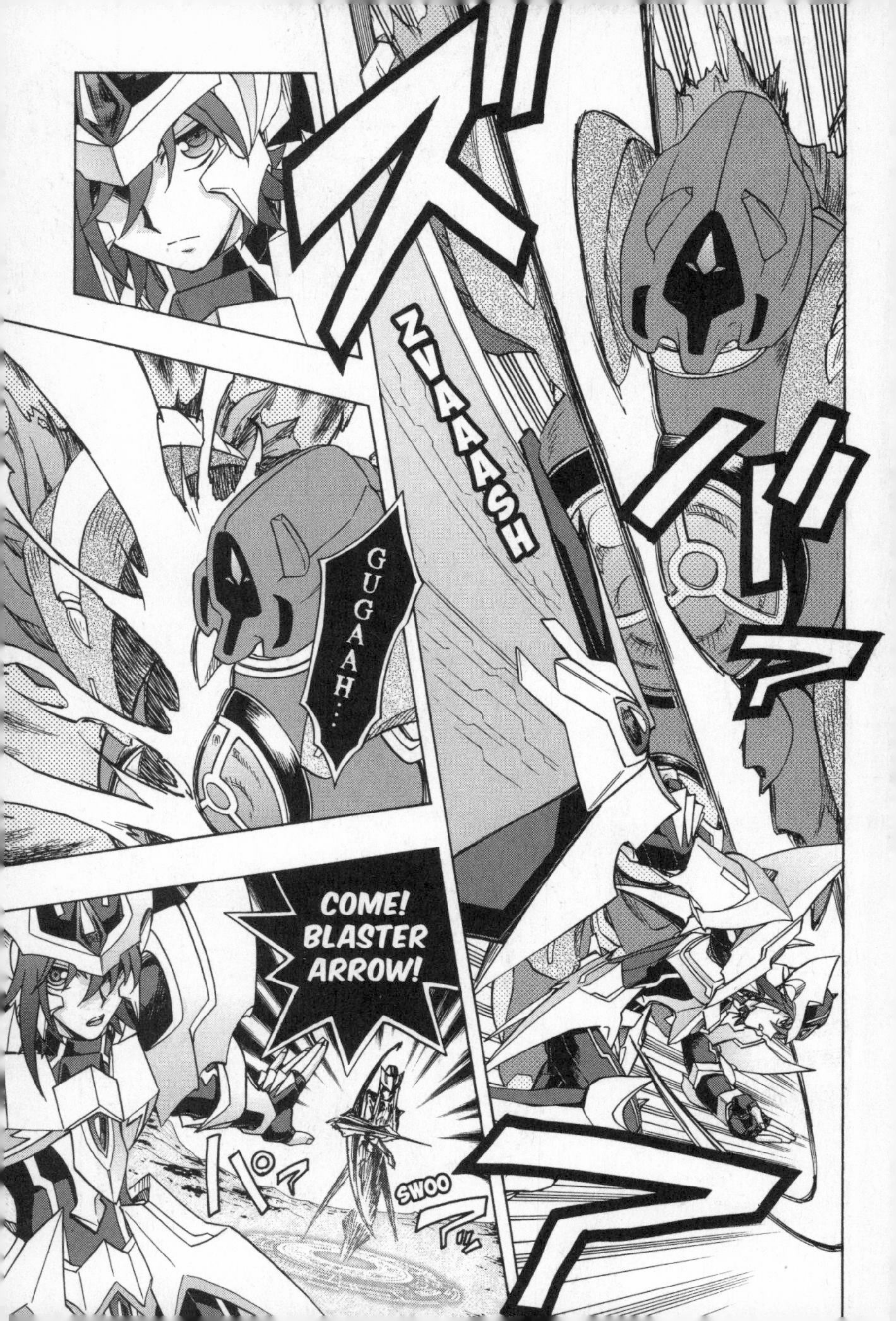
ZVAAAASH
GUGAAH...
COME! BLASTER ARROW!
SWOO

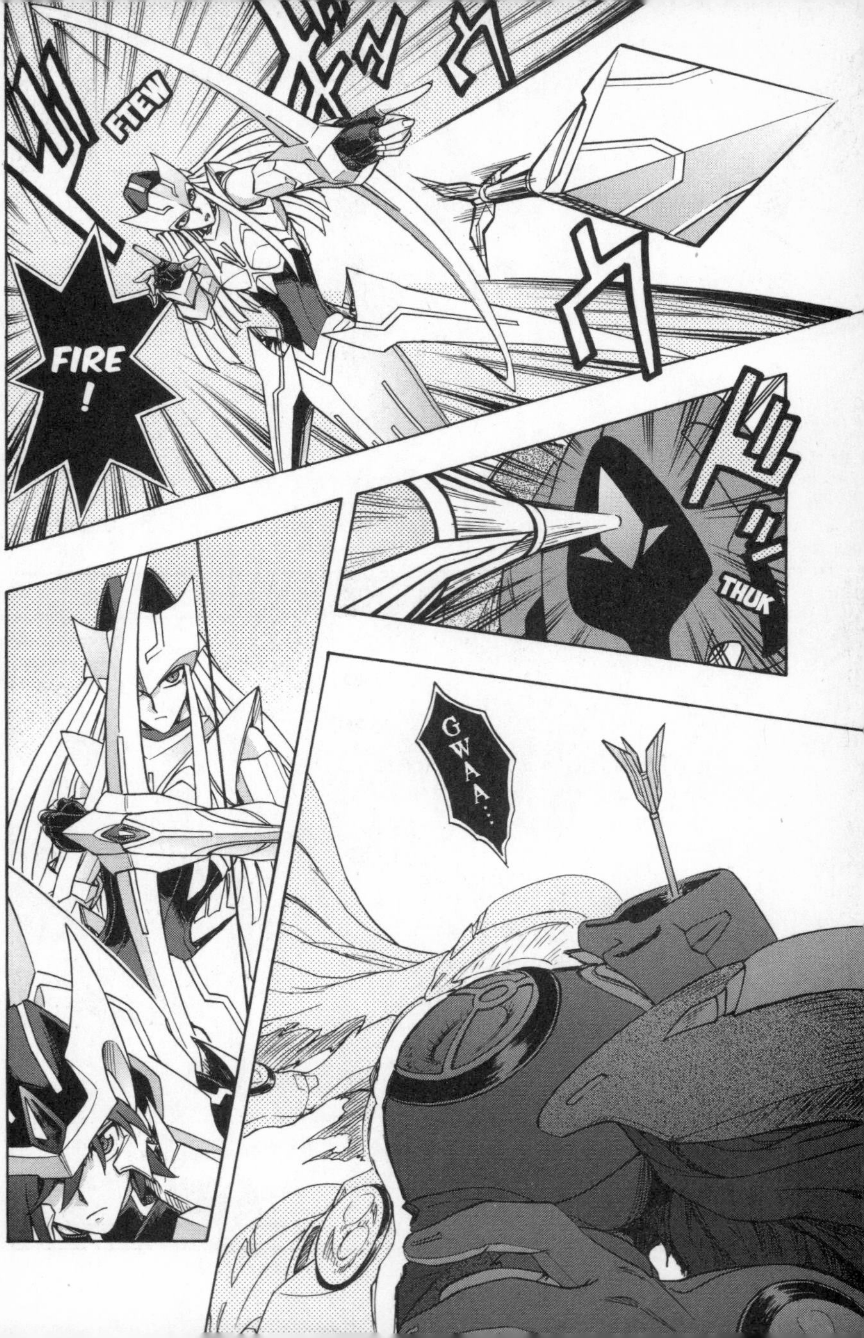
FTEW
FIRE!
THUK
GWAA...

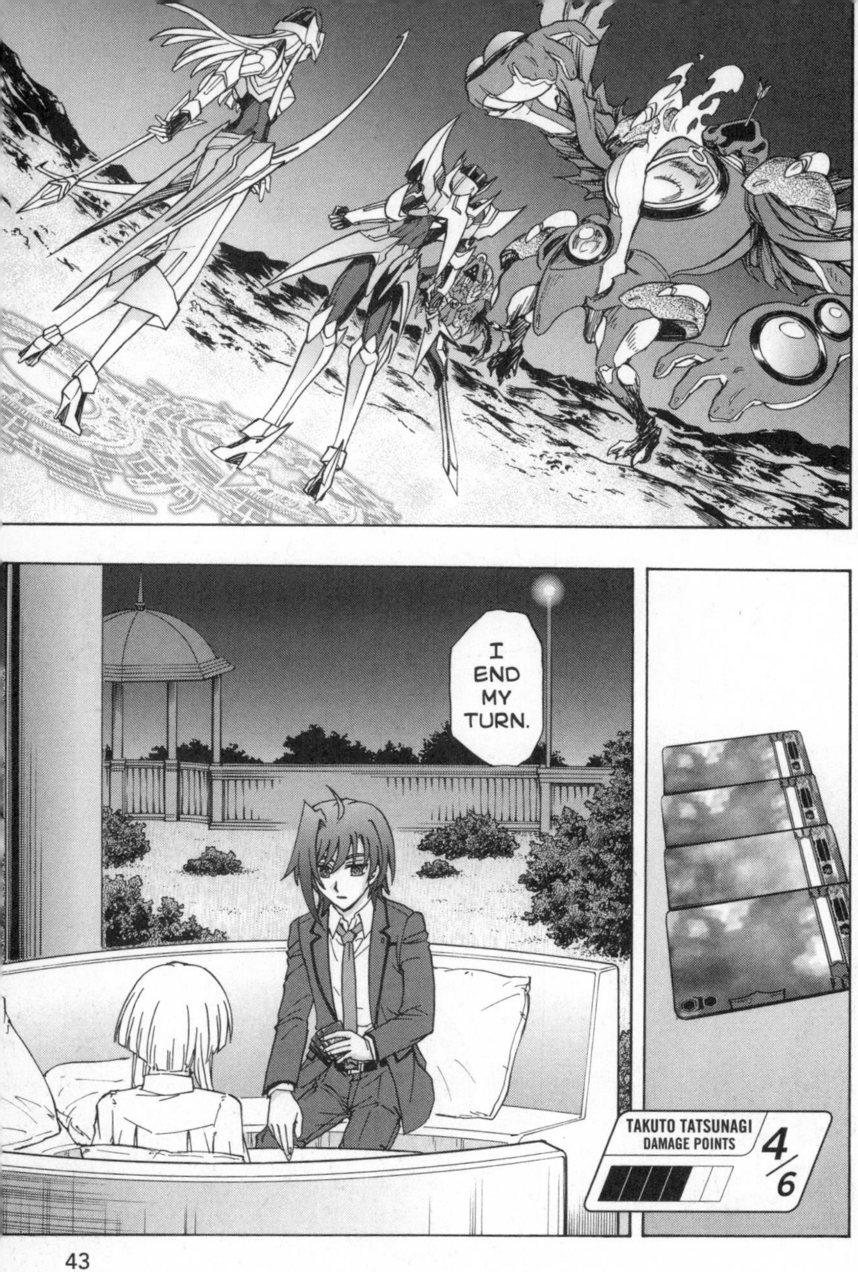
I END MY TURN.
TAKUTO TATSUNAGI
DAMAGE POINTS
4/6

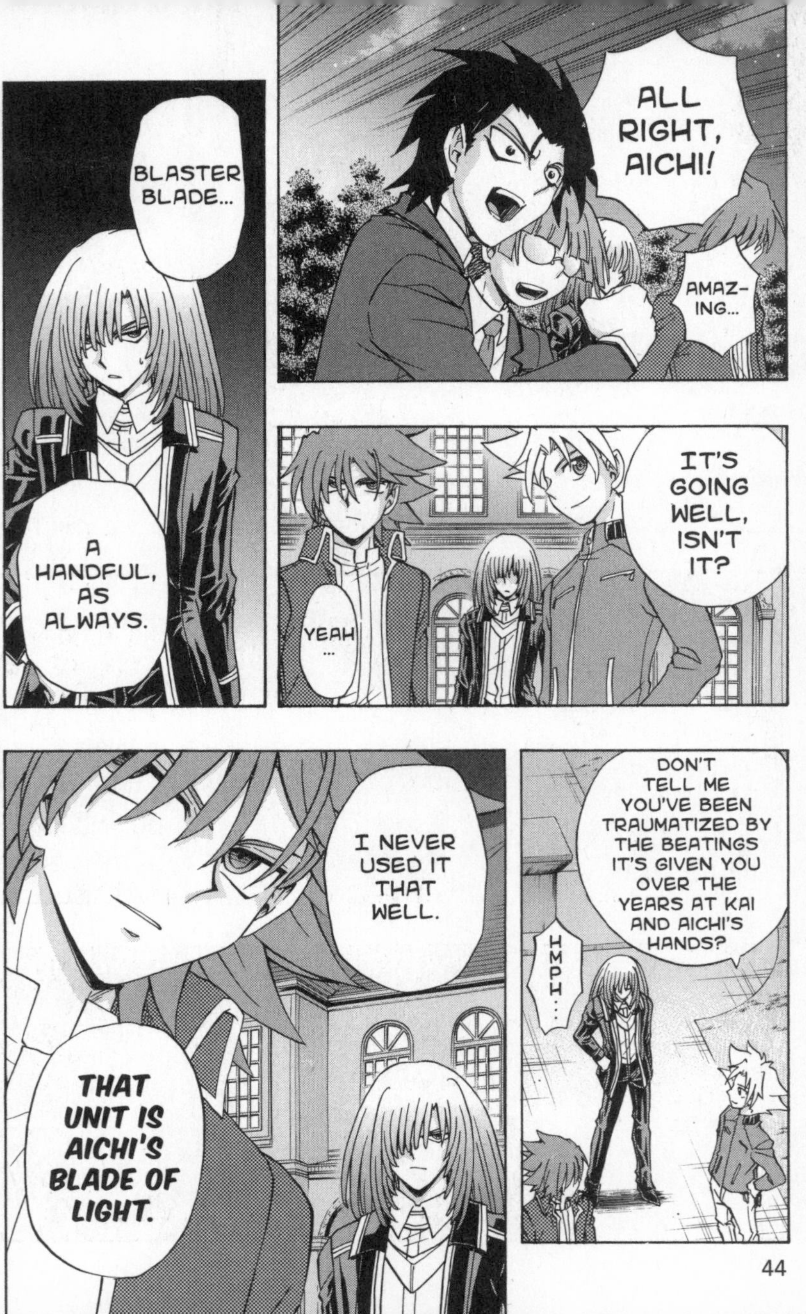
ALL RIGHT, AICHI!
AMAZING...
IT'S GOING WELL, ISN'T IT?
YEAH...
BLASTER BLADE...
A HANDFUL, AS ALWAYS.
DON'T TELL ME YOU'VE BEEN TRAUMATIZED BY THE BEATINGS IT'S GIVEN YOU OVER THE YEARS AT KAI AND AICHI'S HANDS?
HMPH...
I NEVER USED IT THAT WELL.
THAT UNIT IS AICHI'S BLADE OF LIGHT.

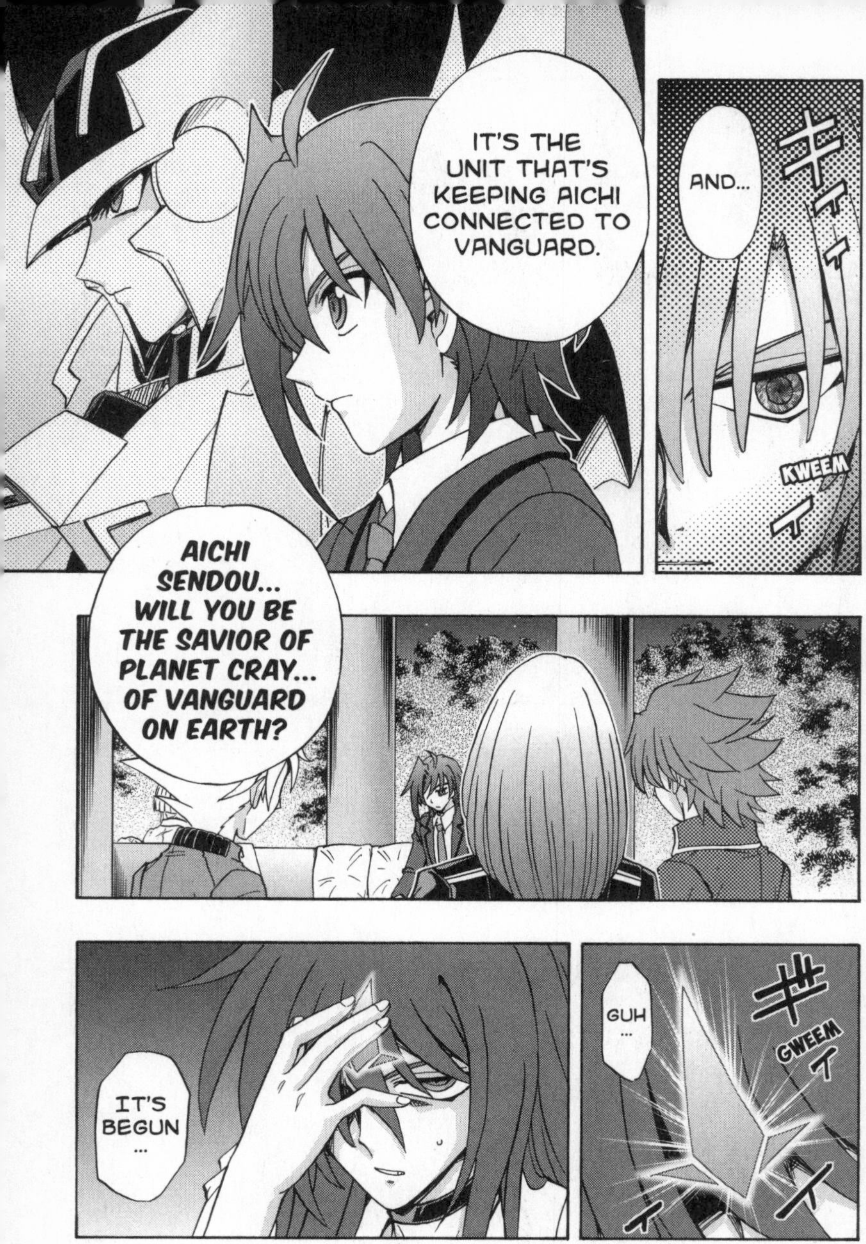
AND...
KWEEM
IT'S THE UNIT THAT'S KEEPING AICHI CONNECTED TO VANGUARD.
AICHI SENDOU... WILL YOU BE THE SAVIOR OF PLANET CRAY... OF VANGUARD ON EARTH?
GUH ...
GWEEM
IT'S BEGUN ...

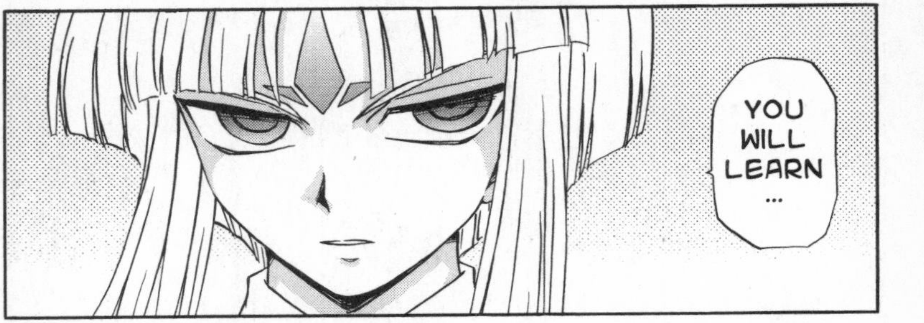
YOU WILL LEARN ...

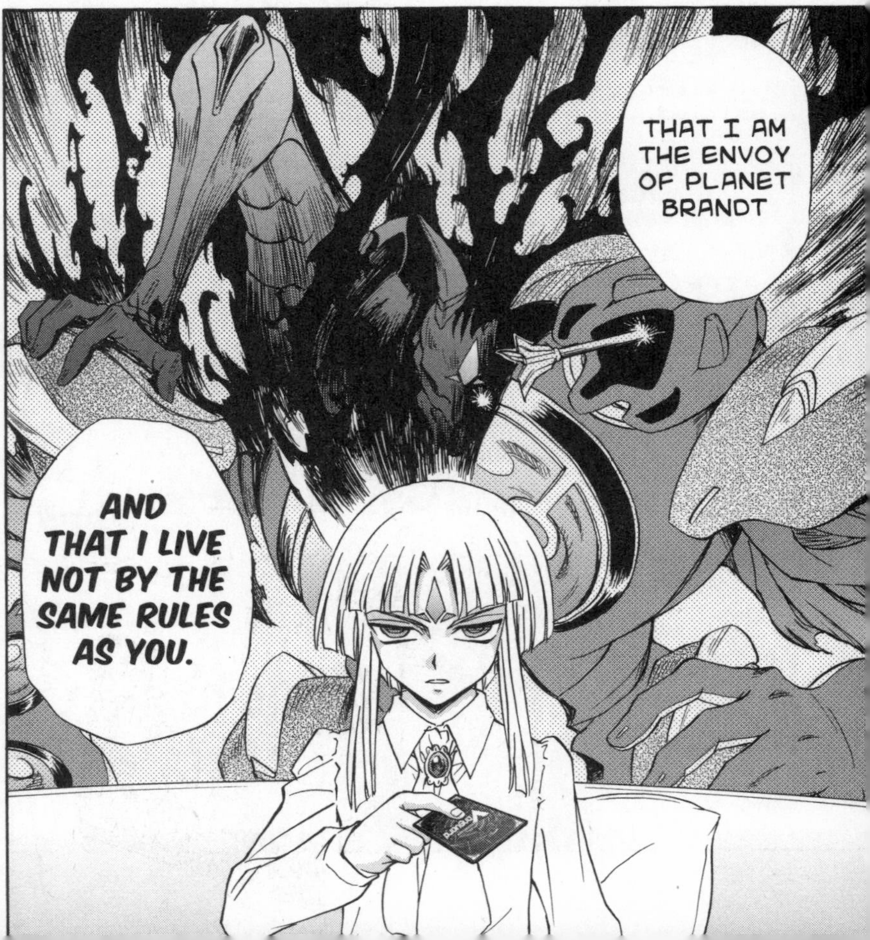
THAT I AM THE ENVOY OF PLANET BRANDT
AND THAT I LIVE NOT BY THE SAME RULES AS YOU.

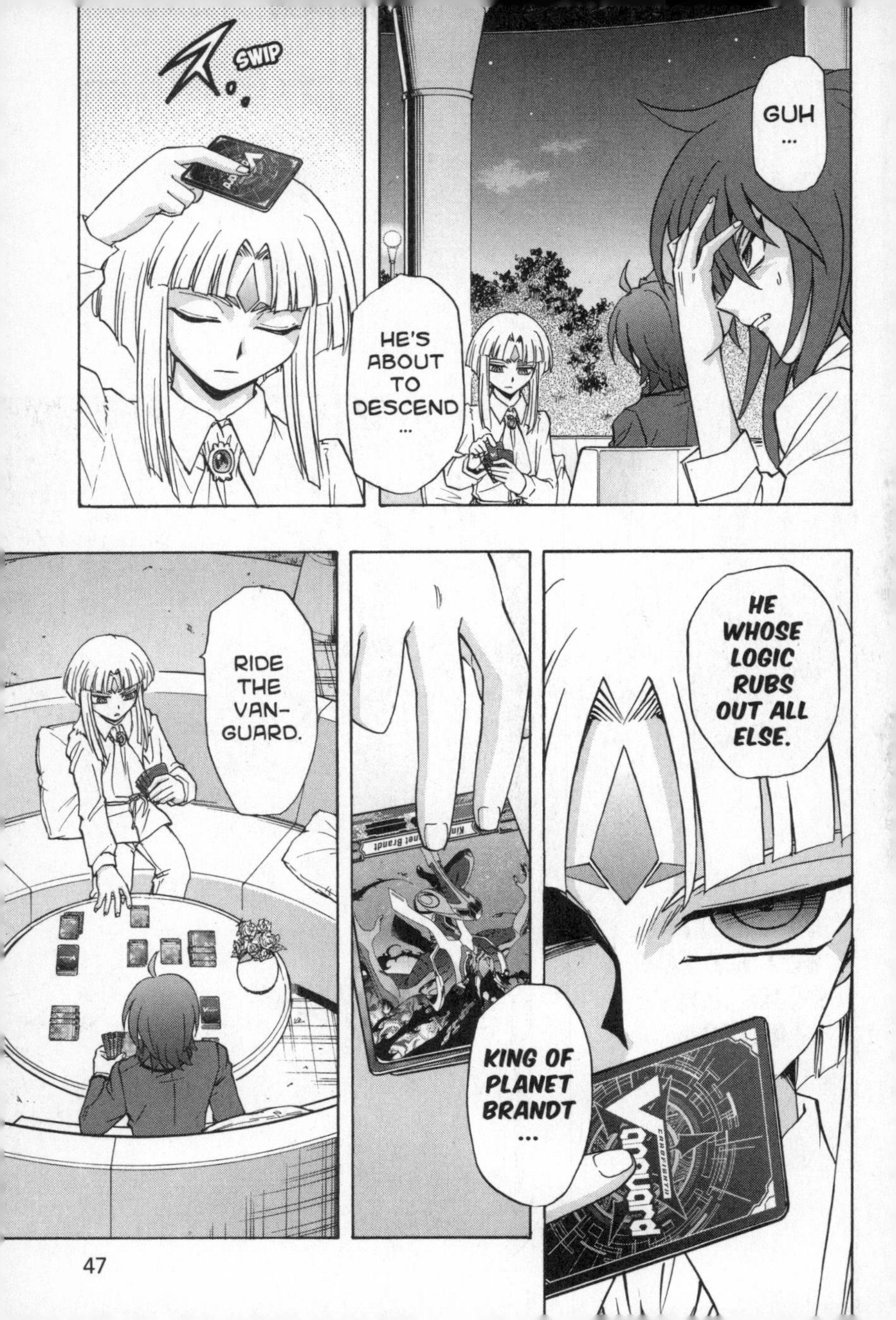
GUH ...
HE'S ABOUT TO DESCEND ...
SWIP
HE WHOSE LOGIC RUBS OUT ALL ELSE.
KING OF PLANET BRANDT ...
RIDE THE VAN-GUARD.

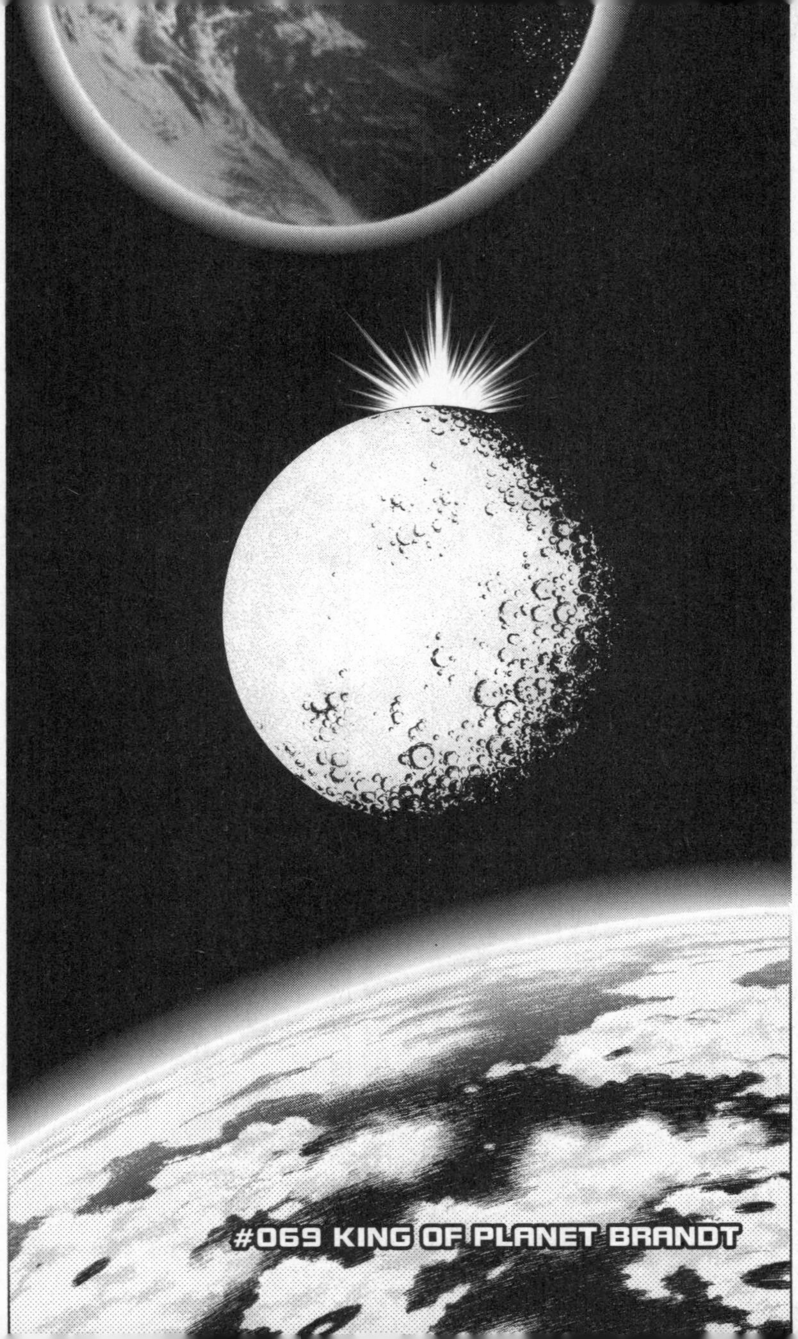
#069 KING OF PLANET BRANDT

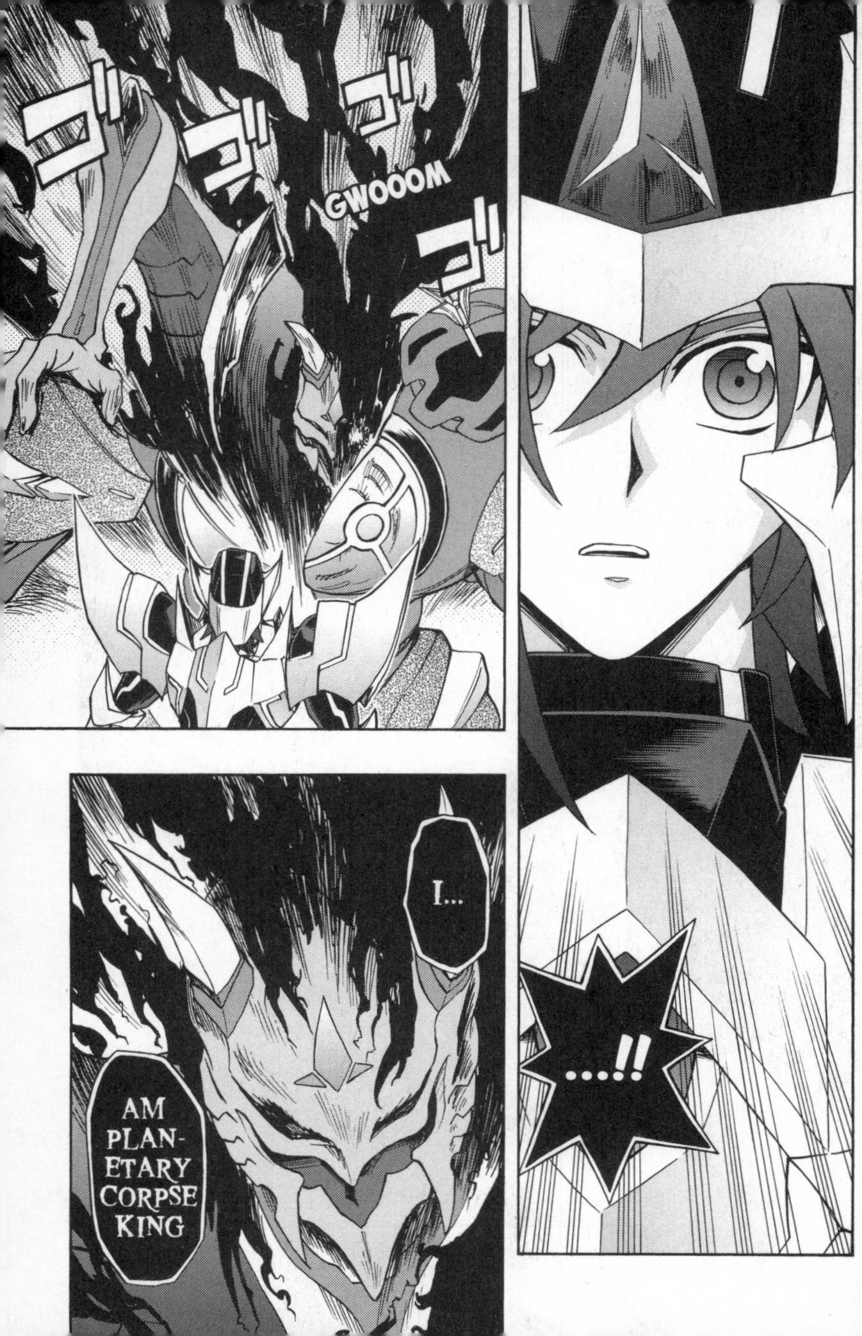
....!!
ゴゴゴゴ
GWOOOM
I...
AM PLAN-ETARY CORPSE KING

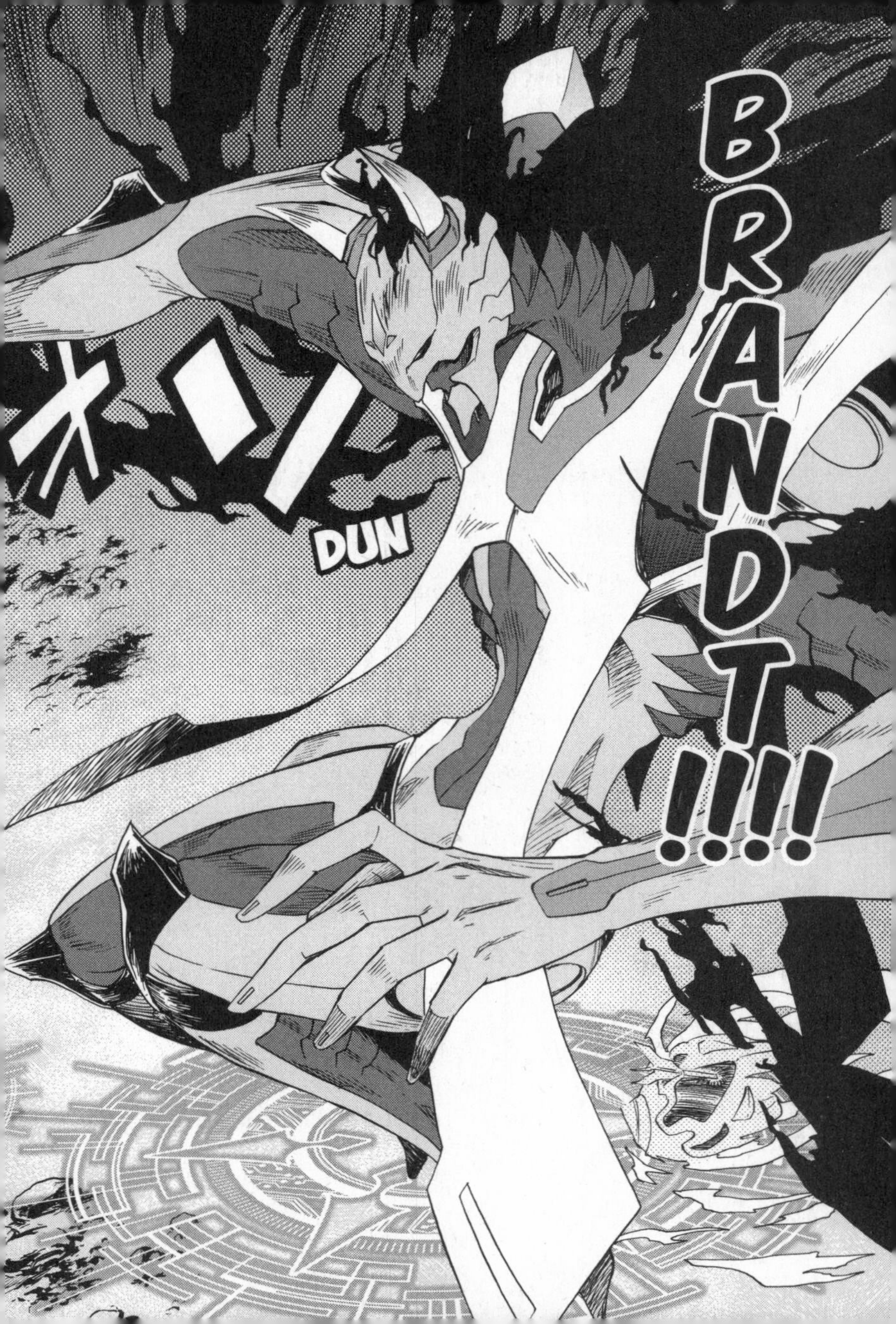
BRANDT!!!!
オーン
DUN

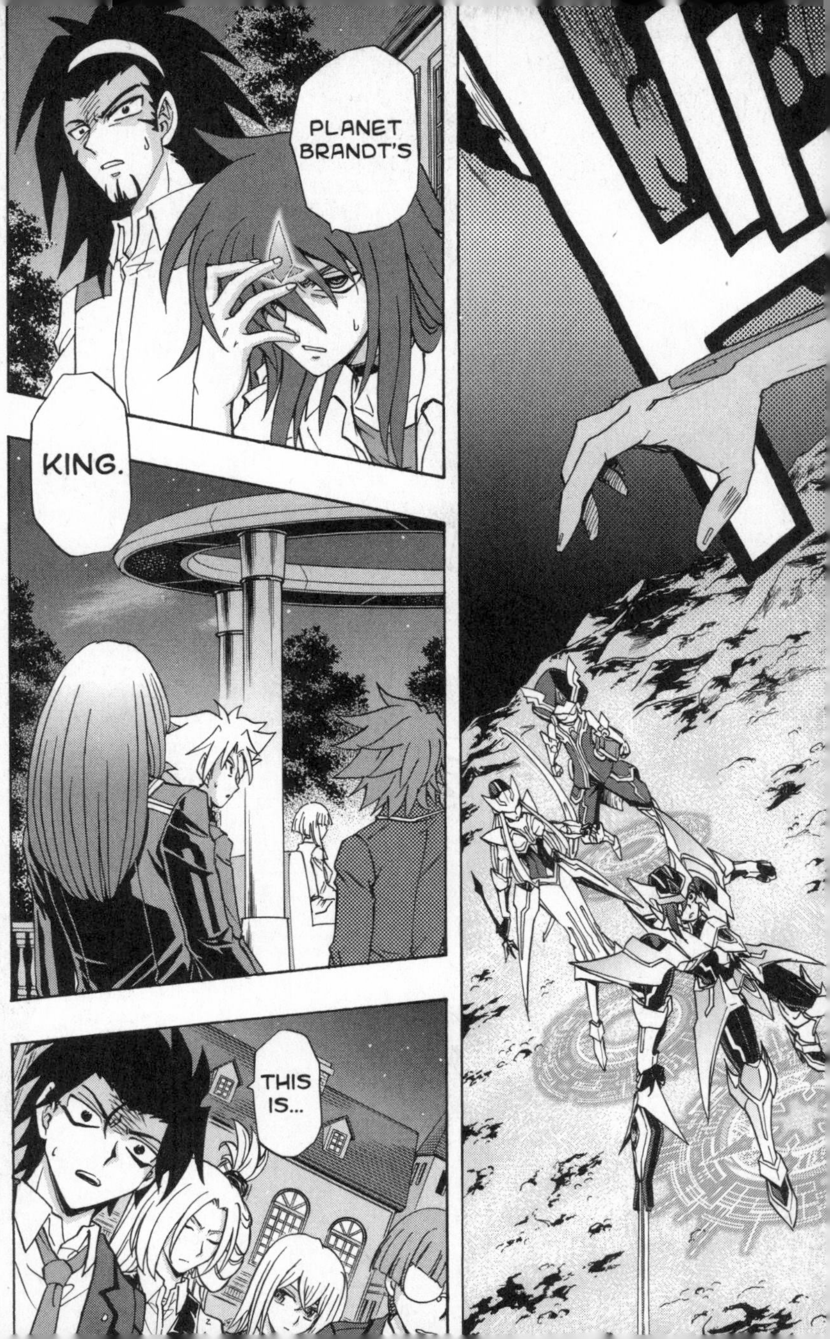
PLANET BRANDT'S
KING.
THIS IS...

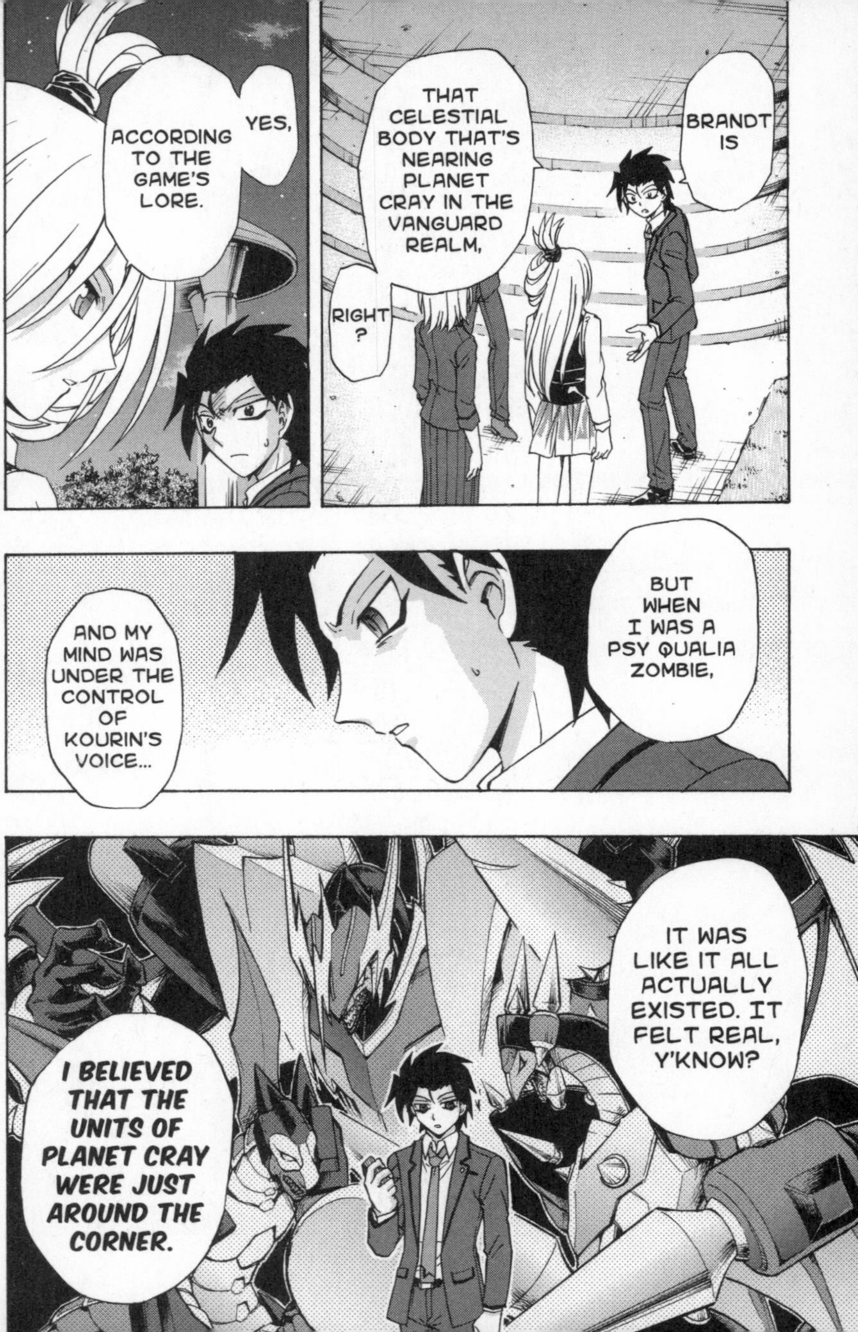
BRANDT IS
THAT CELESTIAL BODY THAT'S NEARING PLANET CRAY IN THE VANGUARD REALM,
RIGHT?
YES,
ACCORDING TO THE GAME'S LORE.
BUT WHEN I WAS A PSY QUALIA ZOMBIE,
AND MY MIND WAS UNDER THE CONTROL OF KOURIN'S VOICE...
IT WAS LIKE IT ALL ACTUALLY EXISTED. IT FELT REAL, Y'KNOW?
I BELIEVED THAT THE UNITS OF PLANET CRAY WERE JUST AROUND THE CORNER.

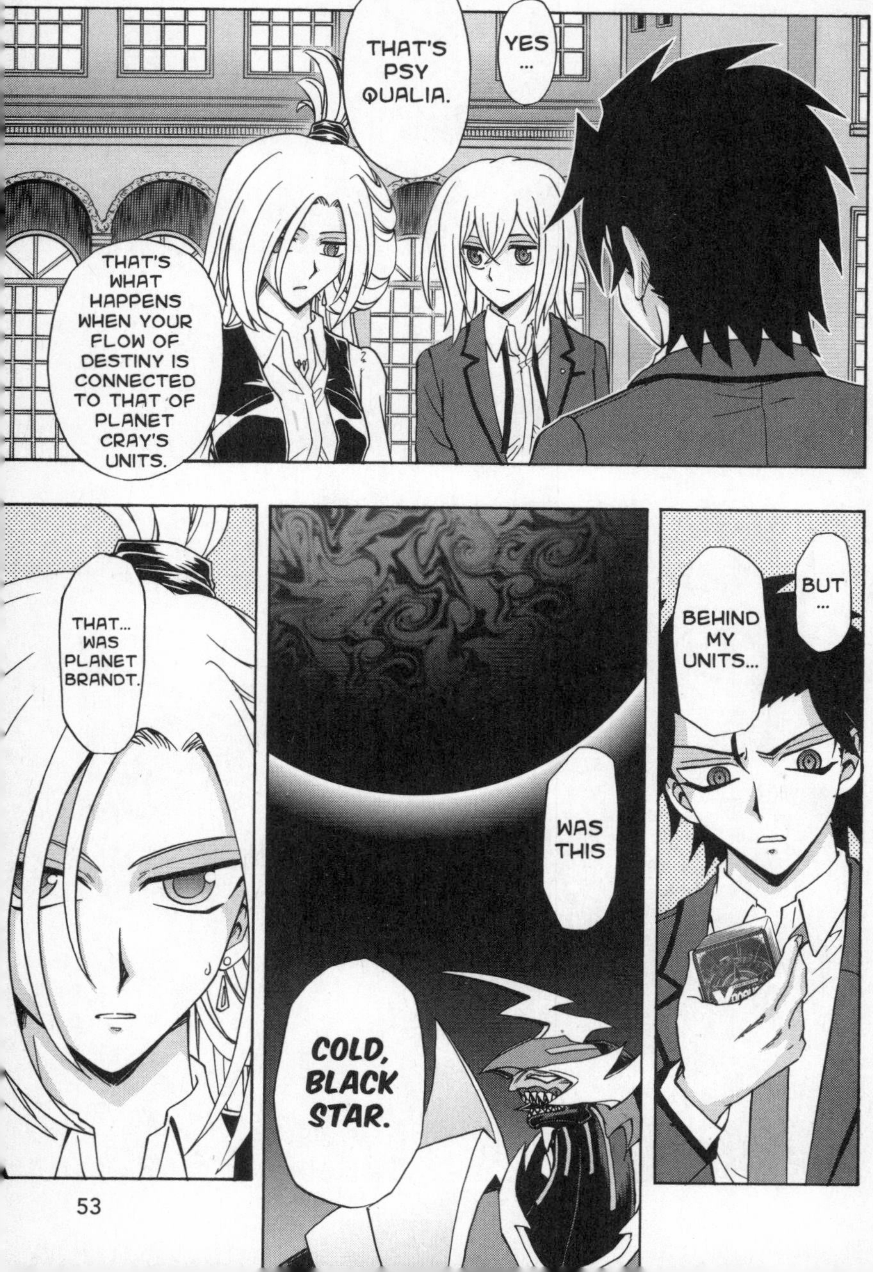
YES ...
THAT'S PSY QUALIA.
THAT'S WHAT HAPPENS WHEN YOUR FLOW OF DESTINY IS CONNECTED TO THAT OF PLANET CRAY'S UNITS.
BUT ...
BEHIND MY UNITS...
WAS THIS
COLD, BLACK STAR.
THAT... WAS PLANET BRANDT.

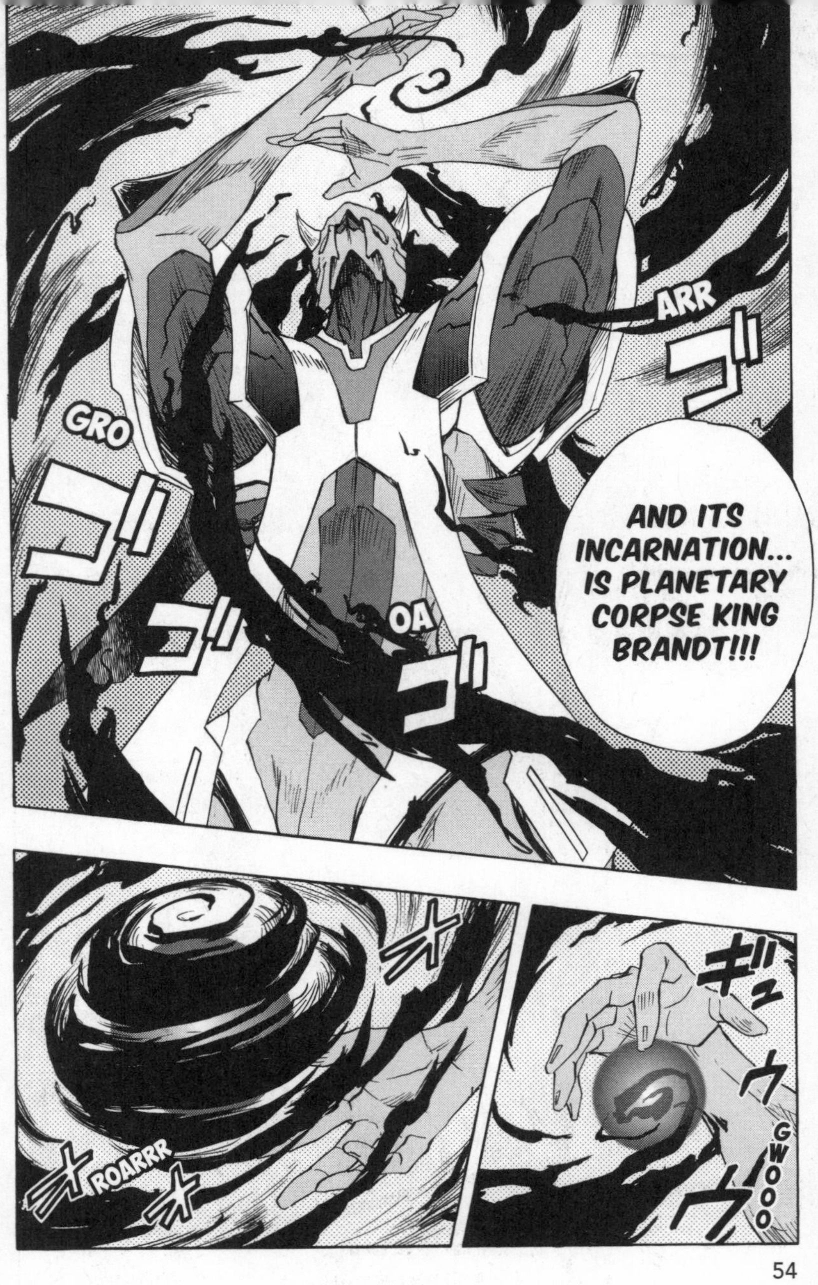
ARR
AND ITS INCARNATION... IS PLANETARY CORPSE KING BRANDT!!!
GRO
OA
GWOOO
ROARRR

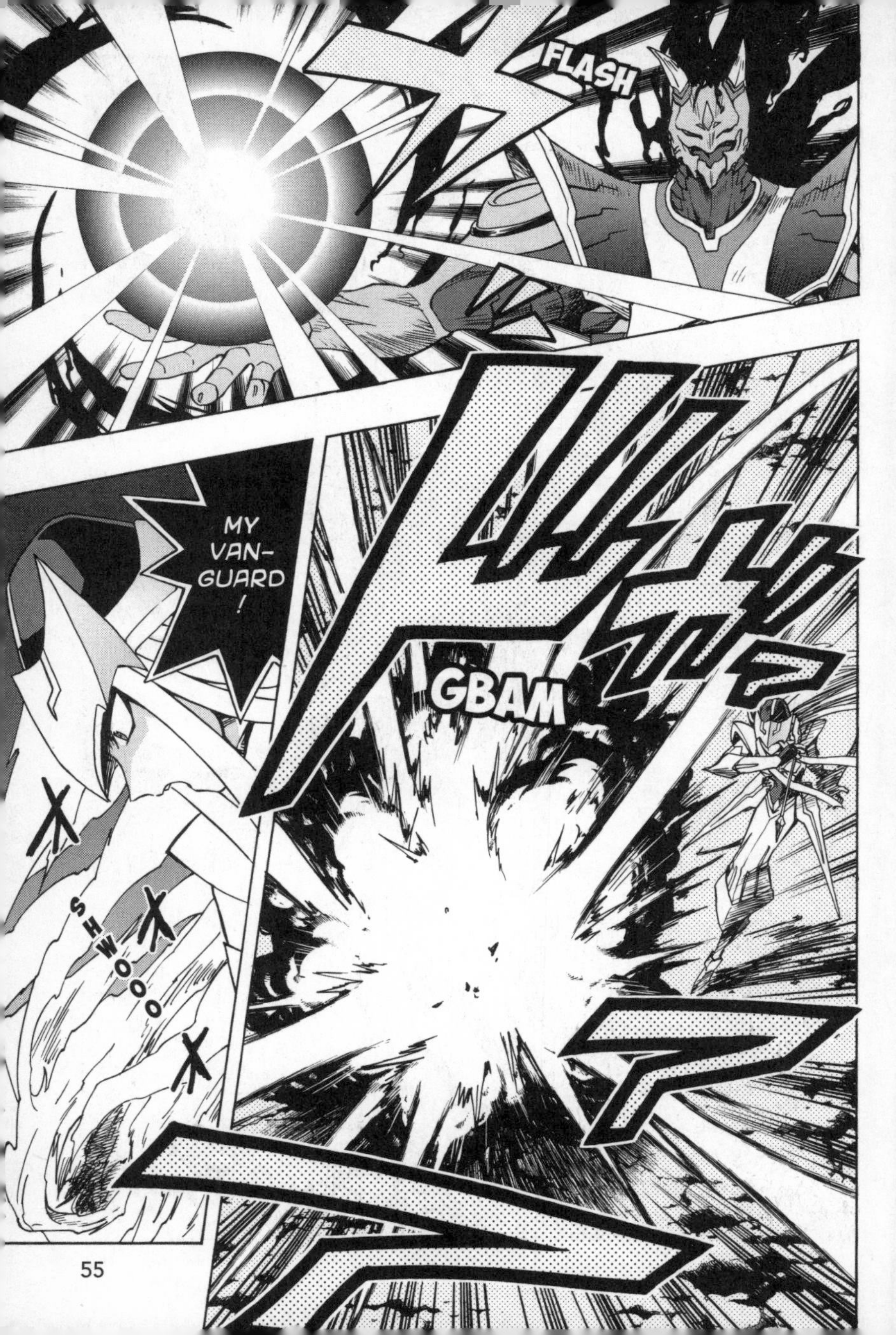
FLASH
GBAM
MY VAN-GUARD !
SHWOOO

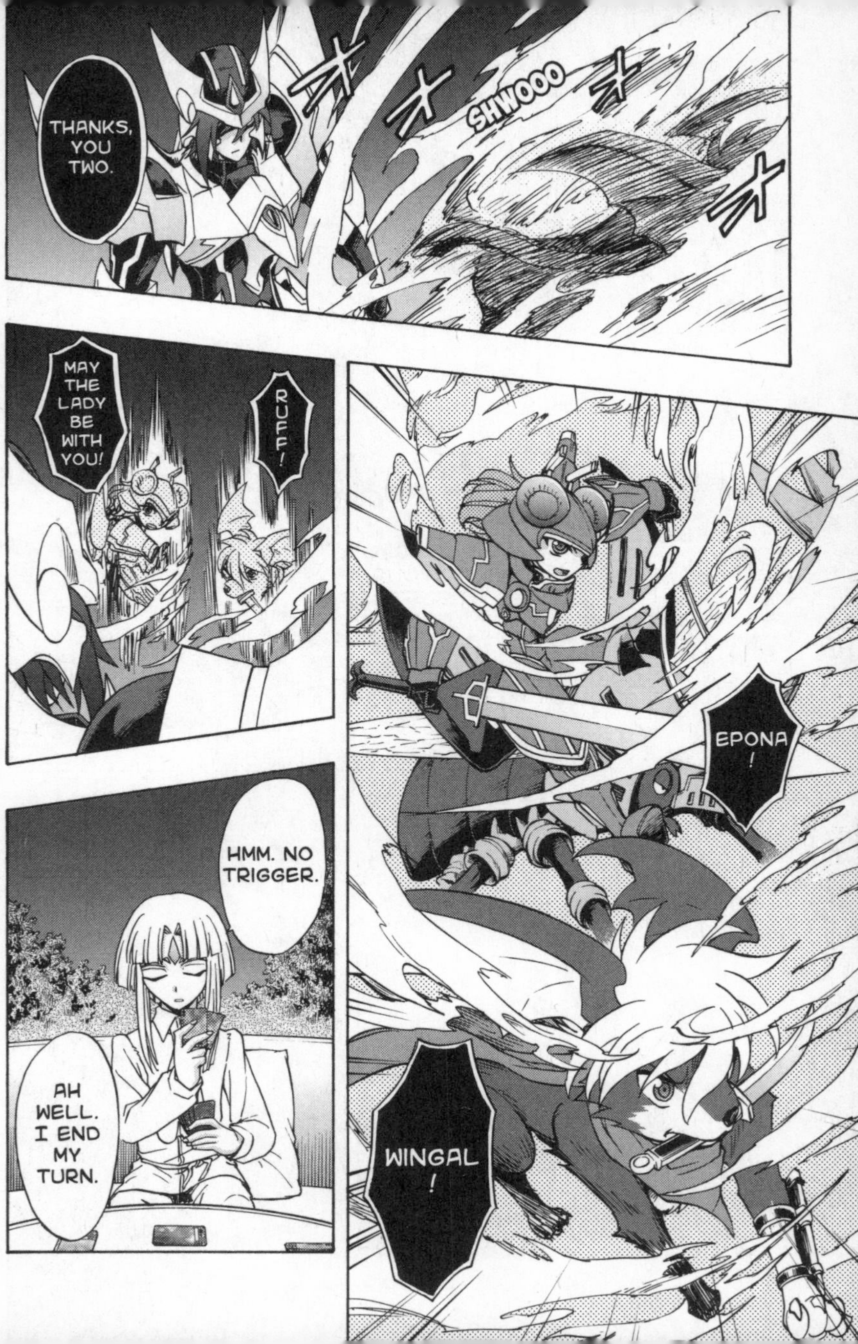
SHWOOO
THANKS, YOU TWO.
EPONA!
WINGAL!
RUFF!
MAY THE LADY BE WITH YOU!
HMM. NO TRIGGER.
AH WELL. I END MY TURN.

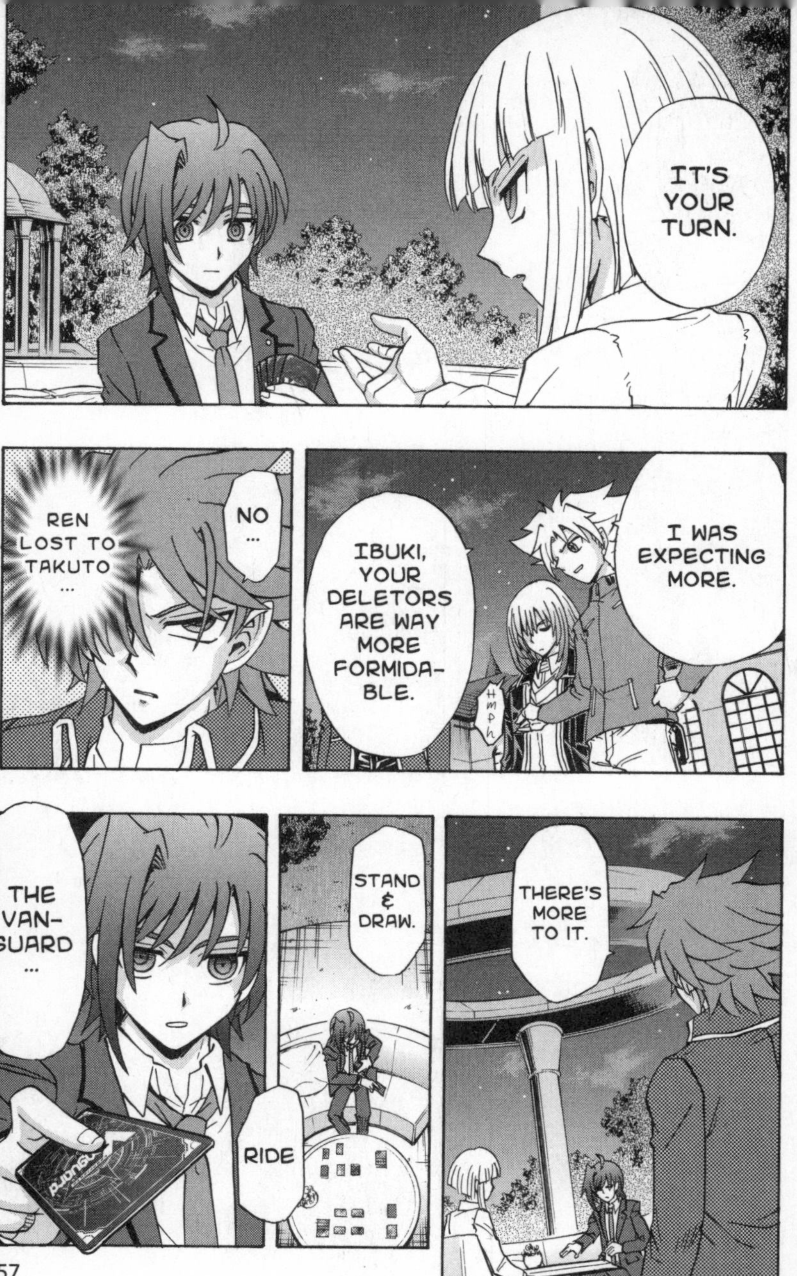
IT'S YOUR TURN.
I WAS EXPECTING MORE.
IBUKI, YOUR DELETORS ARE WAY MORE FORMIDA-BLE.
HMPh
NO ...
REN LOST TO TAKUTO ...
THERE'S MORE TO IT.
STAND & DRAW.
RIDE
THE VAN-GUARD ...

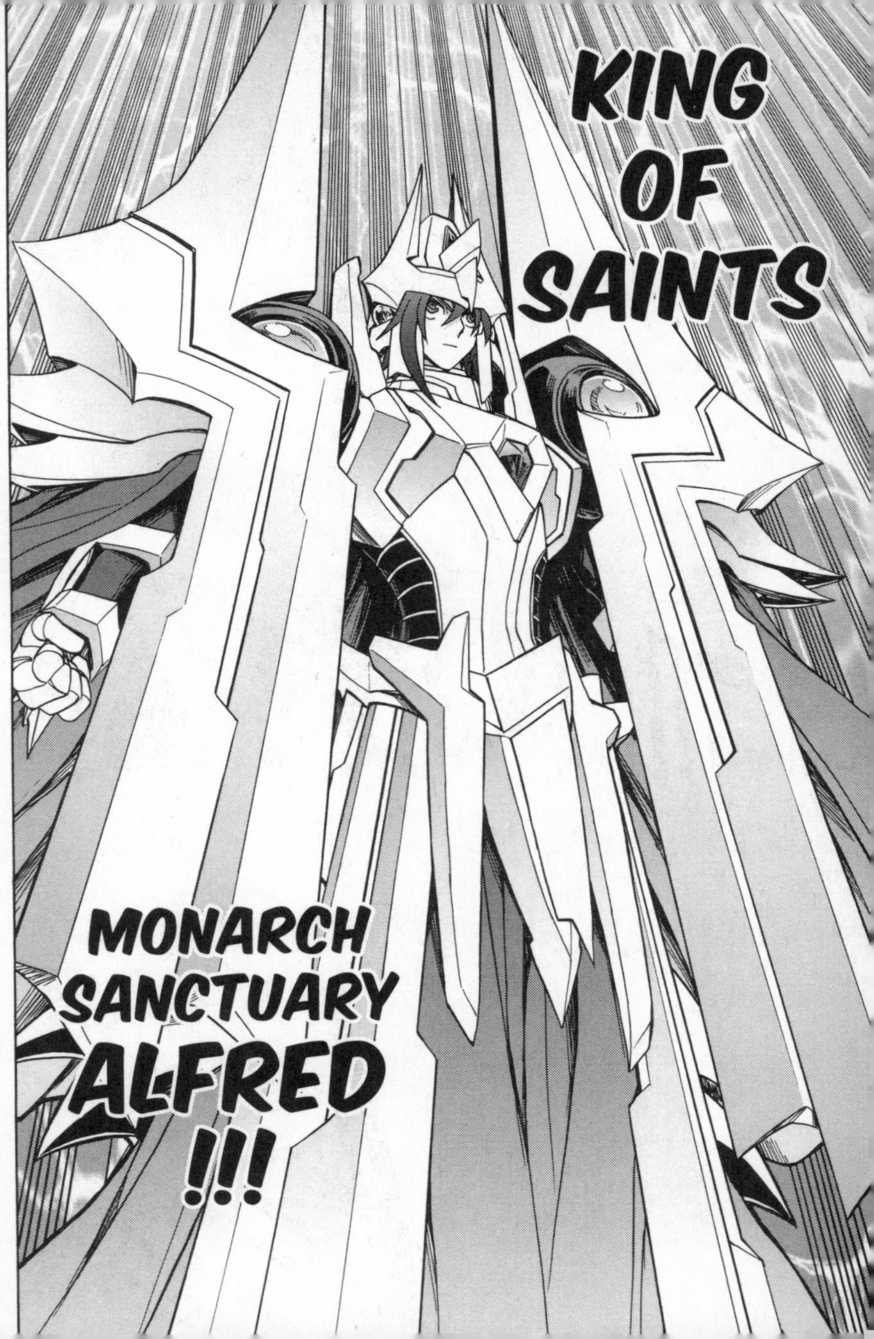
KING OF SAINTS
MONARCH SANCTUARY ALFRED !!!

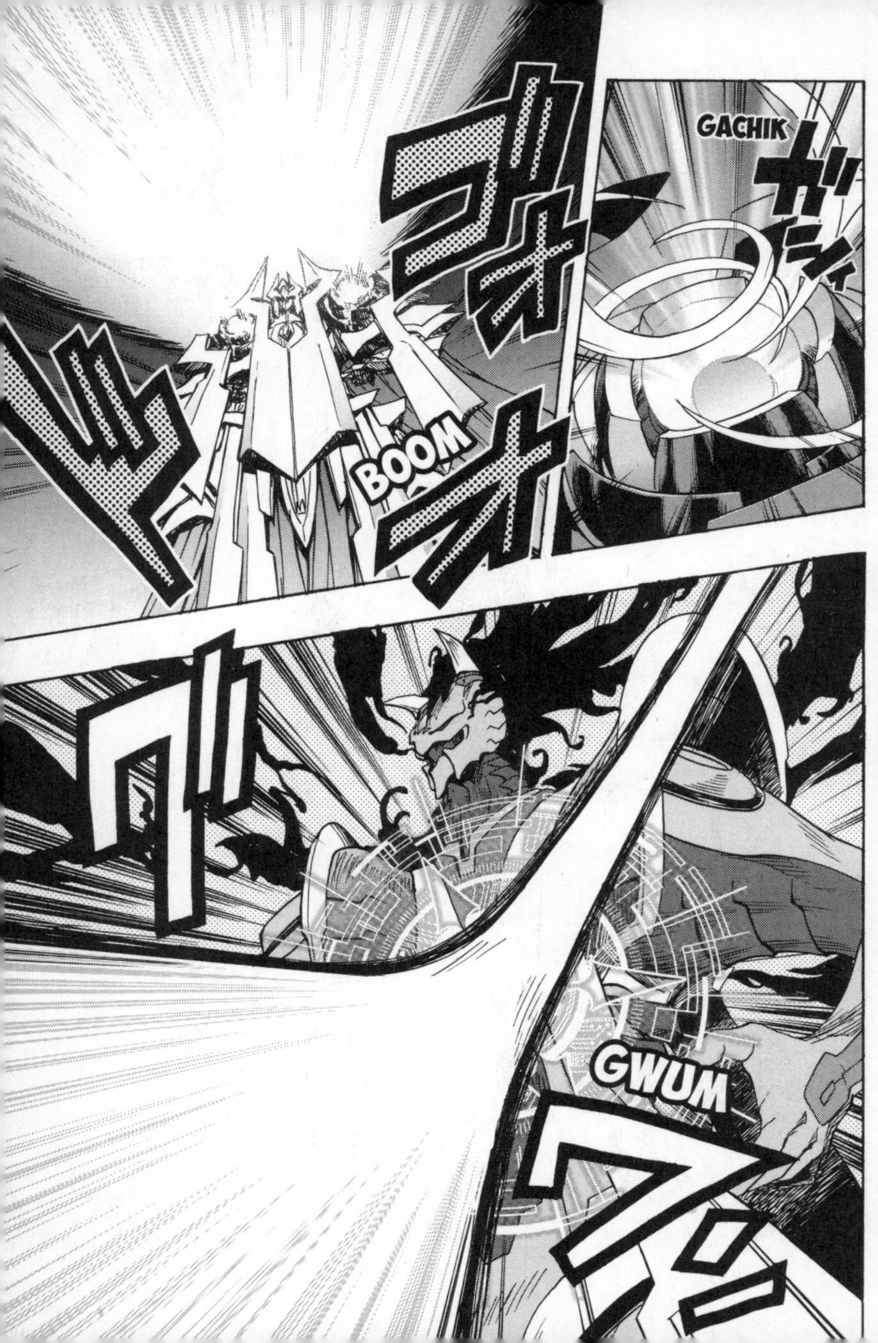
GACHIK
BOOM
GWUM

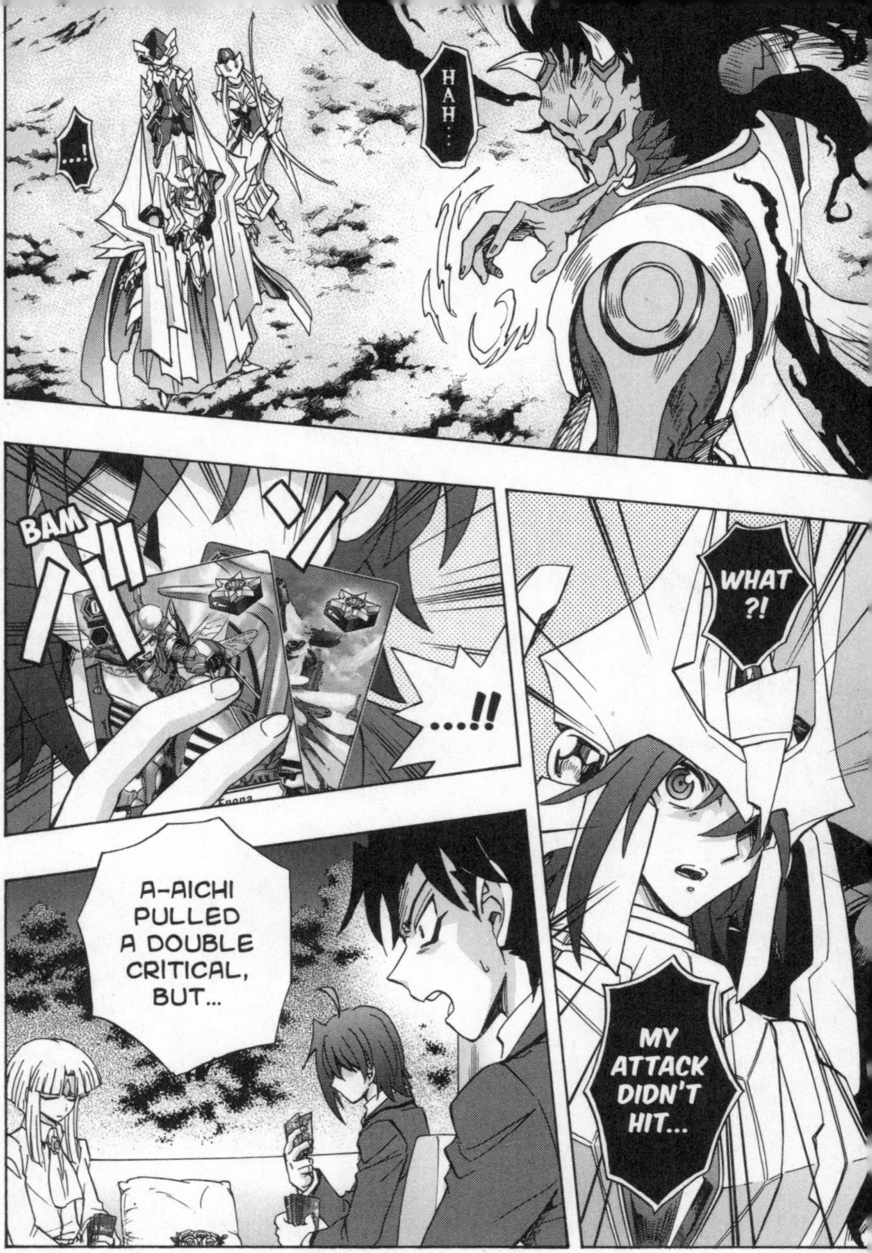
HAH...
...!
WHAT?!
MY ATTACK DIDN'T HIT...
...!!
BAM
A-AICHI PULLED A DOUBLE CRITICAL, BUT...

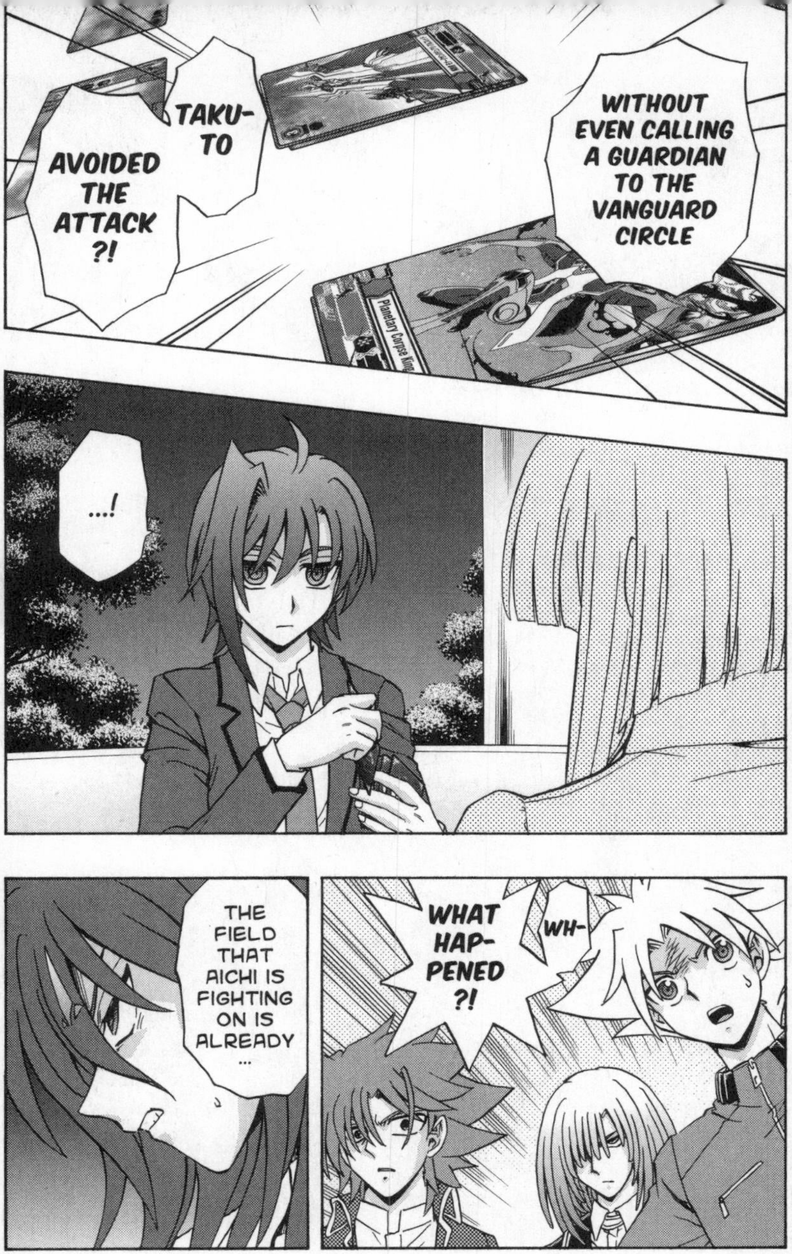
WITHOUT EVEN CALLING A GUARDIAN TO THE VANGUARD CIRCLE
TAKU-TO AVOIDED THE ATTACK ?!
Planetary Corpse King
...!
WH-
WHAT HAP-PENED ?!
THE FIELD THAT AICHI IS FIGHTING ON IS ALREADY ...

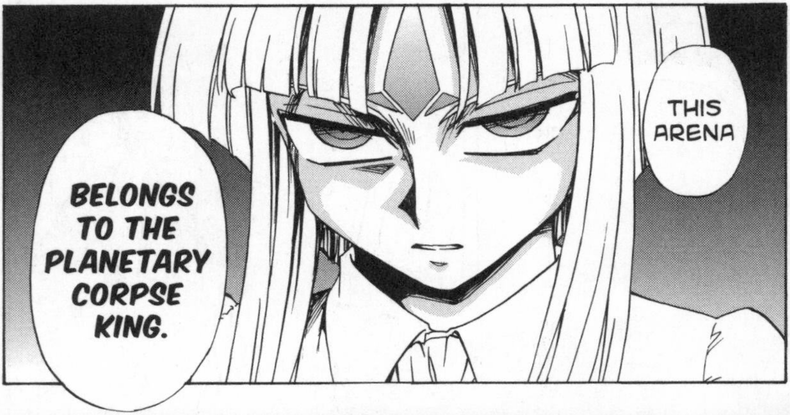
THIS ARENA
BELONGS TO THE PLANETARY CORPSE KING.

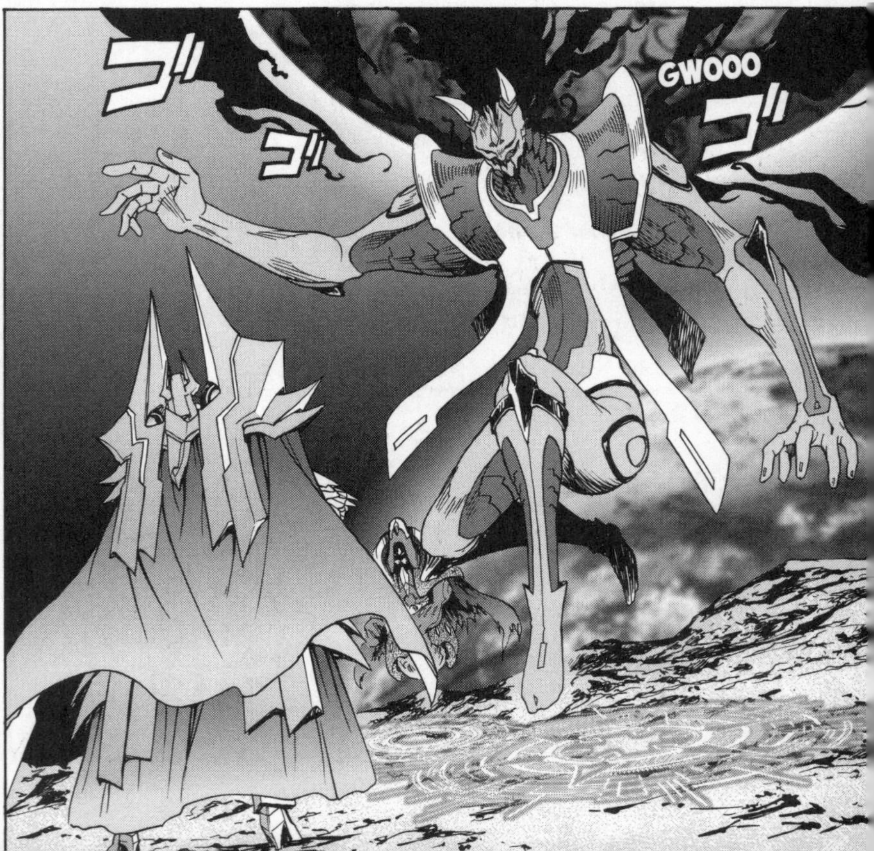
GWOOO
ゴ
ゴ
ゴ

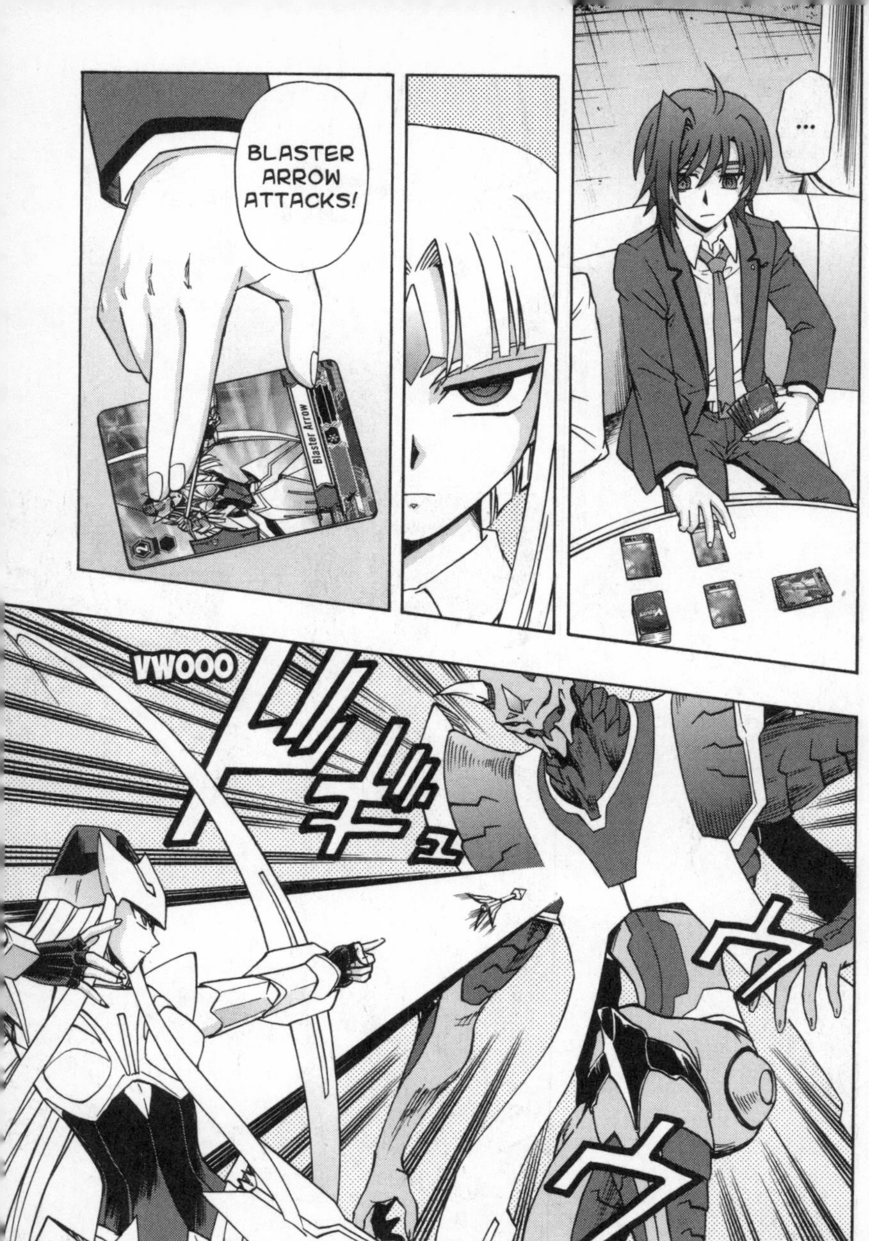
...
BLASTER ARROW ATTACKS!
Blaster Arrow
VWOOO

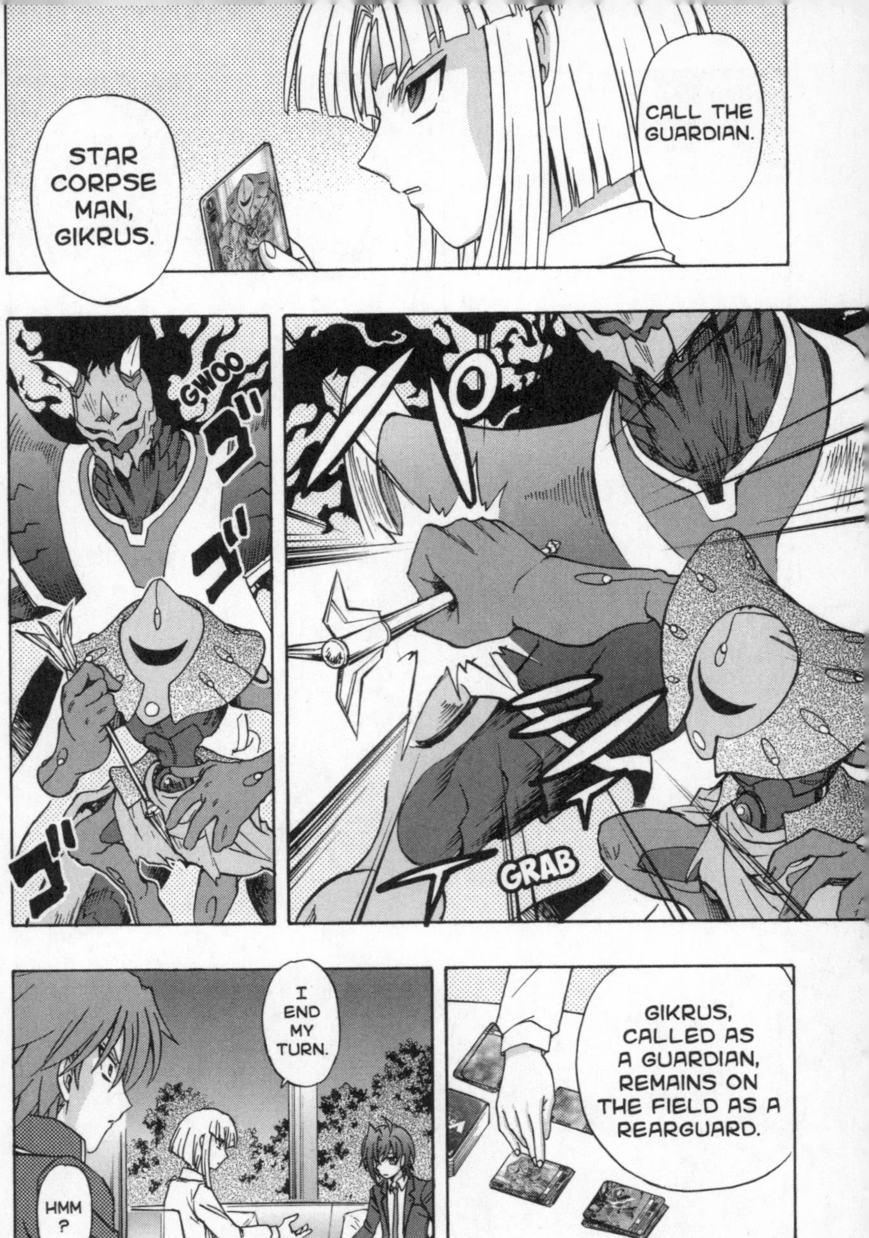
CALL THE GUARDIAN.
STAR CORPSE MAN, GIKRUS.
GRAB
GWOO
ゴゴゴ
GIKRUS, CALLED AS A GUARDIAN, REMAINS ON THE FIELD AS A REARGUARD.
I END MY TURN.
HMM?

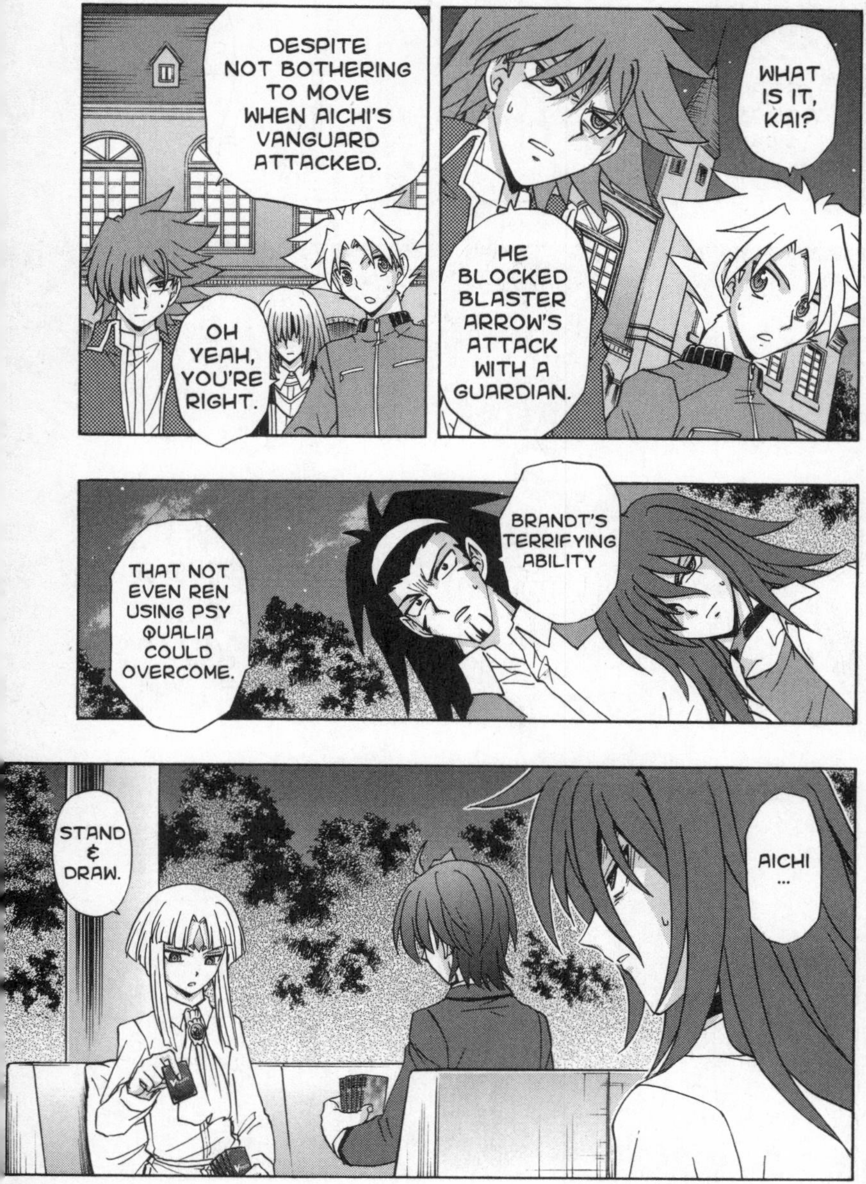
WHAT IS IT, KAI?
HE BLOCKED BLASTER ARROW'S ATTACK WITH A GUARDIAN.
DESPITE NOT BOTHERING TO MOVE WHEN AICHI'S VANGUARD ATTACKED.
OH YEAH, YOU'RE RIGHT.
BRANDT'S TERRIFYING ABILITY
THAT NOT EVEN REN USING PSY QUALIA COULD OVERCOME.
AICHI ...
STAND & DRAW.

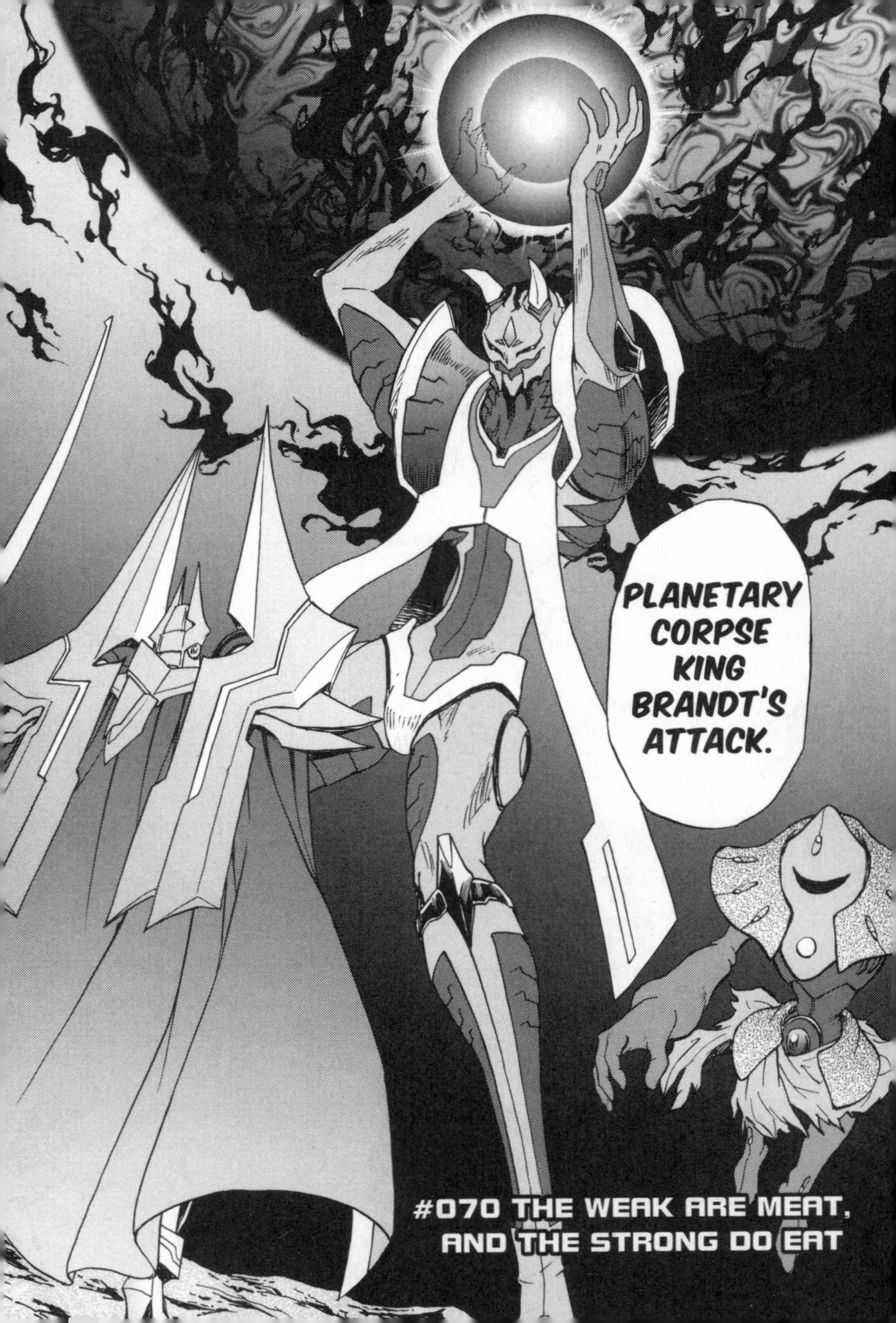
PLANETARY CORPSE KING BRANDT'S ATTACK.
#070 THE WEAK ARE MEAT, AND THE STRONG DO EAT

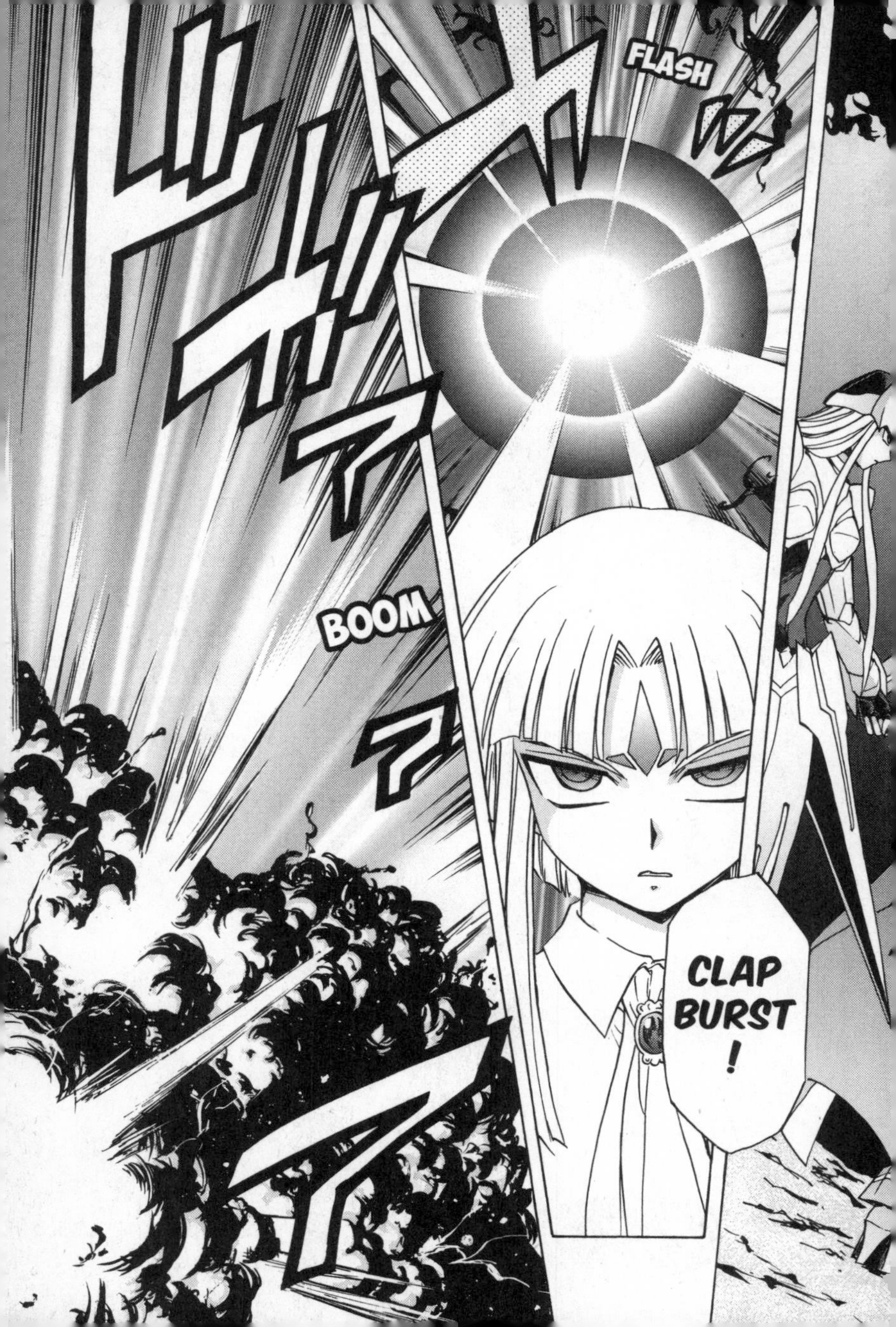
FLASH
BOOM
CLAP BURST!

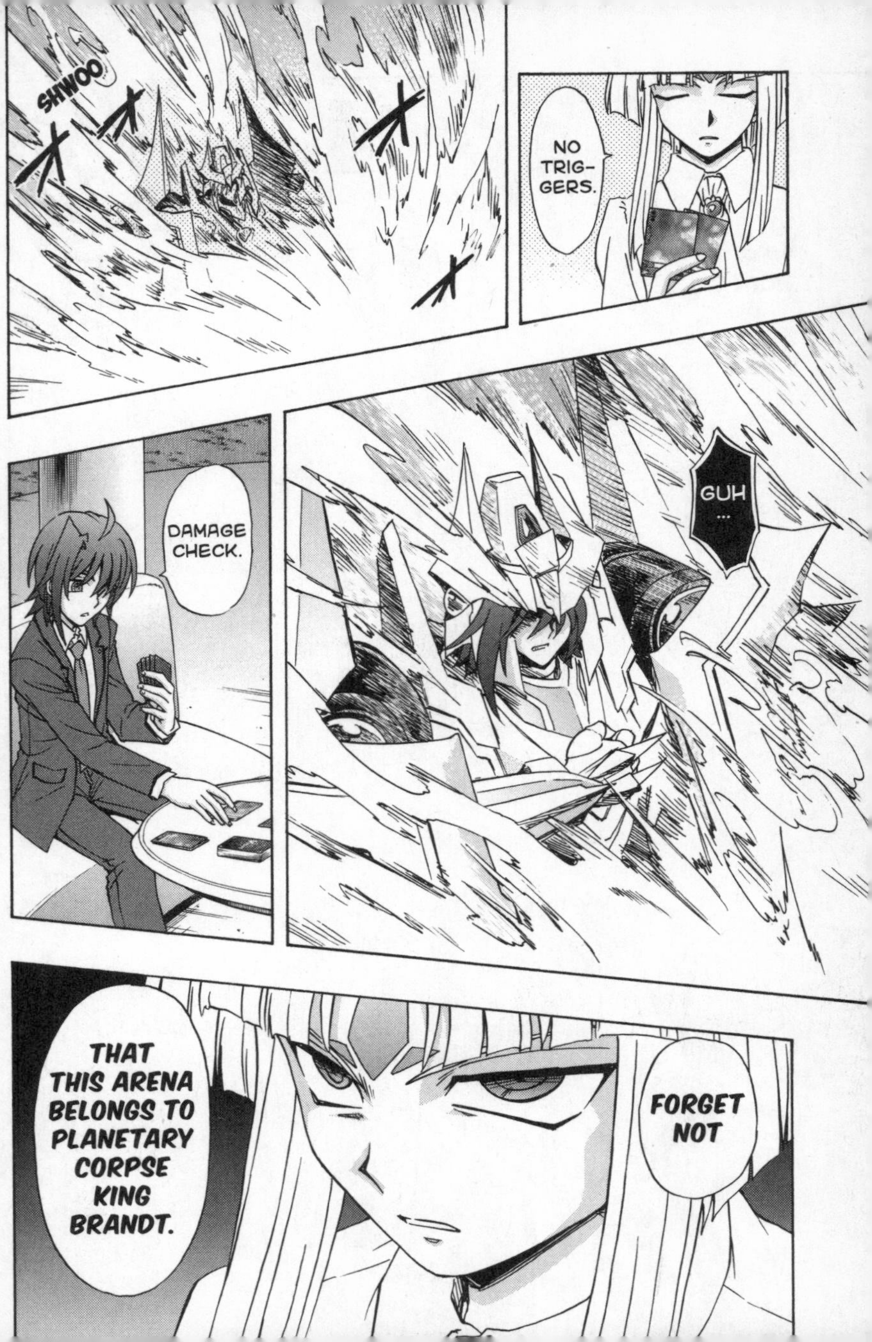
NO TRIGGERS.
SHWOO
GUH ...
DAMAGE CHECK.
FORGET NOT
THAT THIS ARENA BELONGS TO PLANETARY CORPSE KING BRANDT.

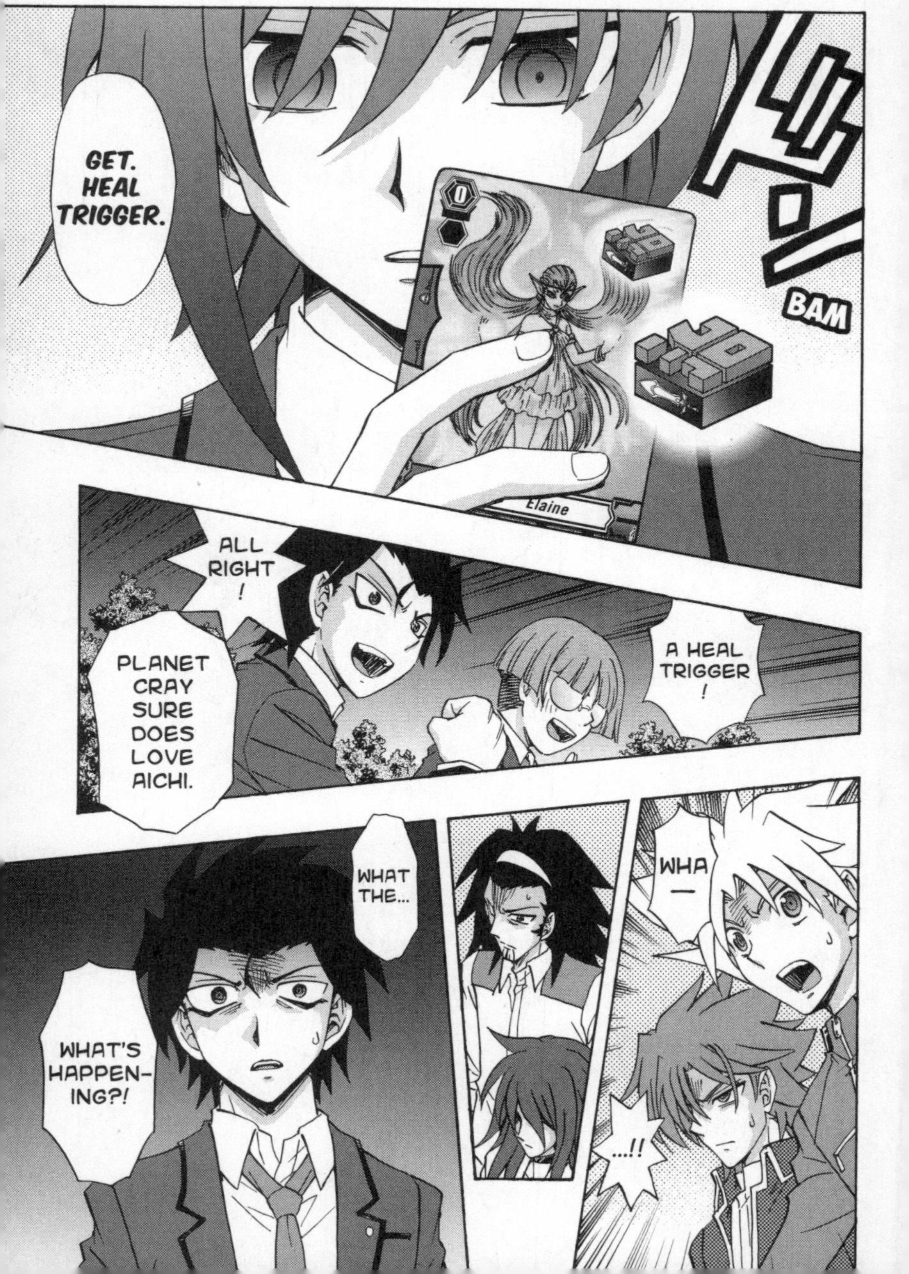

BAM
GET. HEAL TRIGGER.
Elaine
A HEAL TRIGGER!
ALL RIGHT!
PLANET CRAY SURE DOES LOVE AICHI.
WHA—
...!!
WHAT THE...
WHAT'S HAPPEN-ING?!

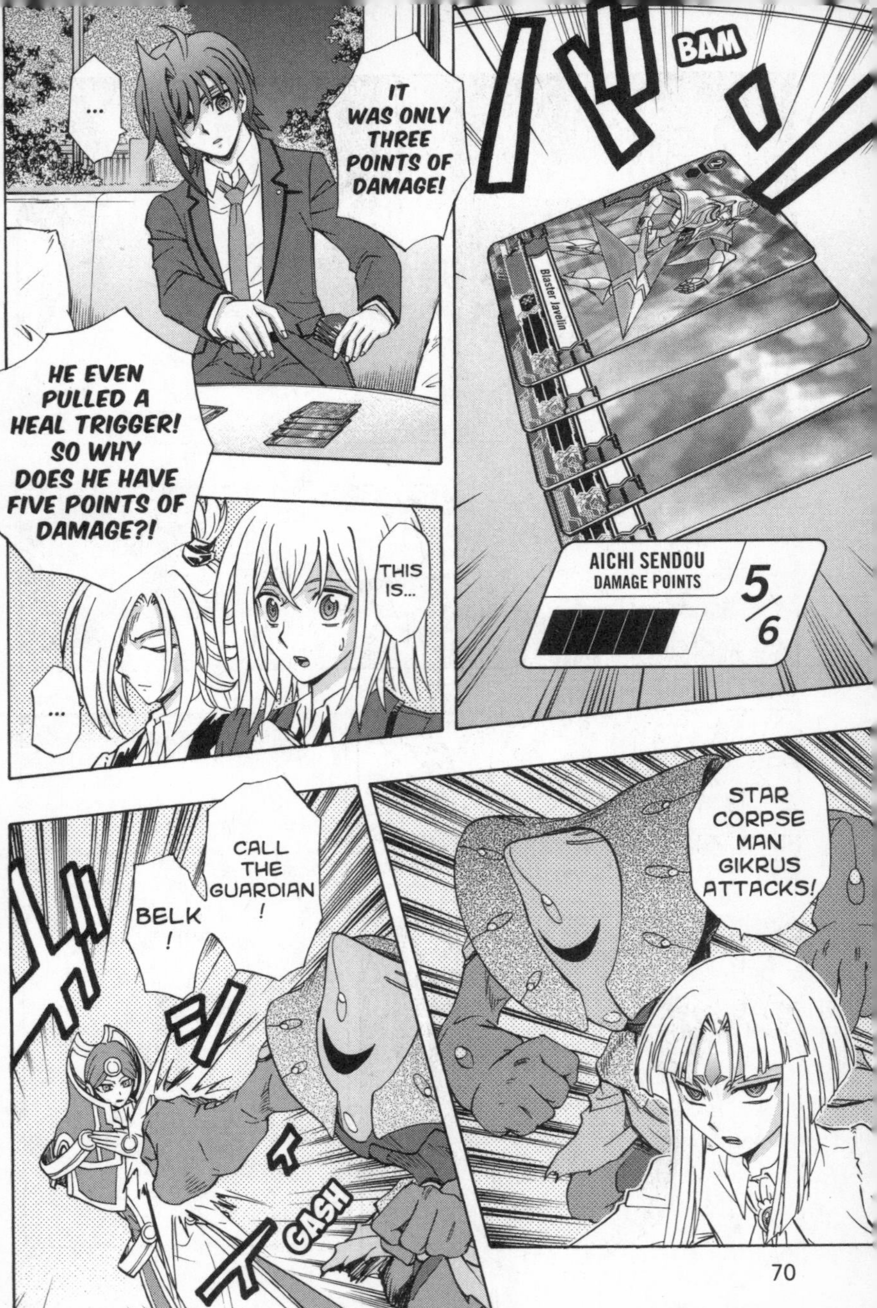
BAM
Blaster Javelin
AICHI SENDOU
DAMAGE POINTS
5/6
IT WAS ONLY THREE POINTS OF DAMAGE!
...
HE EVEN PULLED A HEAL TRIGGER! SO WHY DOES HE HAVE FIVE POINTS OF DAMAGE?!
THIS IS...
...
STAR CORPSE MAN GIKRUS ATTACKS!
CALL THE GUARDIAN!
BELK!
GASH

MY TURN...

STAND & DRAW.

GACHIK

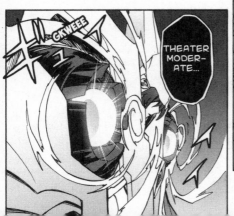

GKSWEEE

THEATER MODER-ATE...

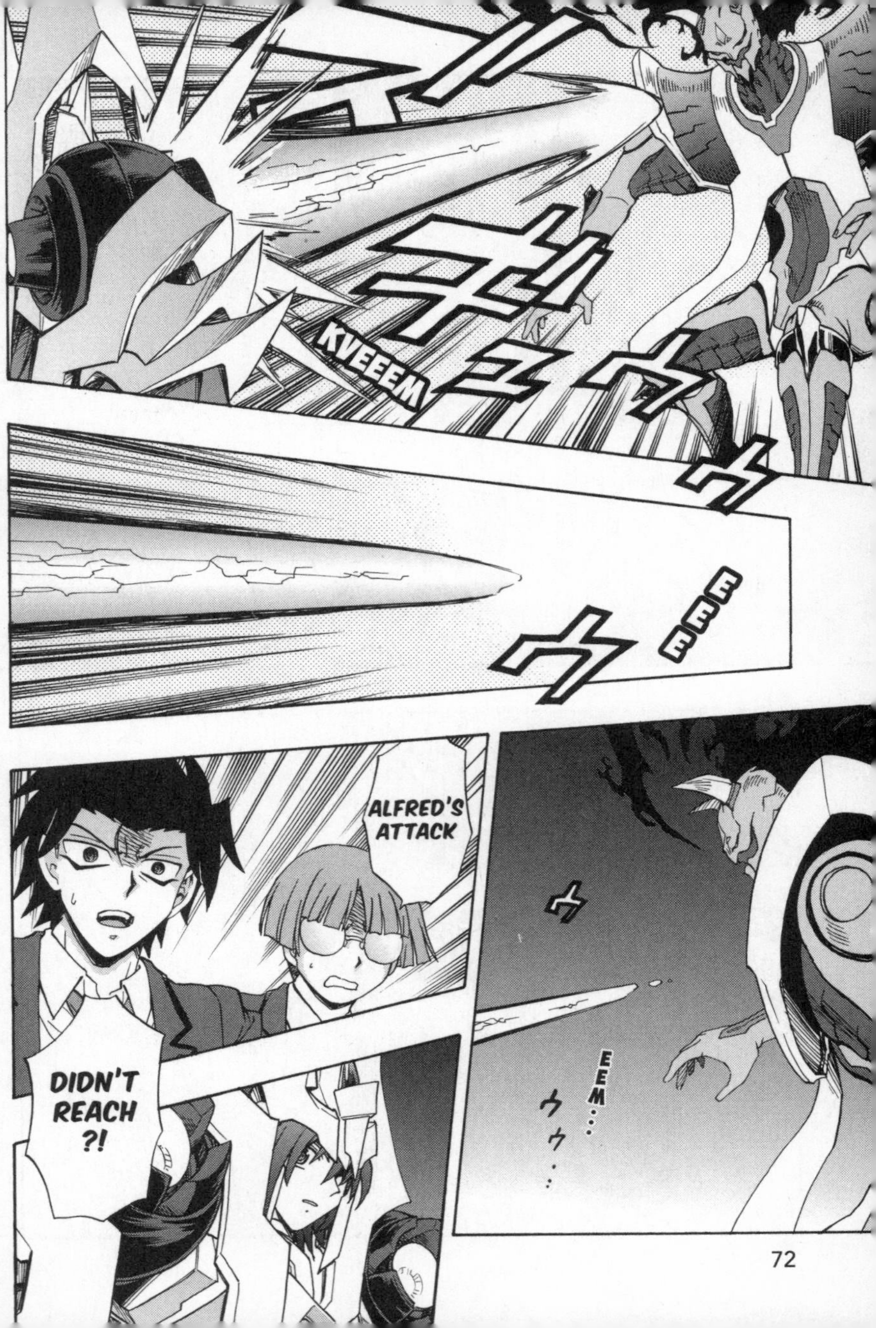
KVEEEEM
EEEE
EEM...
ALFRED'S ATTACK
DIDN'T REACH ?!

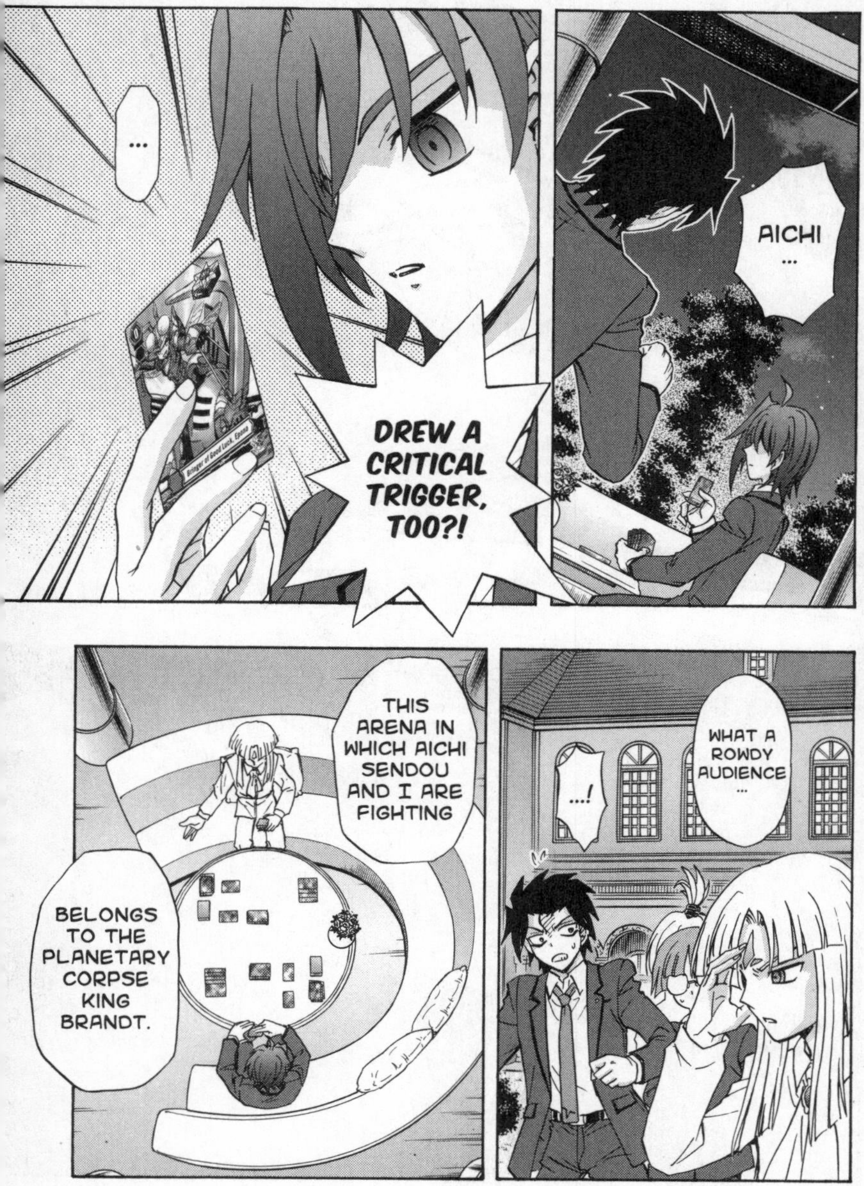
AICHI ...
...
Bringer of Good Luck, Epona
DREW A CRITICAL TRIGGER, TOO?!
WHAT A ROWDY AUDIENCE ...
...!
THIS ARENA IN WHICH AICHI SENDOU AND I ARE FIGHTING
BELONGS TO THE PLANETARY CORPSE KING BRANDT.

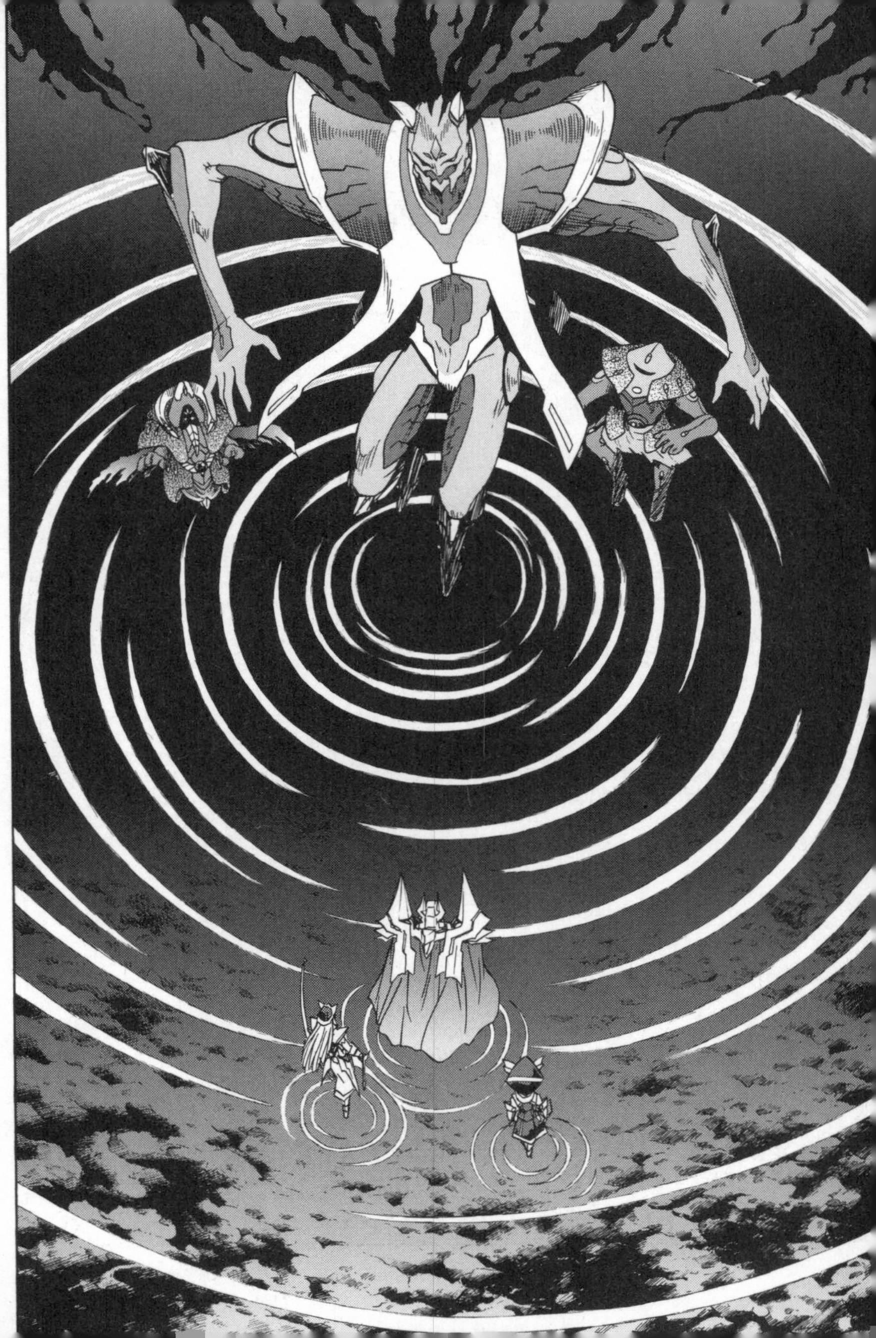

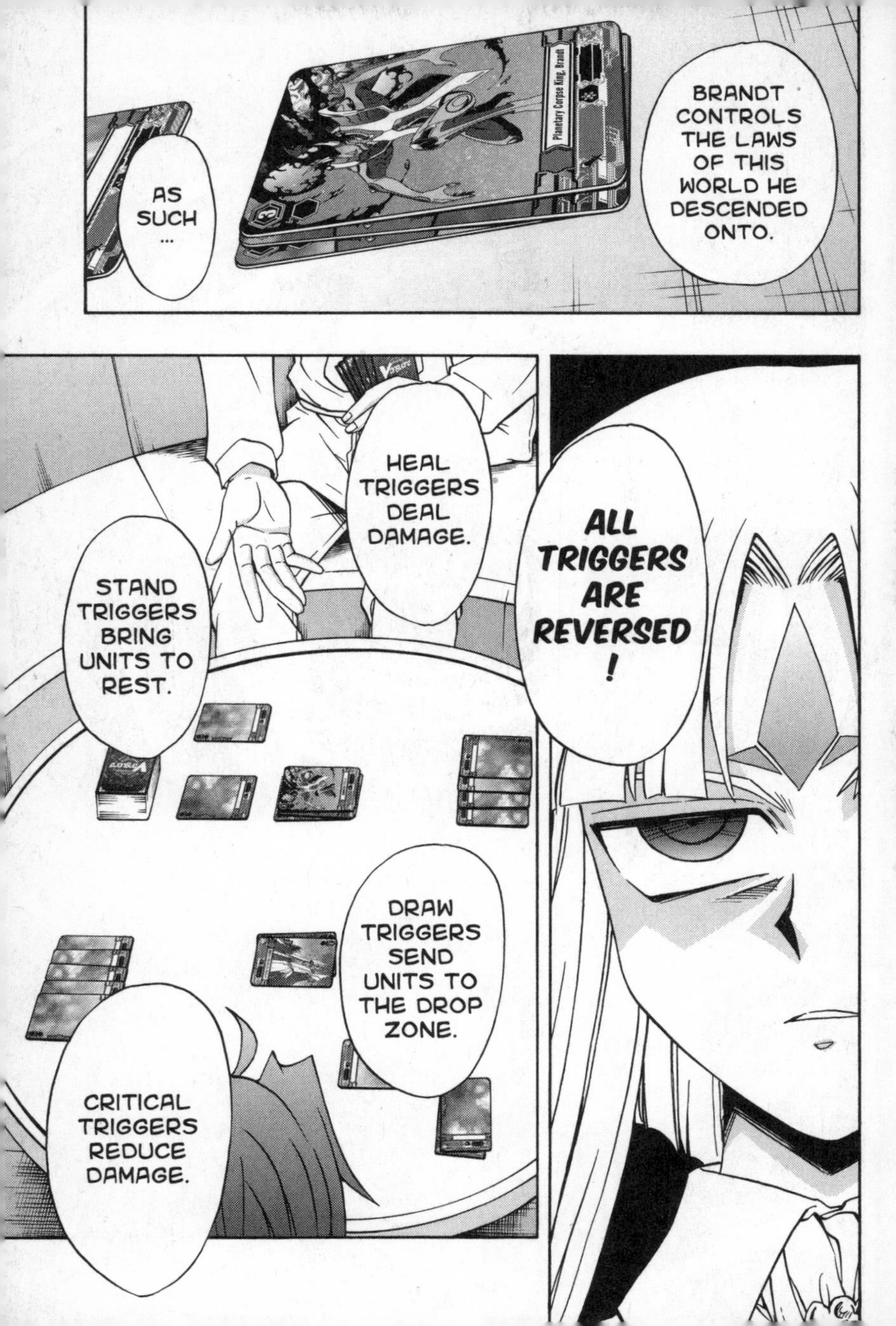

BRANDT CONTROLS THE LAWS OF THIS WORLD HE DESCENDED ONTO.
Planetary Corpse King, Brandt
AS SUCH ...
ALL TRIGGERS ARE REVERSED!
HEAL TRIGGERS DEAL DAMAGE.
STAND TRIGGERS BRING UNITS TO REST.
DRAW TRIGGERS SEND UNITS TO THE DROP ZONE.
CRITICAL TRIGGERS REDUCE DAMAGE.

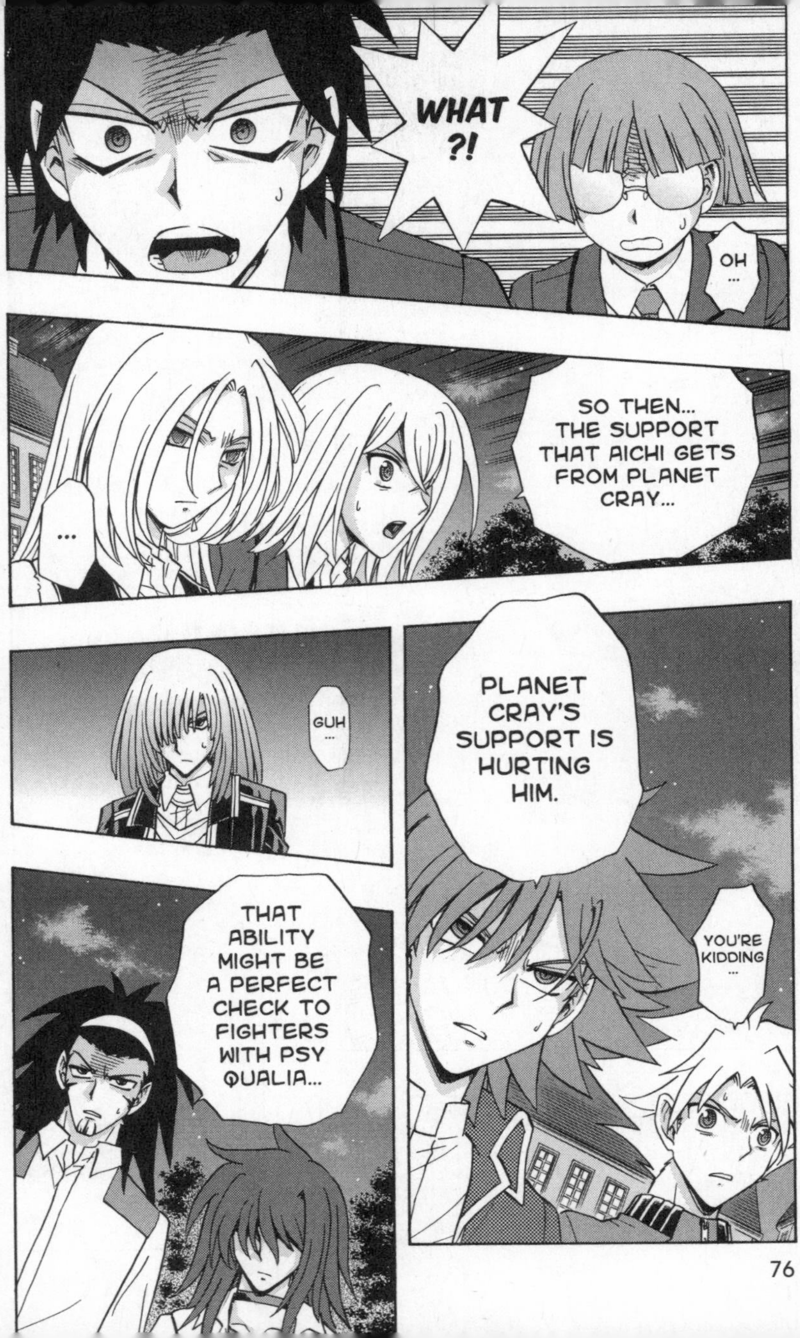
WHAT ?!
OH ...
SO THEN... THE SUPPORT THAT AICHI GETS FROM PLANET CRAY...
...
PLANET CRAY'S SUPPORT IS HURTING HIM.
YOU'RE KIDDING ...
GUH ...
THAT ABILITY MIGHT BE A PERFECT CHECK TO FIGHTERS WITH PSY QUALIA...

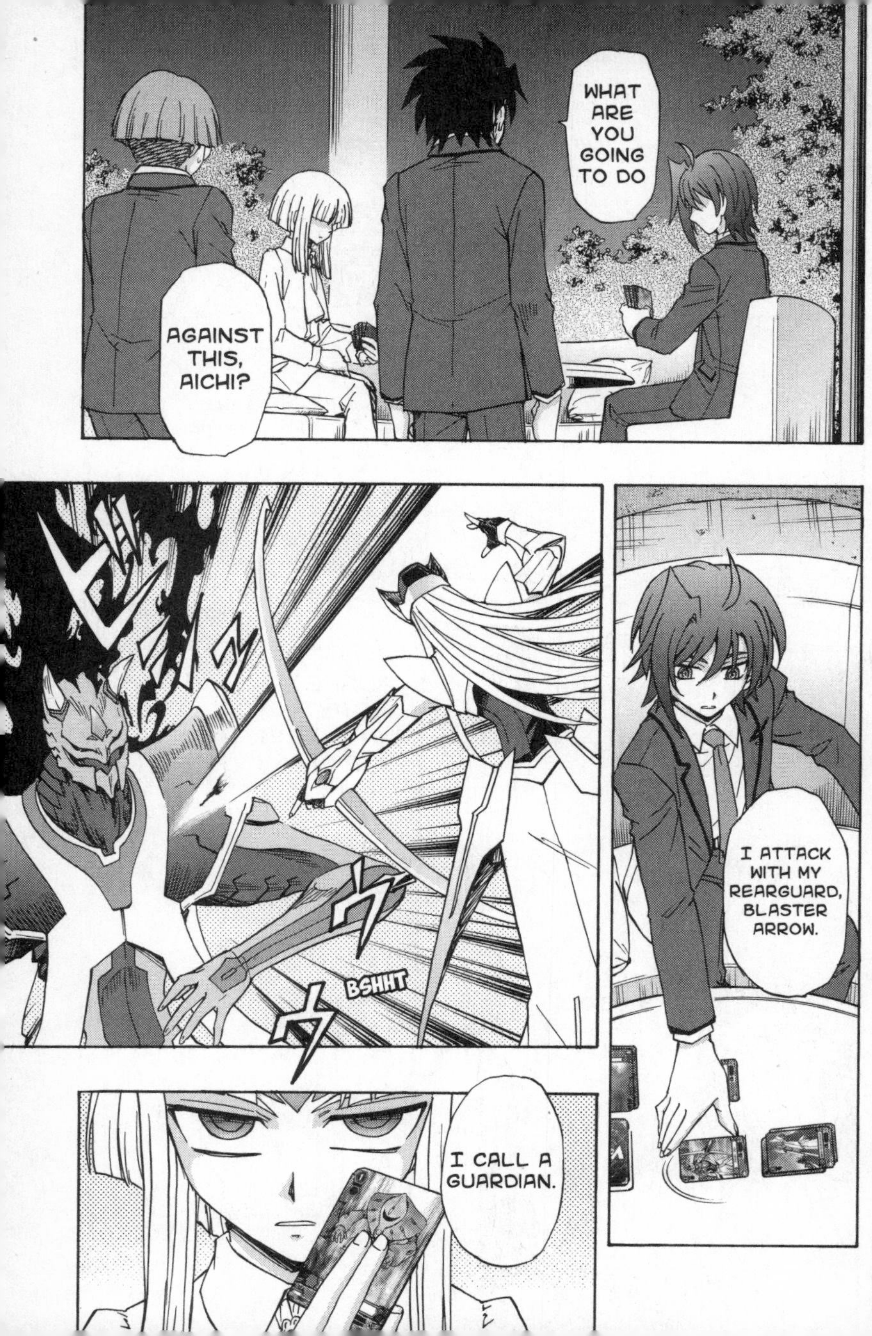
WHAT ARE YOU GOING TO DO
AGAINST THIS, AICHI?
I ATTACK WITH MY REARGUARD, BLASTER ARROW.
BSHHT
I CALL A GUARDIAN.

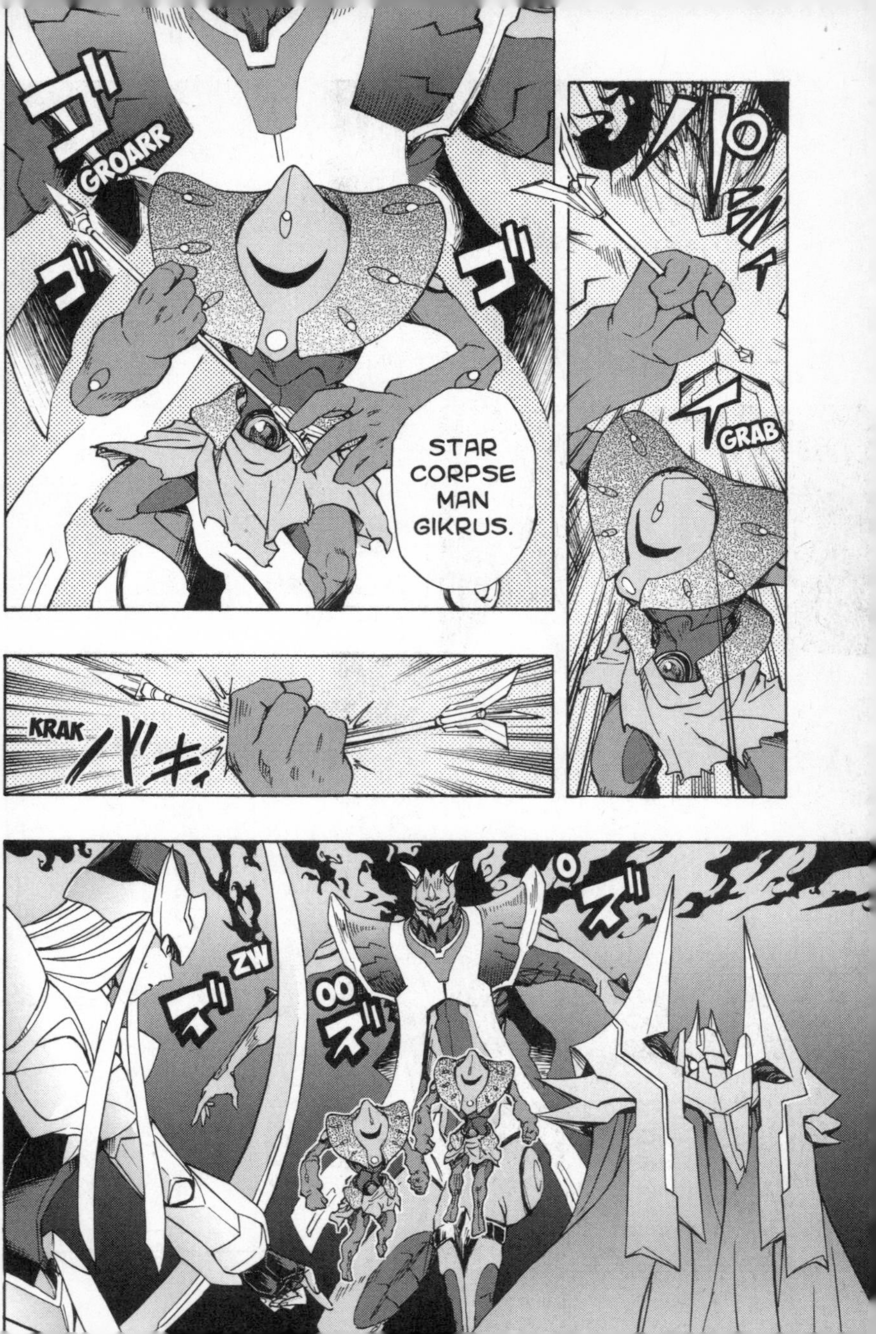
GRAB
GROARR
STAR CORPSE MAN GIKRUS.
KRAK
ZW
OO

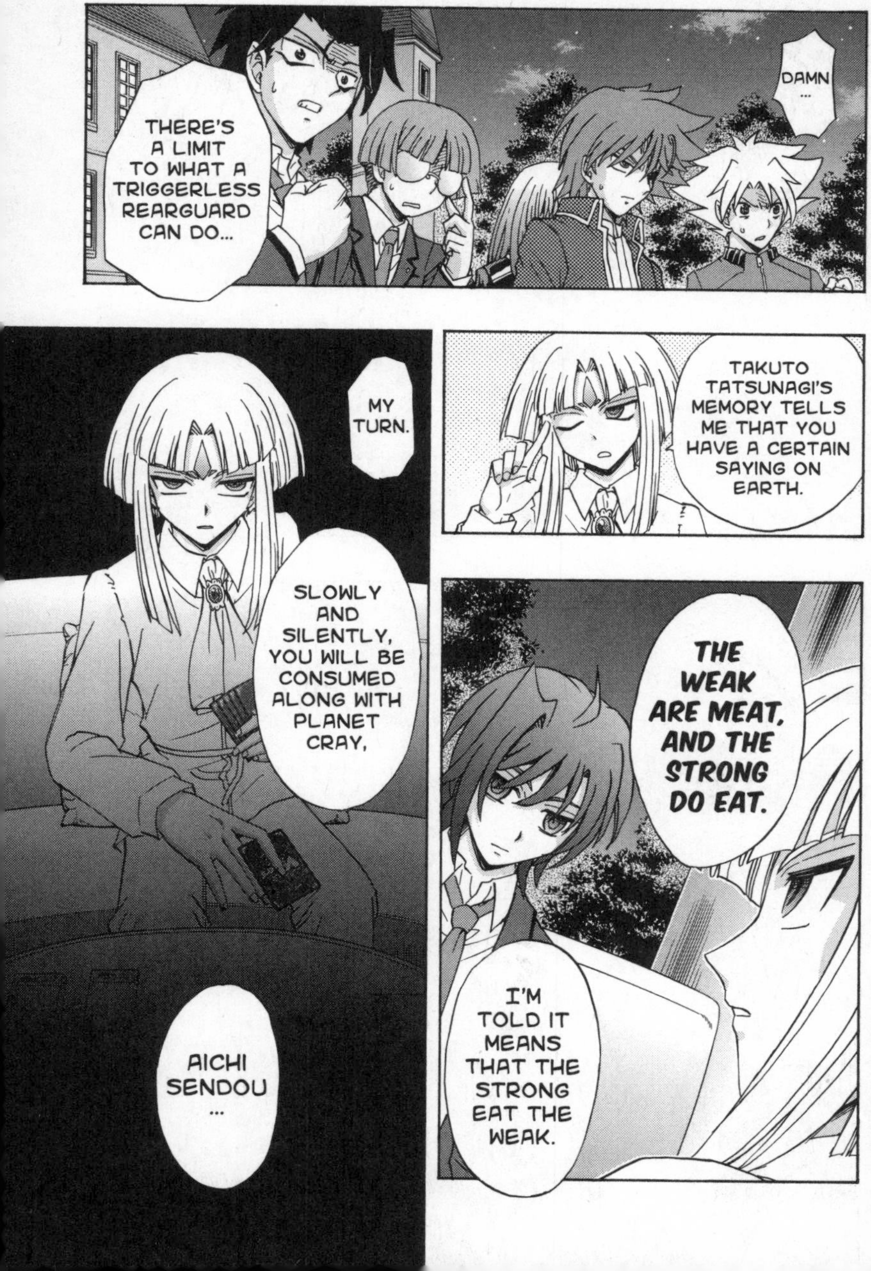
DAMN...
THERE'S A LIMIT TO WHAT A TRIGGERLESS REARGUARD CAN DO...
TAKUTO TATSUNAGI'S MEMORY TELLS ME THAT YOU HAVE A CERTAIN SAYING ON EARTH.
THE WEAK ARE MEAT, AND THE STRONG DO EAT.
I'M TOLD IT MEANS THAT THE STRONG EAT THE WEAK.
MY TURN.
SLOWLY AND SILENTLY, YOU WILL BE CONSUMED ALONG WITH PLANET CRAY,
AICHI SENDOU...

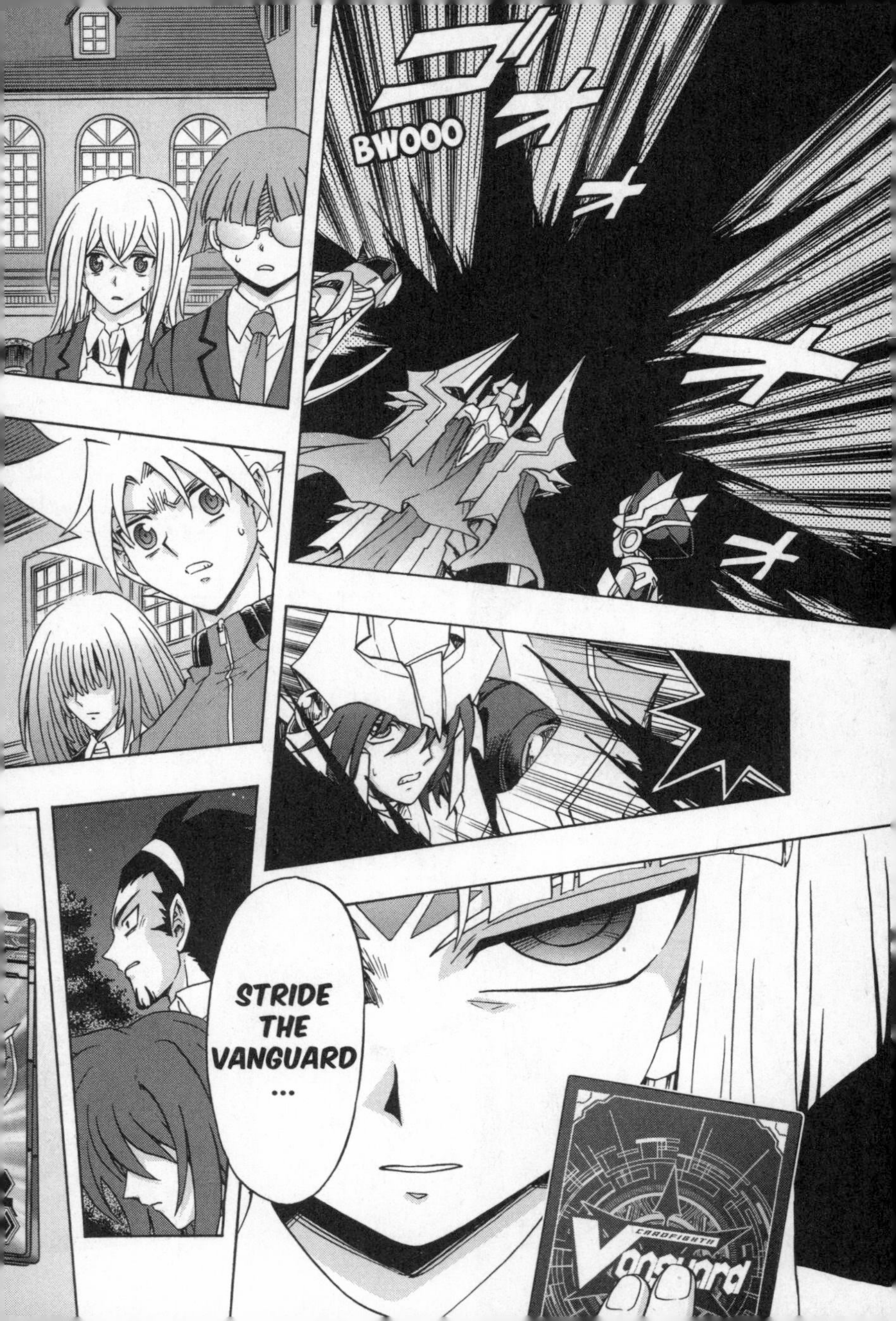
BWOOO
STRIDE THE VANGUARD ...

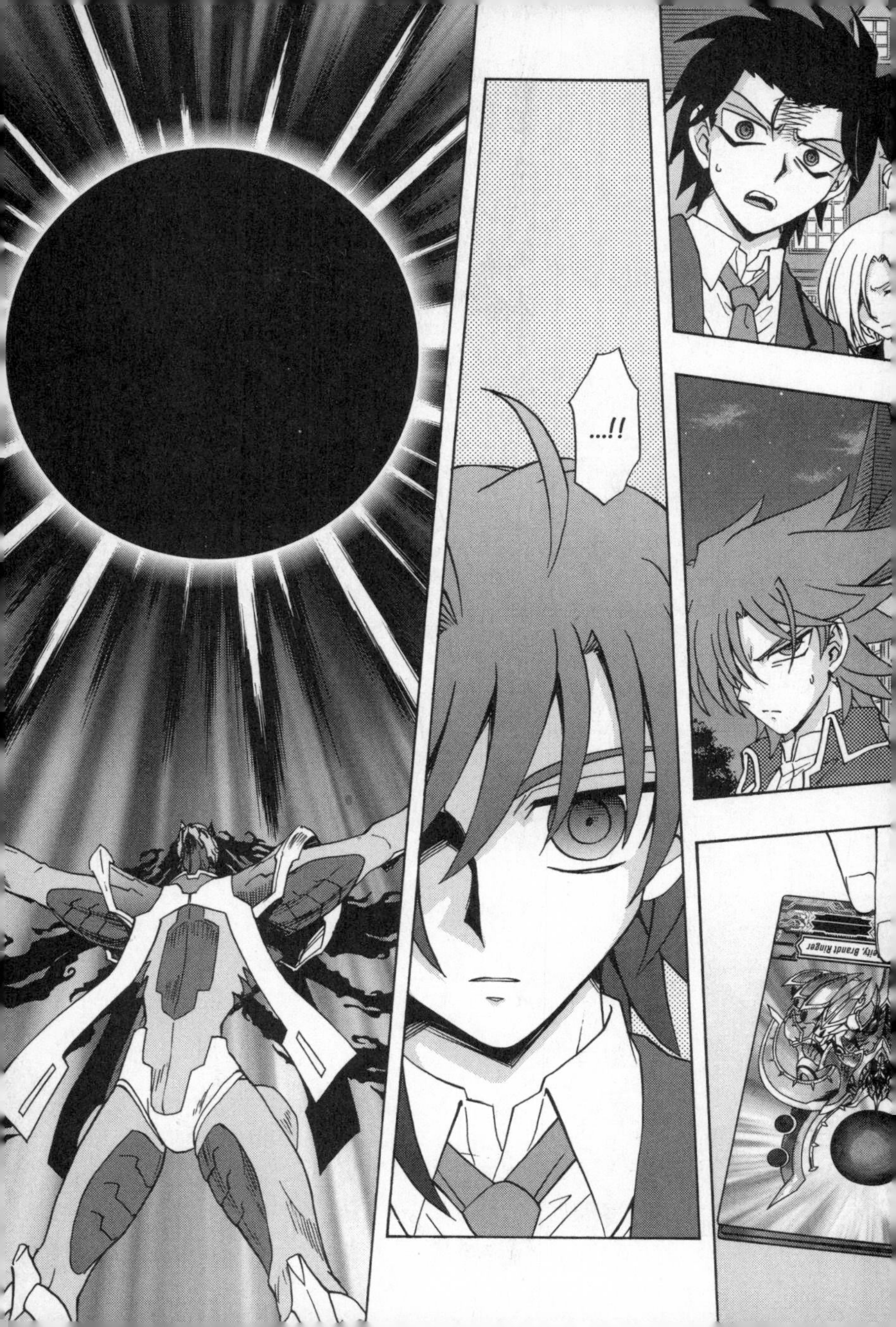
...!!

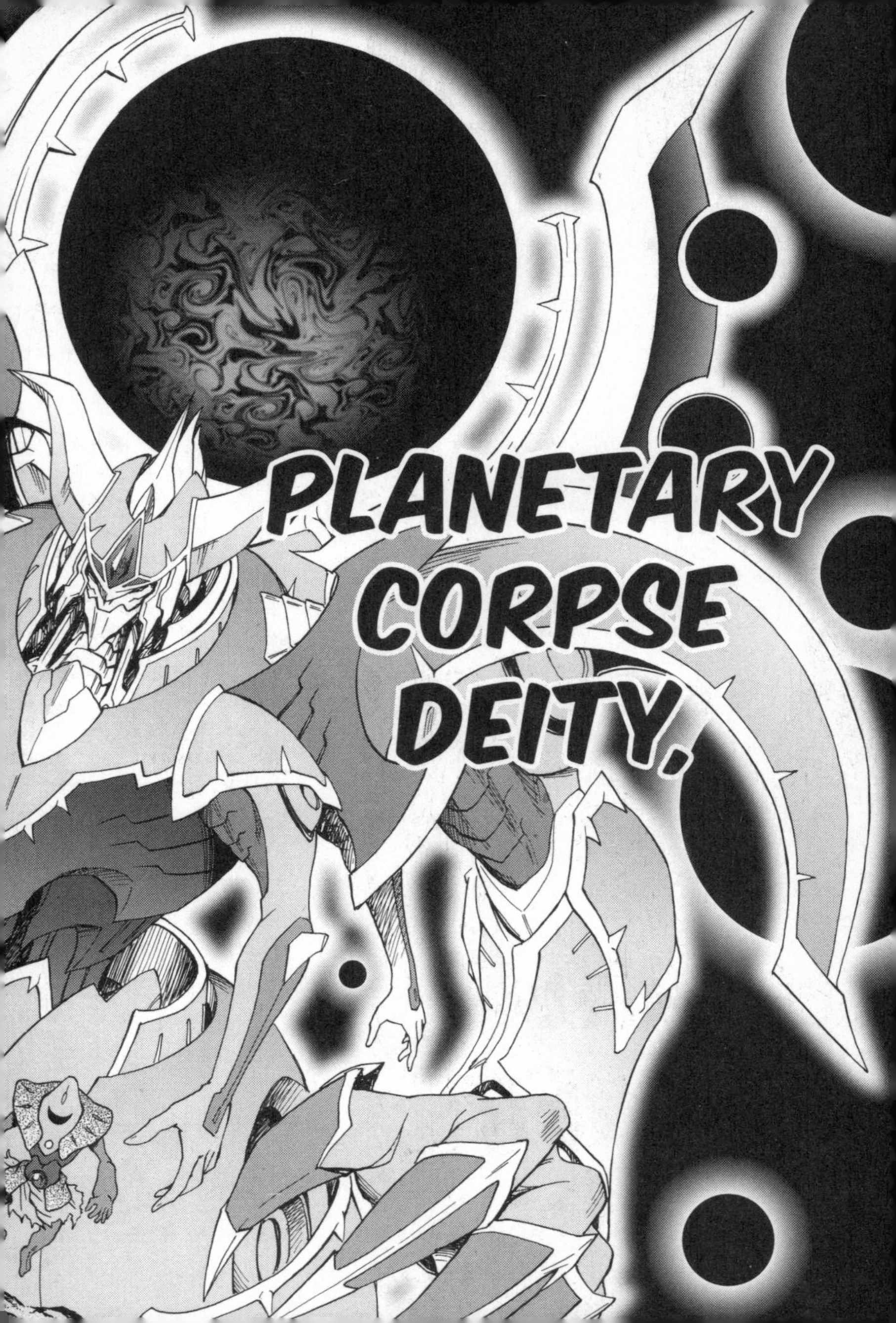
PLANETARY CORPSE DEITY.

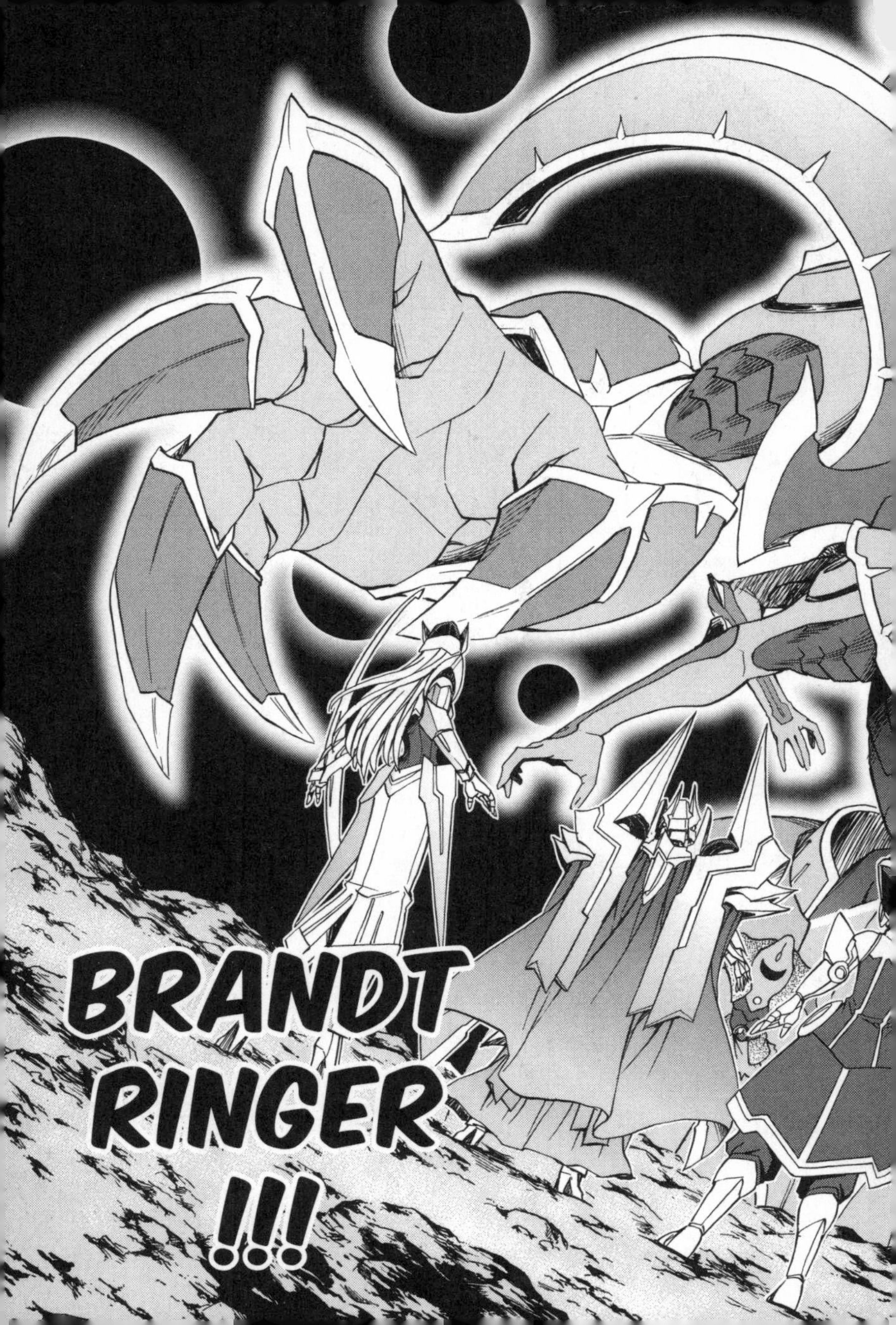
BRANDT RINGER !!!

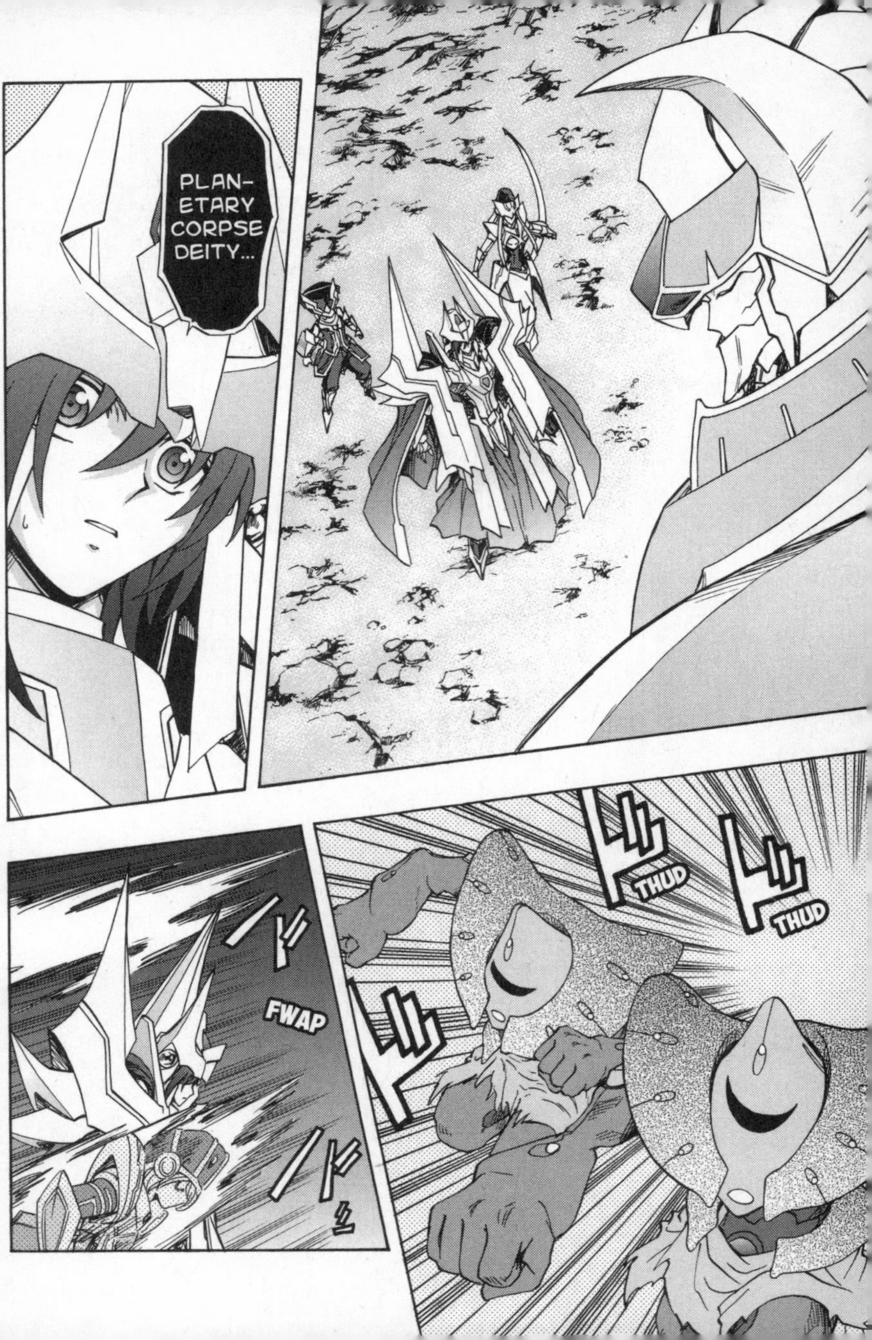
PLAN-ETARY CORPSE DEITY...
THUD
THUD
FWAP

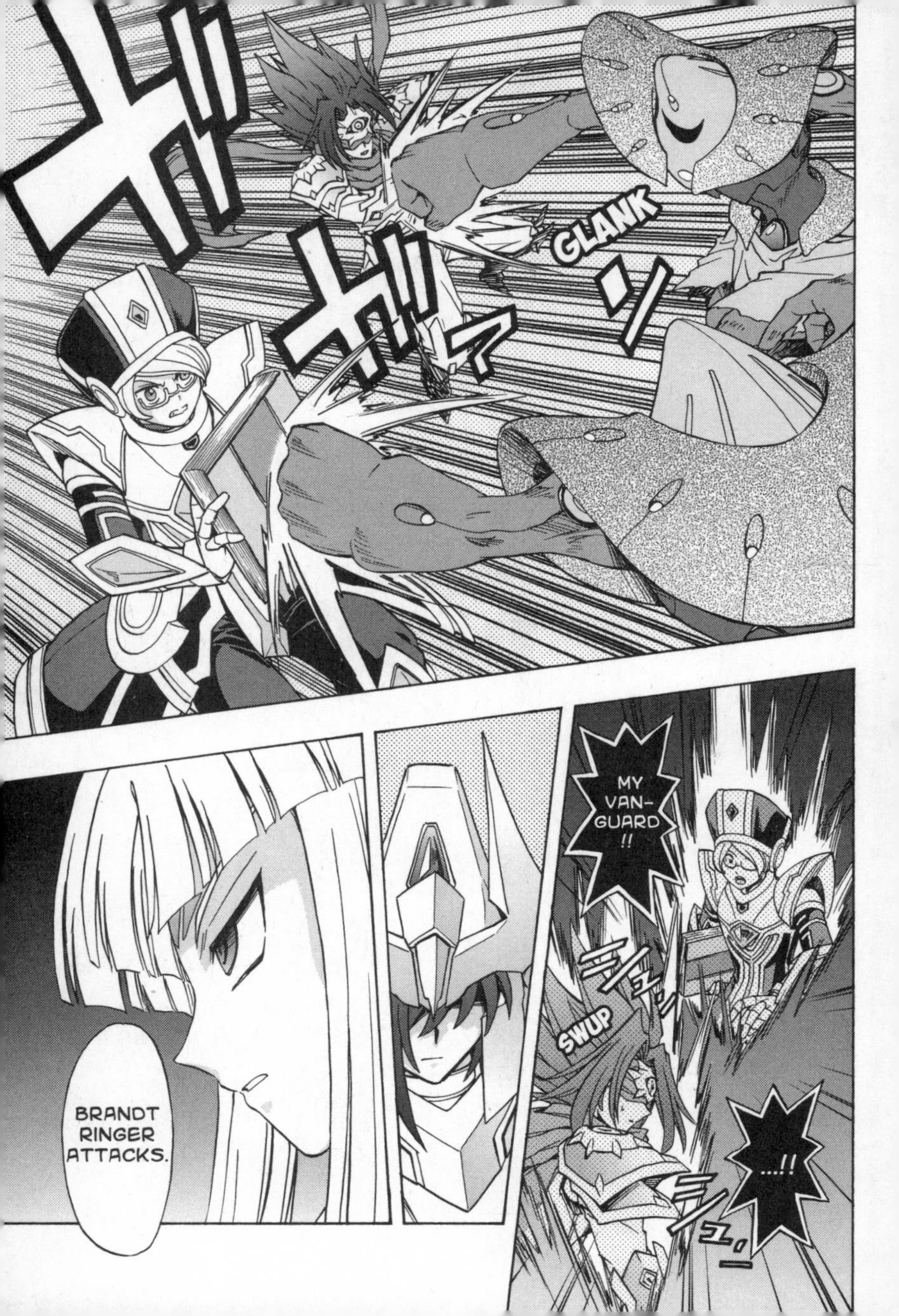
GLANK
MY VAN-GUARD!!
SWUP
...!!
BRANDT RINGER ATTACKS.

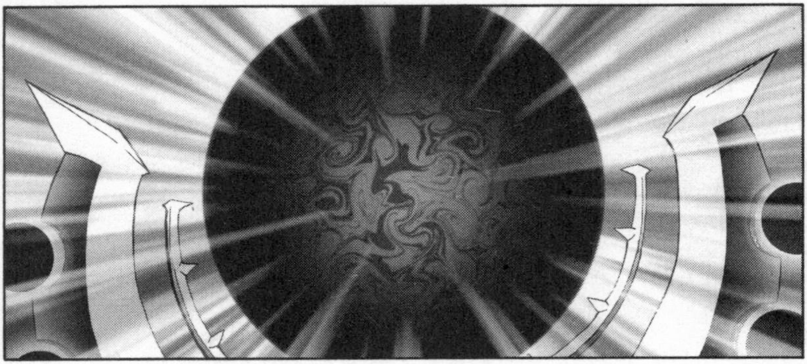

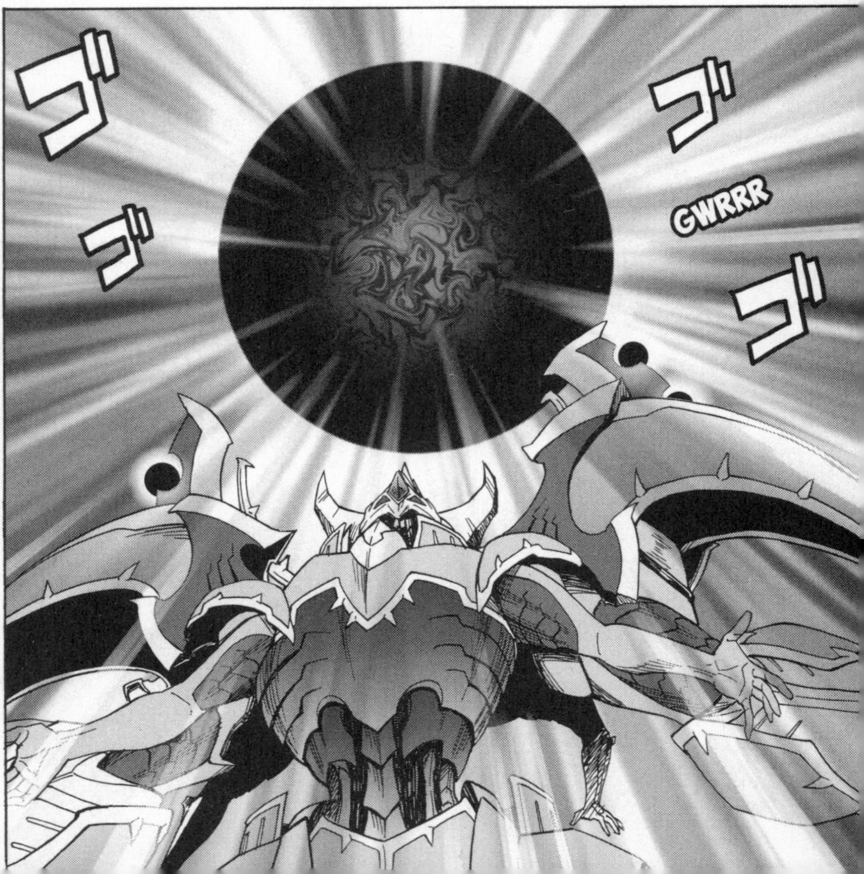
ゴ
ゴ
GWRRR
ゴ
ゴ

CARDFIGHT!!
Vanguard

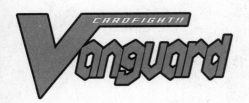

BONUS! CARDFIGHT!! Vanguard

NEVER-BEFORE-SEEN IMAGE BOARDS

Releasing Mr. Akira Itou's Rough Sketches!

All riled up...
A.

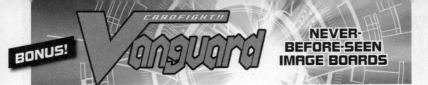

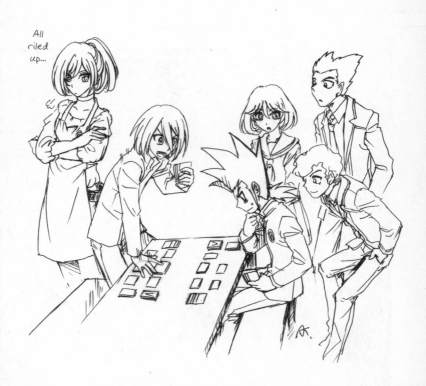

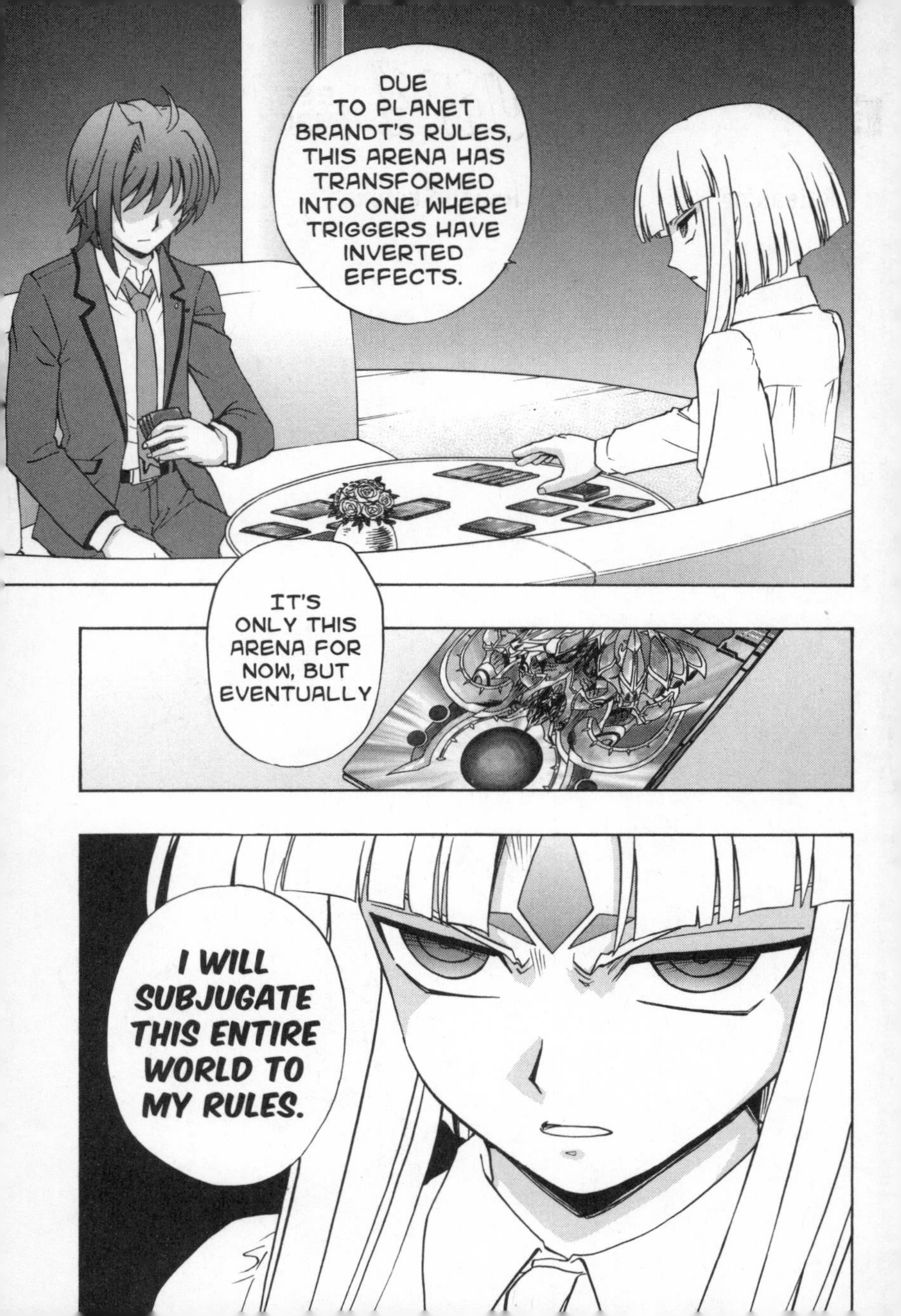
DUE TO PLANET BRANDT'S RULES, THIS ARENA HAS TRANSFORMED INTO ONE WHERE TRIGGERS HAVE INVERTED EFFECTS.
IT'S ONLY THIS ARENA FOR NOW, BUT EVENTUALLY
I WILL SUBJUGATE THIS ENTIRE WORLD TO MY RULES.

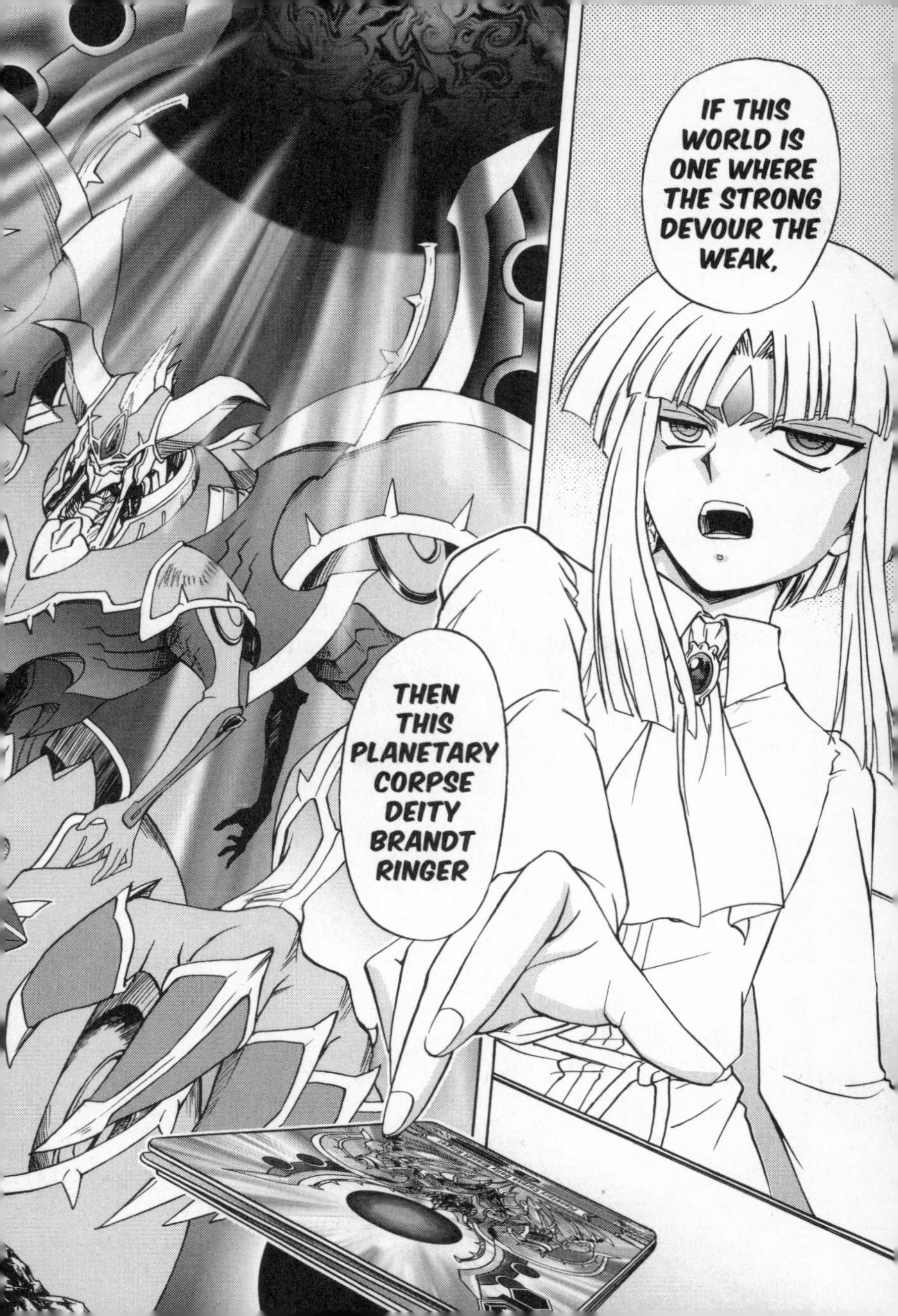
IF THIS WORLD IS ONE WHERE THE STRONG DEVOUR THE WEAK,
THEN THIS PLANETARY CORPSE DEITY BRANDT RINGER

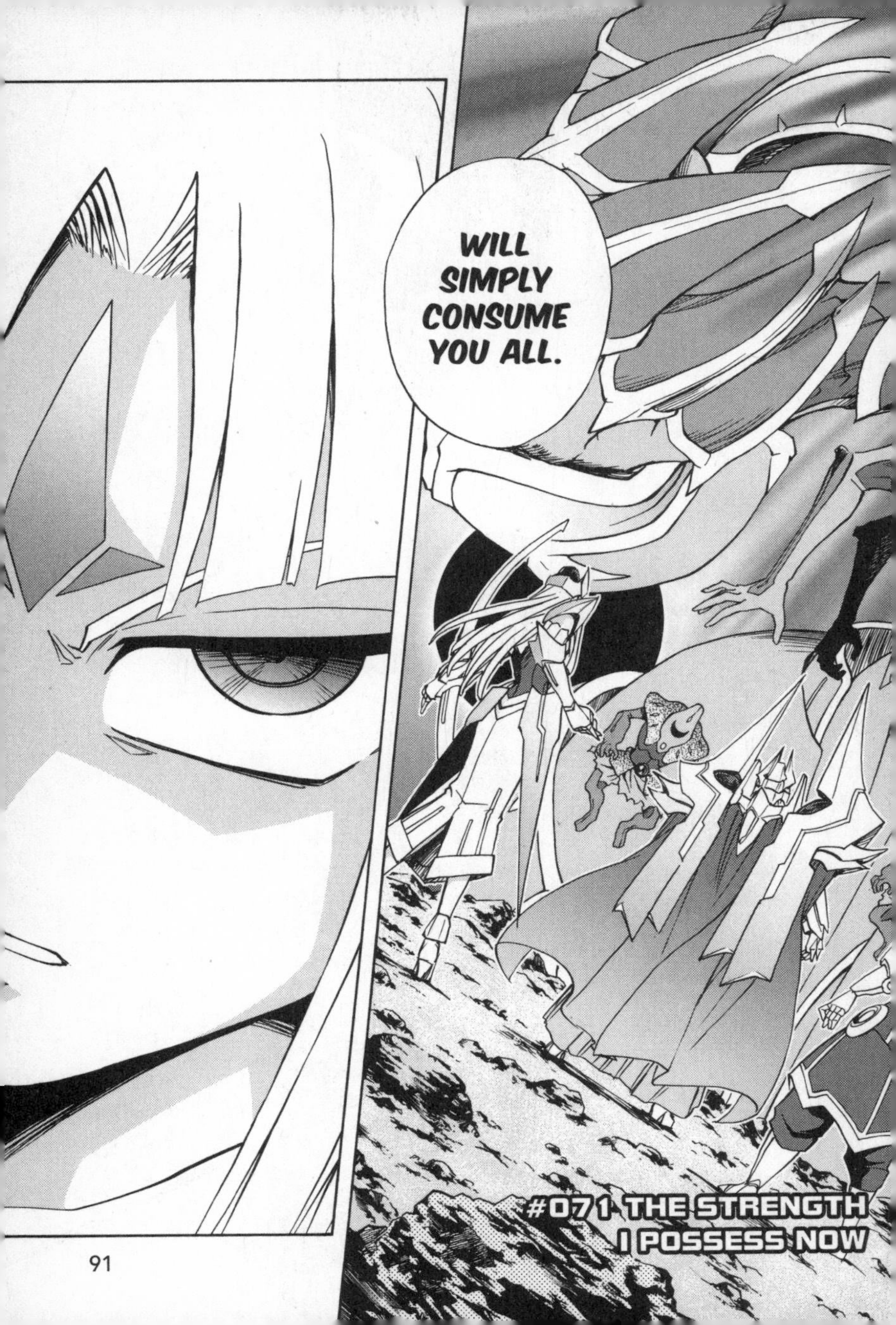
WILL SIMPLY CONSUME YOU ALL.
#071 THE STRENGTH I POSSESS NOW

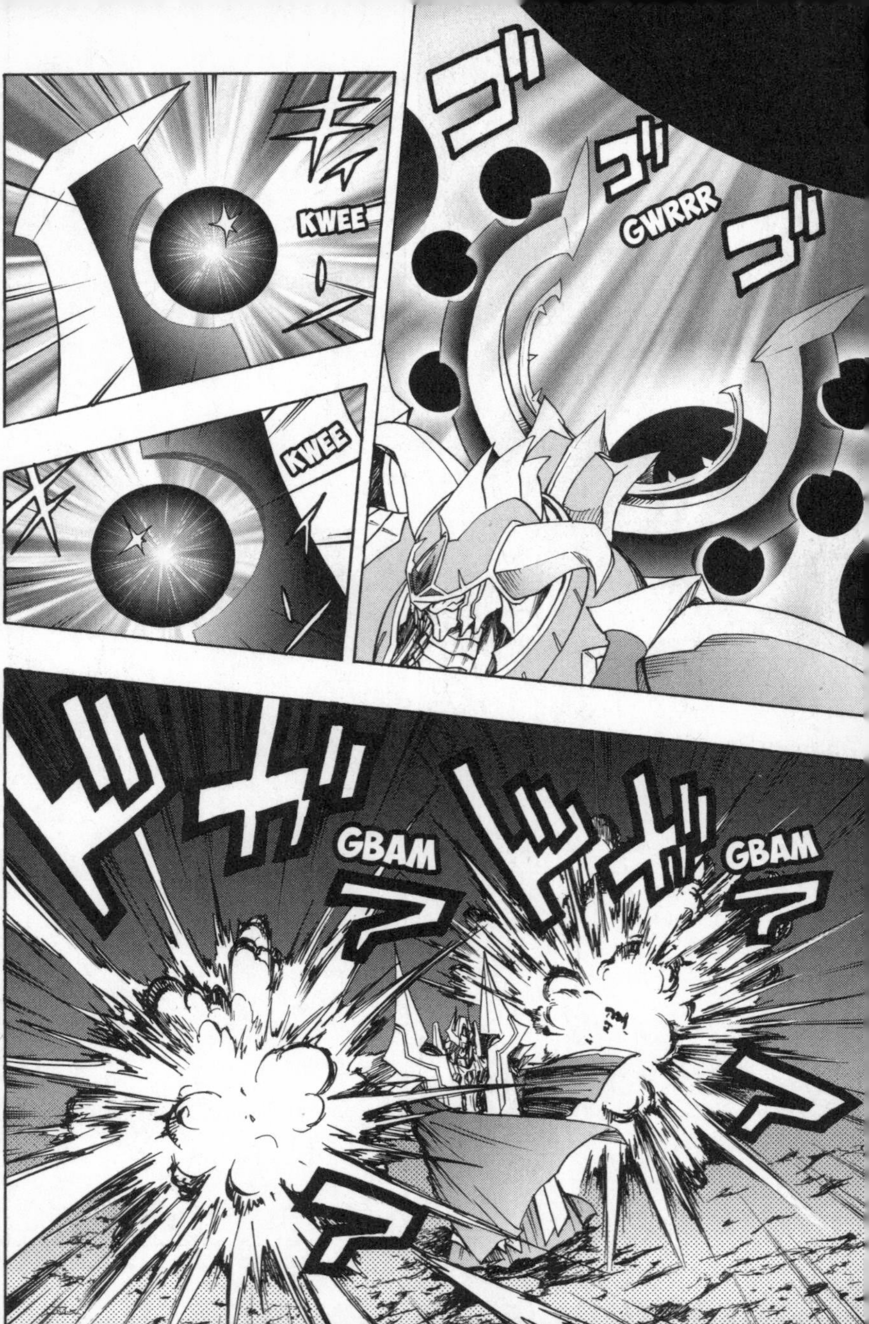
GWRRR
KWEE
KWEE
GBAM
GBAM

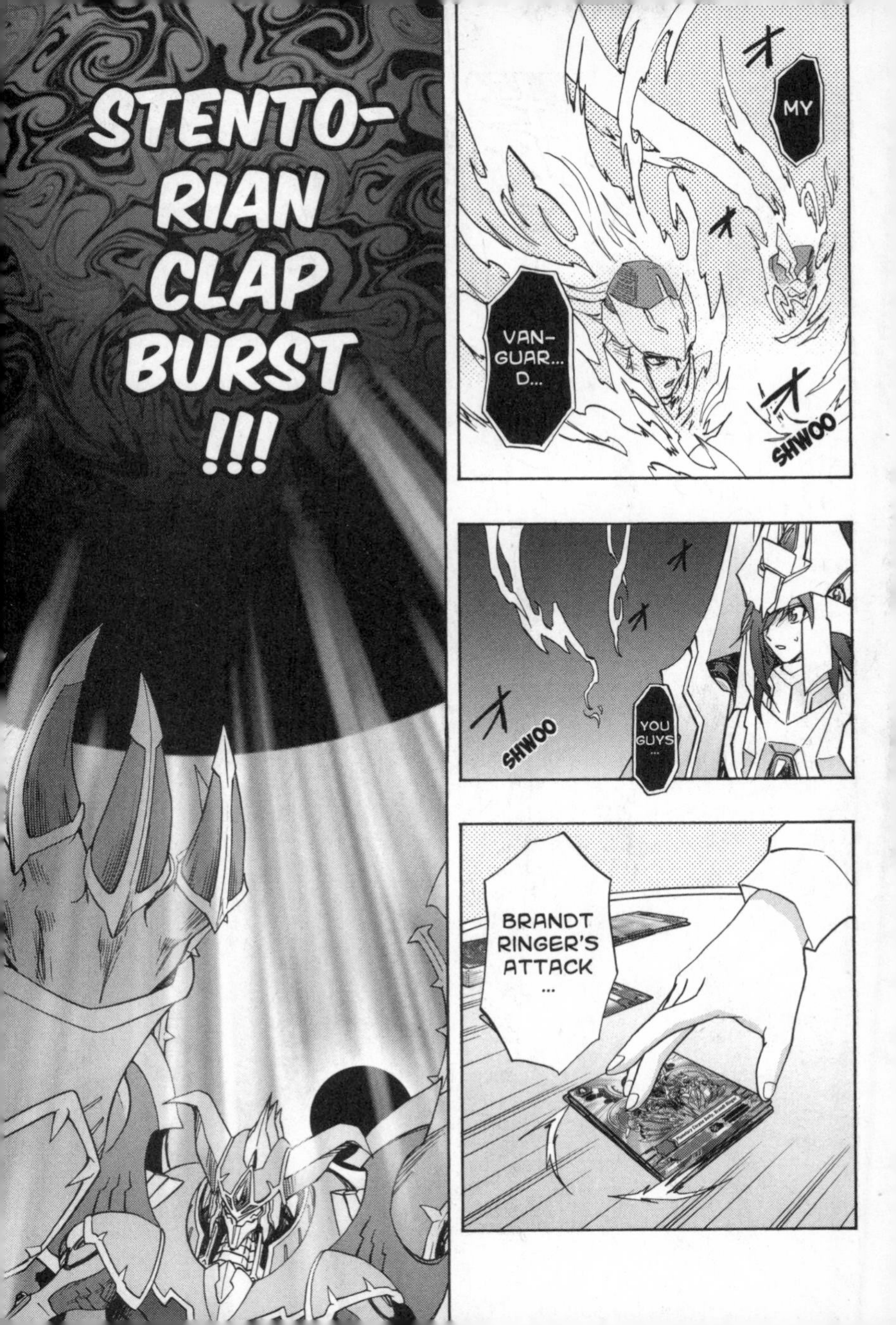
MY
VAN-GUAR... D...
SHWOO
YOU GUYS ...
SHWOO
BRANDT RINGER'S ATTACK ...
STENTO-RIAN CLAP BURST !!!

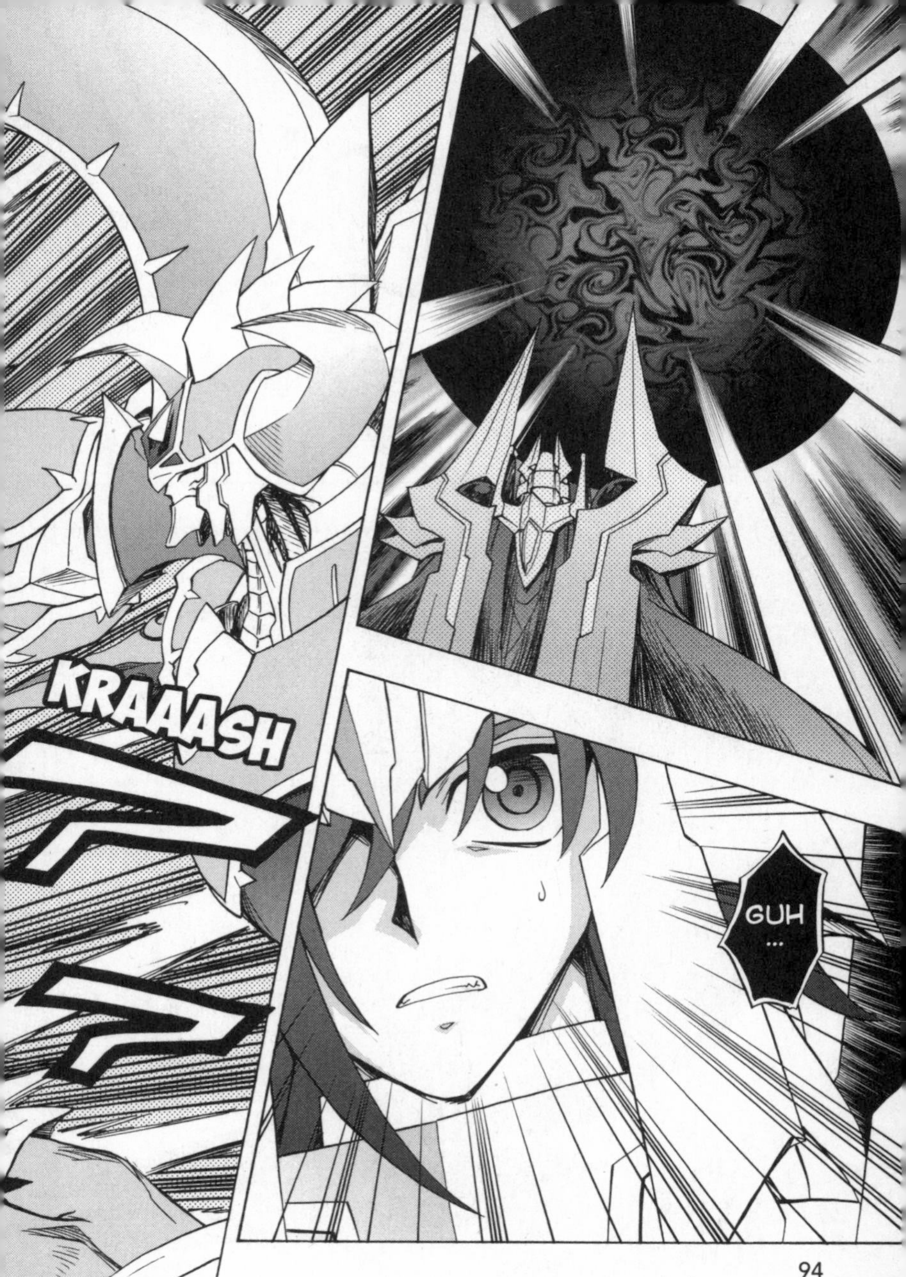
GUH ...
KRAAASH

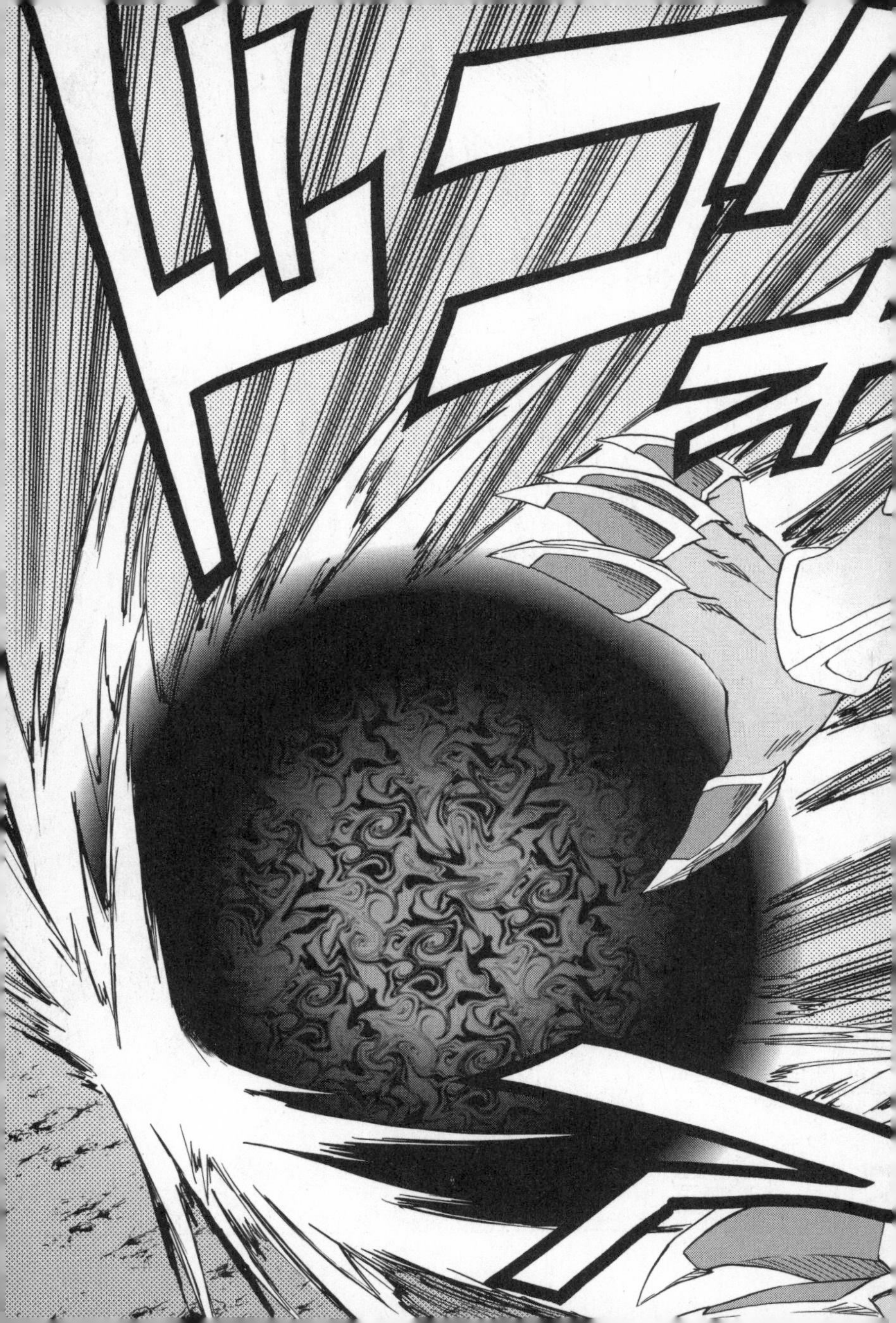

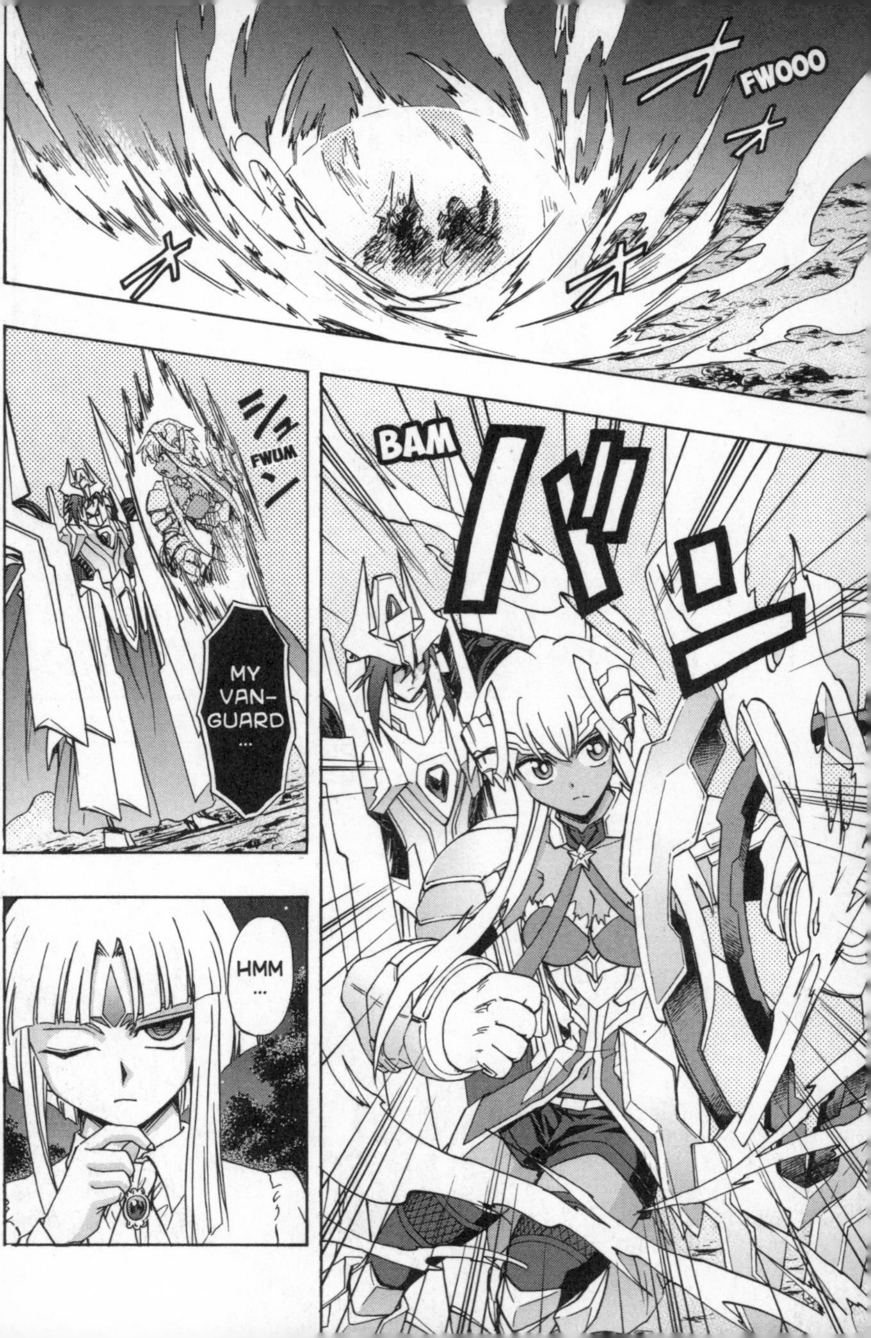
FWOOO
BAM
FWUM
MY VAN-GUARD ...
HMM ...

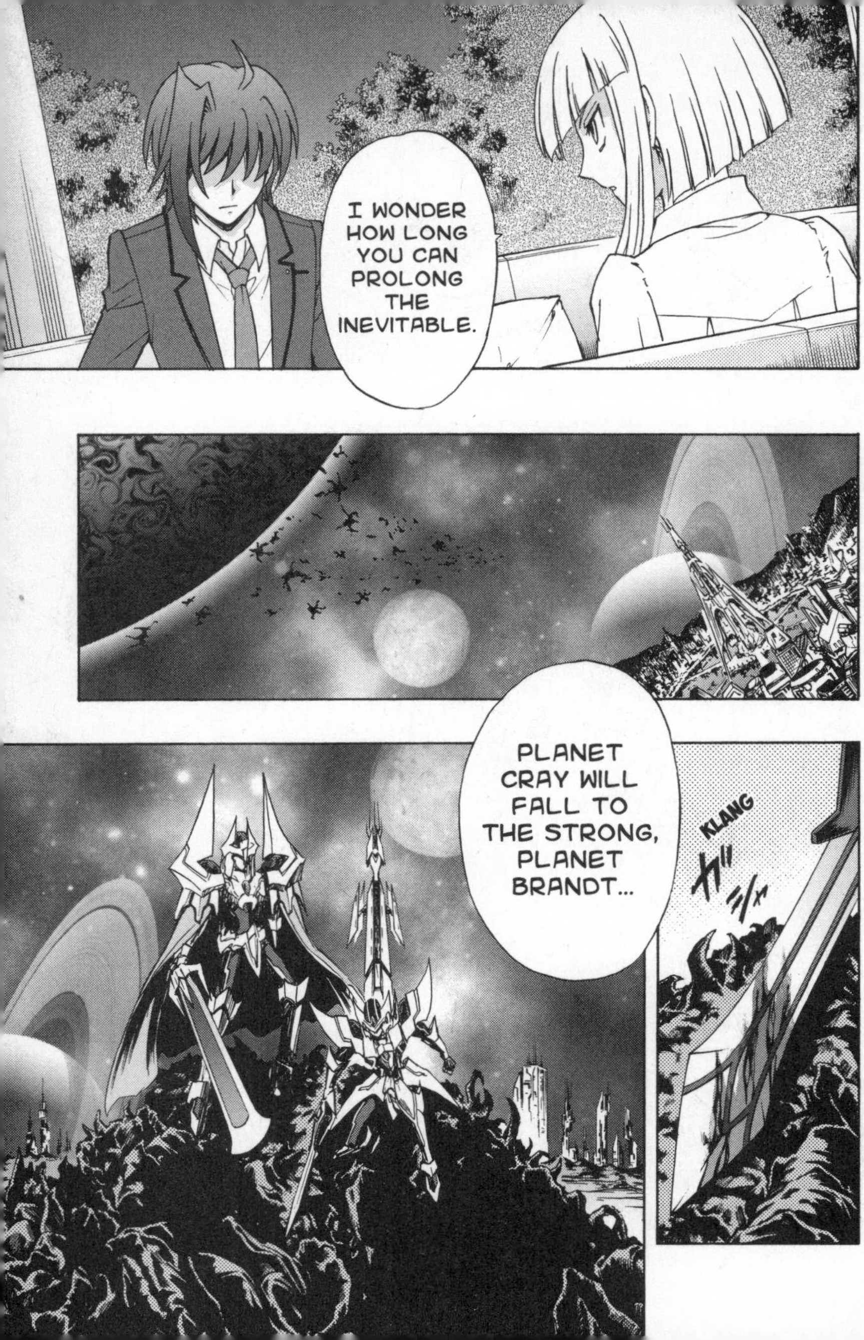
I WONDER HOW LONG YOU CAN PROLONG THE INEVITABLE.
PLANET CRAY WILL FALL TO THE STRONG, PLANET BRANDT...
KLANG

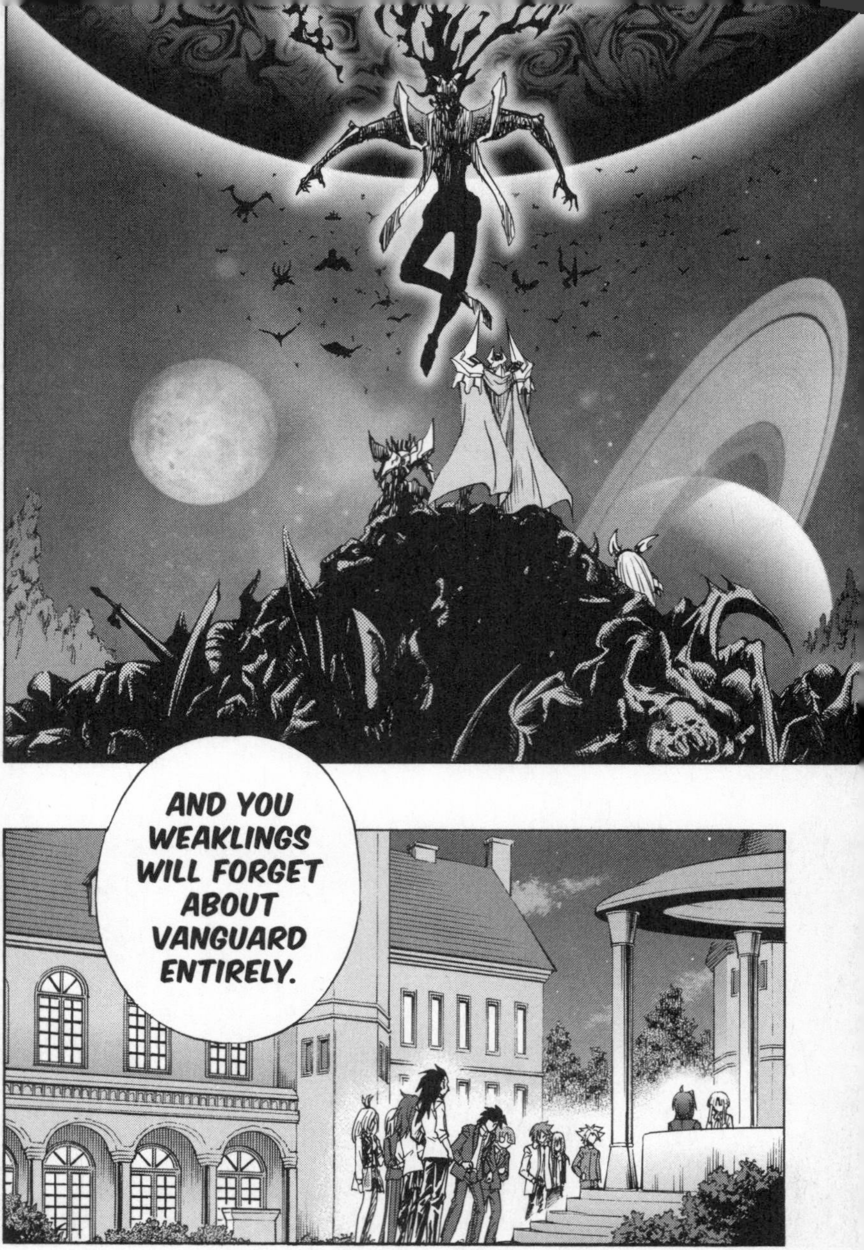
AND YOU WEAKLINGS WILL FORGET ABOUT VANGUARD ENTIRELY.

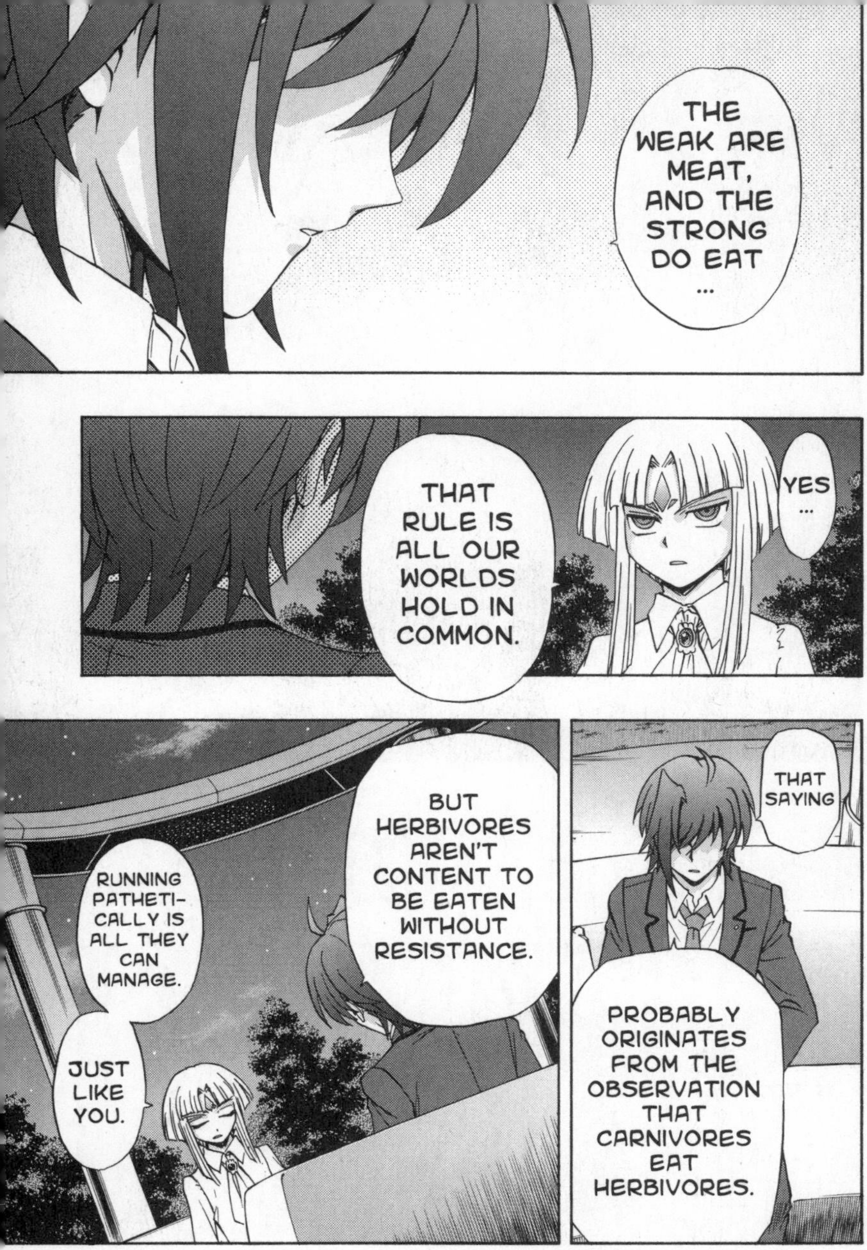
THE WEAK ARE MEAT, AND THE STRONG DO EAT ...
YES ...
THAT RULE IS ALL OUR WORLDS HOLD IN COMMON.
THAT SAYING
PROBABLY ORIGINATES FROM THE OBSERVATION THAT CARNIVORES EAT HERBIVORES.
BUT HERBIVORES AREN'T CONTENT TO BE EATEN WITHOUT RESISTANCE.
RUNNING PATHETICALLY IS ALL THEY CAN MANAGE.
JUST LIKE YOU.

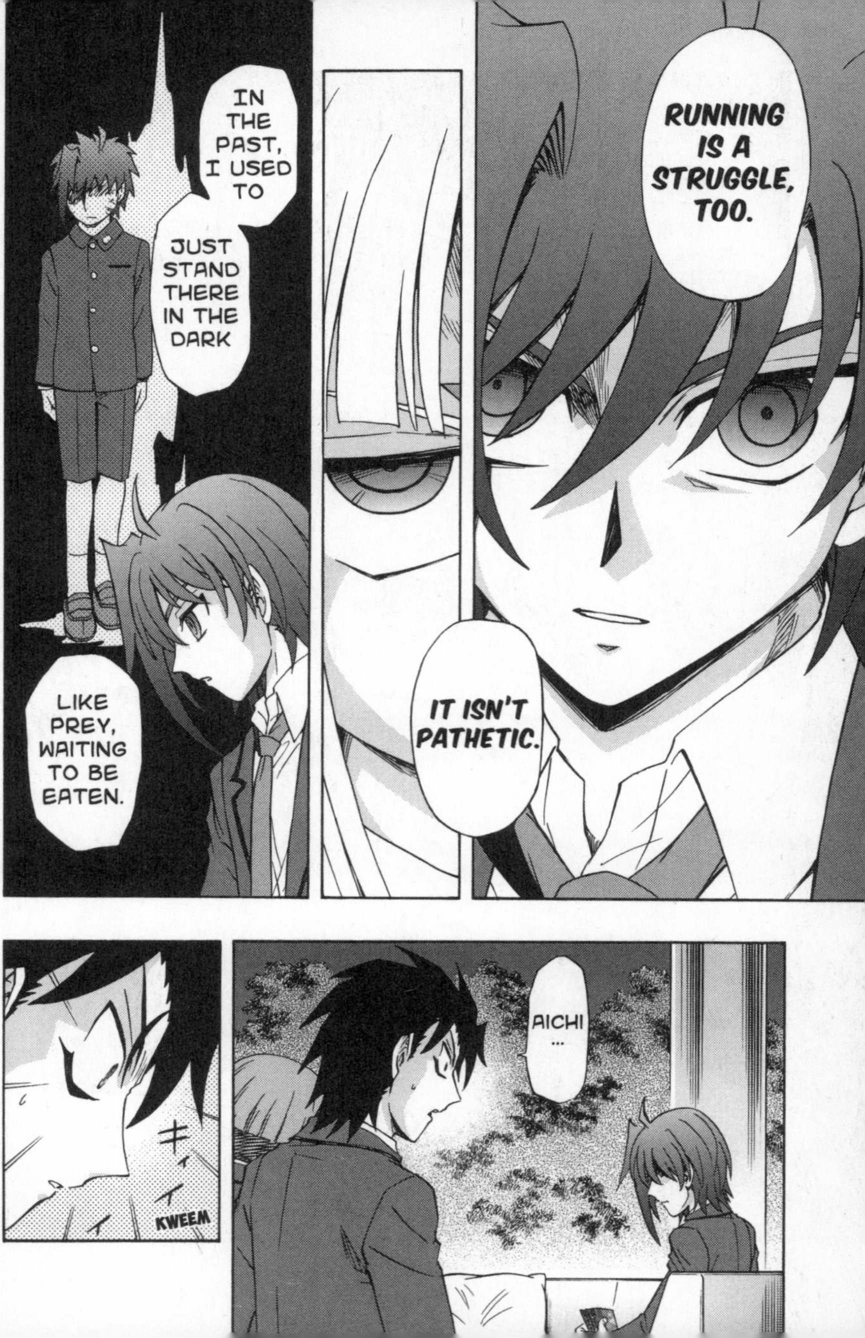
RUNNING IS A STRUGGLE, TOO.
IT ISN'T PATHETIC.
IN THE PAST, I USED TO
JUST STAND THERE IN THE DARK
LIKE PREY, WAITING TO BE EATEN.
AICHI ...
KWEEM

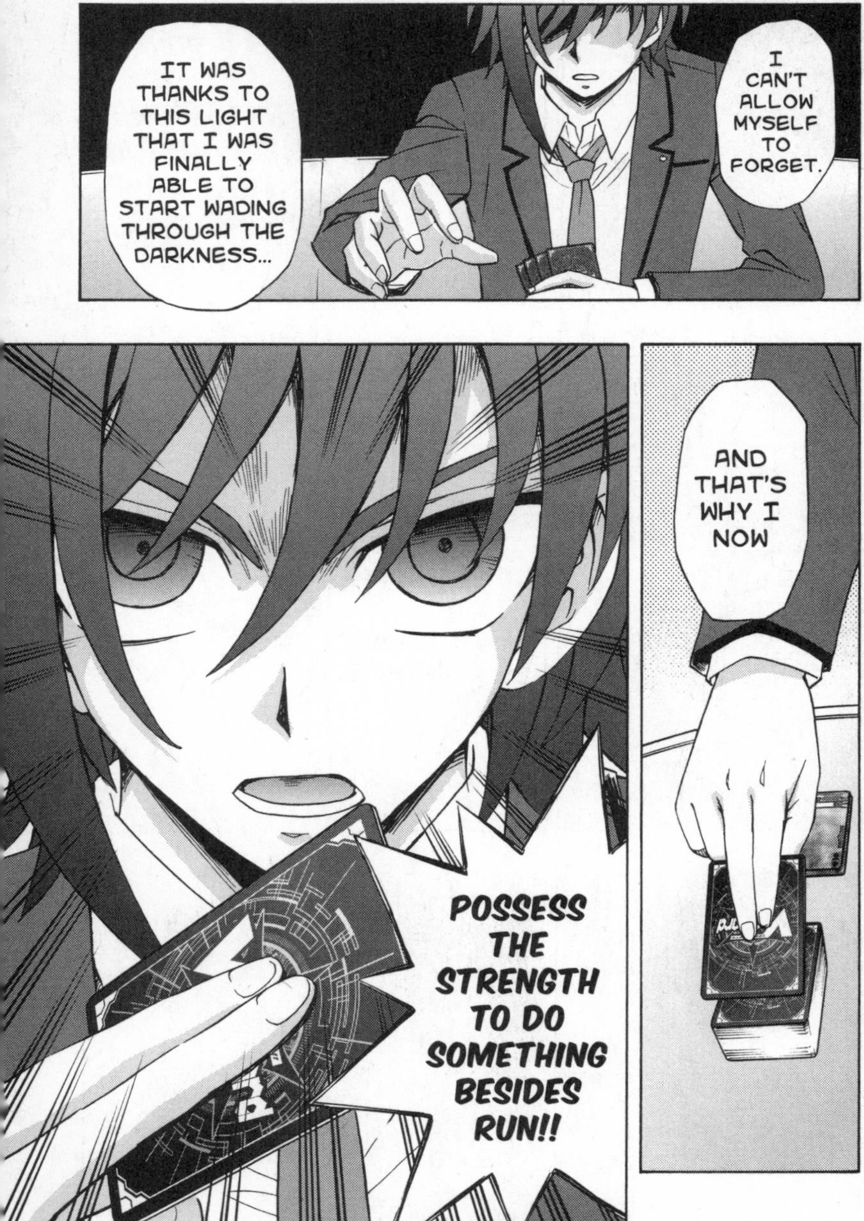
I CAN'T ALLOW MYSELF TO FORGET.
IT WAS THANKS TO THIS LIGHT THAT I WAS FINALLY ABLE TO START WADING THROUGH THE DARKNESS...
AND THAT'S WHY I NOW
POSSESS THE STRENGTH TO DO SOMETHING BESIDES RUN!!

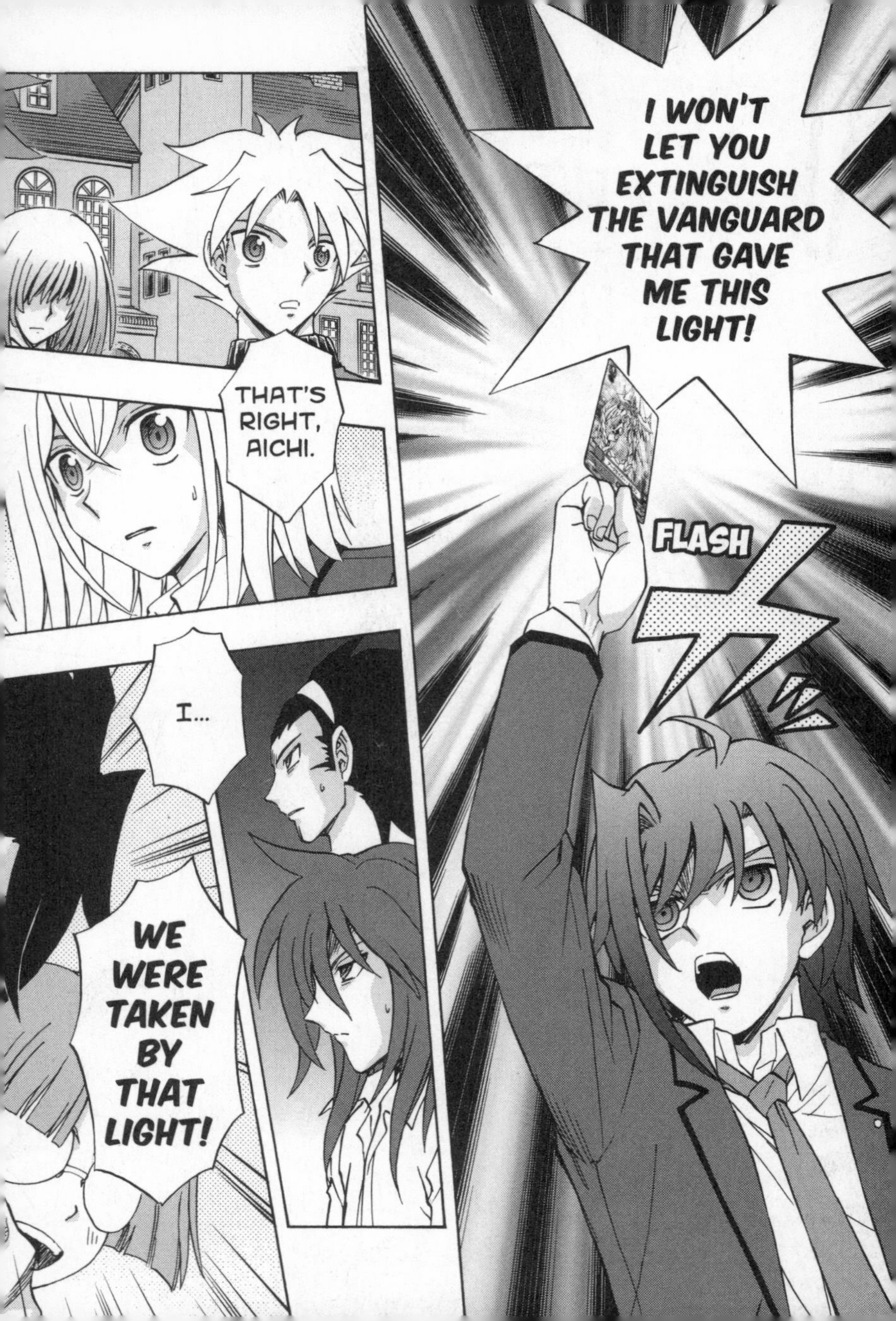
I WON'T LET YOU EXTINGUISH THE VANGUARD THAT GAVE ME THIS LIGHT!
FLASH
THAT'S RIGHT, AICHI.
I...
WE WERE TAKEN BY THAT LIGHT!

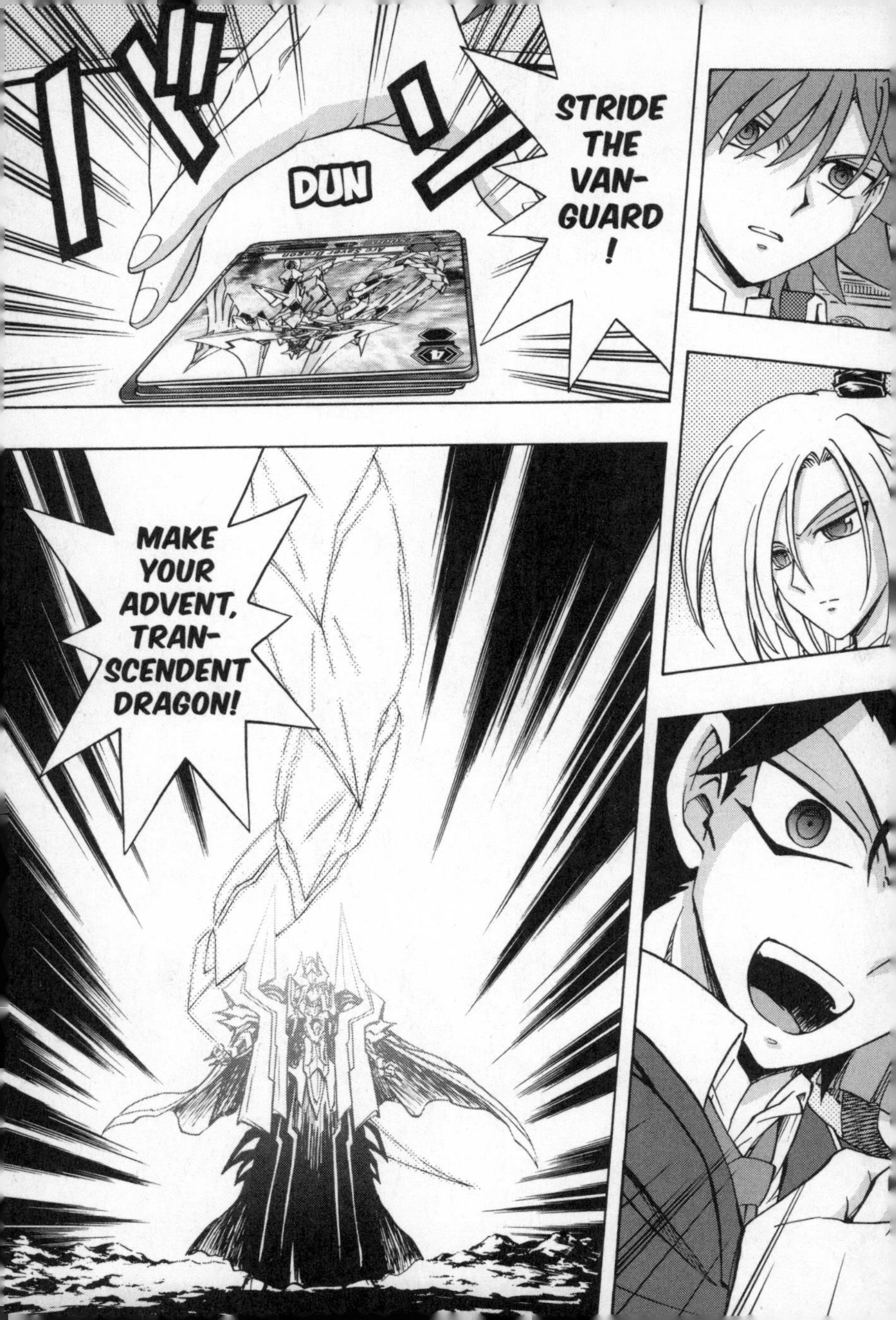
STRIDE THE VAN-GUARD!
DUN
MAKE YOUR ADVENT, TRAN-SCENDENT DRAGON!

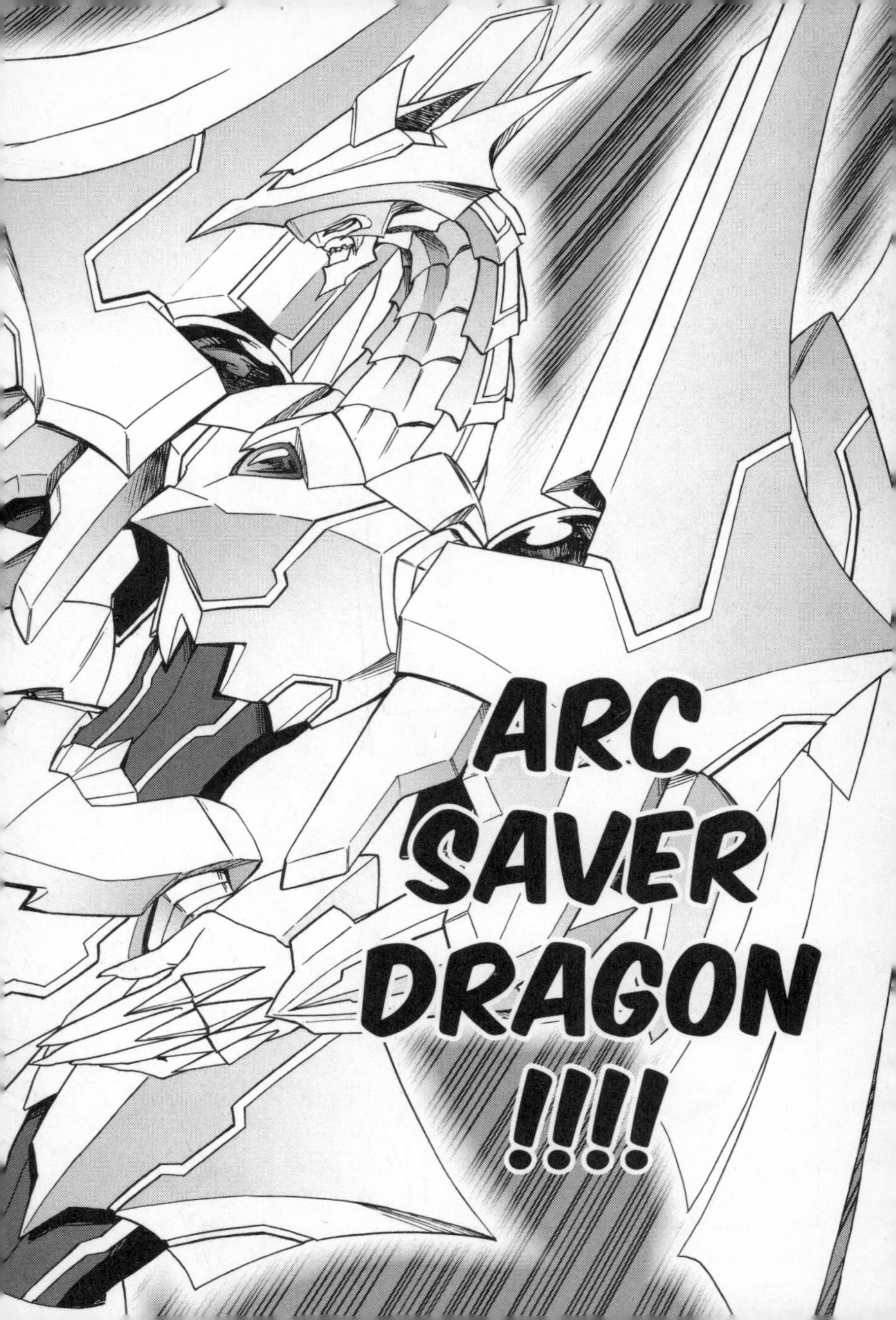
ARC SAVER DRAGON !!!!

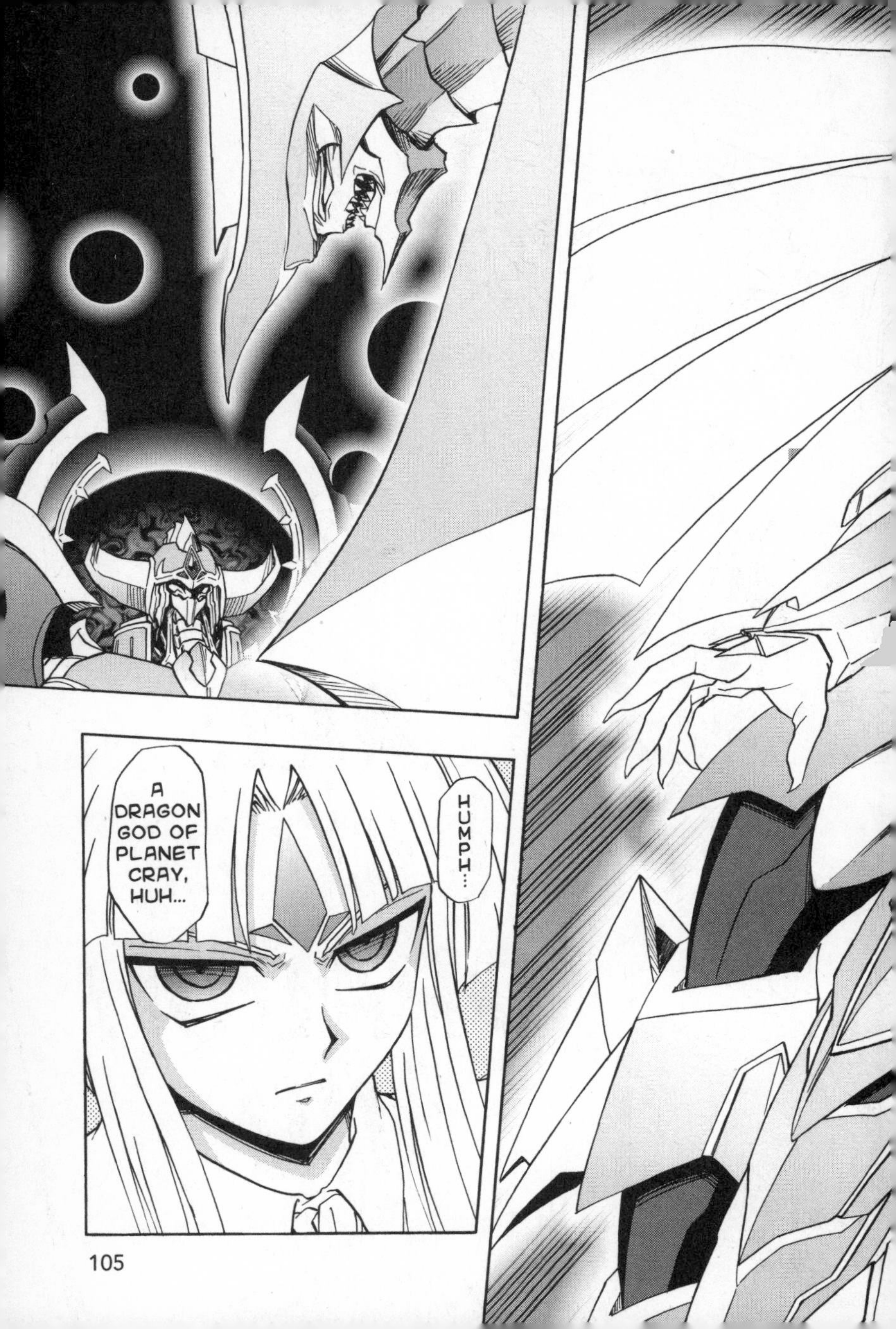
HUMPH...
A DRAGON GOD OF PLANET CRAY, HUH...

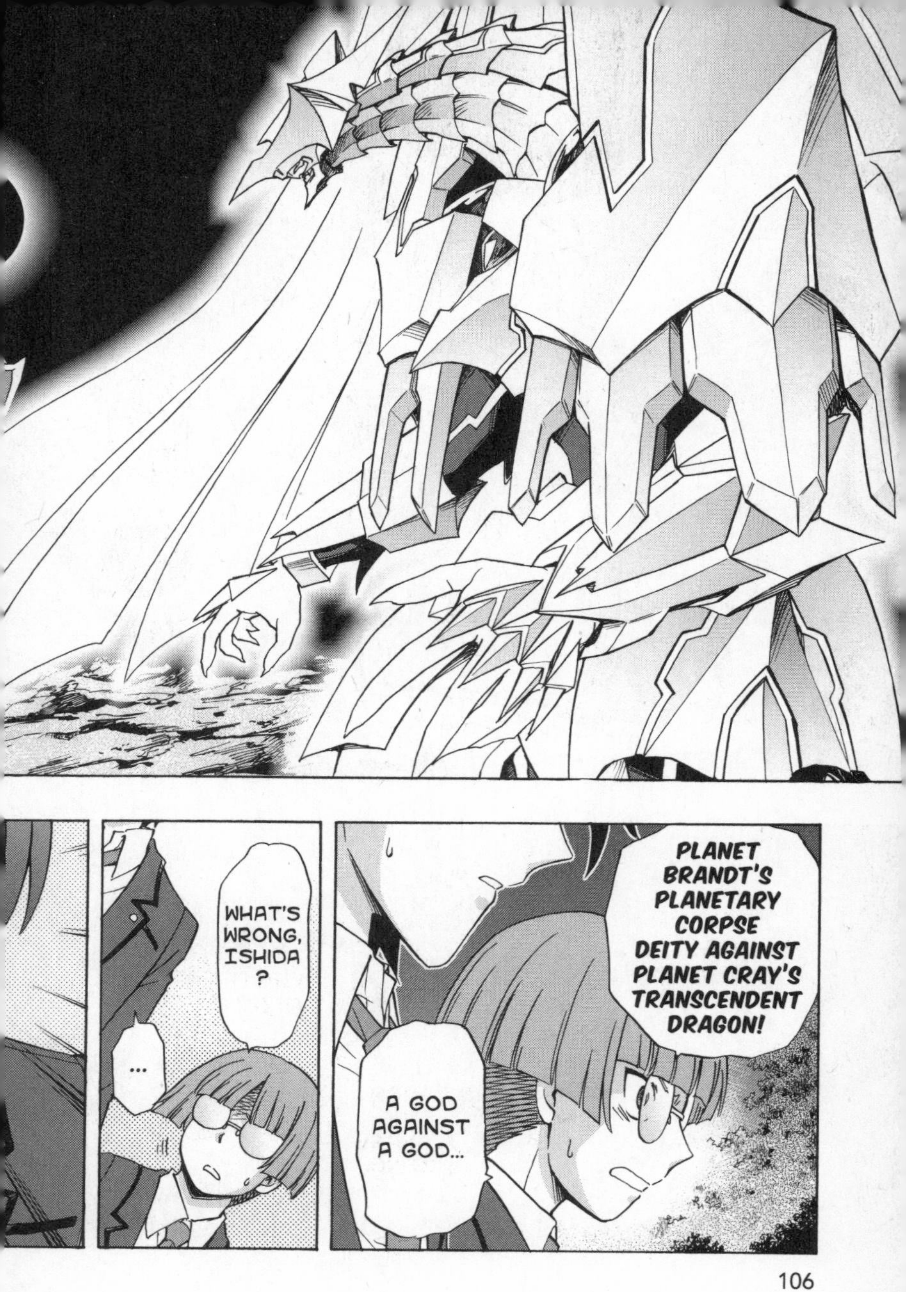
PLANET BRANDT'S PLANETARY CORPSE DEITY AGAINST PLANET CRAY'S TRANSCENDENT DRAGON!
A GOD AGAINST A GOD...
WHAT'S WRONG, ISHIDA?
...

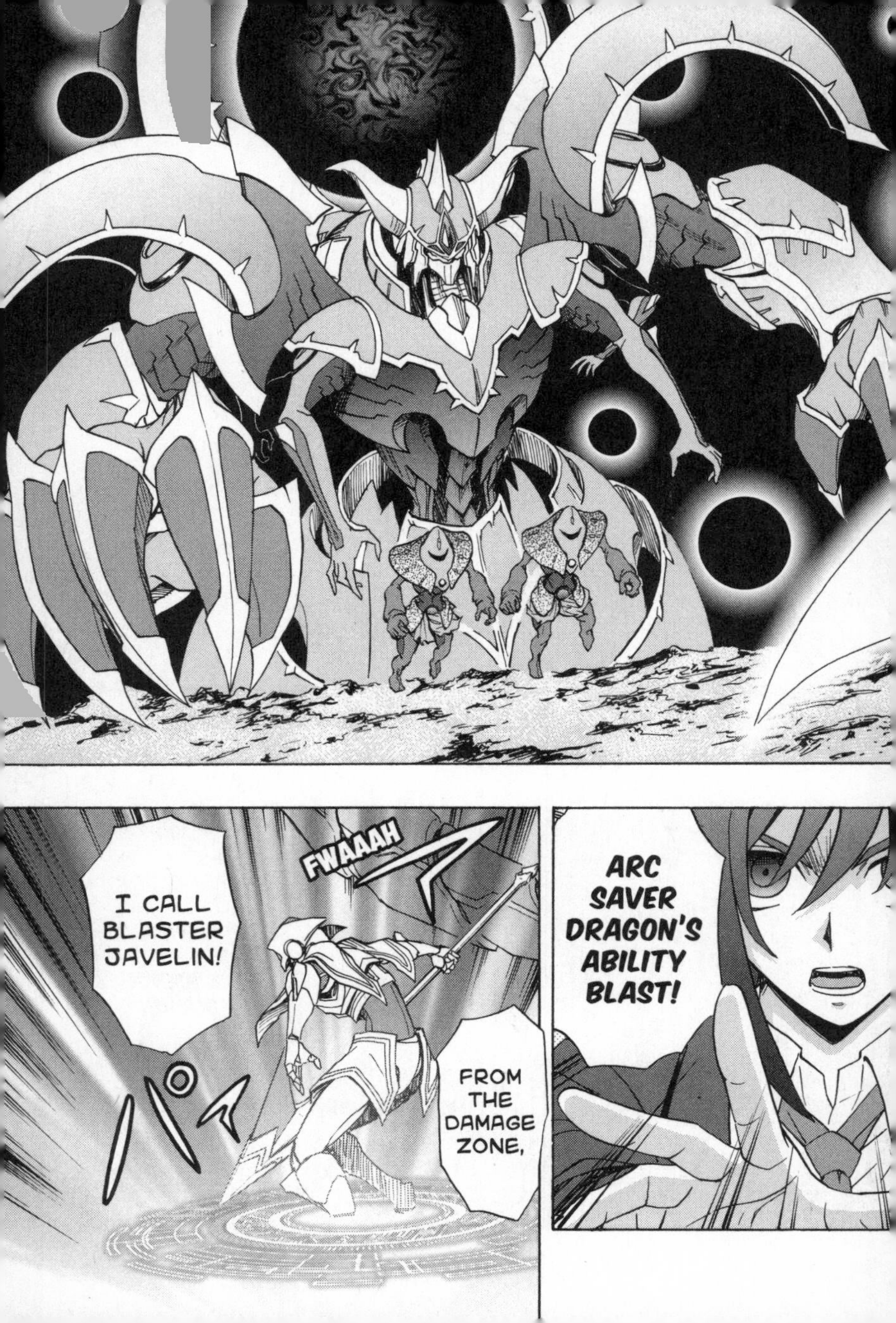
ARC SAVER DRAGON'S ABILITY BLAST!
FWAAAH
FROM THE DAMAGE ZONE,
I CALL BLASTER JAVELIN!

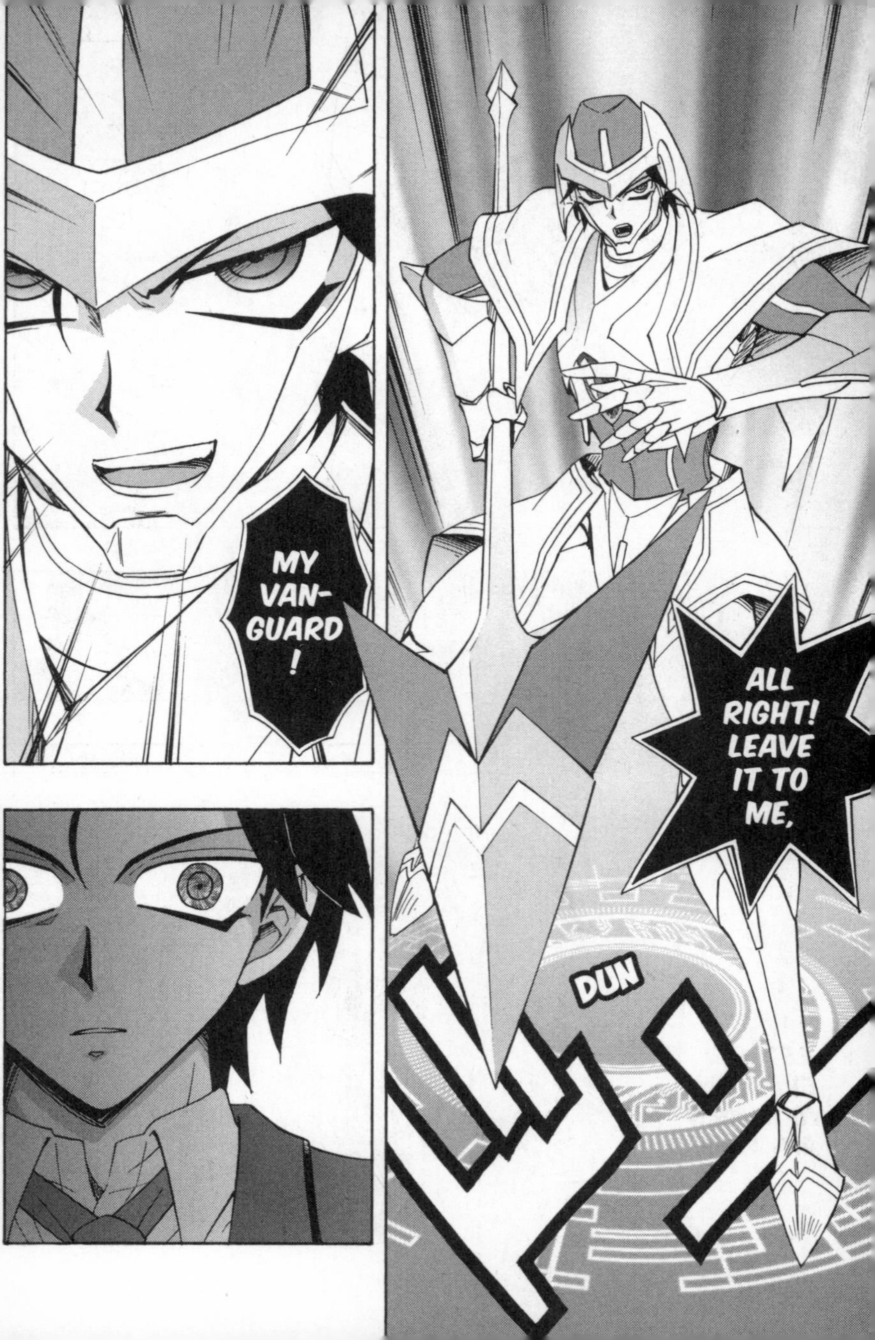
ALL RIGHT! LEAVE IT TO ME,
DUN
MY VAN-GUARD!

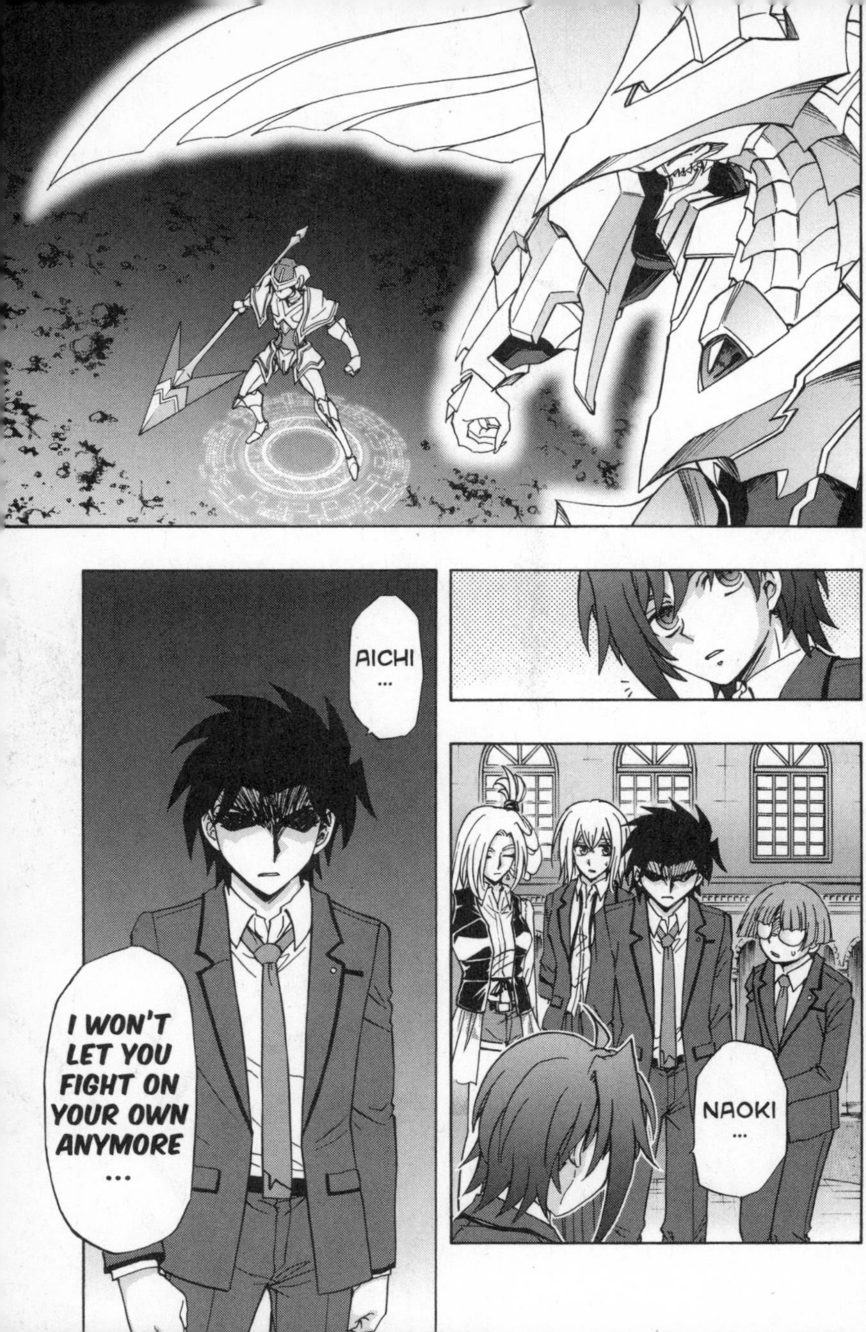
NAOKI ...
AICHI ...
I WON'T LET YOU FIGHT ON YOUR OWN ANYMORE ...

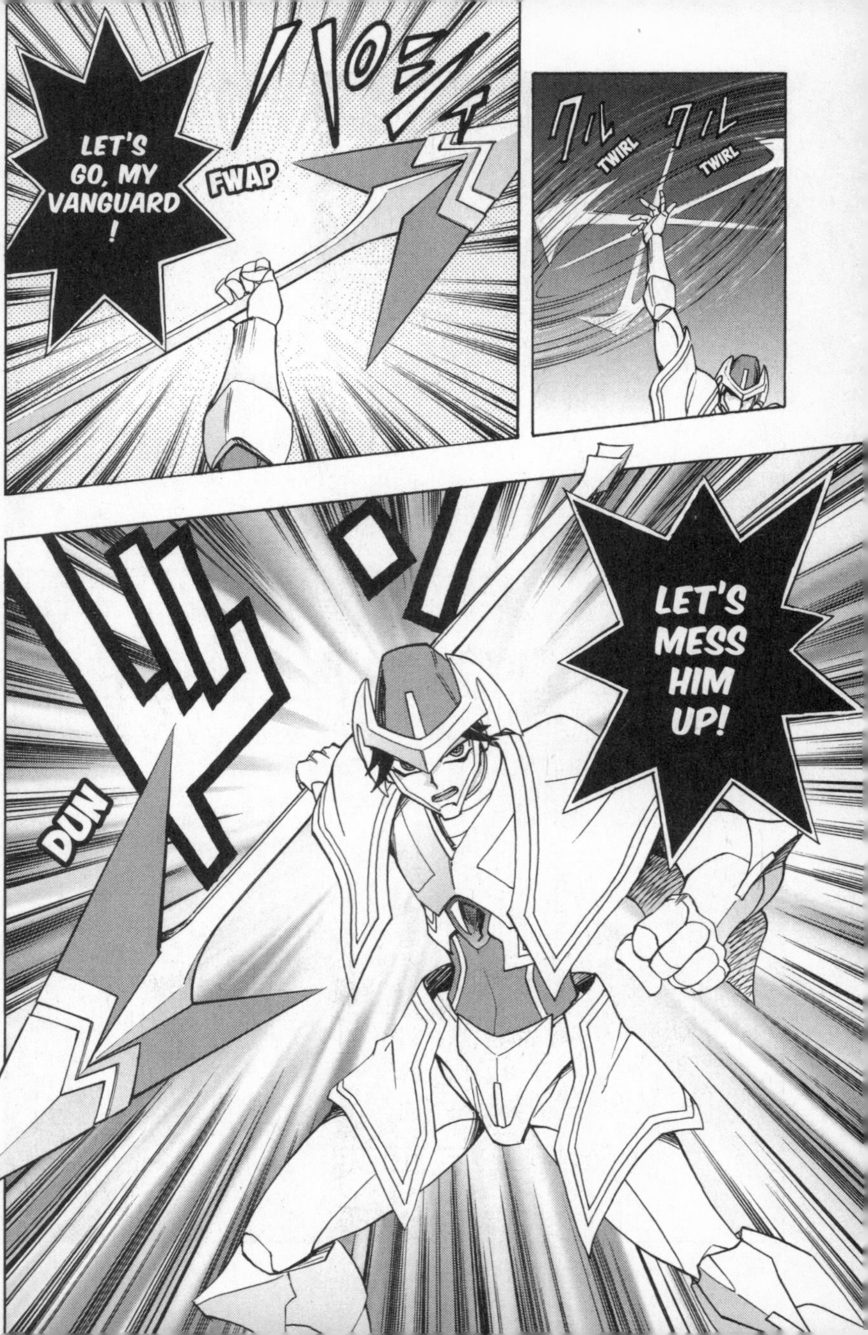
クル
TWIRL
クル
TWIRL
LET'S GO, MY VANGUARD!
FWAP
LET'S MESS HIM UP!
DUN

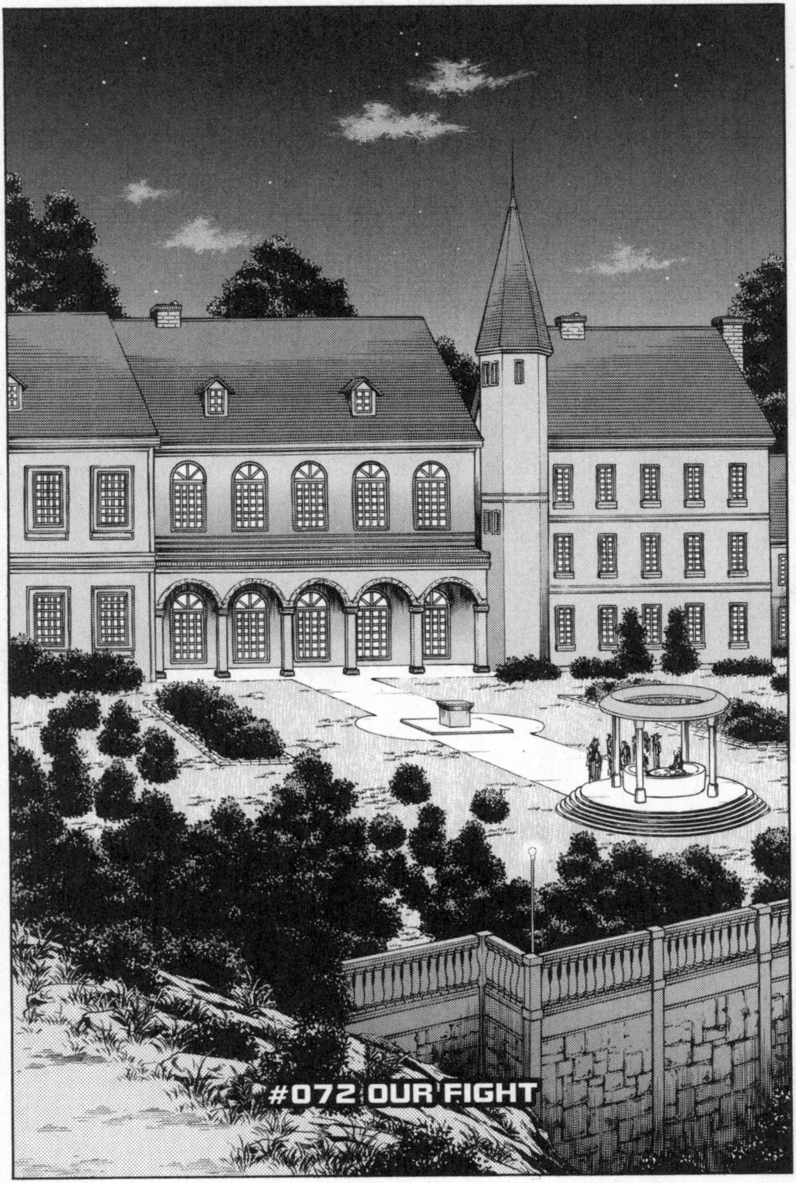
#072 OUR FIGHT

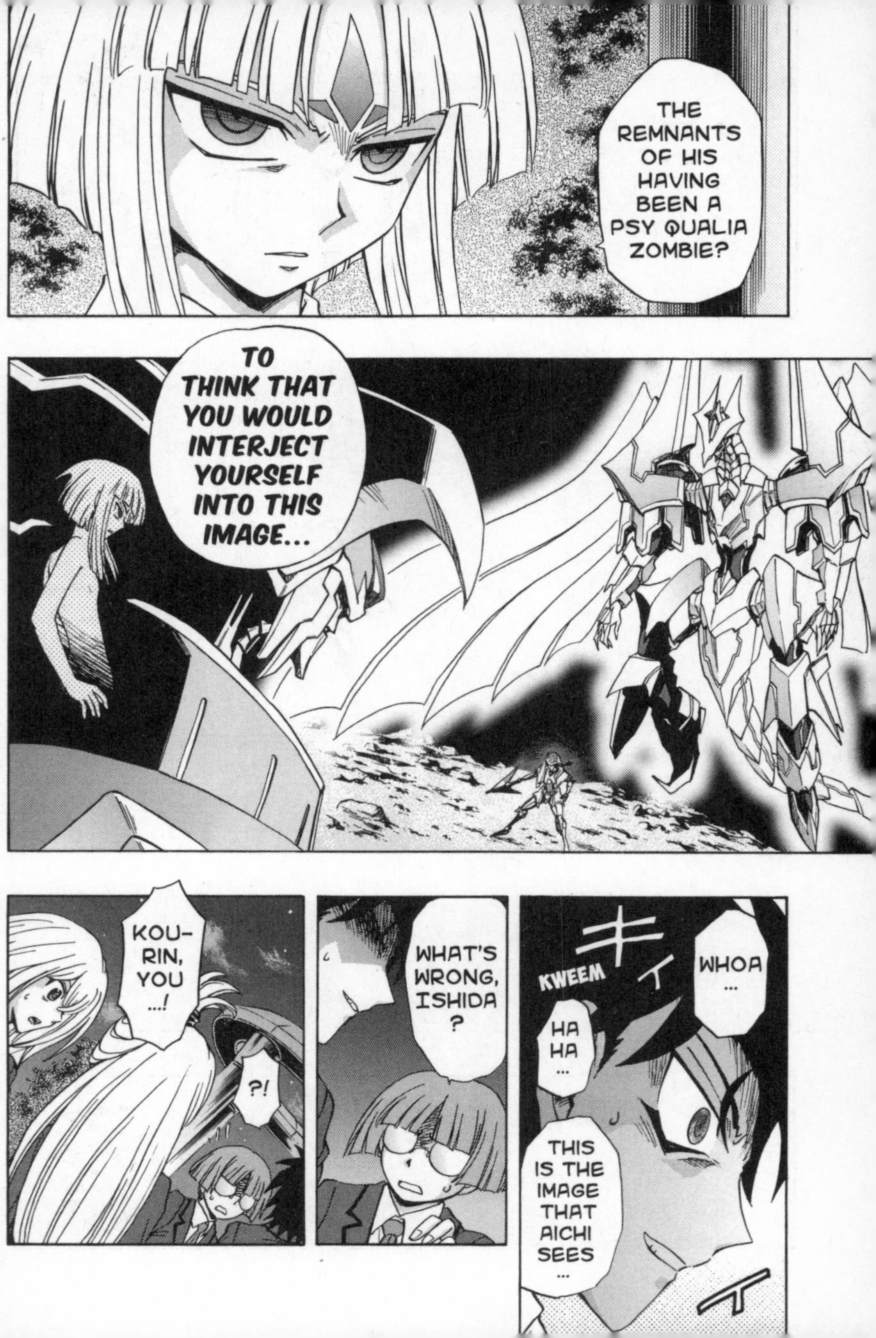
THE REMNANTS OF HIS HAVING BEEN A PSY QUALIA ZOMBIE?
TO THINK THAT YOU WOULD INTERJECT YOURSELF INTO THIS IMAGE...
WHOA ...
KWEEM
キイ
HA HA ...
THIS IS THE IMAGE THAT AICHI SEES ...
WHAT'S WRONG, ISHIDA ?
KOU-RIN, YOU ...!
?!

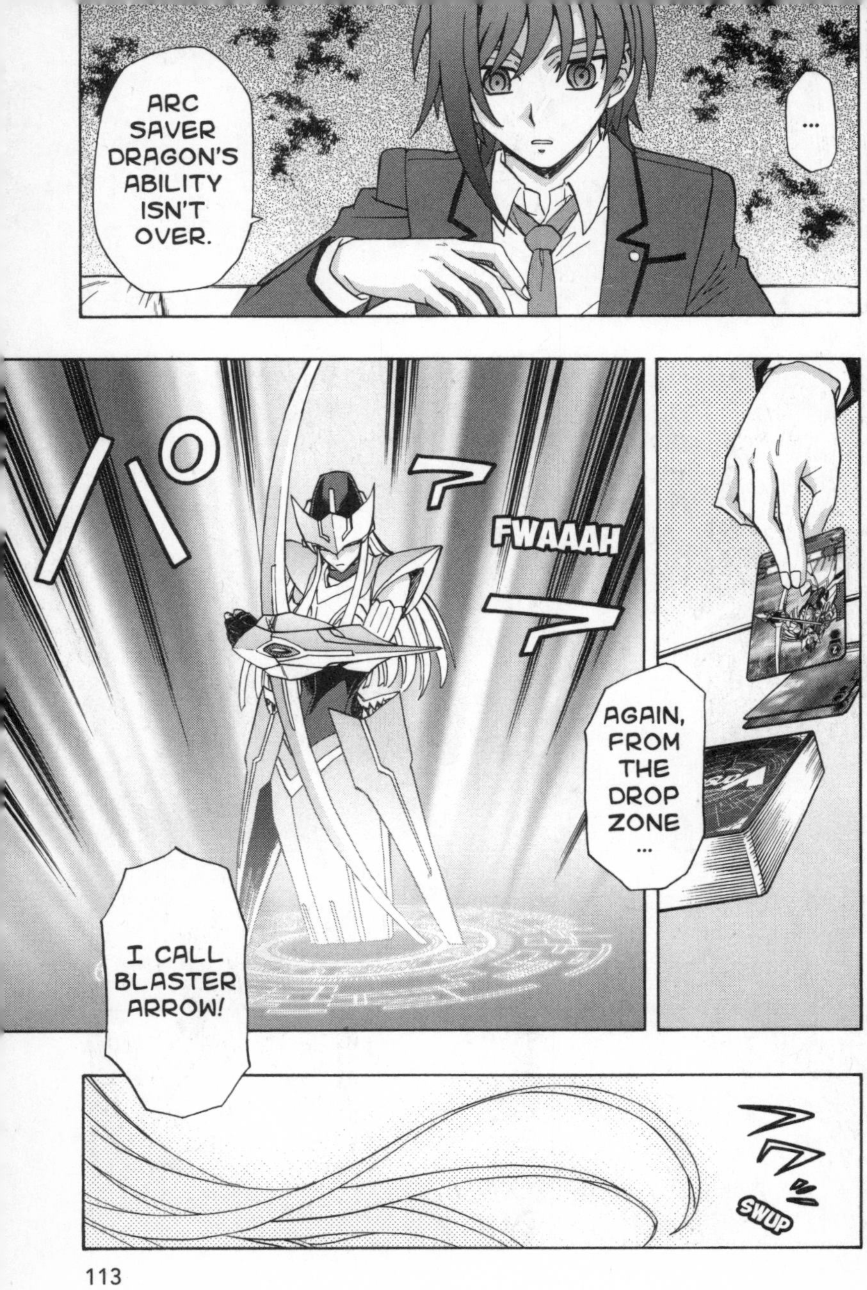

...
ARC SAVER DRAGON'S ABILITY ISN'T OVER.
AGAIN, FROM THE DROP ZONE ...
FWAAAH
I CALL BLASTER ARROW!
SWUP

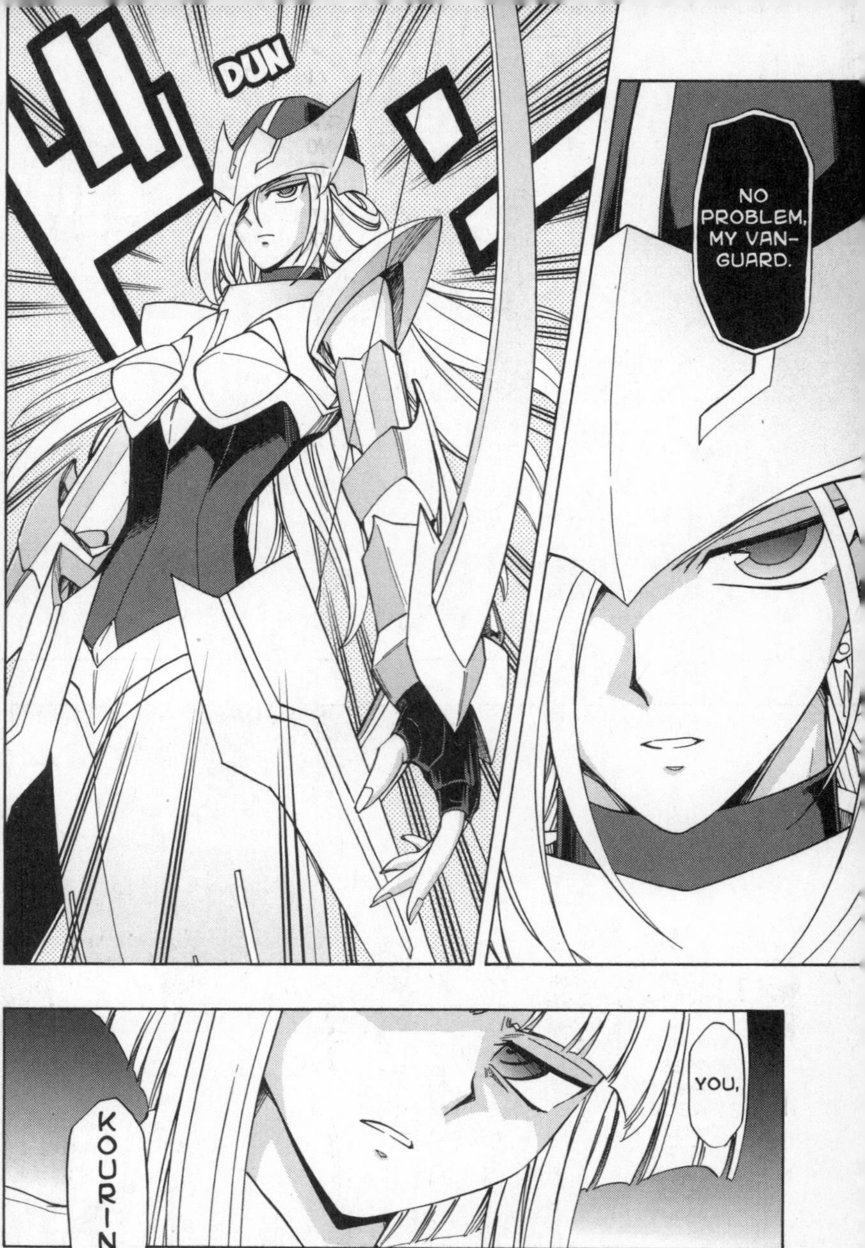
NO PROBLEM, MY VAN-GUARD.
DUN
YOU,
KOURIN?

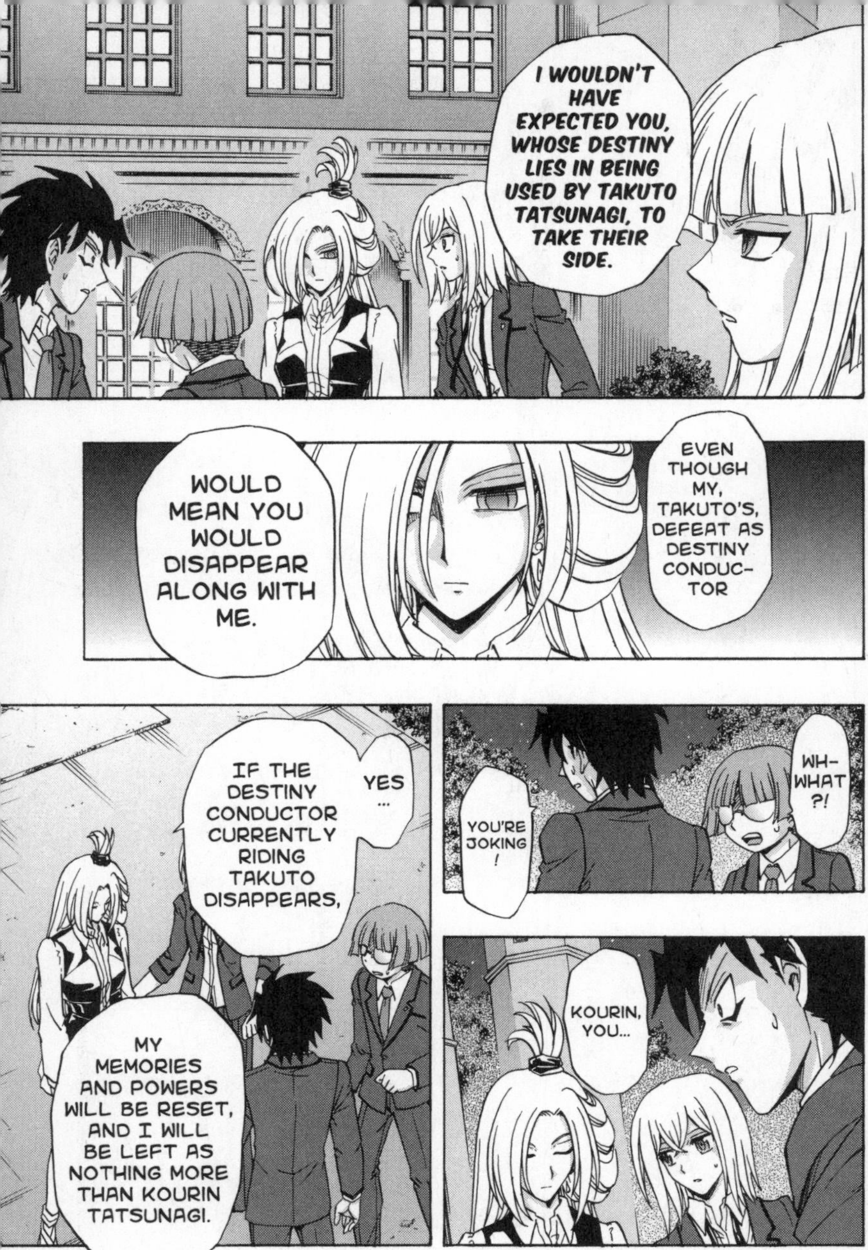
I WOULDN'T HAVE EXPECTED YOU, WHOSE DESTINY LIES IN BEING USED BY TAKUTO TATSUNAGI, TO TAKE THEIR SIDE.
EVEN THOUGH MY, TAKUTO'S, DEFEAT AS DESTINY CONDUC-TOR
WOULD MEAN YOU WOULD DISAPPEAR ALONG WITH ME.
WH-WHAT?!
YOU'RE JOKING!
KOURIN, YOU...
YES...
IF THE DESTINY CONDUCTOR CURRENTLY RIDING TAKUTO DISAPPEARS,
MY MEMORIES AND POWERS WILL BE RESET, AND I WILL BE LEFT AS NOTHING MORE THAN KOURIN TATSUNAGI.

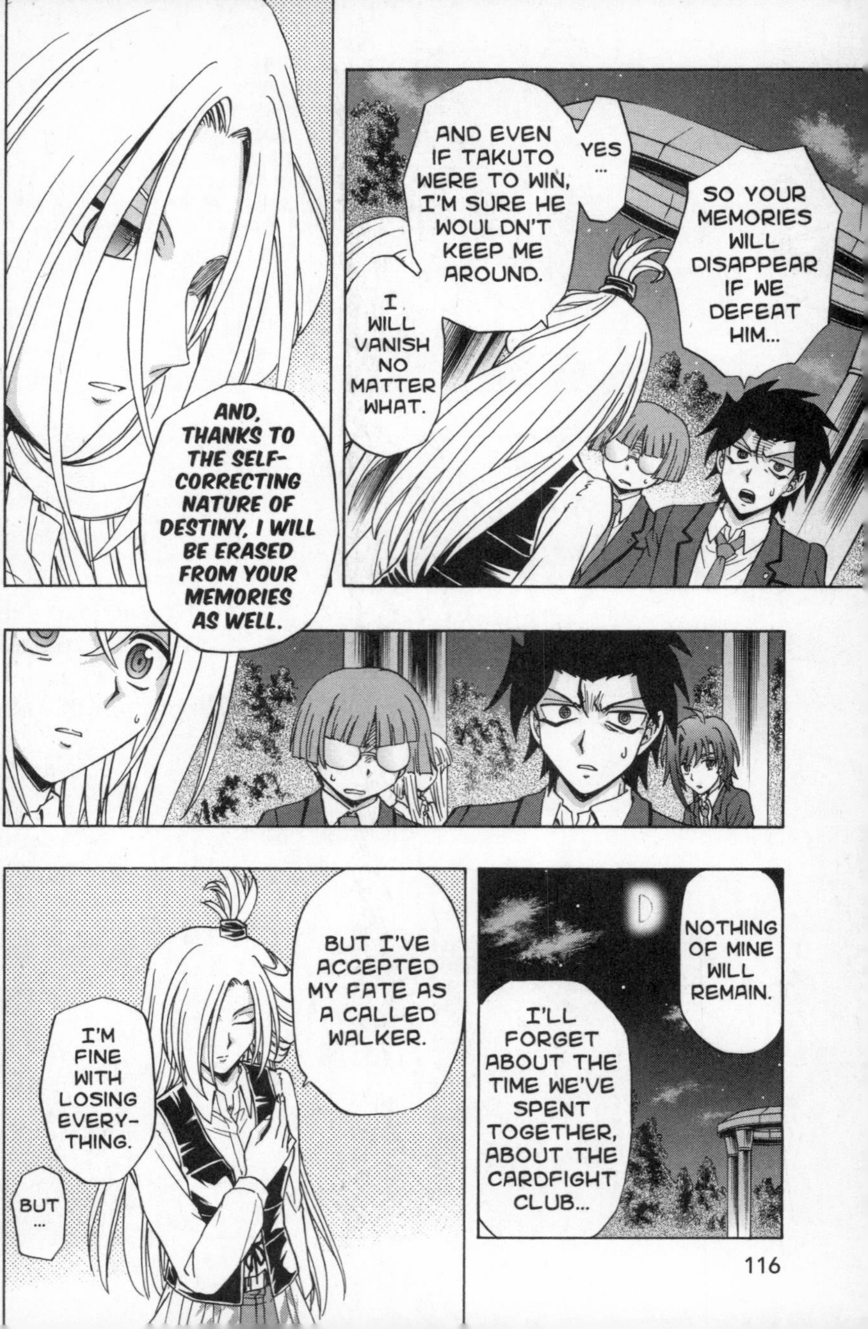
SO YOUR MEMORIES WILL DISAPPEAR IF WE DEFEAT HIM...
YES ...
AND EVEN IF TAKUTO WERE TO WIN, I'M SURE HE WOULDN'T KEEP ME AROUND.
I WILL VANISH NO MATTER WHAT.
AND, THANKS TO THE SELF-CORRECTING NATURE OF DESTINY, I WILL BE ERASED FROM YOUR MEMORIES AS WELL.
NOTHING OF MINE WILL REMAIN.
I'LL FORGET ABOUT THE TIME WE'VE SPENT TOGETHER, ABOUT THE CARDFIGHT CLUB...
BUT I'VE ACCEPTED MY FATE AS A CALLED WALKER.
I'M FINE WITH LOSING EVERYTHING.
BUT ...

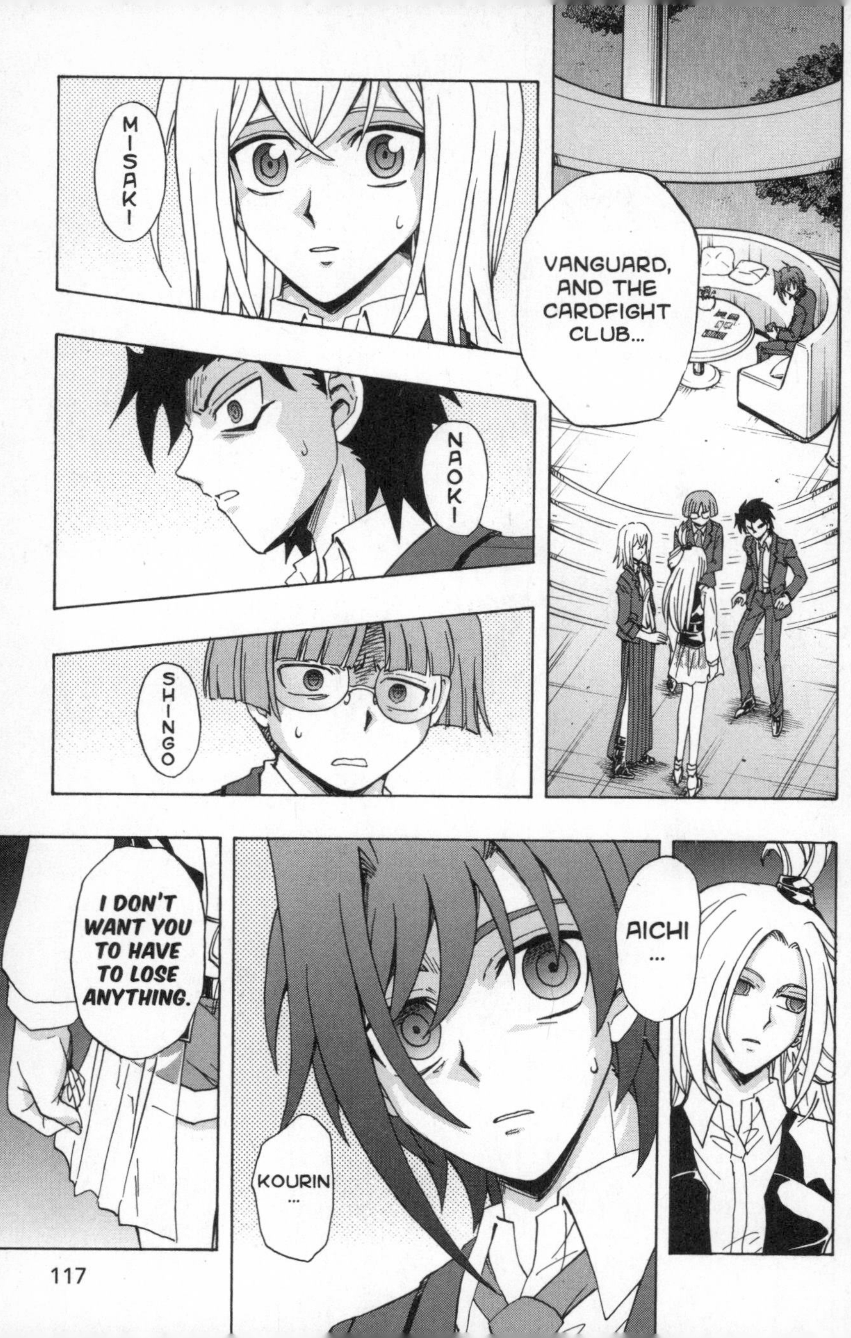
VANGUARD, AND THE CARDFIGHT CLUB...
MISAKI
NAOKI
SHINGO
AICHI ...
KOURIN ...
I DON'T WANT YOU TO HAVE TO LOSE ANYTHING.

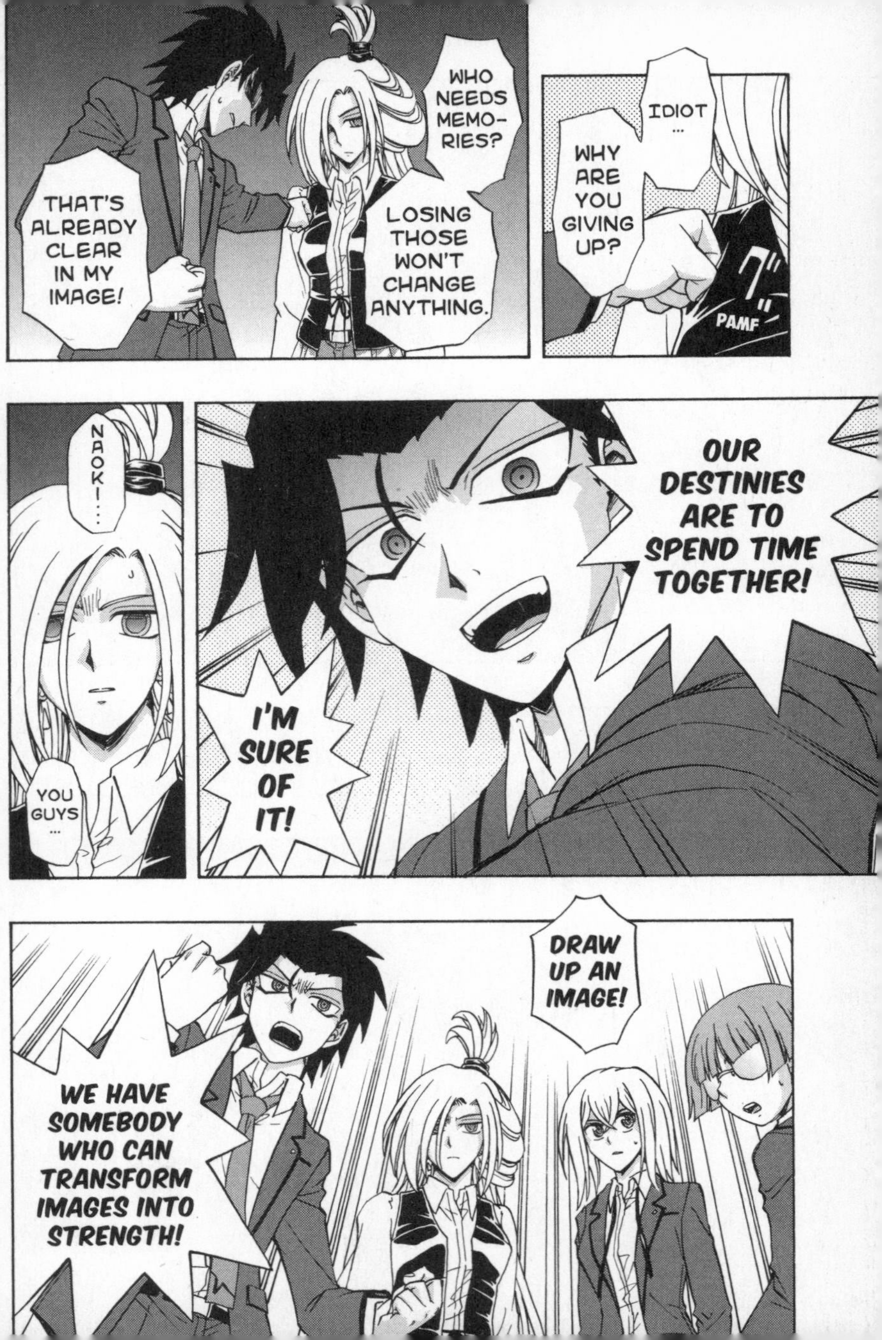
IDIOT ...
WHY ARE YOU GIVING UP?
PAMF
WHO NEEDS MEMO-RIES?
LOSING THOSE WON'T CHANGE ANYTHING.
THAT'S ALREADY CLEAR IN MY IMAGE!
OUR DESTINIES ARE TO SPEND TIME TOGETHER!
I'M SURE OF IT!
NAOKI ...
YOU GUYS ...
DRAW UP AN IMAGE!
WE HAVE SOMEBODY WHO CAN TRANSFORM IMAGES INTO STRENGTH!

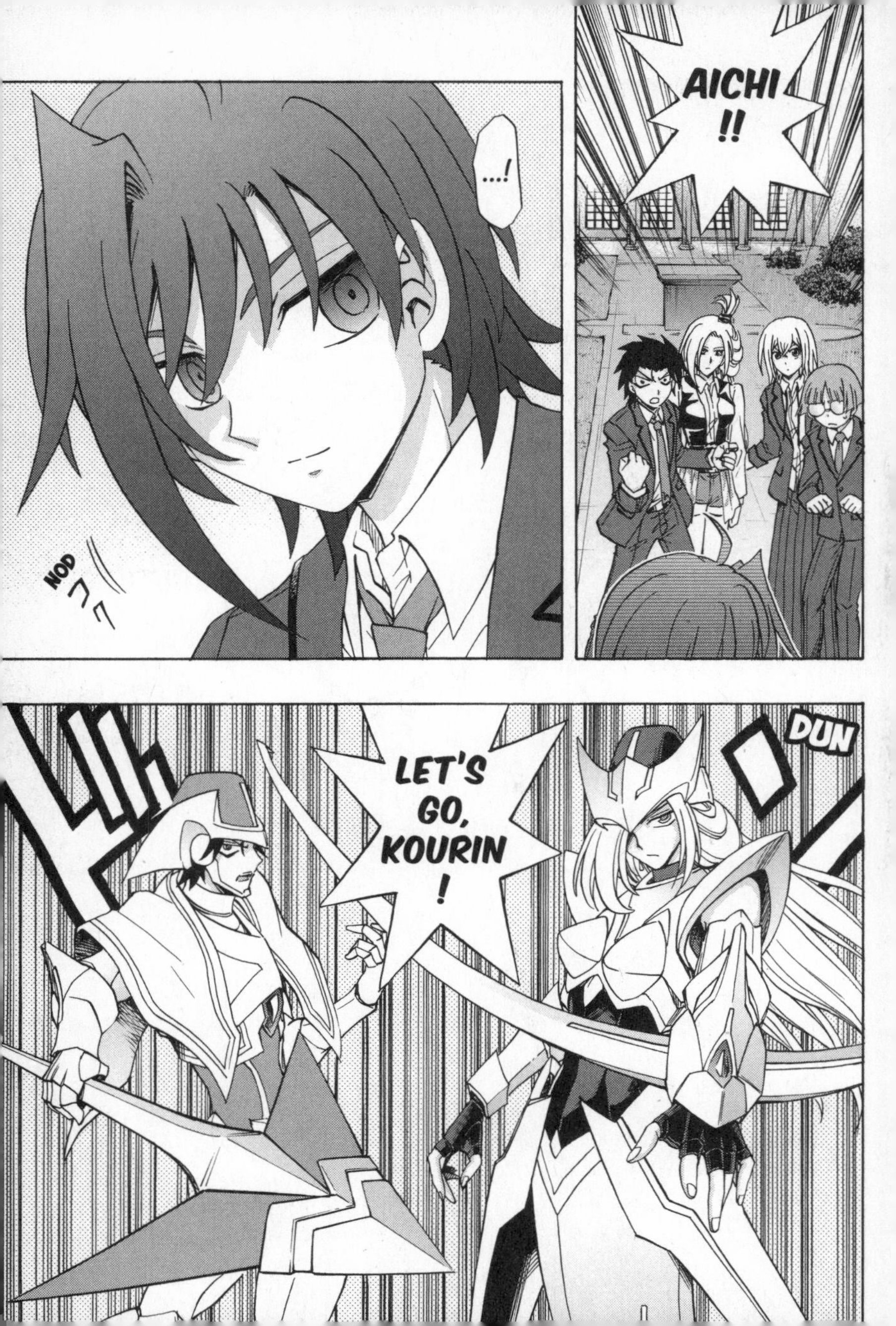
AICHI !!
...!
NOD
DUN
LET'S GO, KOURIN !

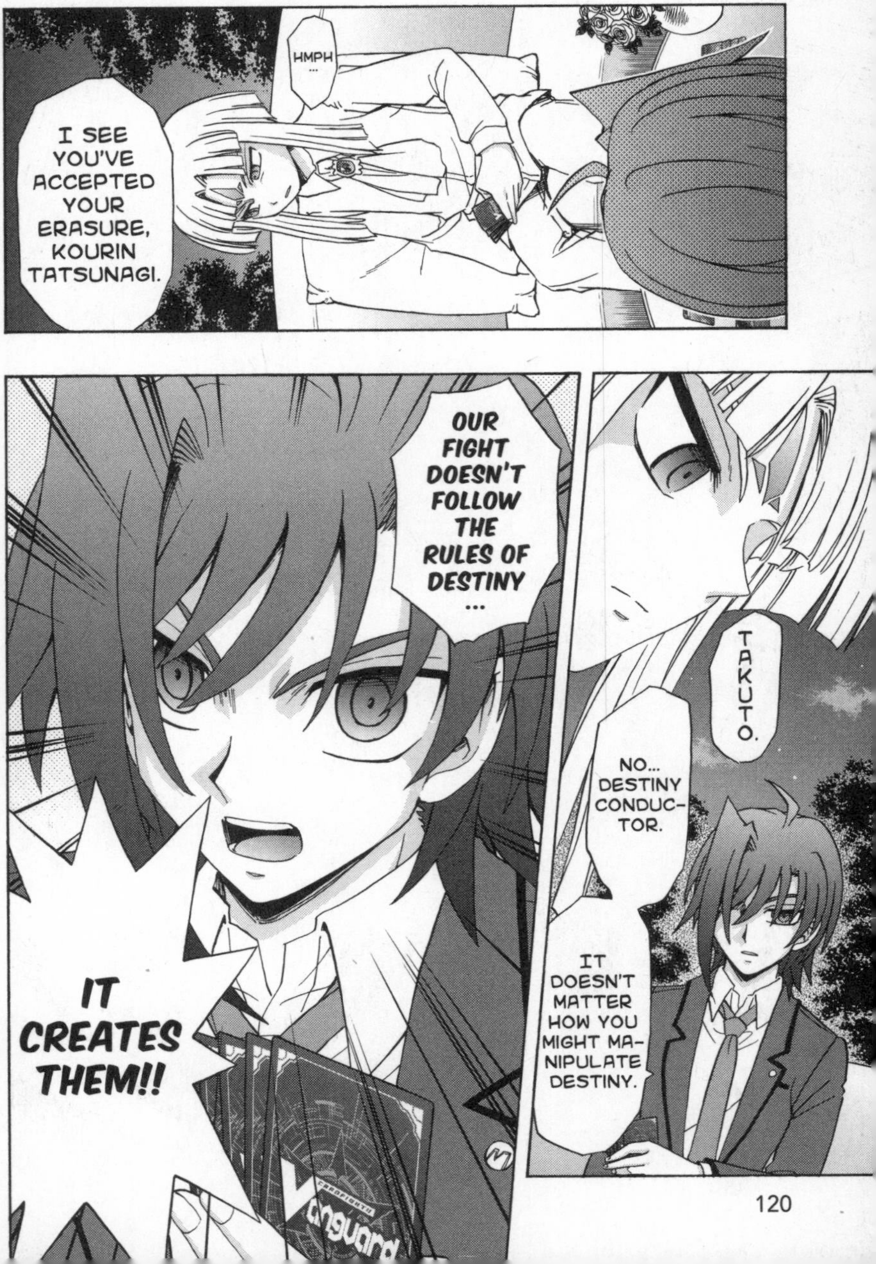
HMPH...
I SEE YOU'VE ACCEPTED YOUR ERASURE, KOURIN TATSUNAGI.
TAKUTO.
NO... DESTINY CONDUCTOR.
IT DOESN'T MATTER HOW YOU MIGHT MANIPULATE DESTINY.
OUR FIGHT DOESN'T FOLLOW THE RULES OF DESTINY...
IT CREATES THEM!!
Vanguard

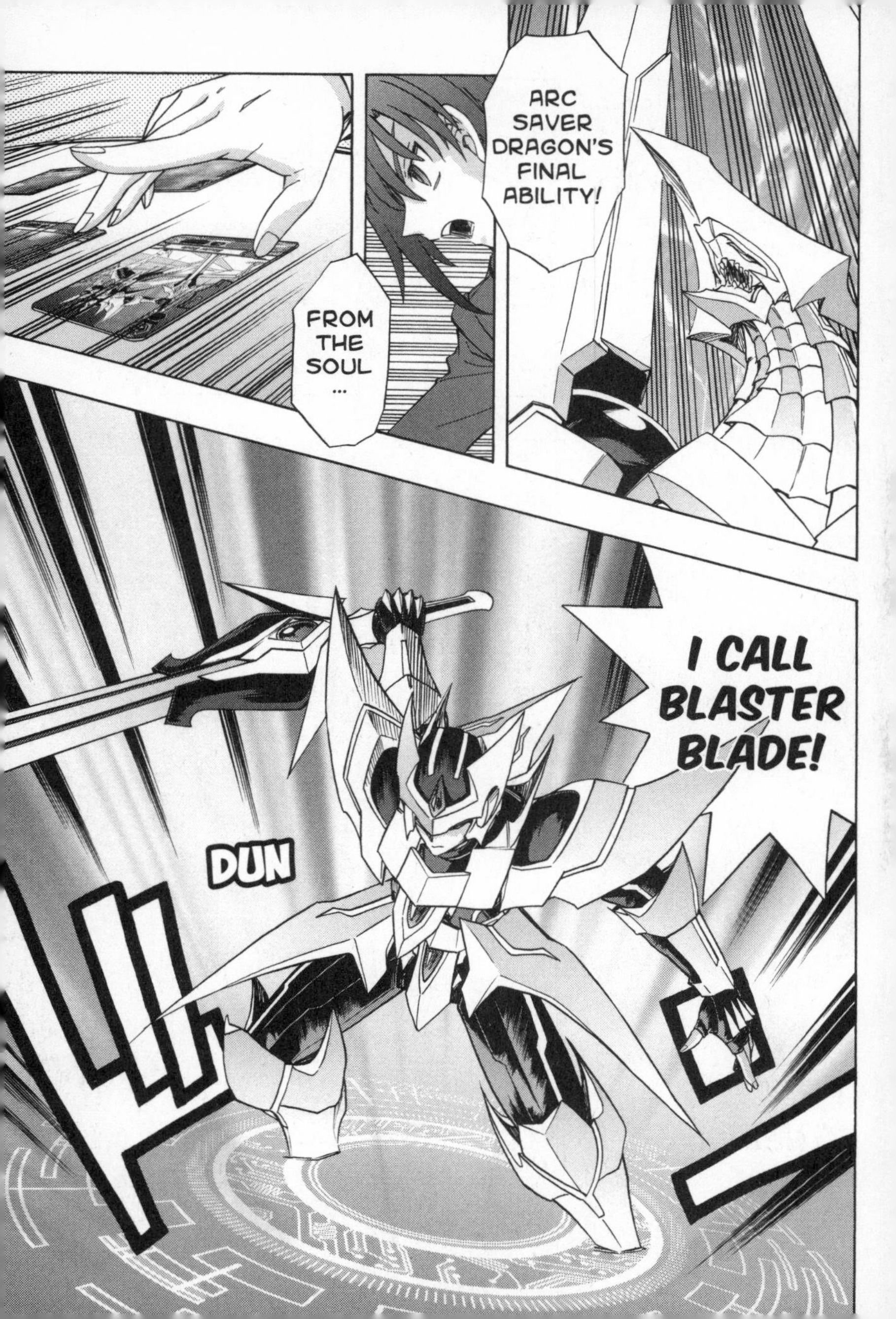
ARC SAVER DRAGON'S FINAL ABILITY!
FROM THE SOUL ...
I CALL BLASTER BLADE!
DUN

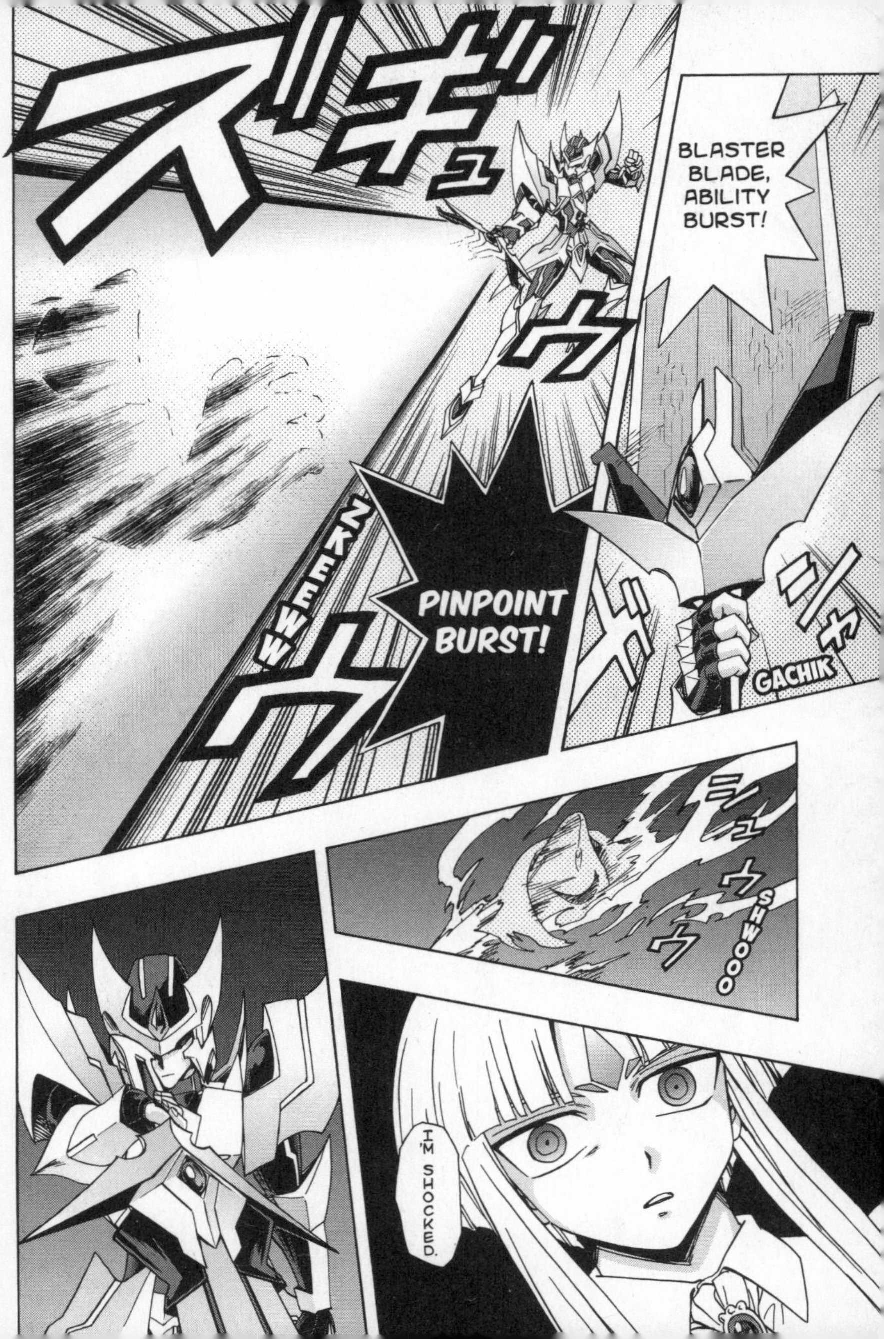
BLASTER BLADE, ABILITY BURST!
GACHIK
PINPOINT BURST!
ZKEEEWW
SHWOOO
I'M SHOCKED.

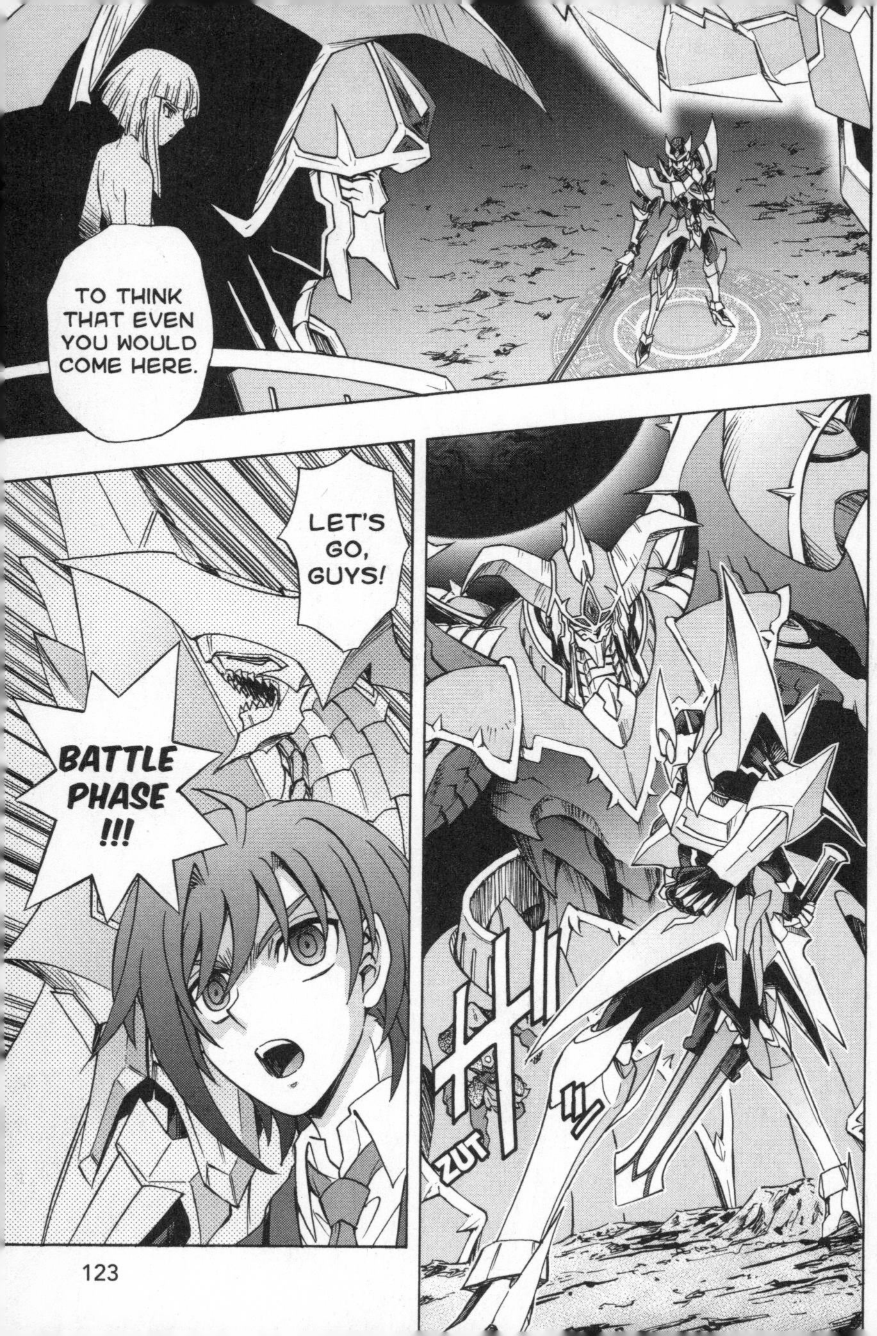
TO THINK THAT EVEN YOU WOULD COME HERE.
ZUT
LET'S GO, GUYS!
BATTLE PHASE !!!

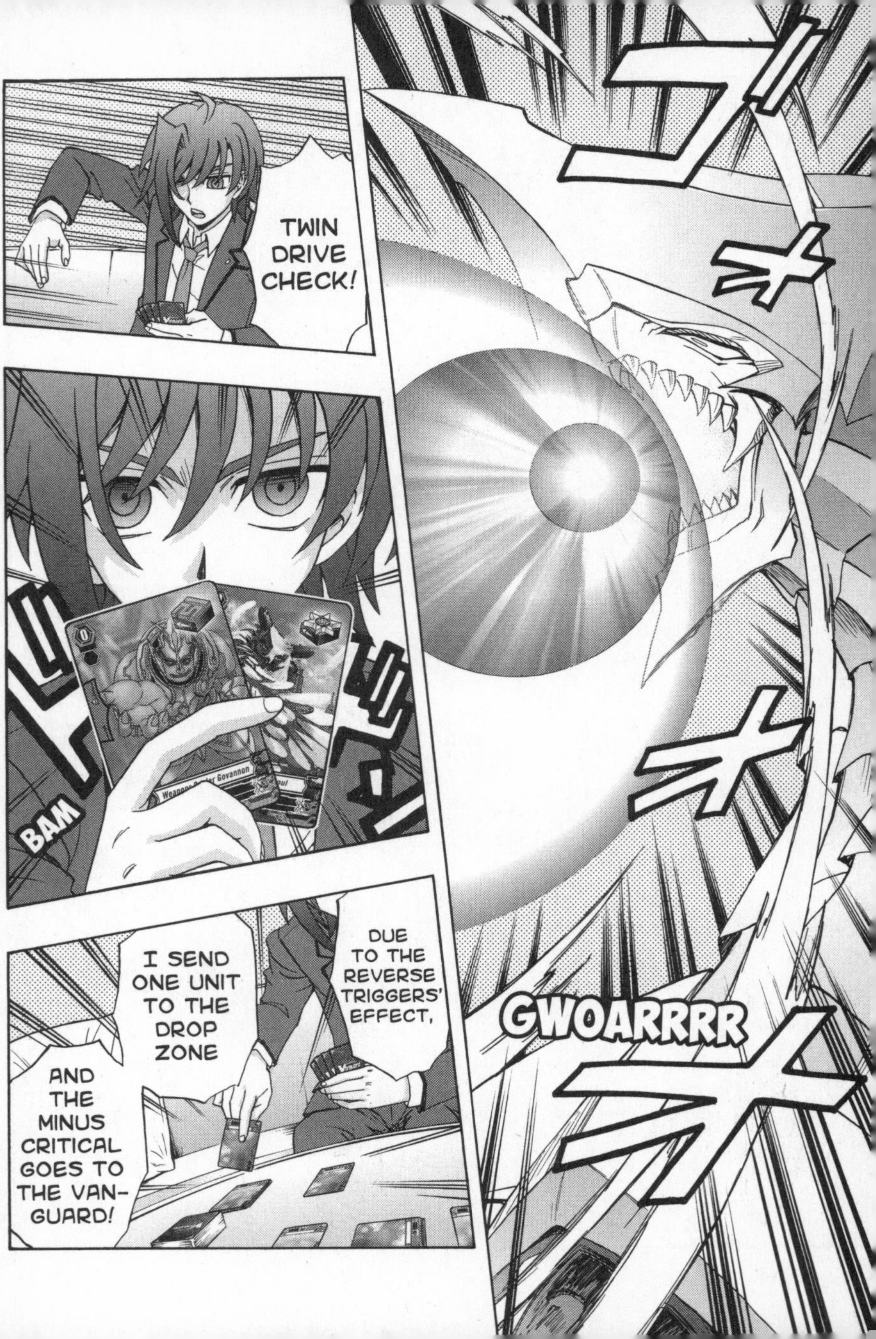
GWOARRRR
TWIN DRIVE CHECK!
BAM
DUE TO THE REVERSE TRIGGERS' EFFECT,
I SEND ONE UNIT TO THE DROP ZONE
AND THE MINUS CRITICAL GOES TO THE VAN-GUARD!

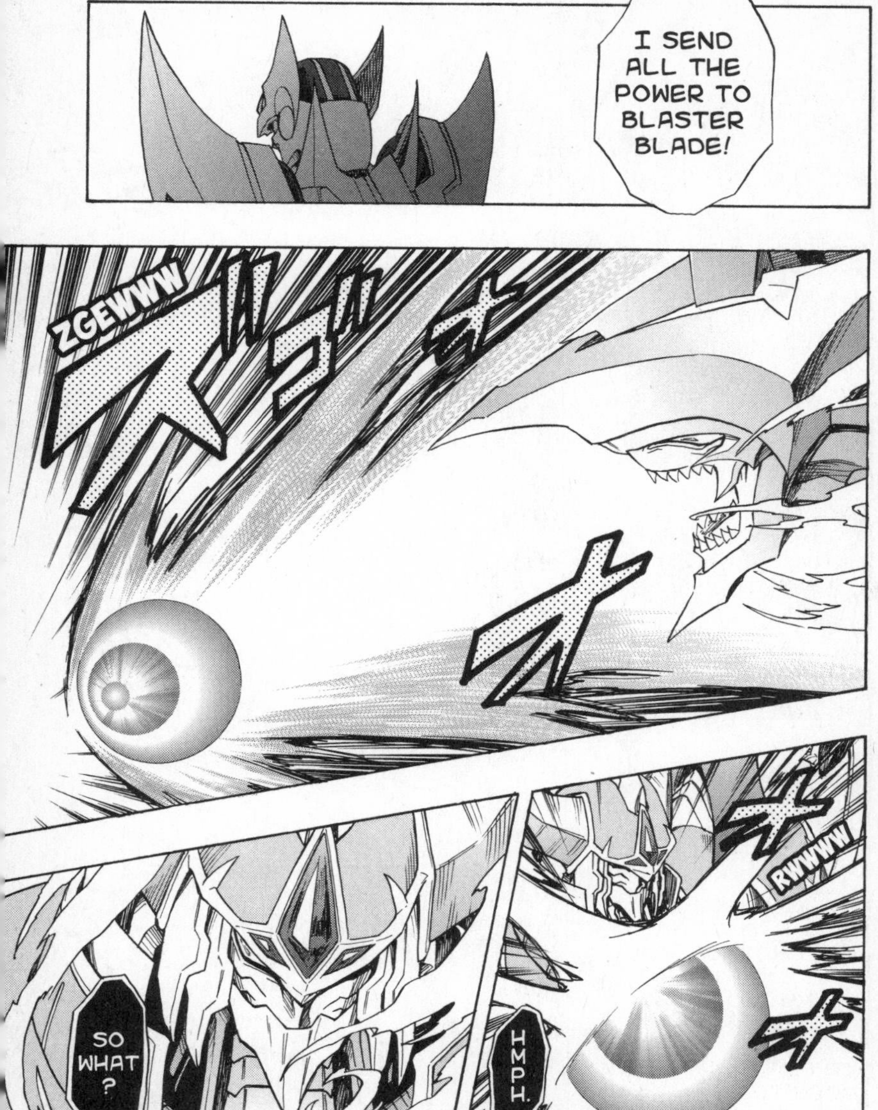
I SEND ALL THE POWER TO BLASTER BLADE!
ZGEWWW
RWWWW
HMPH.
SO WHAT?

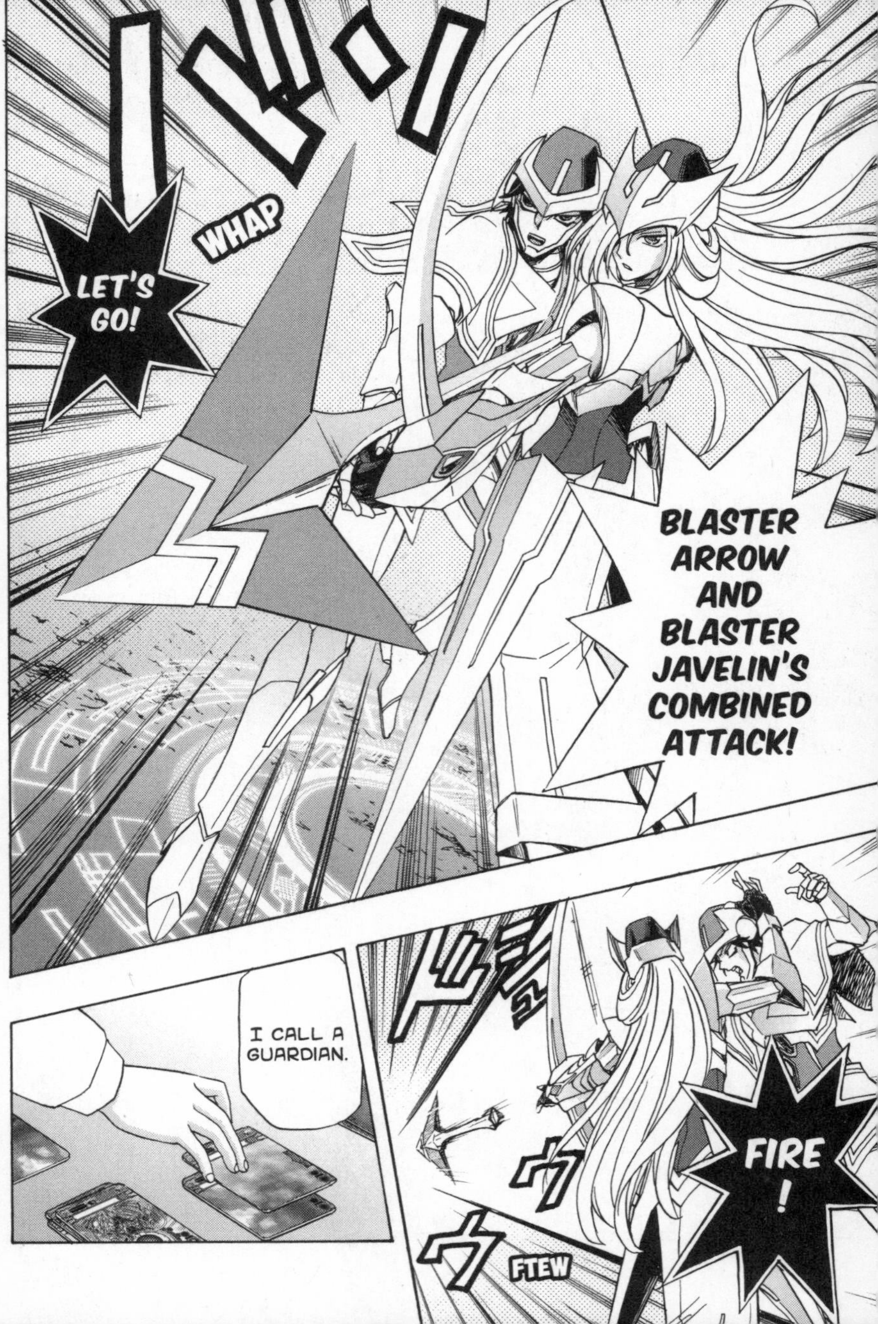
WHAP
LET'S GO!
BLASTER ARROW AND BLASTER JAVELIN'S COMBINED ATTACK!
FIRE!
FTEW
I CALL A GUARDIAN.

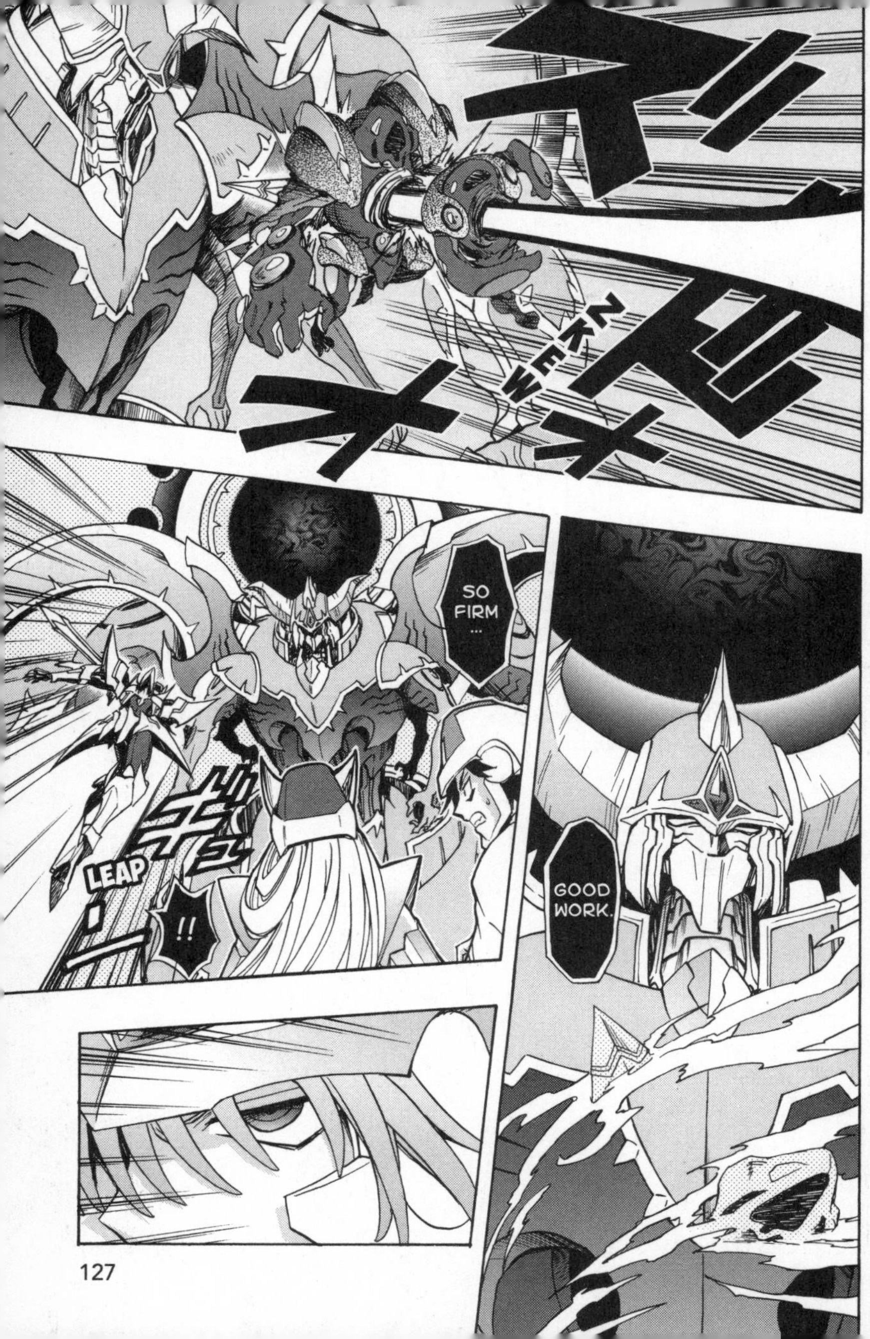

ZKEEW
GOOD WORK.
SO FIRM ...
LEAP
!!

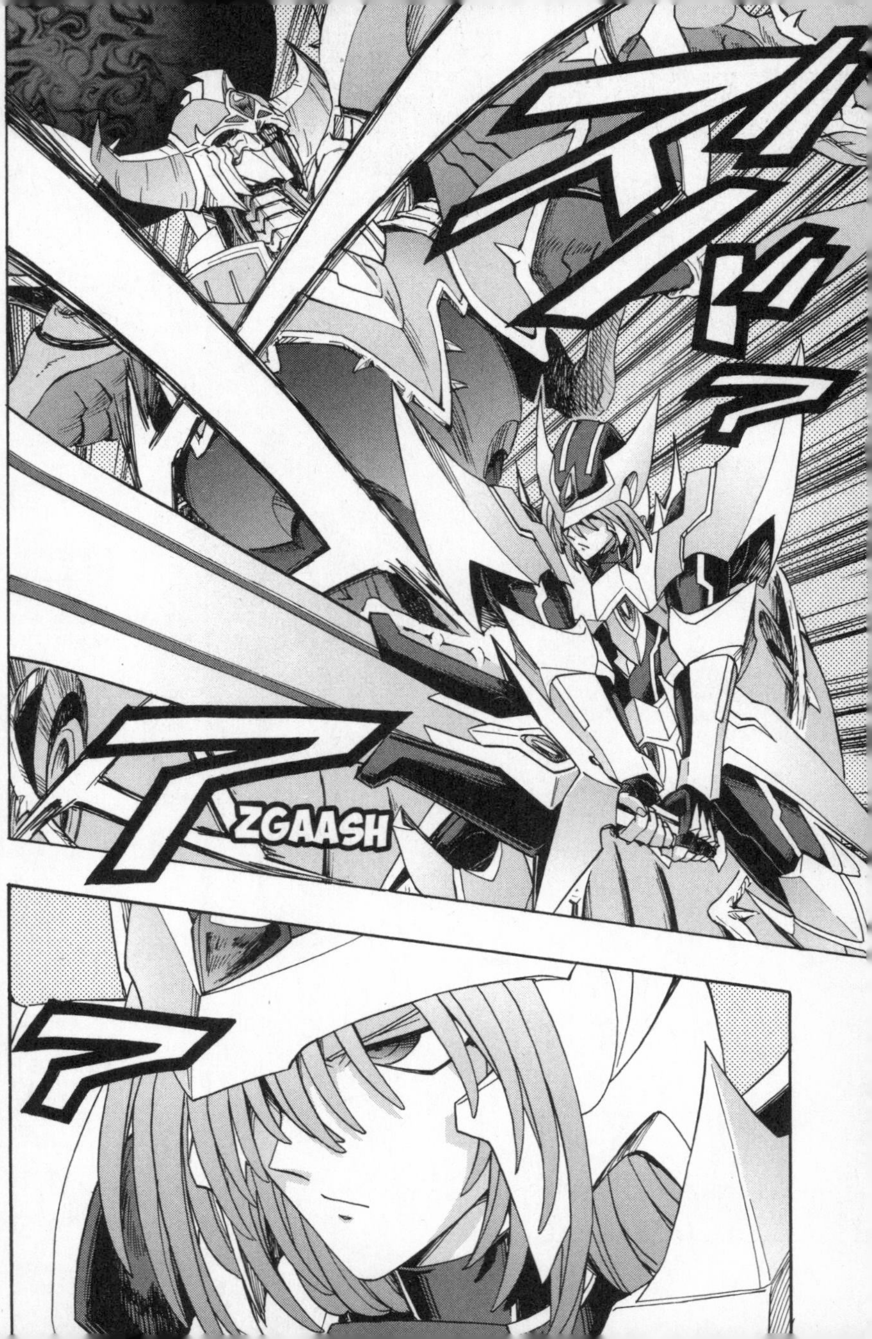
ZGAASH

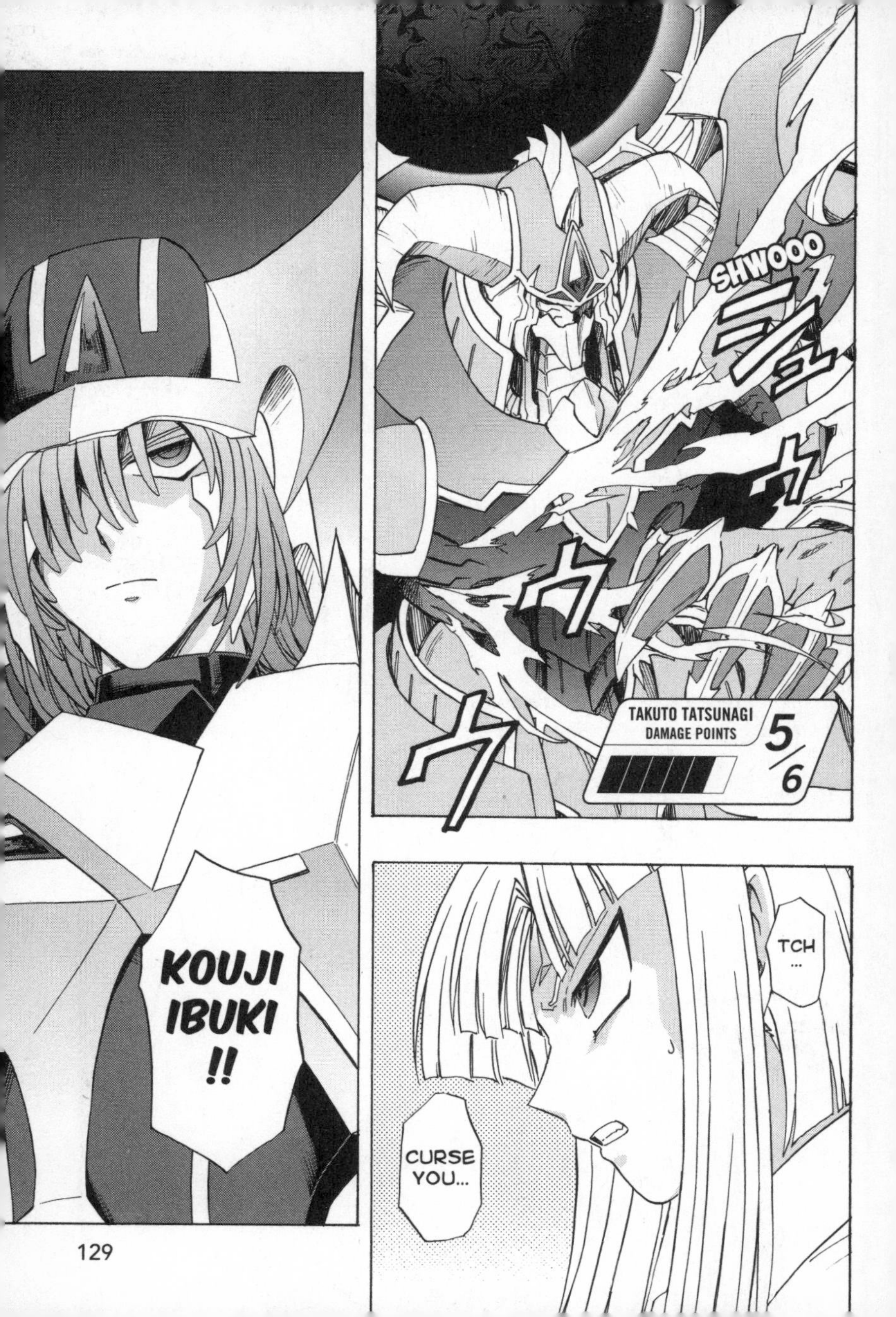
SHWOOO
TAKUTO TATSUNAGI DAMAGE POINTS
5/6
TCH...
CURSE YOU...
KOUJI IBUKI!!

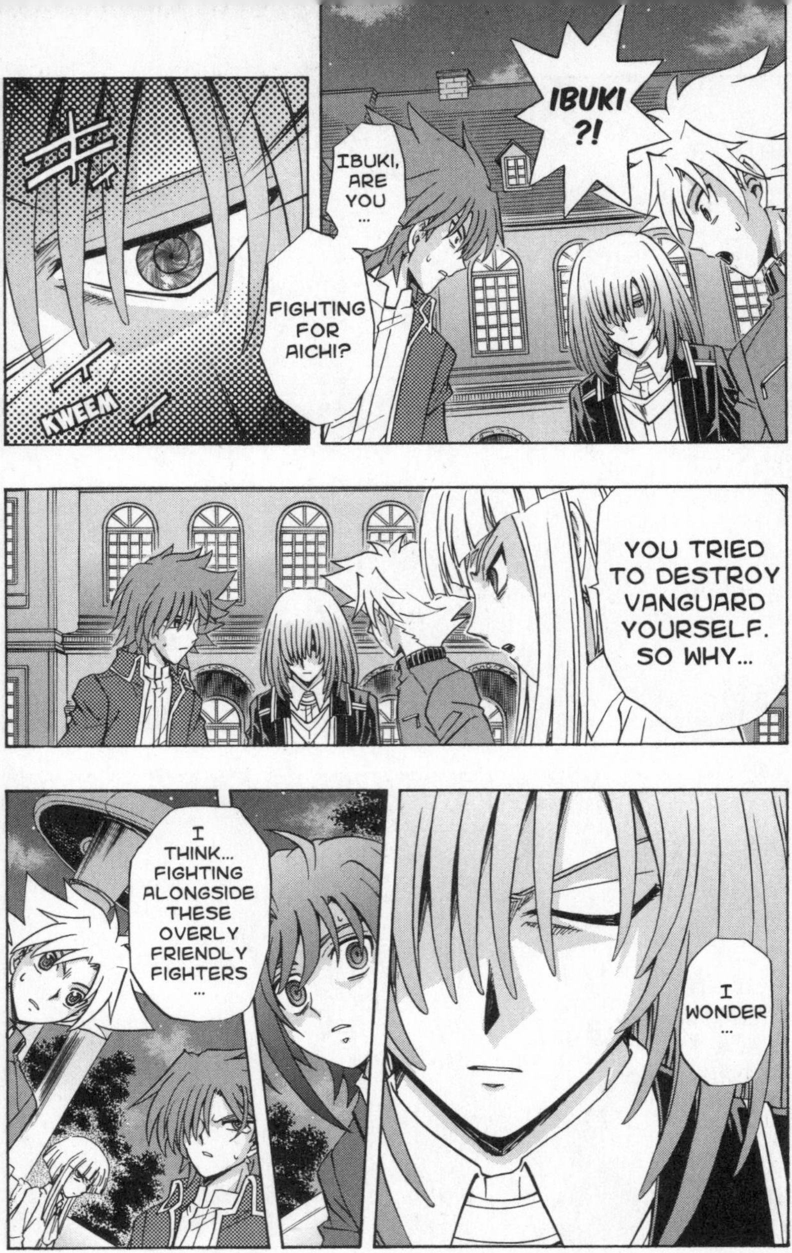
IBUKI ?!
IBUKI, ARE YOU ...
FIGHTING FOR AICHI?
KWEEM
YOU TRIED TO DESTROY VANGUARD YOURSELF. SO WHY...
I WONDER ...
I THINK... FIGHTING ALONGSIDE THESE OVERLY FRIENDLY FIGHTERS ...

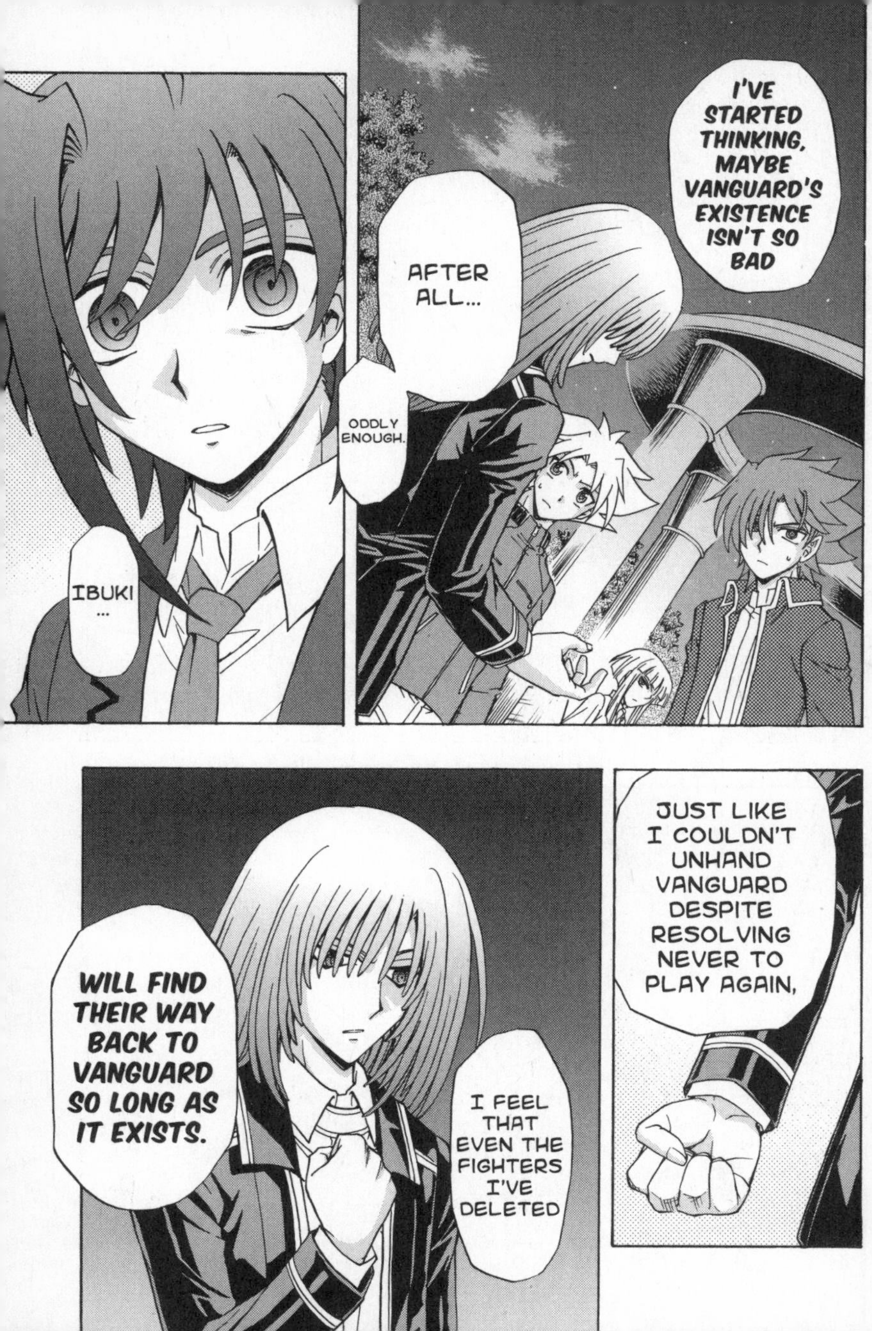
I'VE STARTED THINKING, MAYBE VANGUARD'S EXISTENCE ISN'T SO BAD
AFTER ALL...
ODDLY ENOUGH.
IBUKI ...
JUST LIKE I COULDN'T UNHAND VANGUARD DESPITE RESOLVING NEVER TO PLAY AGAIN,
I FEEL THAT EVEN THE FIGHTERS I'VE DELETED
WILL FIND THEIR WAY BACK TO VANGUARD SO LONG AS IT EXISTS.

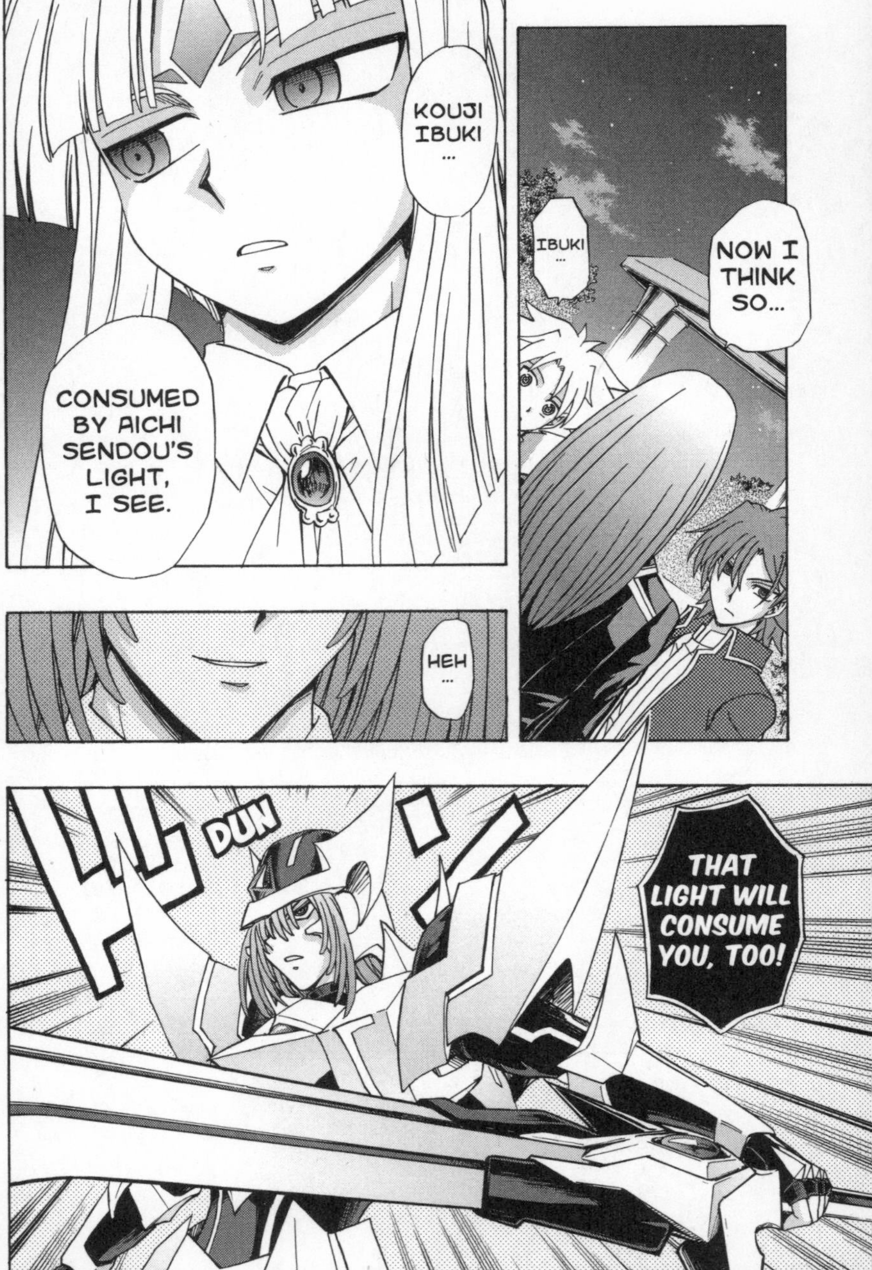
NOW I THINK SO...
IBUKI ...
KOUJI IBUKI ...
CONSUMED BY AICHI SENDOU'S LIGHT, I SEE.
HEH ...
THAT LIGHT WILL CONSUME YOU, TOO!
DUN

CARDFIGHT!!
Vanguard

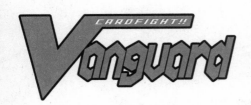

BONUS!

CARDFIGHT!! Vanguard

NEVER-BEFORE-SEEN IMAGE BOARDS

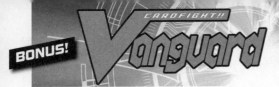

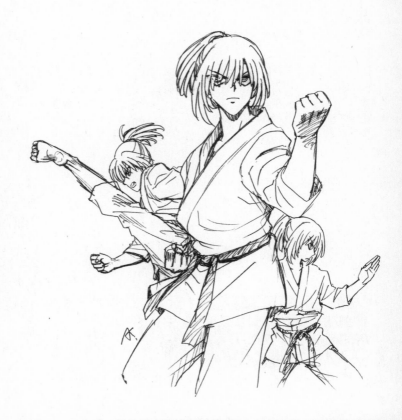

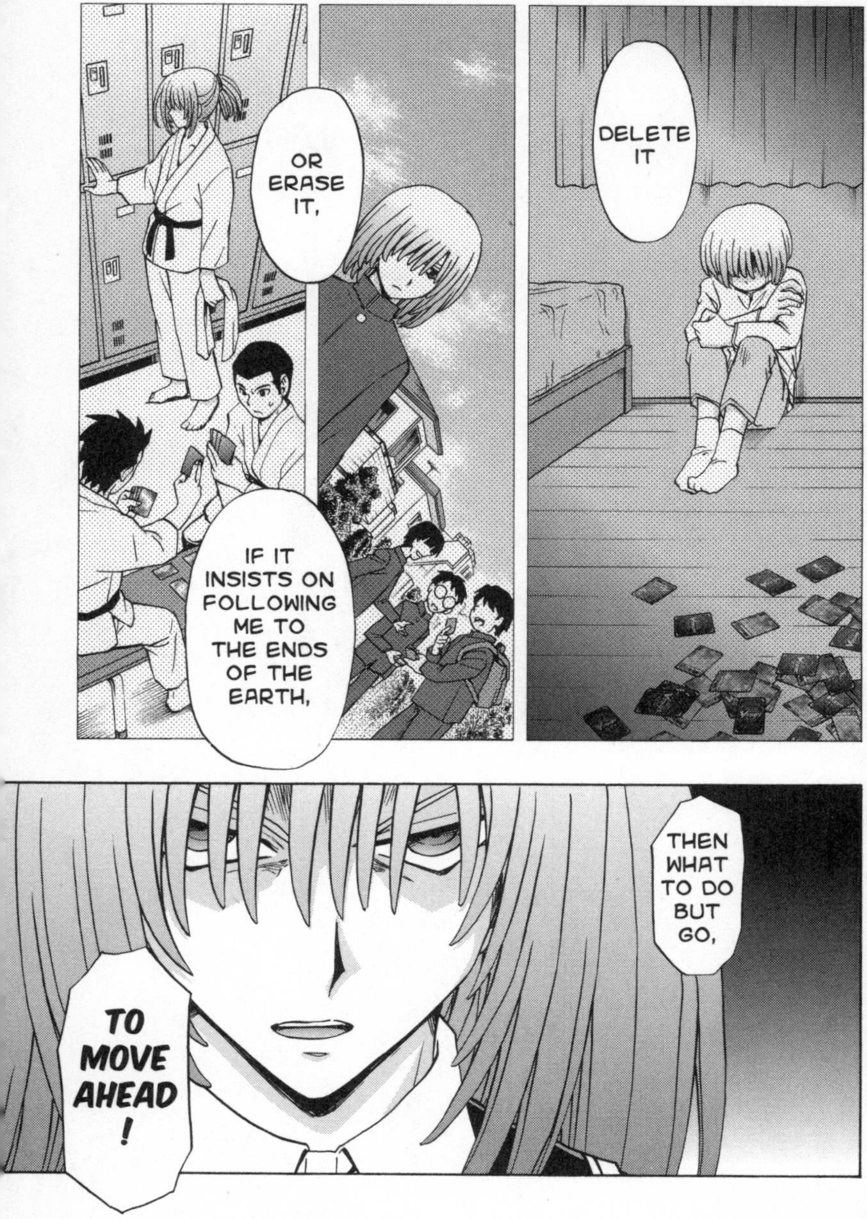
DELETE IT
OR ERASE IT,
IF IT INSISTS ON FOLLOWING ME TO THE ENDS OF THE EARTH,
THEN WHAT TO DO BUT GO,
TO MOVE AHEAD!

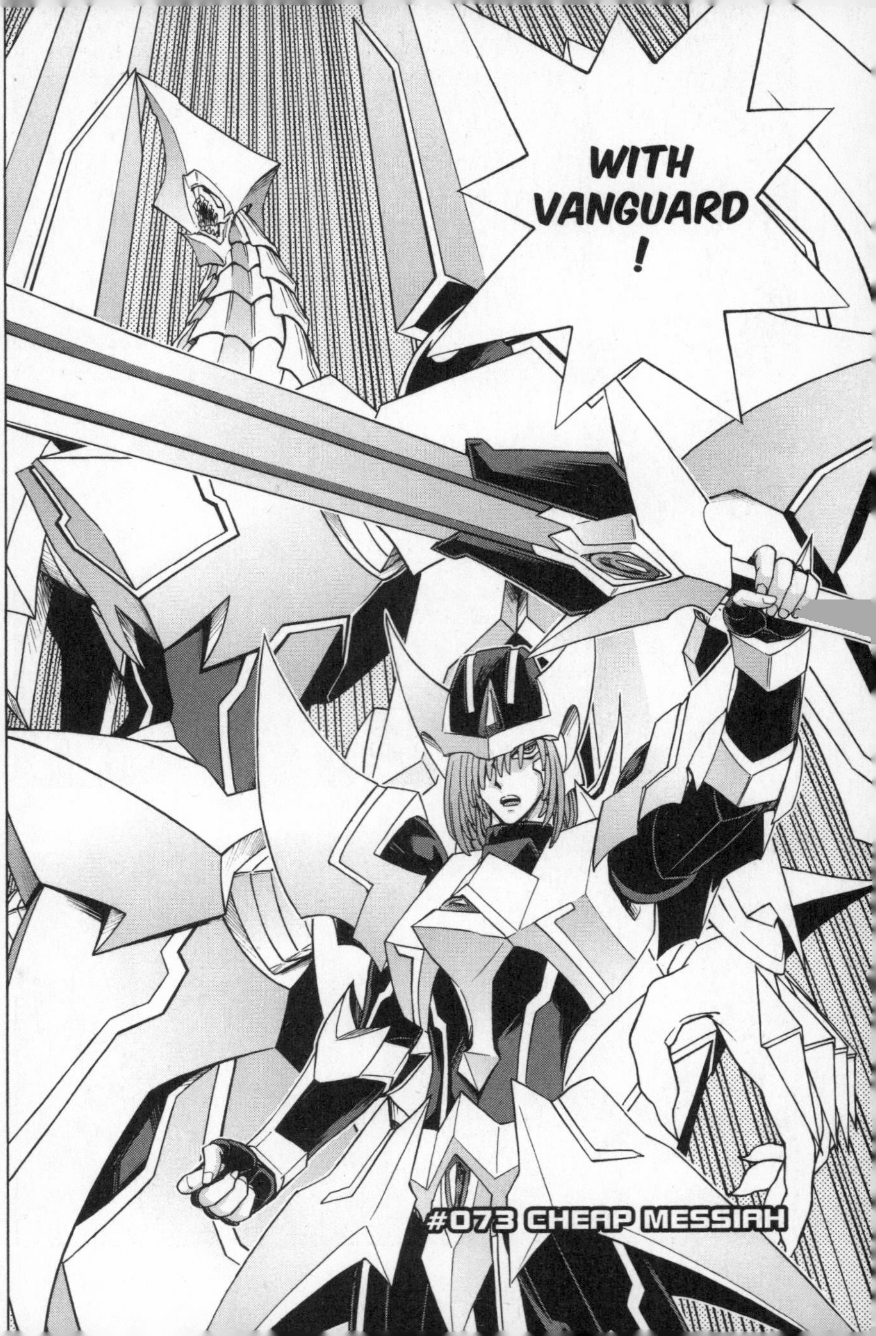
WITH VANGUARD!
#073 CHEAP MESSIAH

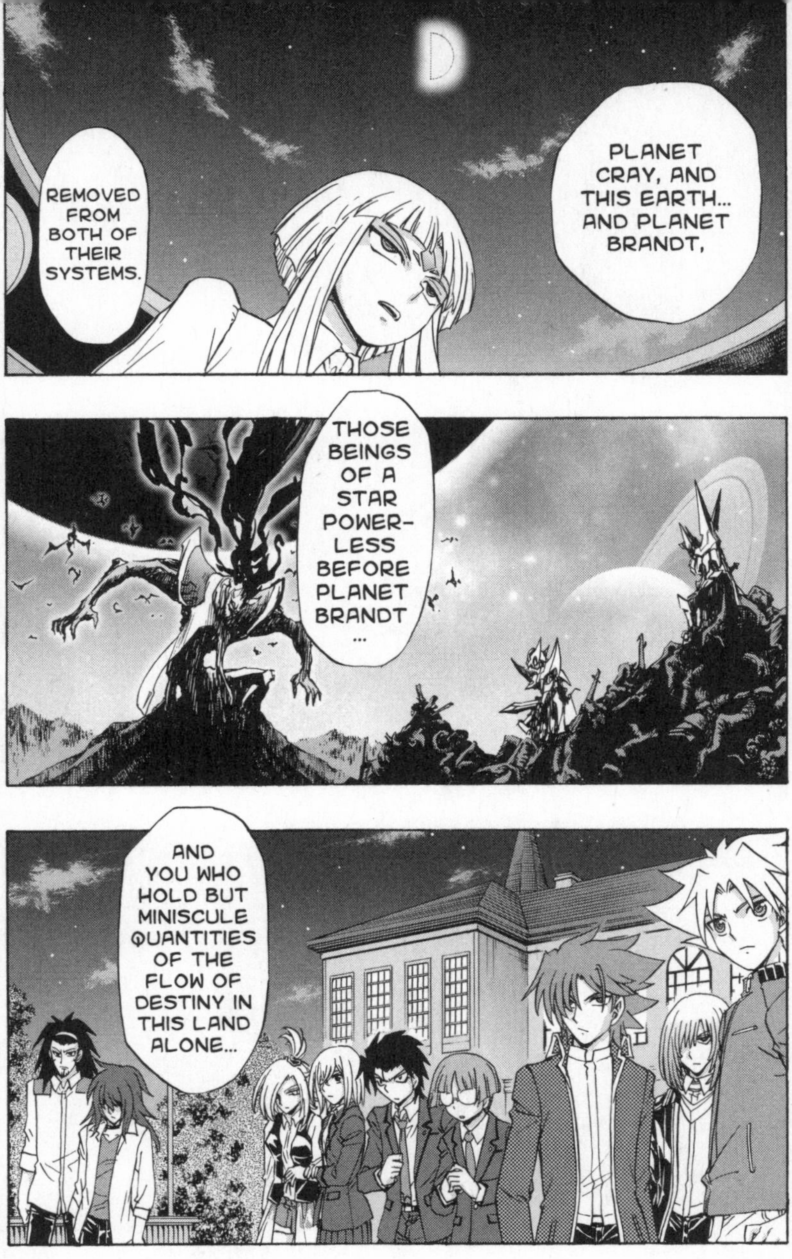
PLANET CRAY, AND THIS EARTH... AND PLANET BRANDT,
REMOVED FROM BOTH OF THEIR SYSTEMS.
THOSE BEINGS OF A STAR POWER-LESS BEFORE PLANET BRANDT...
AND YOU WHO HOLD BUT MINISCULE QUANTITIES OF THE FLOW OF DESTINY IN THIS LAND ALONE...

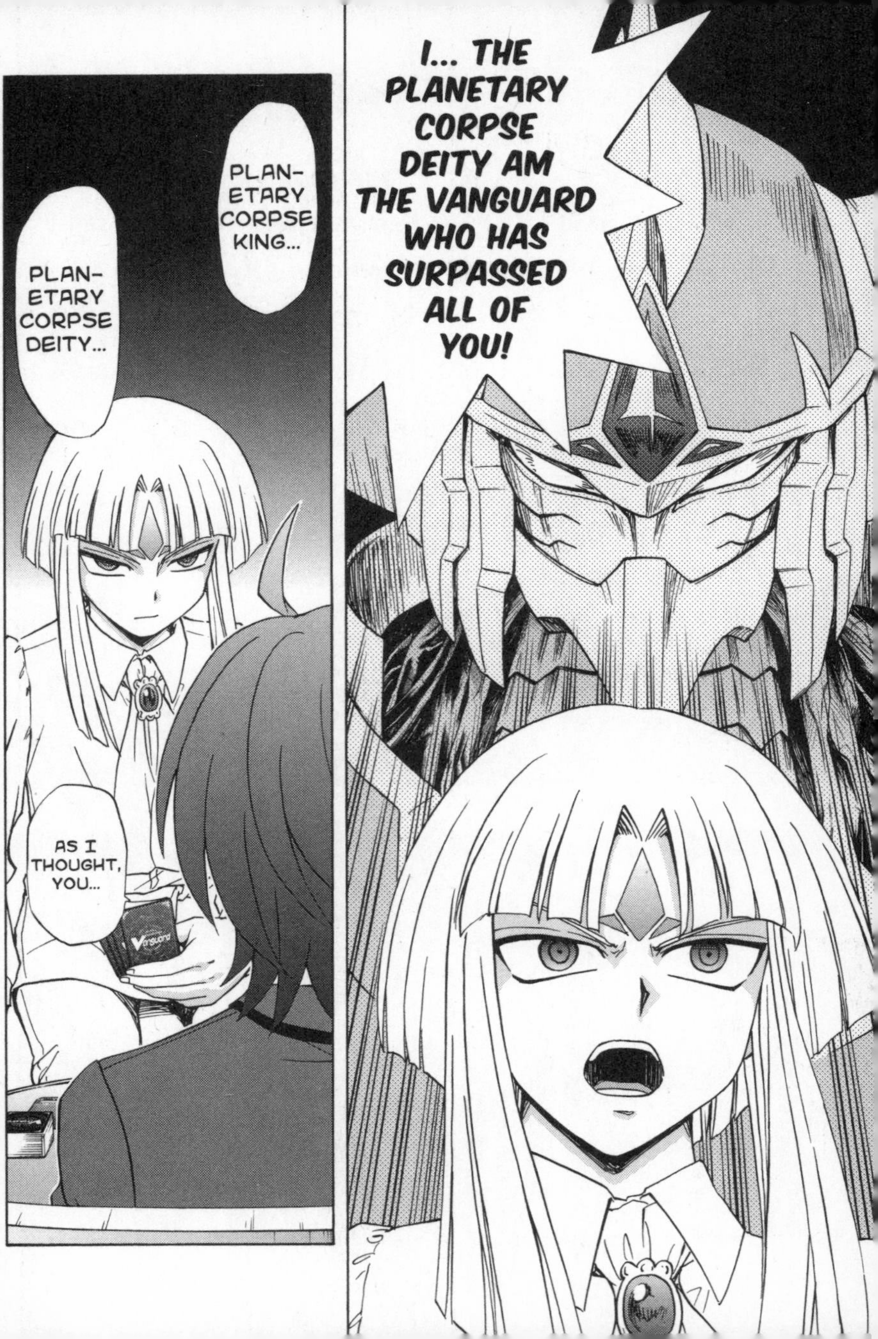
I... THE PLANETARY CORPSE DEITY AM THE VANGUARD WHO HAS SURPASSED ALL OF YOU!
PLAN-ETARY CORPSE KING...
PLAN-ETARY CORPSE DEITY...
AS I THOUGHT, YOU...

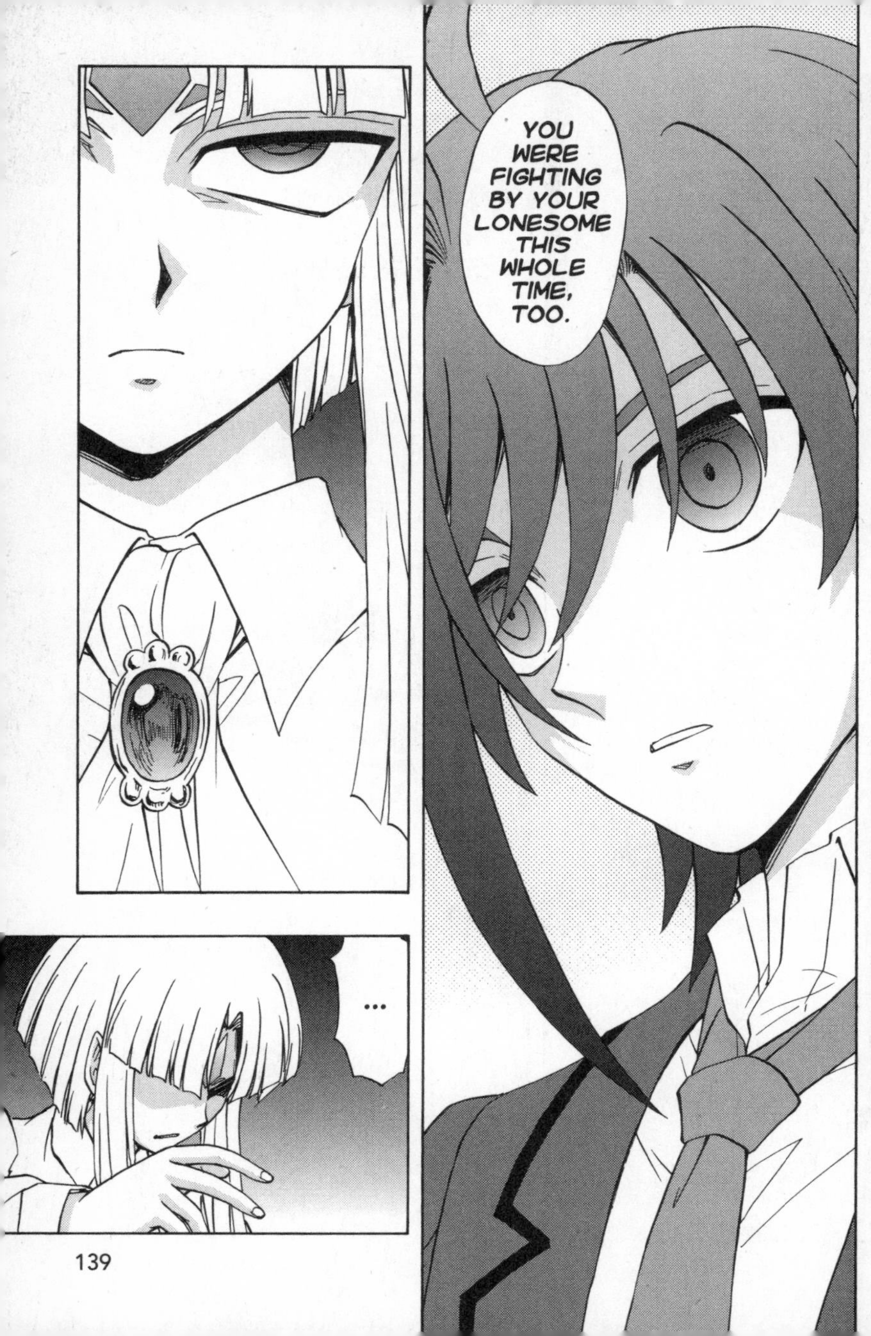
YOU WERE FIGHTING BY YOUR LONESOME THIS WHOLE TIME, TOO.
...

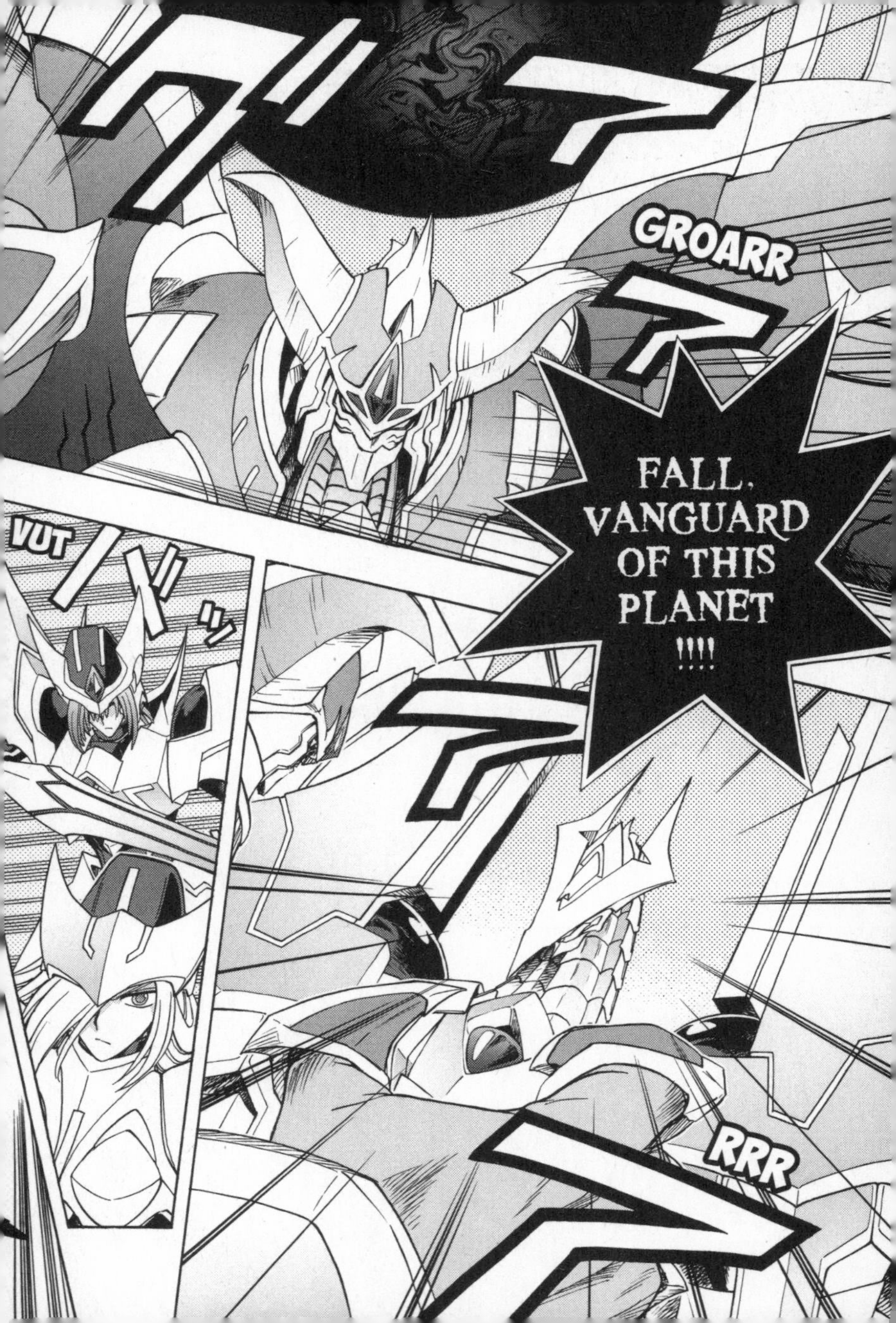
GROARR
FALL, VANGUARD OF THIS PLANET !!!!
RRR
VUT

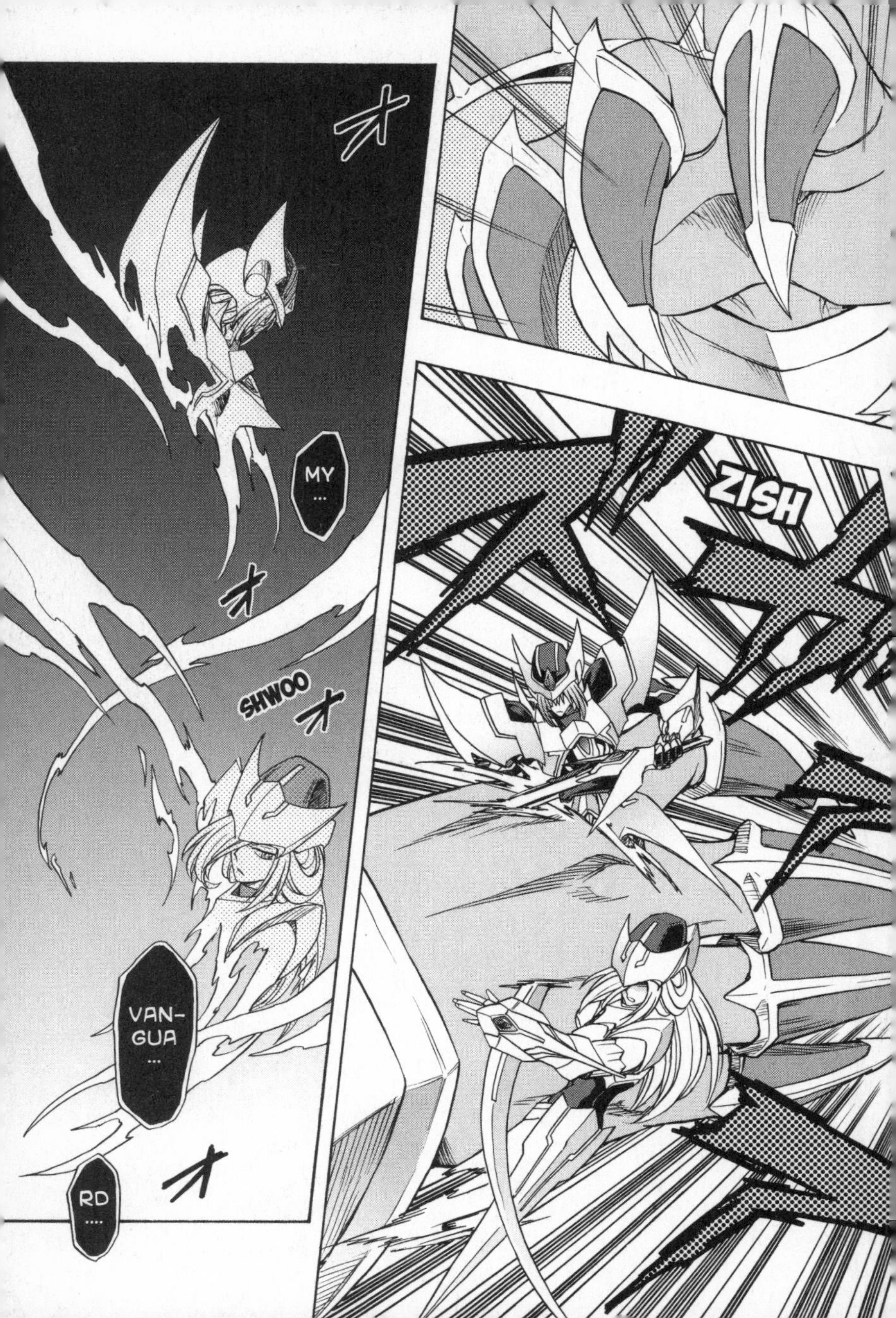
ZISH
MY ...
SHWOO
VAN-GUA ...
RD ....

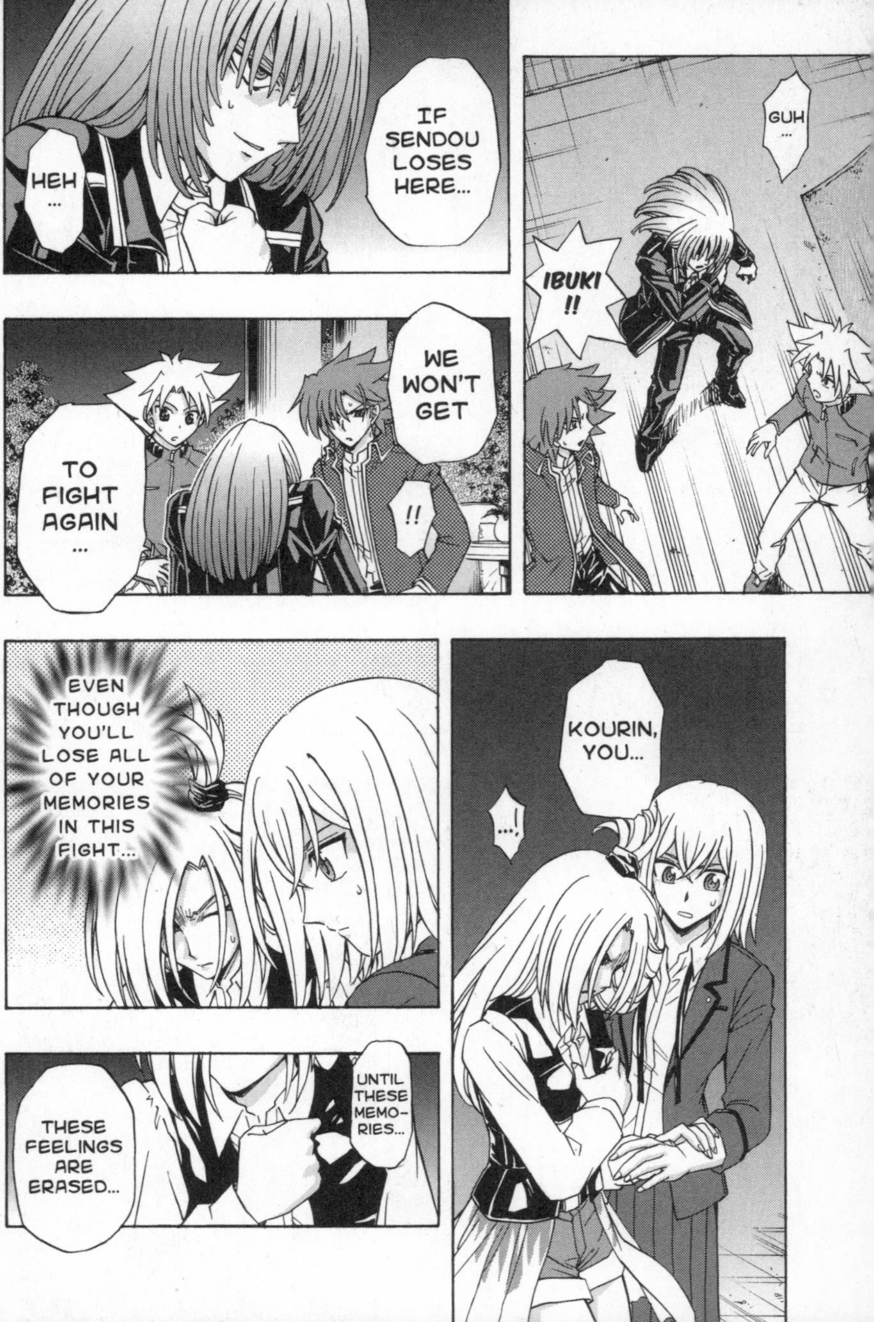
GUH...
IBUKI!!
IF SENDOU LOSES HERE...
HEH...
WE WON'T GET
TO FIGHT AGAIN...
!!
KOURIN, YOU...
...!
EVEN THOUGH YOU'LL LOSE ALL OF YOUR MEMORIES IN THIS FIGHT...
UNTIL THESE MEMORIES...
THESE FEELINGS ARE ERASED...

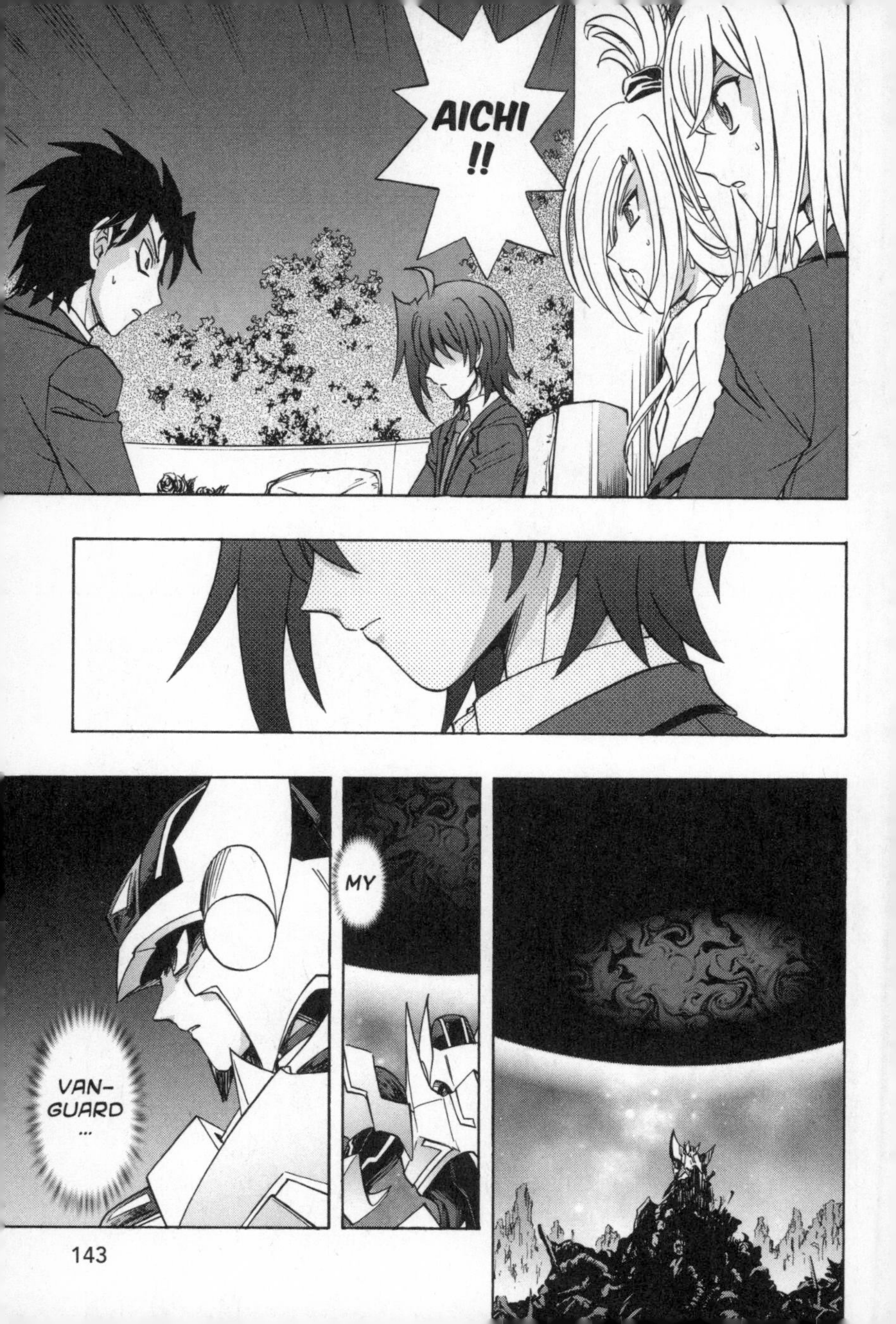
AICHI !!
MY
VAN-GUARD ...

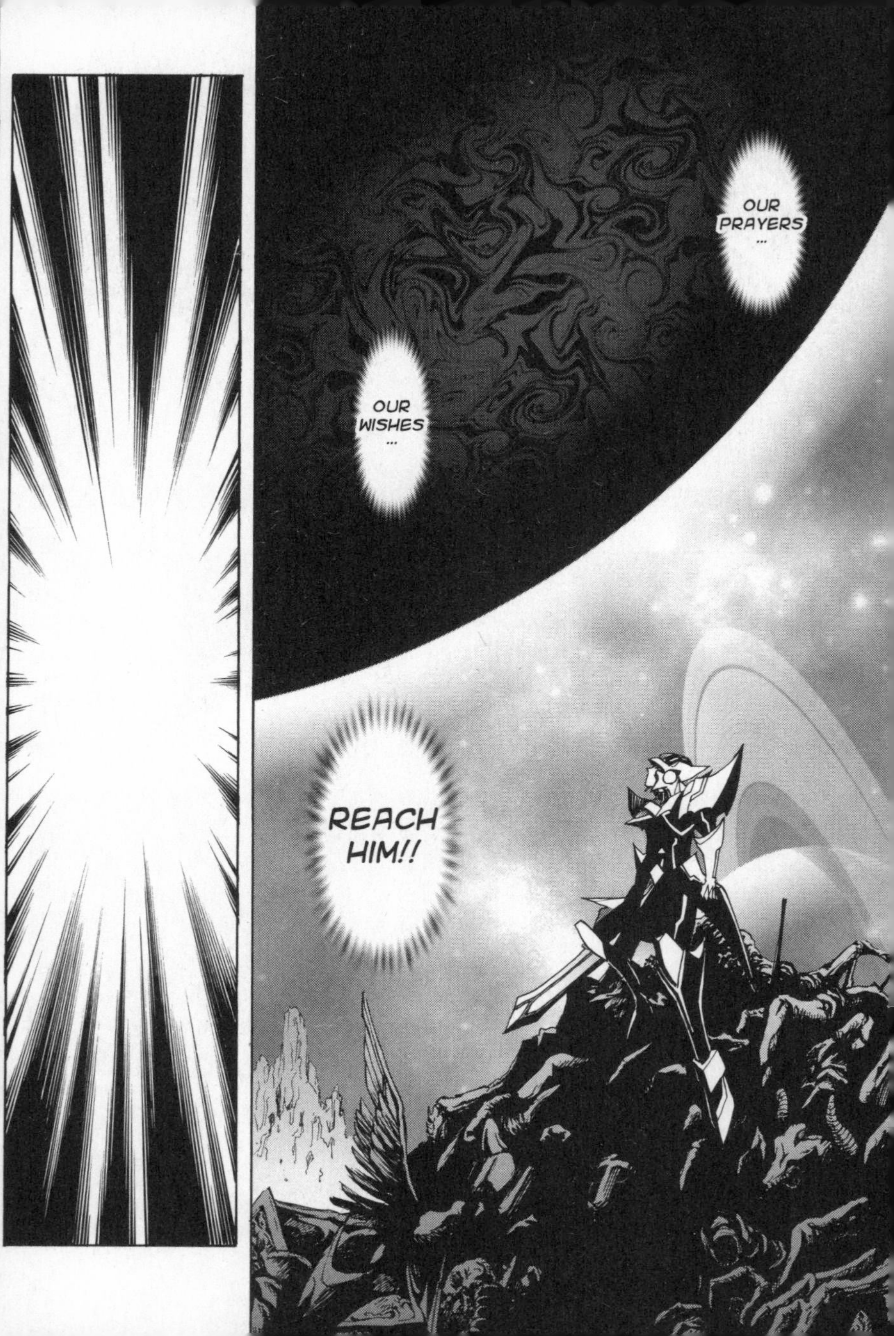
OUR PRAYERS ...
OUR WISHES ...
REACH HIM!!

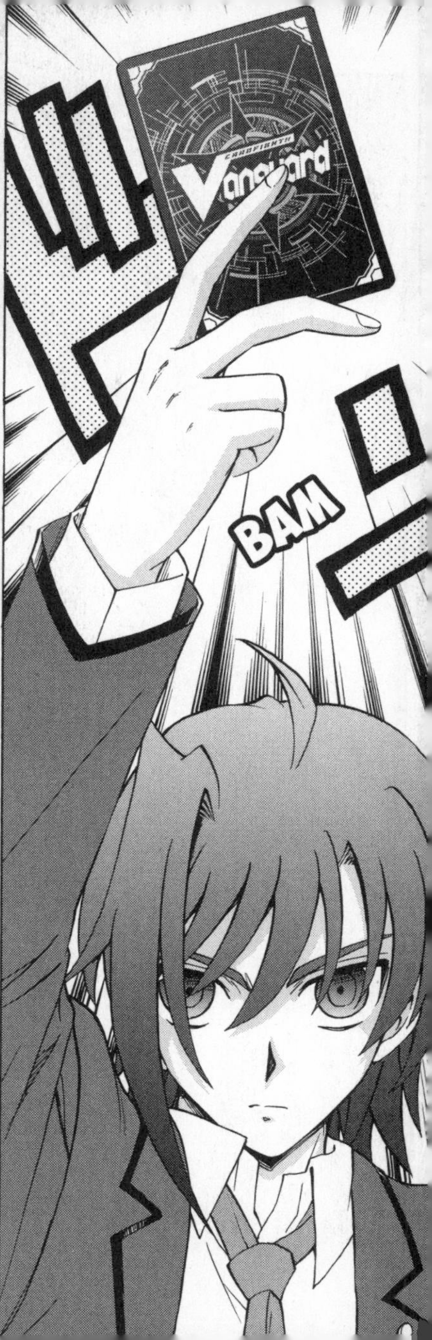
Vanguard
BAM

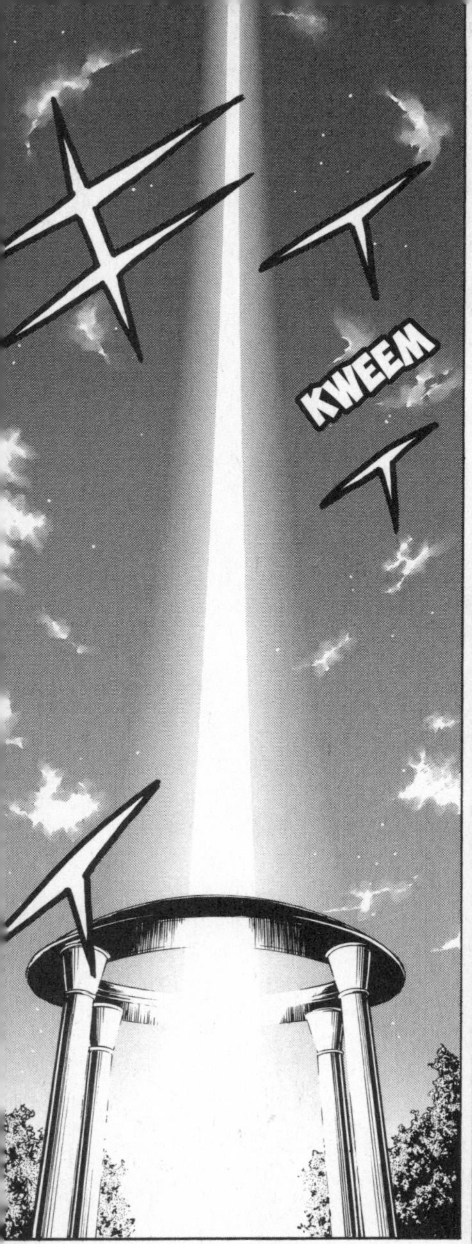
KWEEM

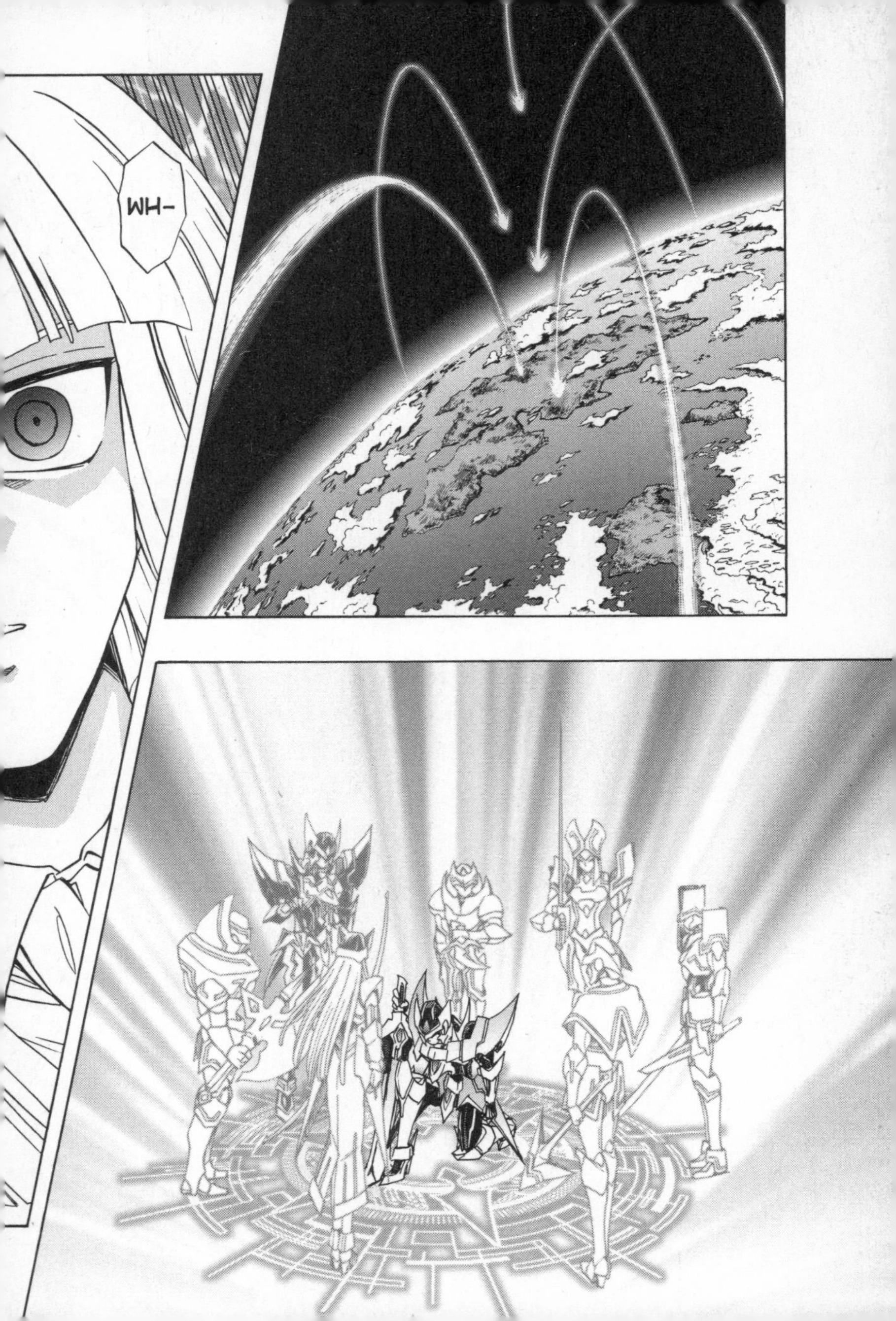
WH-

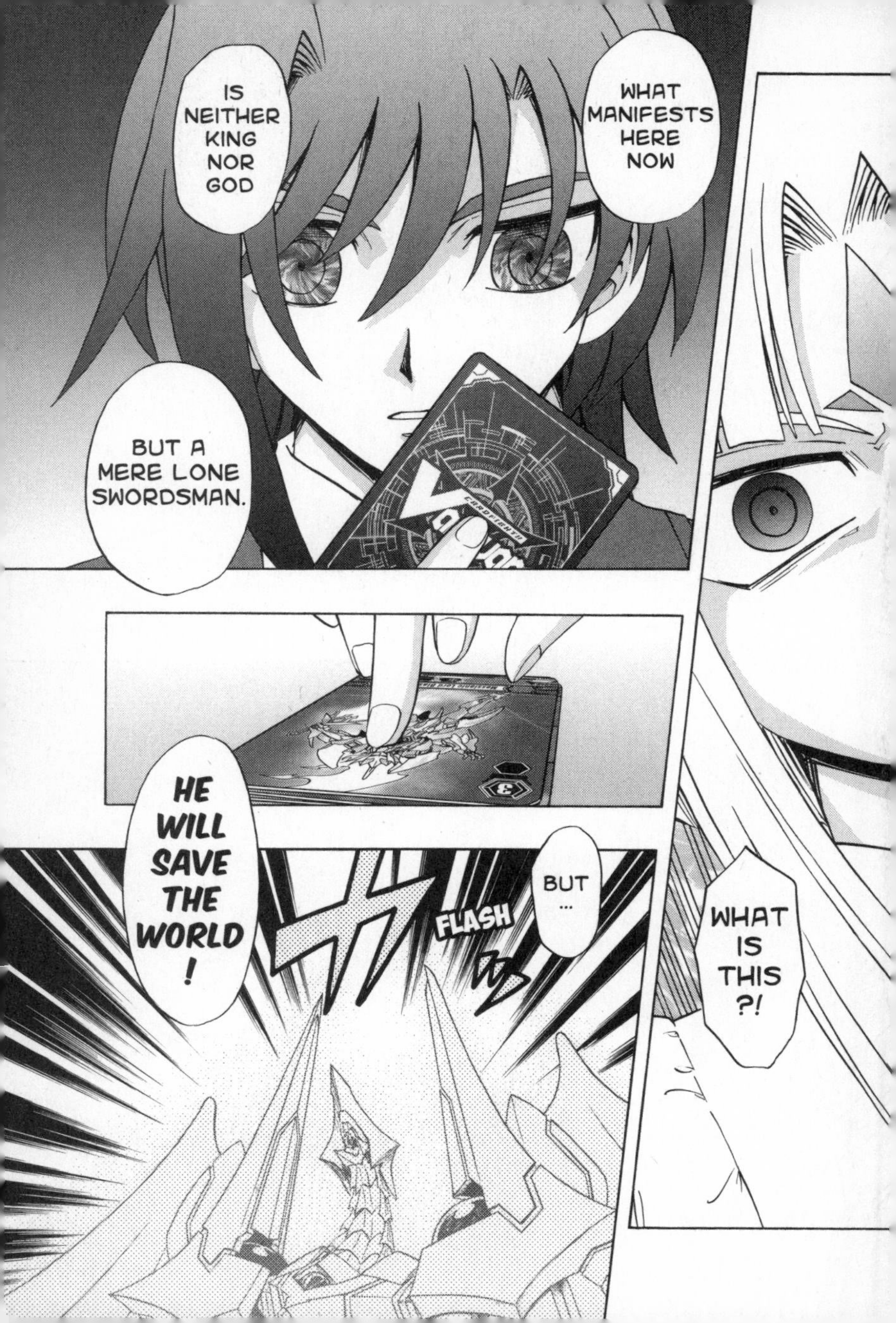
WHAT IS THIS ?!
WHAT MANIFESTS HERE NOW
IS NEITHER KING NOR GOD
BUT A MERE LONE SWORDSMAN.
BUT ...
FLASH
HE WILL SAVE THE WORLD !

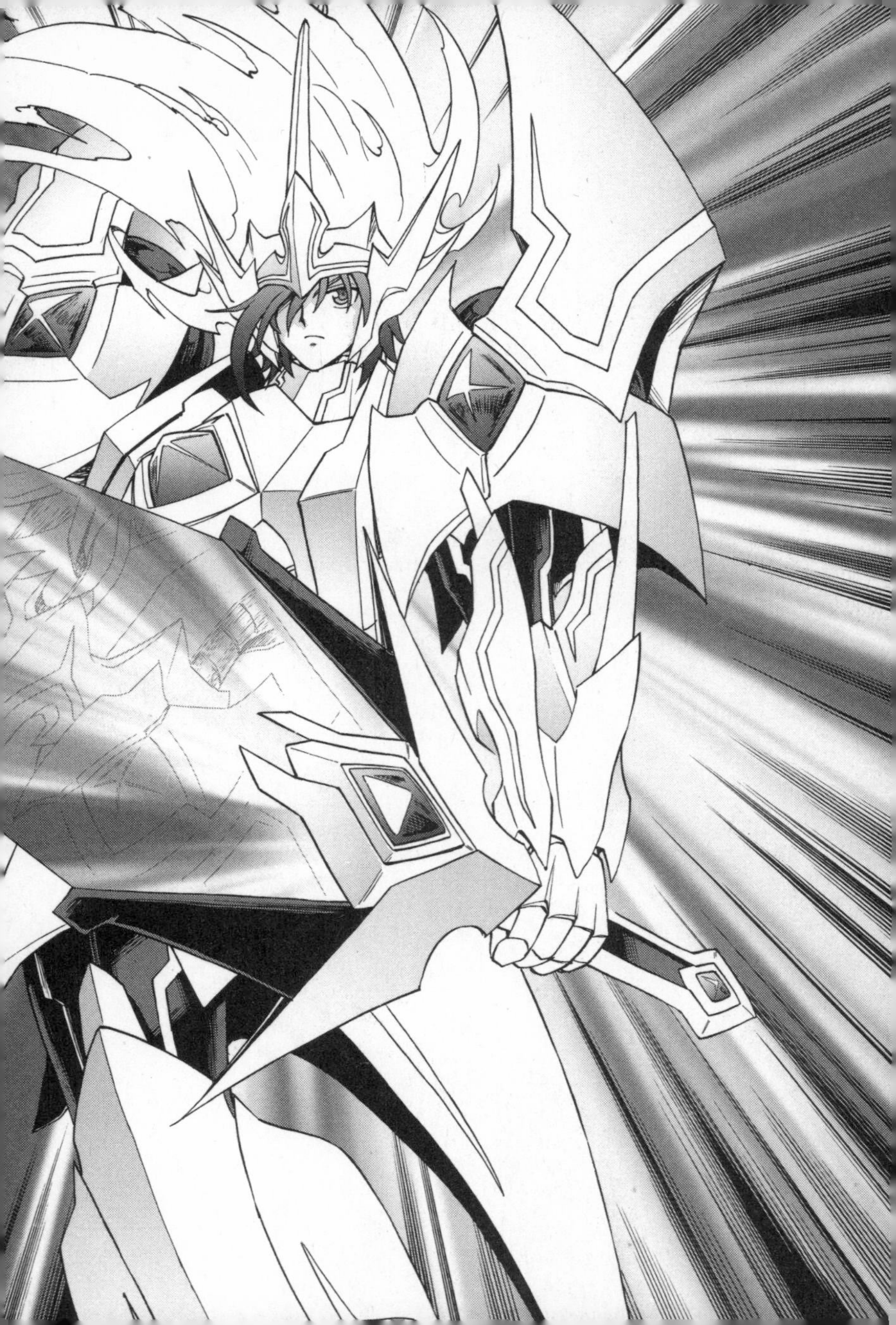

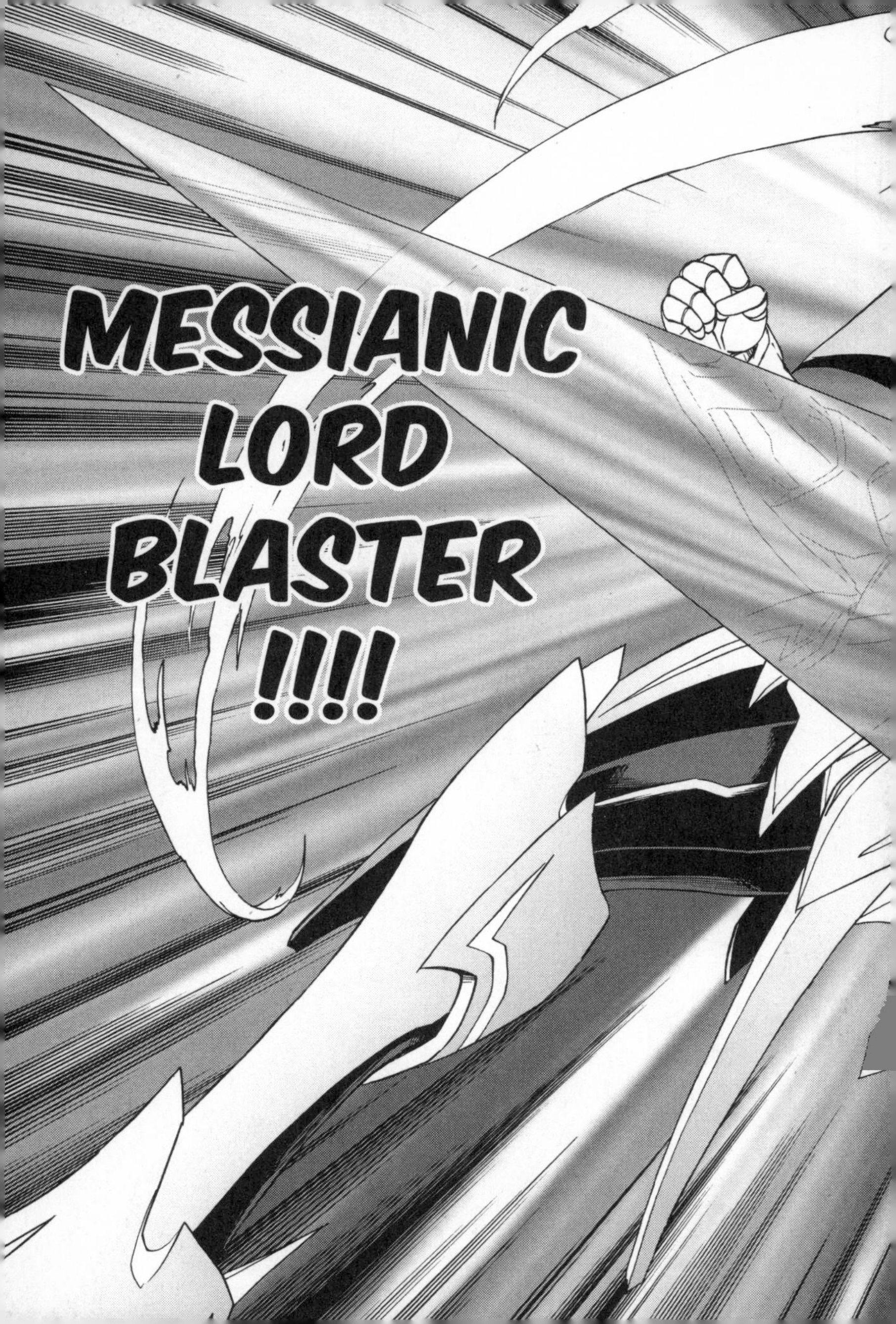
MESSIANIC LORD BLASTER !!!!

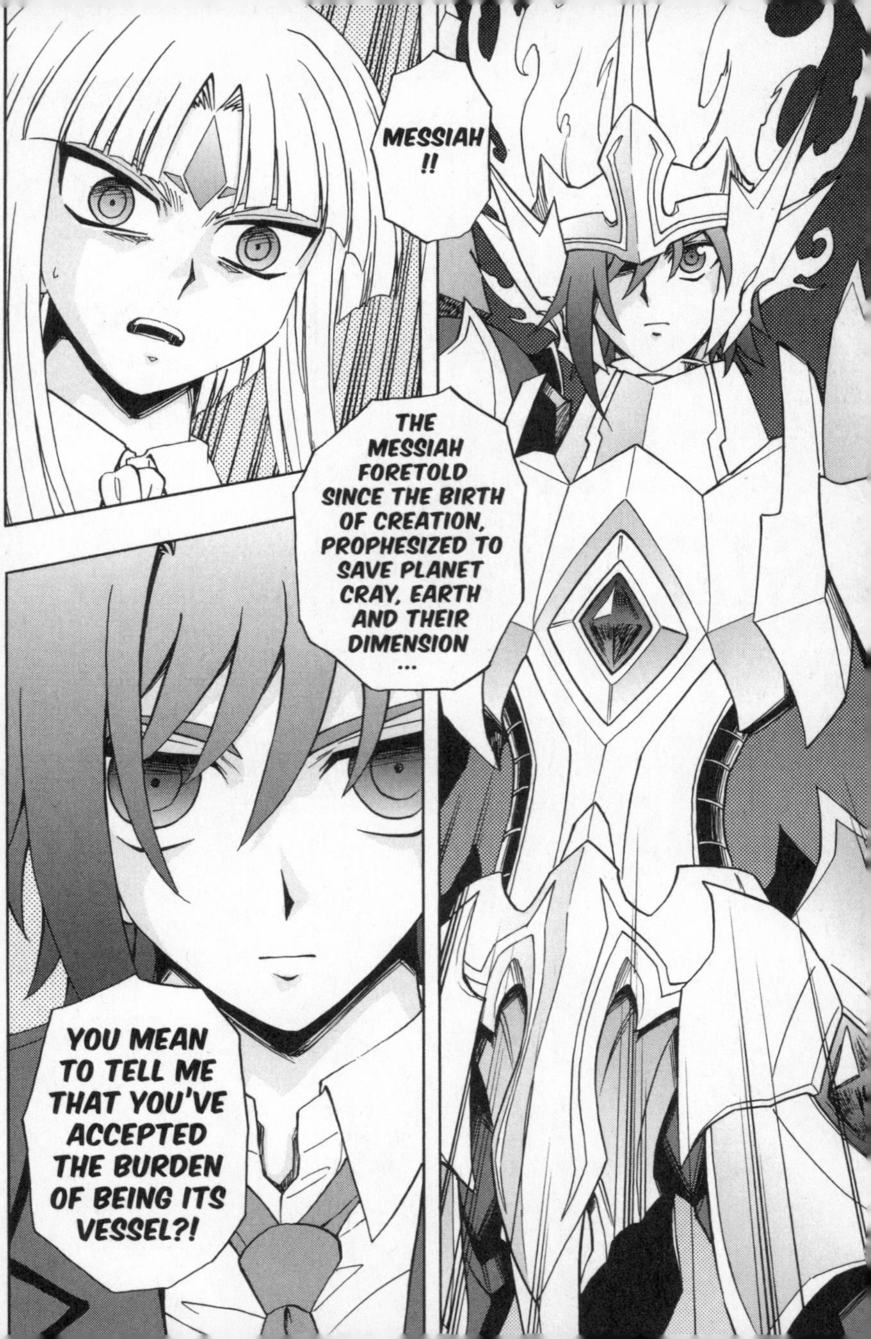
MESSIAH !!
THE MESSIAH FORETOLD SINCE THE BIRTH OF CREATION, PROPHESIZED TO SAVE PLANET CRAY, EARTH AND THEIR DIMENSION ...
YOU MEAN TO TELL ME THAT YOU'VE ACCEPTED THE BURDEN OF BEING ITS VESSEL?!

TRIGGER CHECK.

MESSIANIC LORD BLASTER ATTACKS.

BAM

Rapier

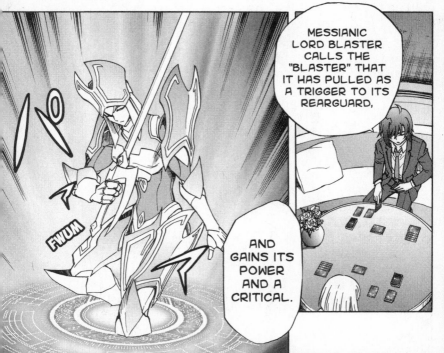

MESSIANIC LORD BLASTER CALLS THE "BLASTER" THAT IT HAS PULLED AS A TRIGGER TO ITS REARGUARD,

AND GAINS ITS POWER AND A CRITICAL.

FWUM

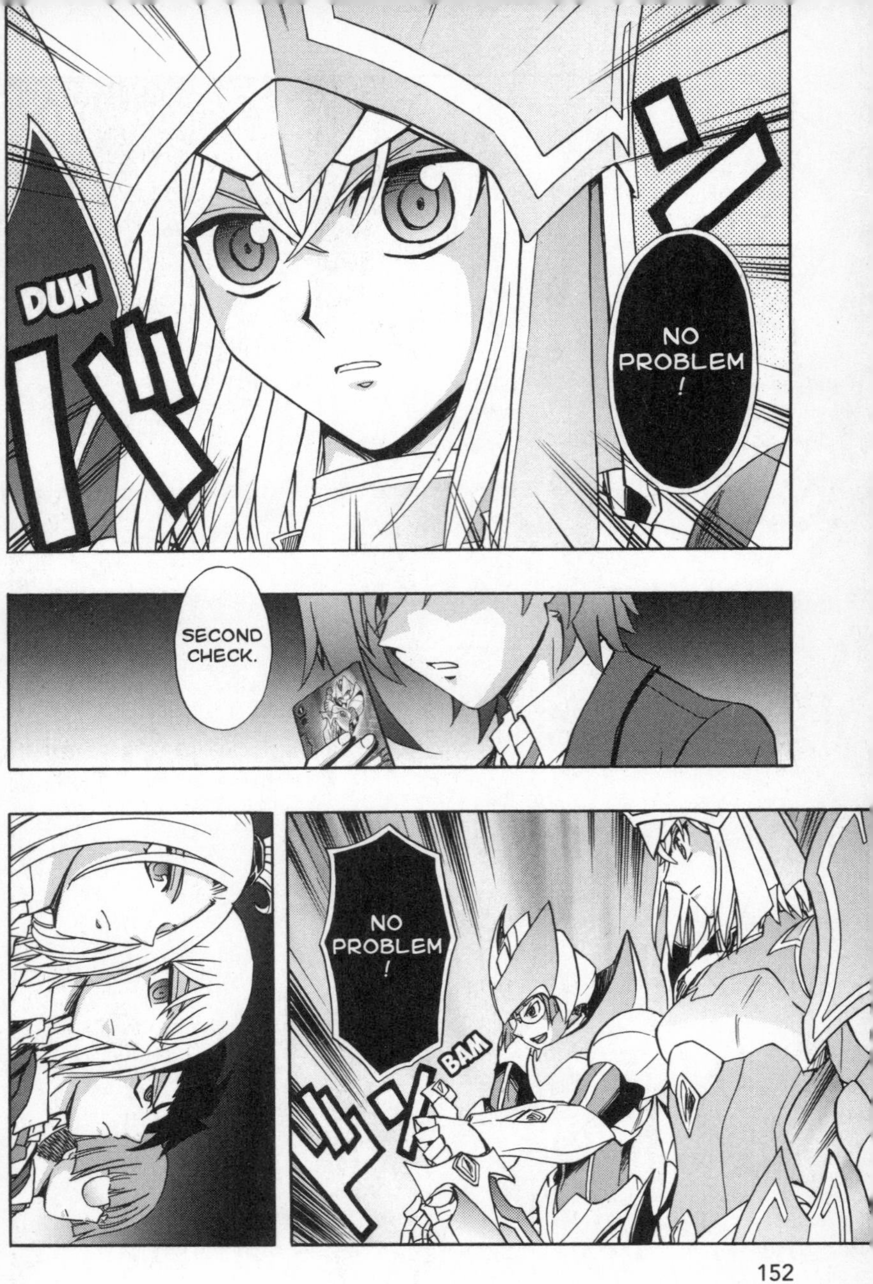
NO PROBLEM!
DUN
SECOND CHECK.
NO PROBLEM!
BAM

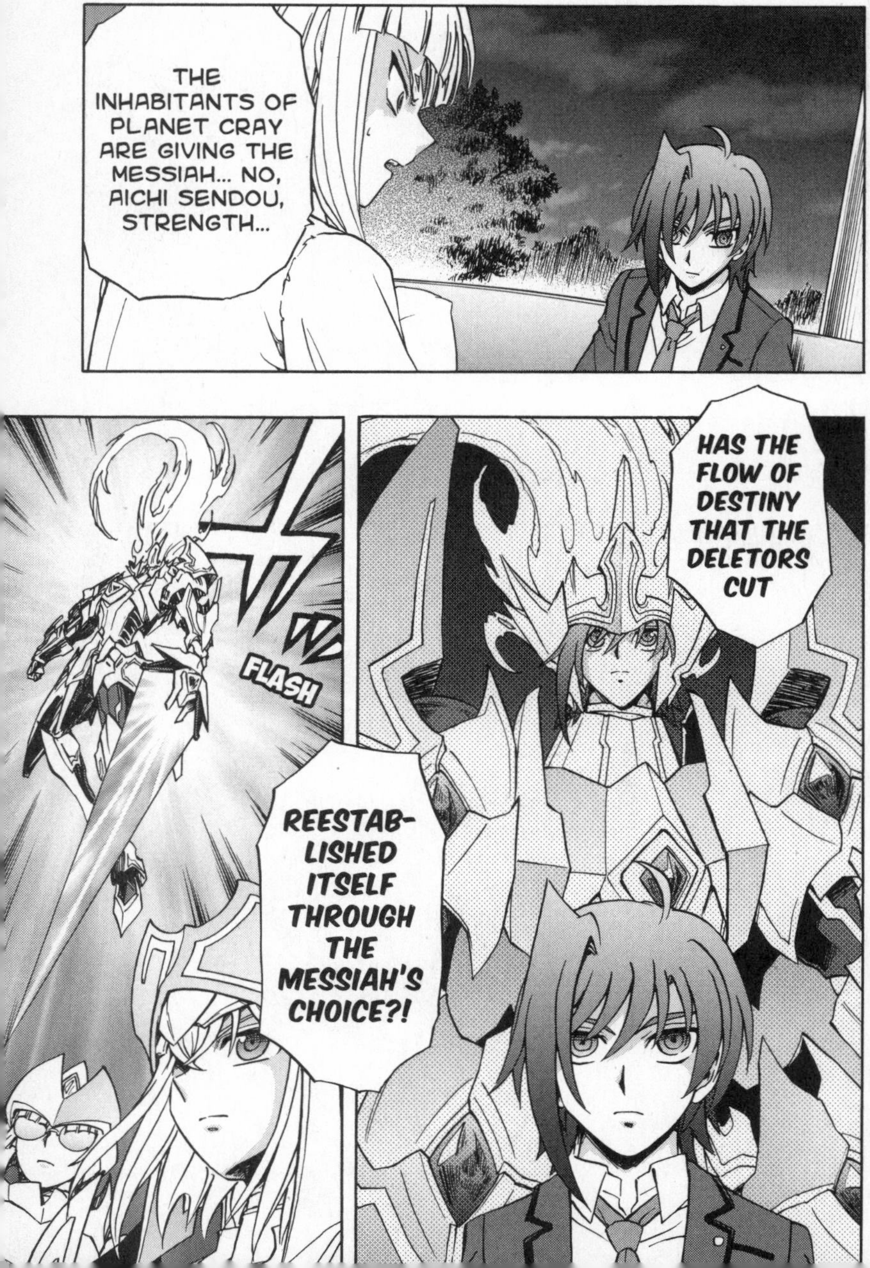
THE INHABITANTS OF PLANET CRAY ARE GIVING THE MESSIAH... NO, AICHI SENDOU, STRENGTH...
HAS THE FLOW OF DESTINY THAT THE DELETORS CUT
REESTAB-LISHED ITSELF THROUGH THE MESSIAH'S CHOICE?!
FLASH

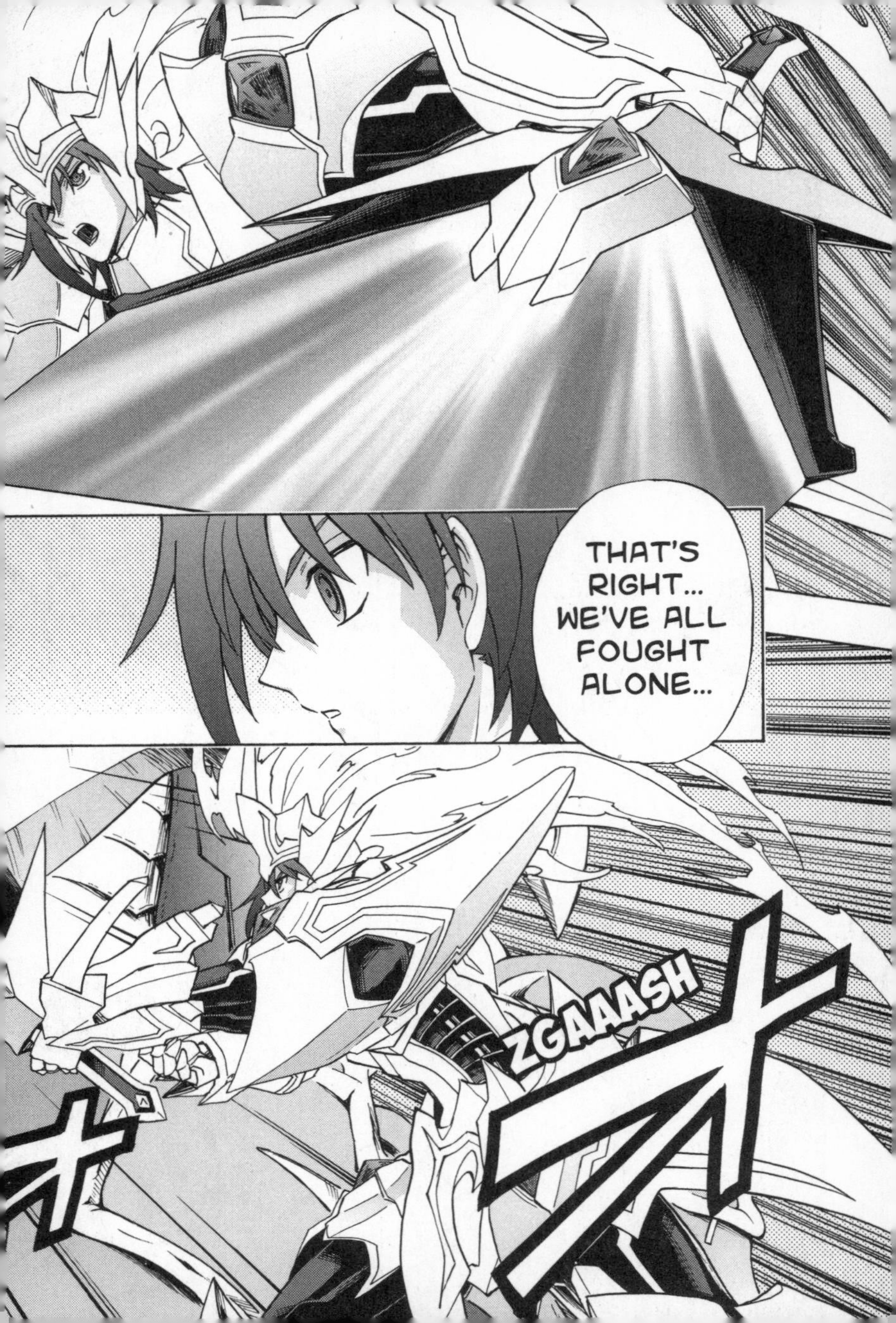
THAT'S RIGHT... WE'VE ALL FOUGHT ALONE...
ZGAAASH

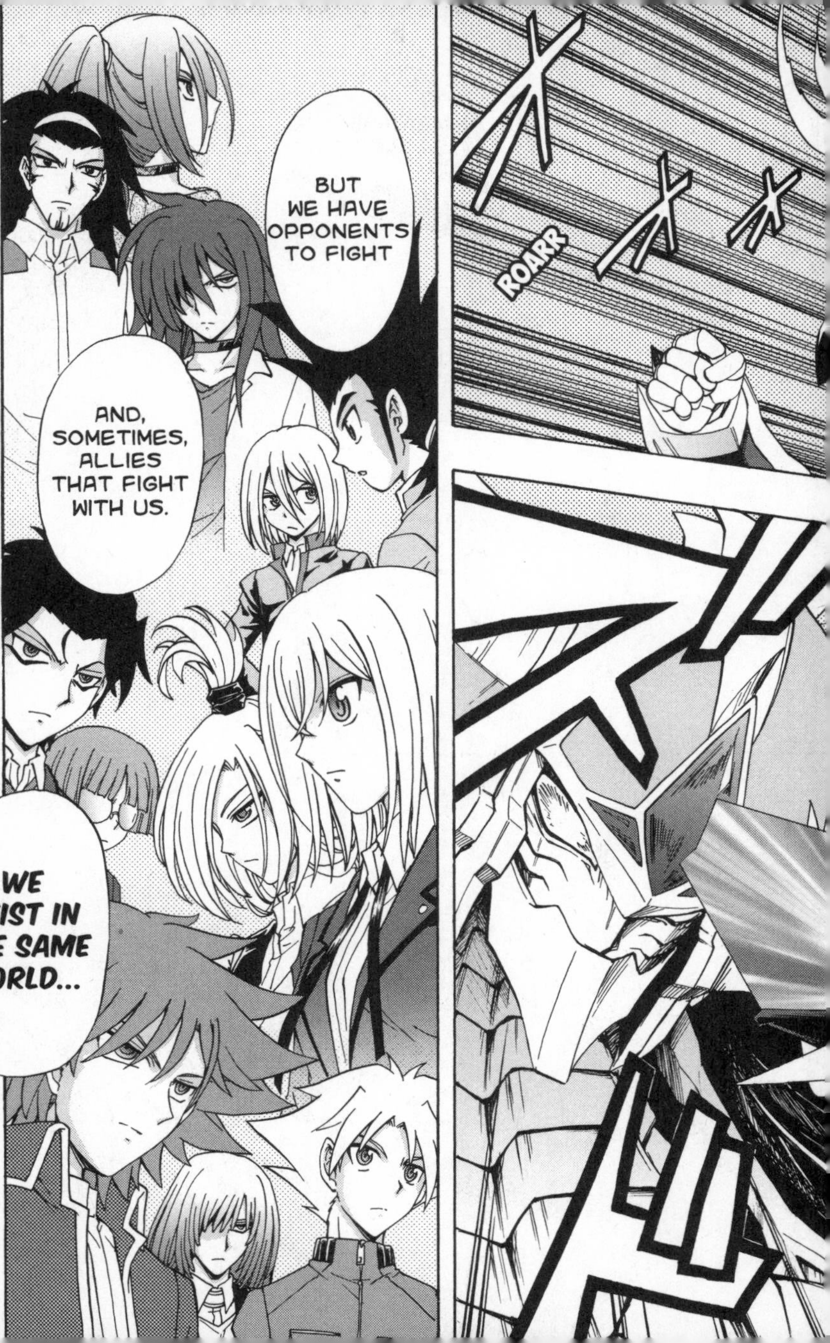
ROARR
BUT WE HAVE OPPONENTS TO FIGHT
AND, SOMETIMES, ALLIES THAT FIGHT WITH US.
WE EXIST IN THE SAME WORLD...

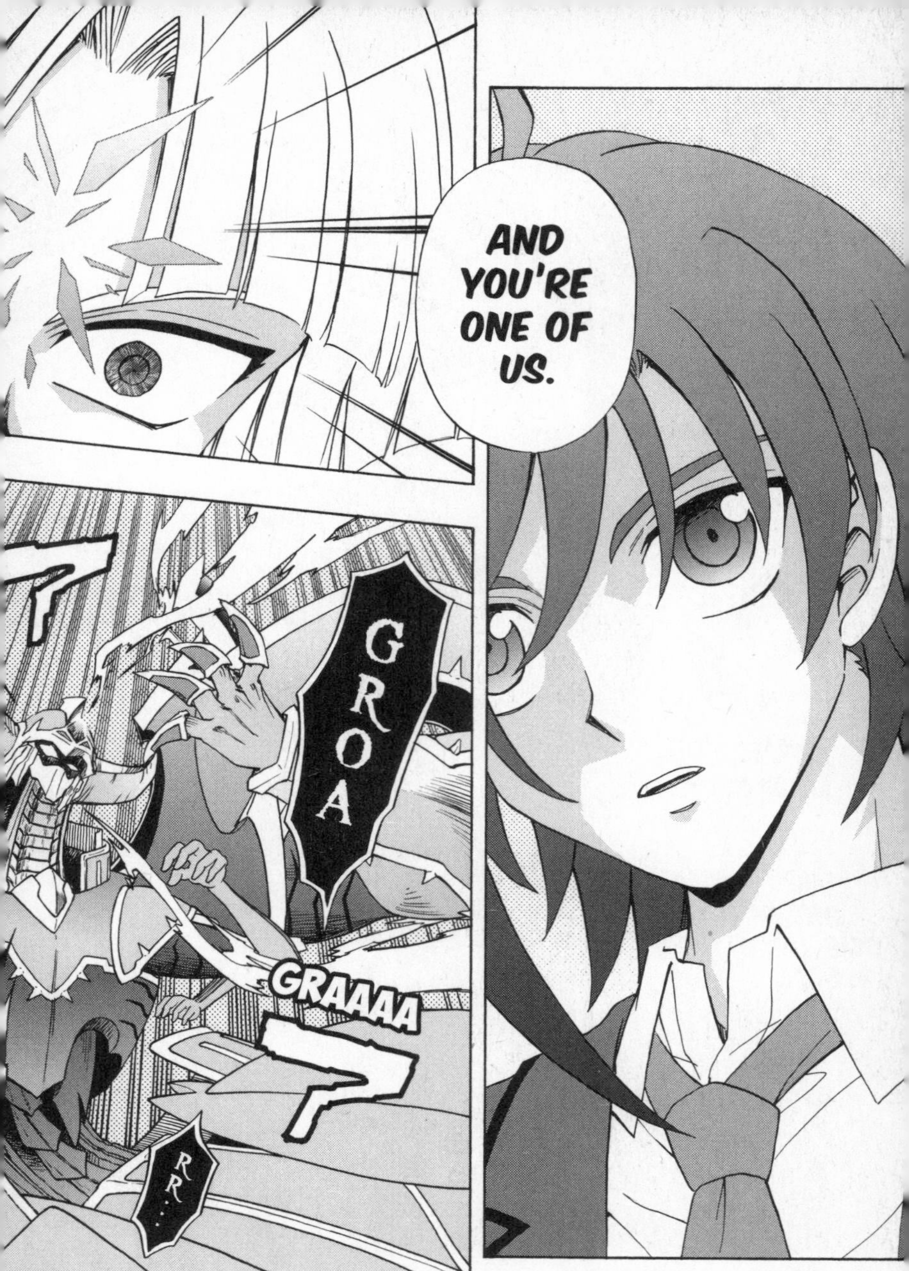
AND YOU'RE ONE OF US.
GROA
GRAAAA
RR...

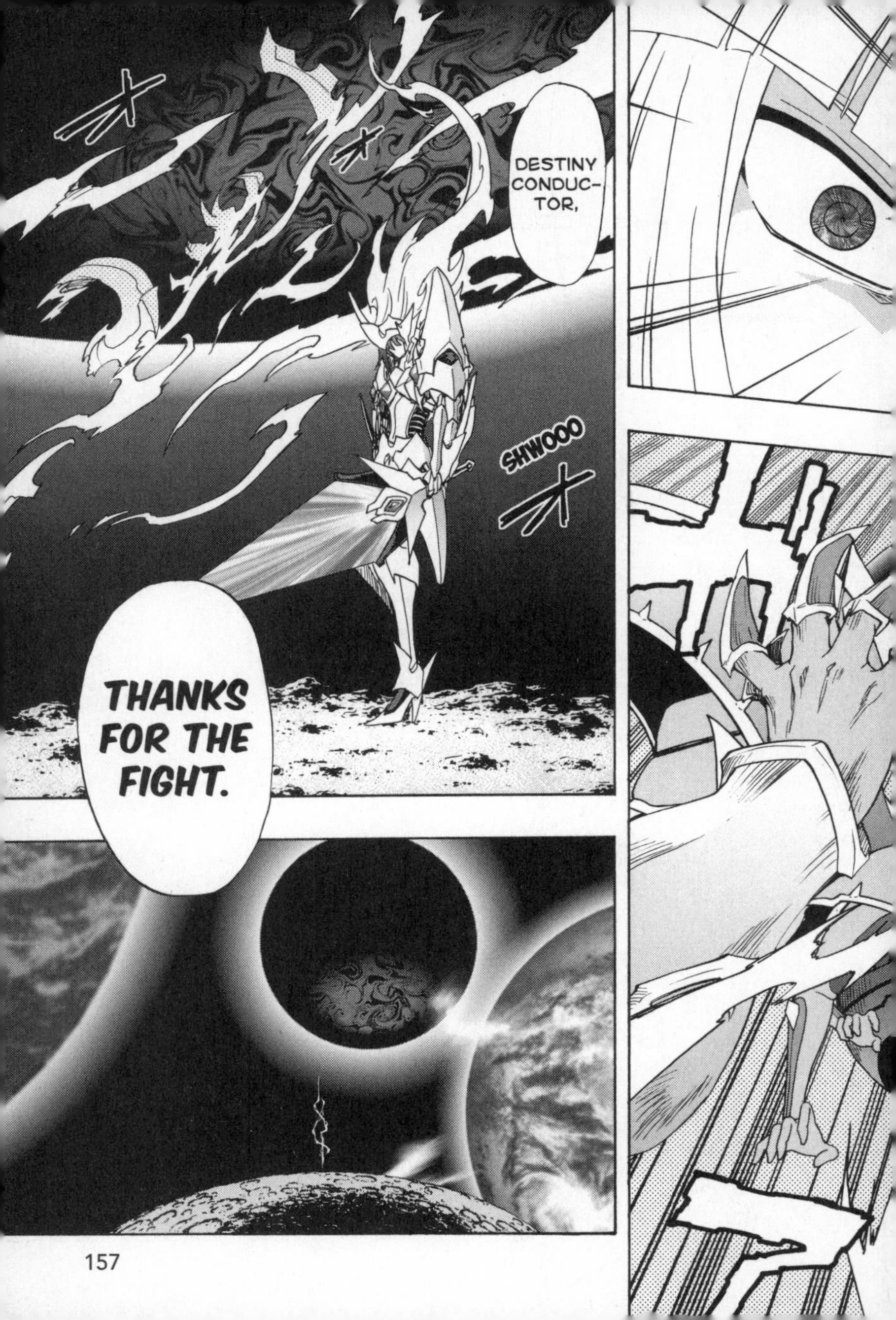
DESTINY CONDUCTOR,
SHWOOO
THANKS FOR THE FIGHT.

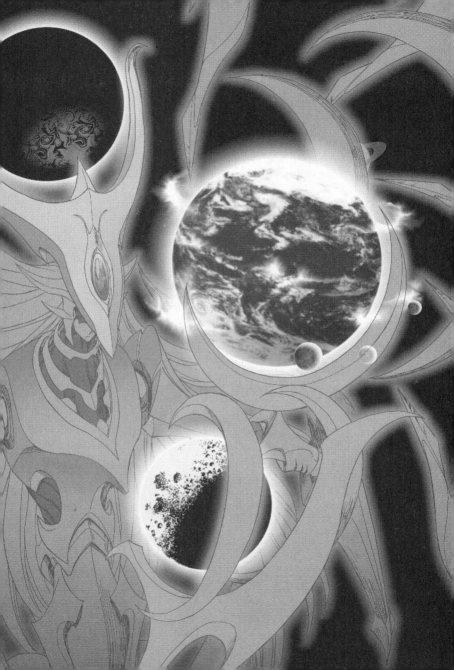

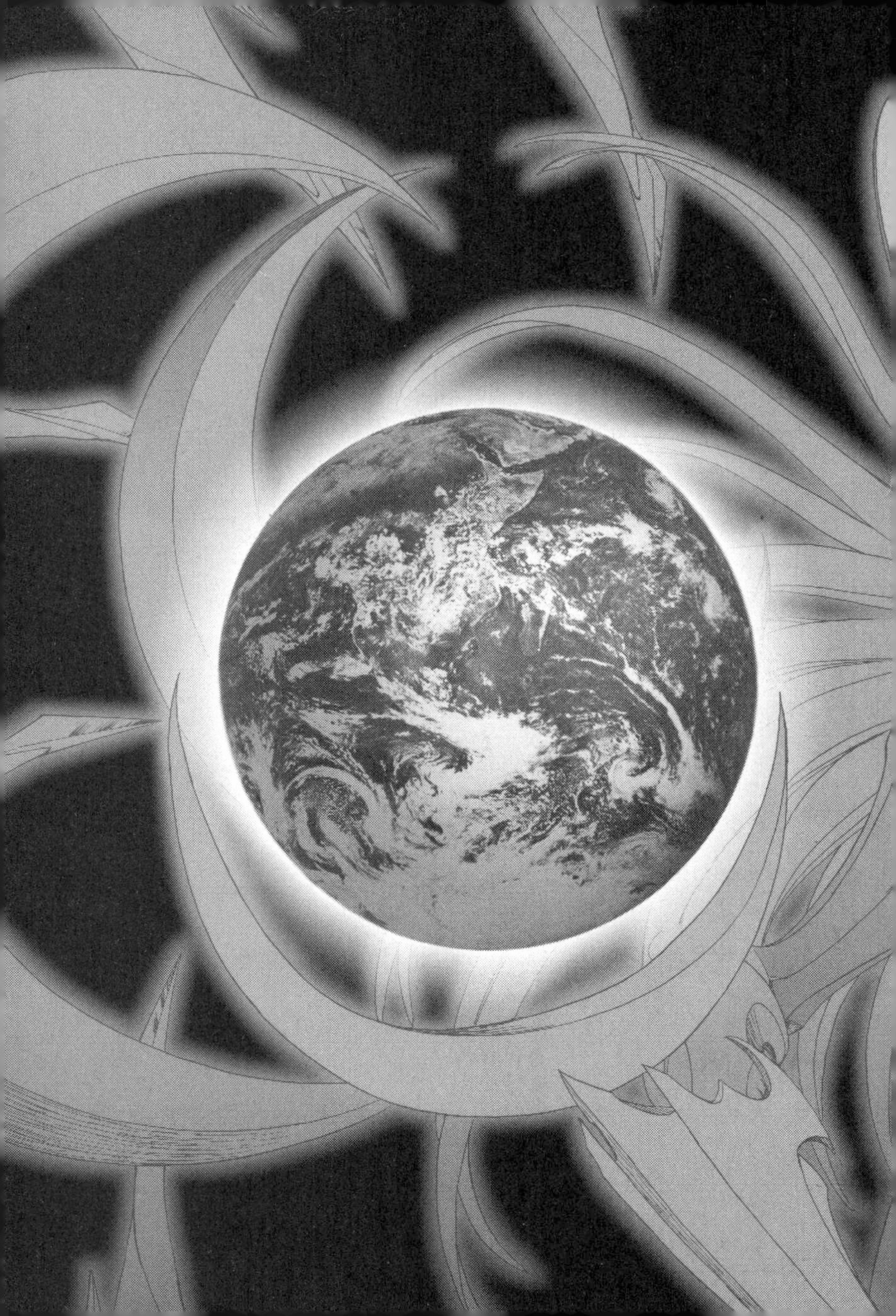

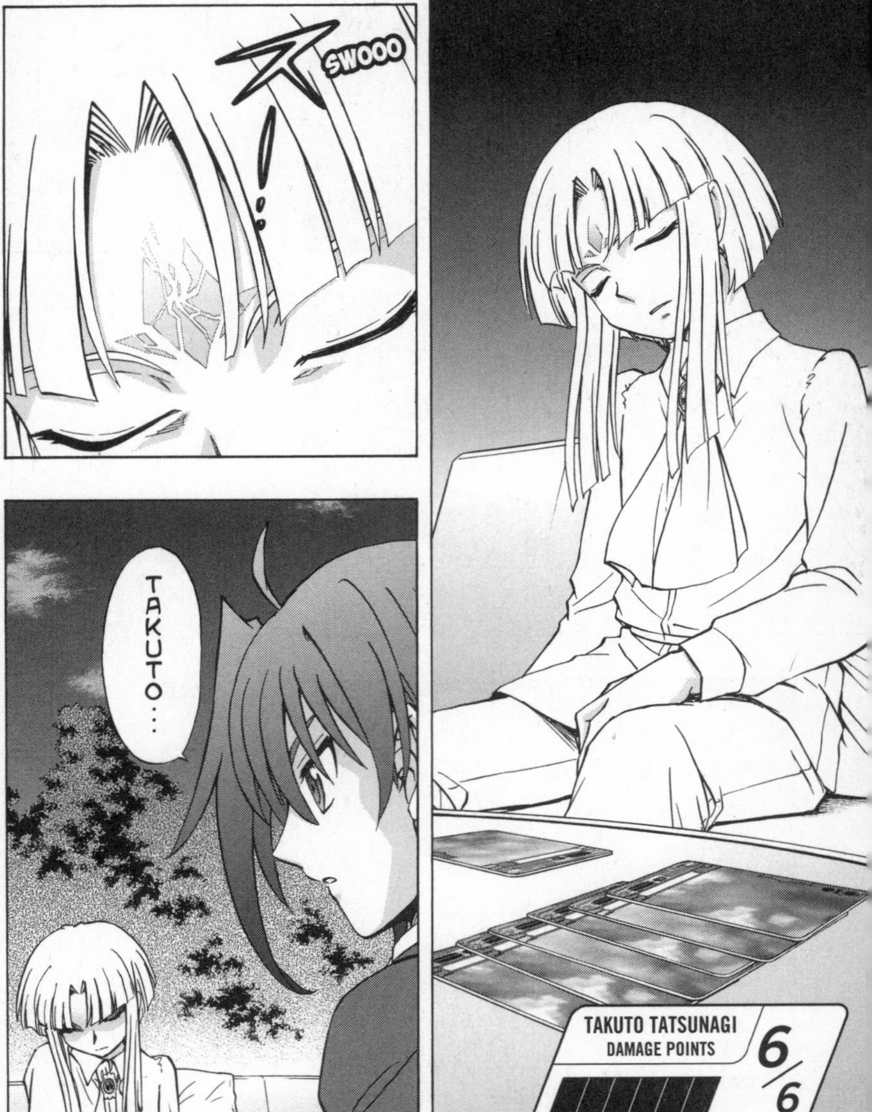
TAKUTO TATSUNAGI
DAMAGE POINTS
6/6
SWOOO
TAKUTO...

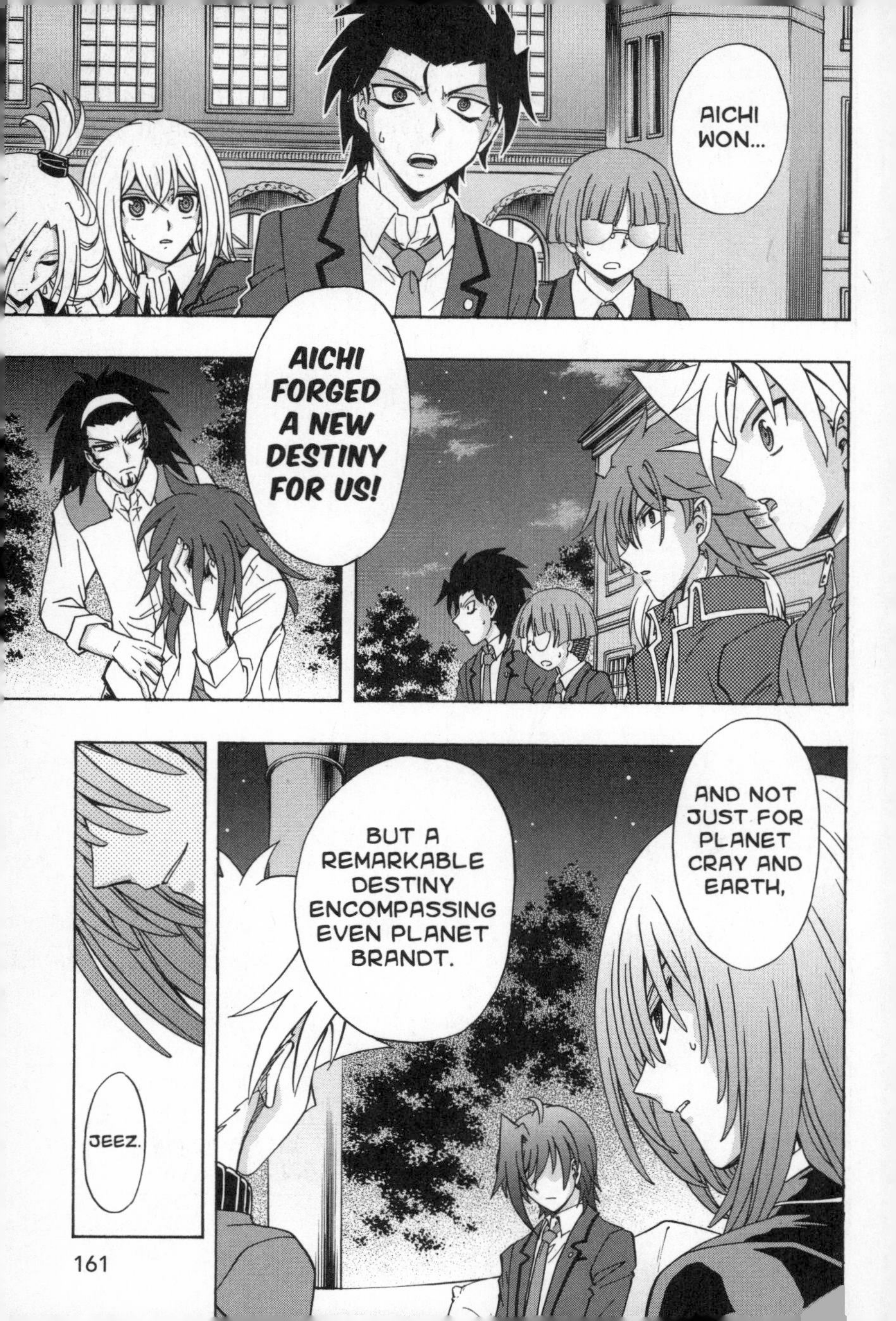
AICHI WON...
AICHI FORGED A NEW DESTINY FOR US!
AND NOT JUST FOR PLANET CRAY AND EARTH,
BUT A REMARKABLE DESTINY ENCOMPASSING EVEN PLANET BRANDT.
JEEZ.

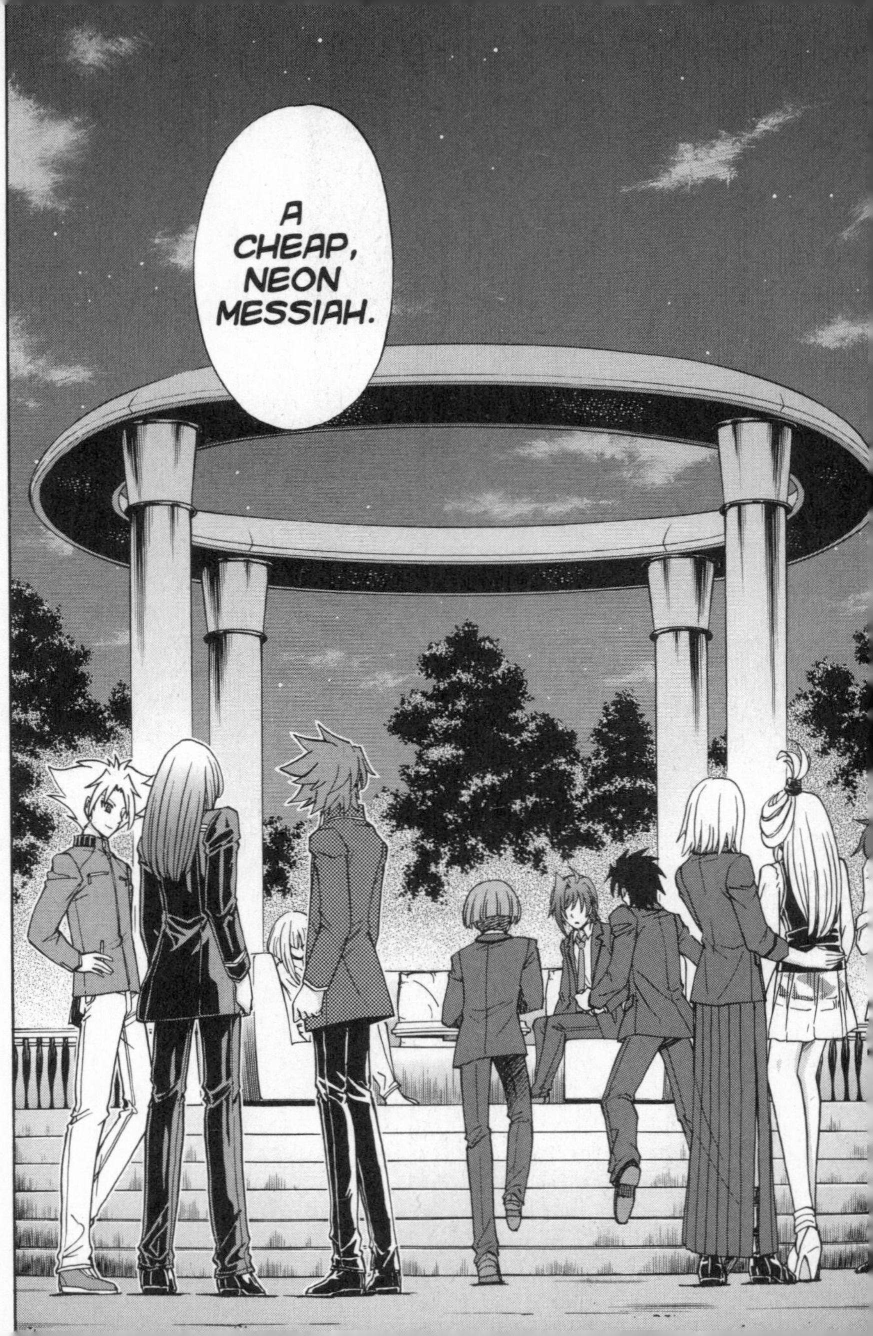
A CHEAP, NEON MESSIAH.

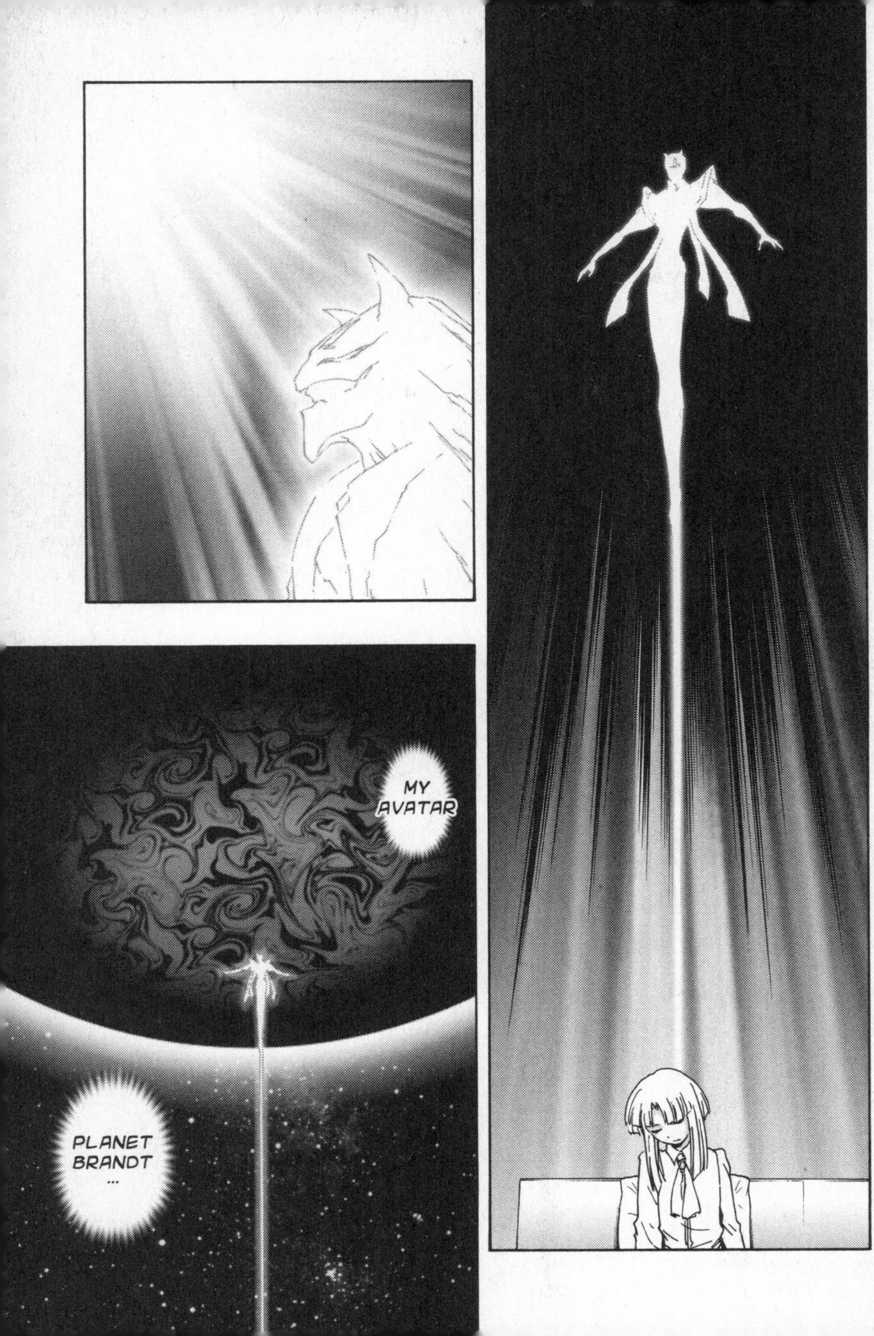
MY AVATAR
PLANET BRANDT ...

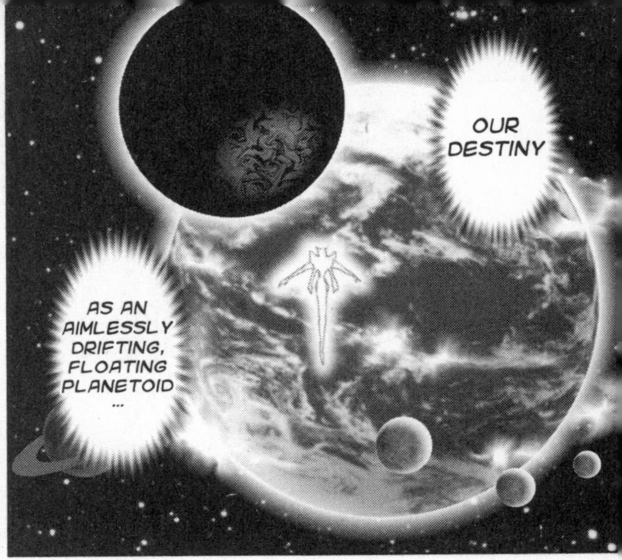
OUR DESTINY
AS AN AIMLESSLY DRIFTING, FLOATING PLANETOID ...
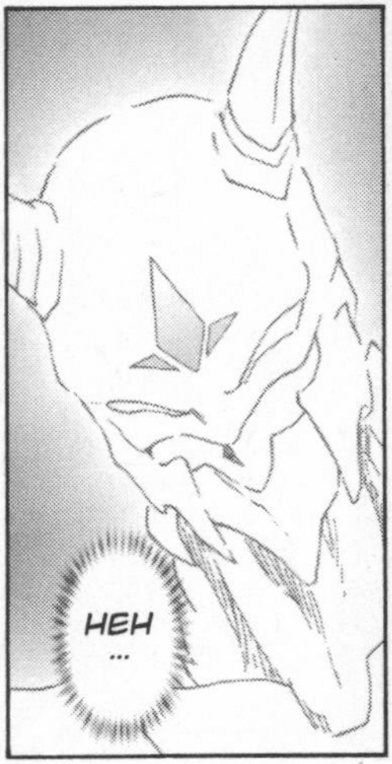
HEH ...
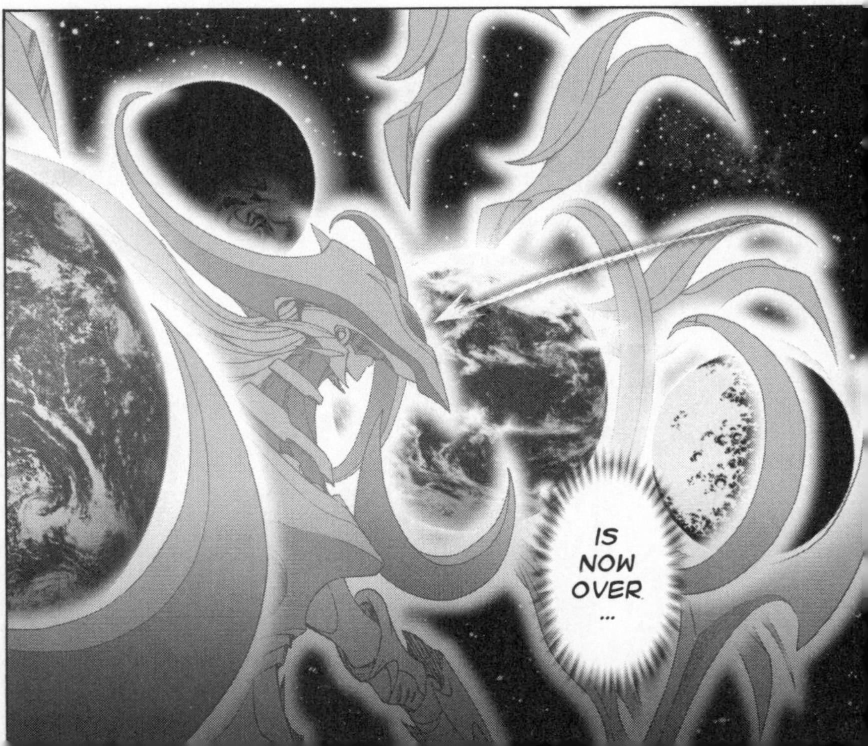
IS NOW OVER ...

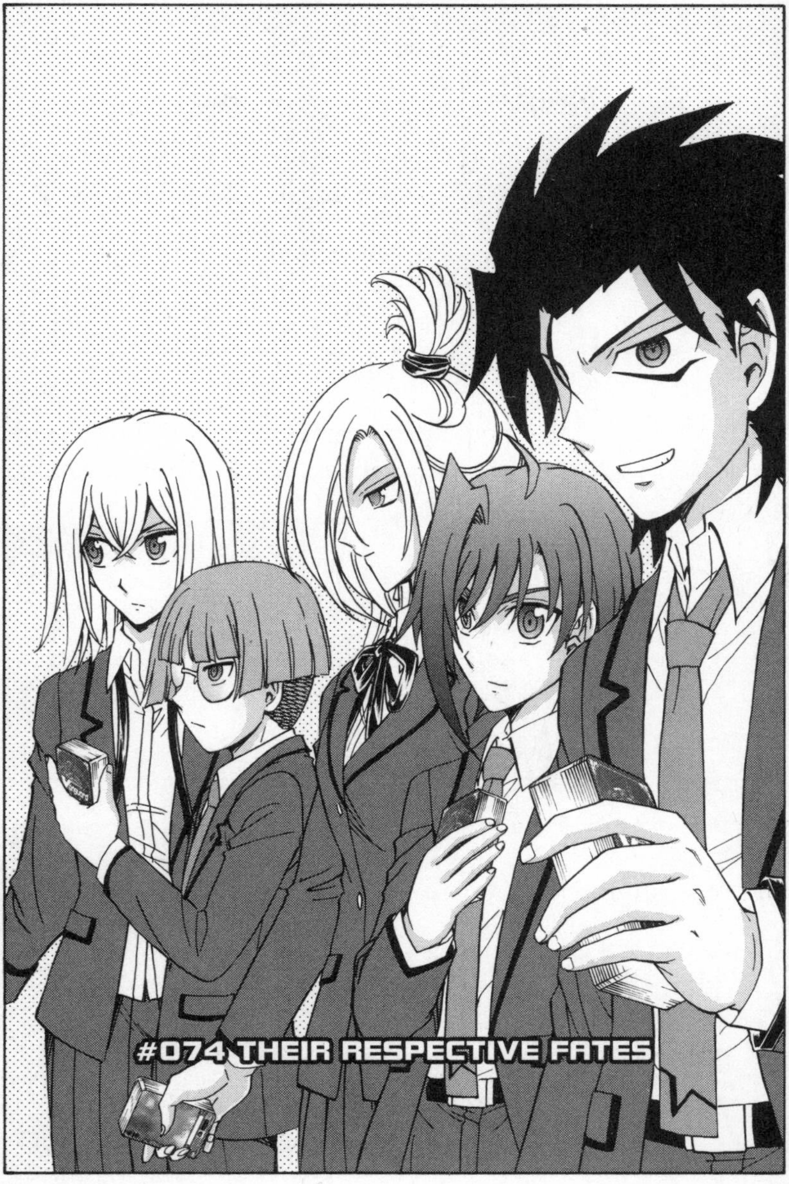
#074 THEIR RESPECTIVE FATES

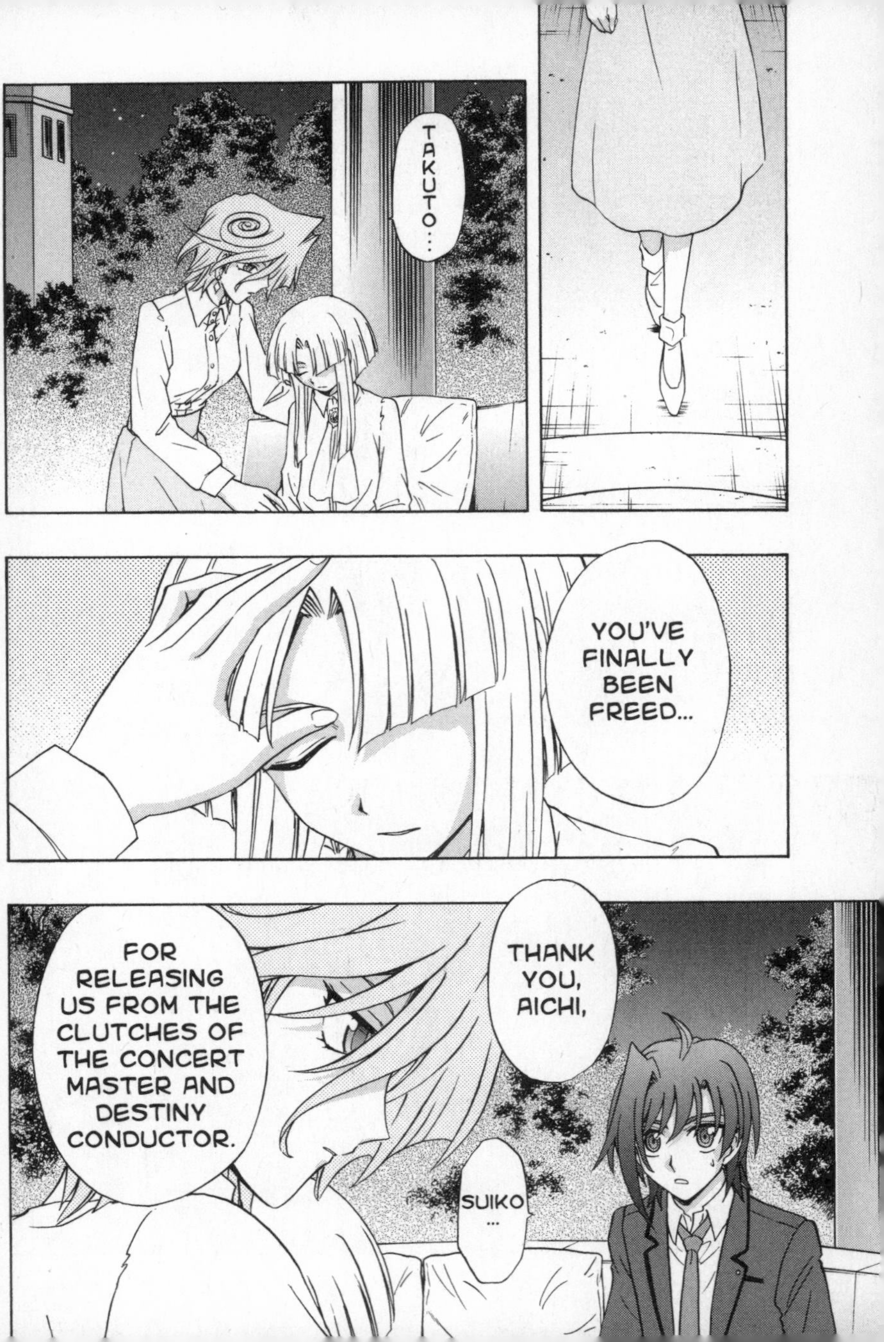
TAKUTO...
YOU'VE FINALLY BEEN FREED...
THANK YOU, AICHI,
FOR RELEASING US FROM THE CLUTCHES OF THE CONCERT MASTER AND DESTINY CONDUCTOR.
SUIKO...

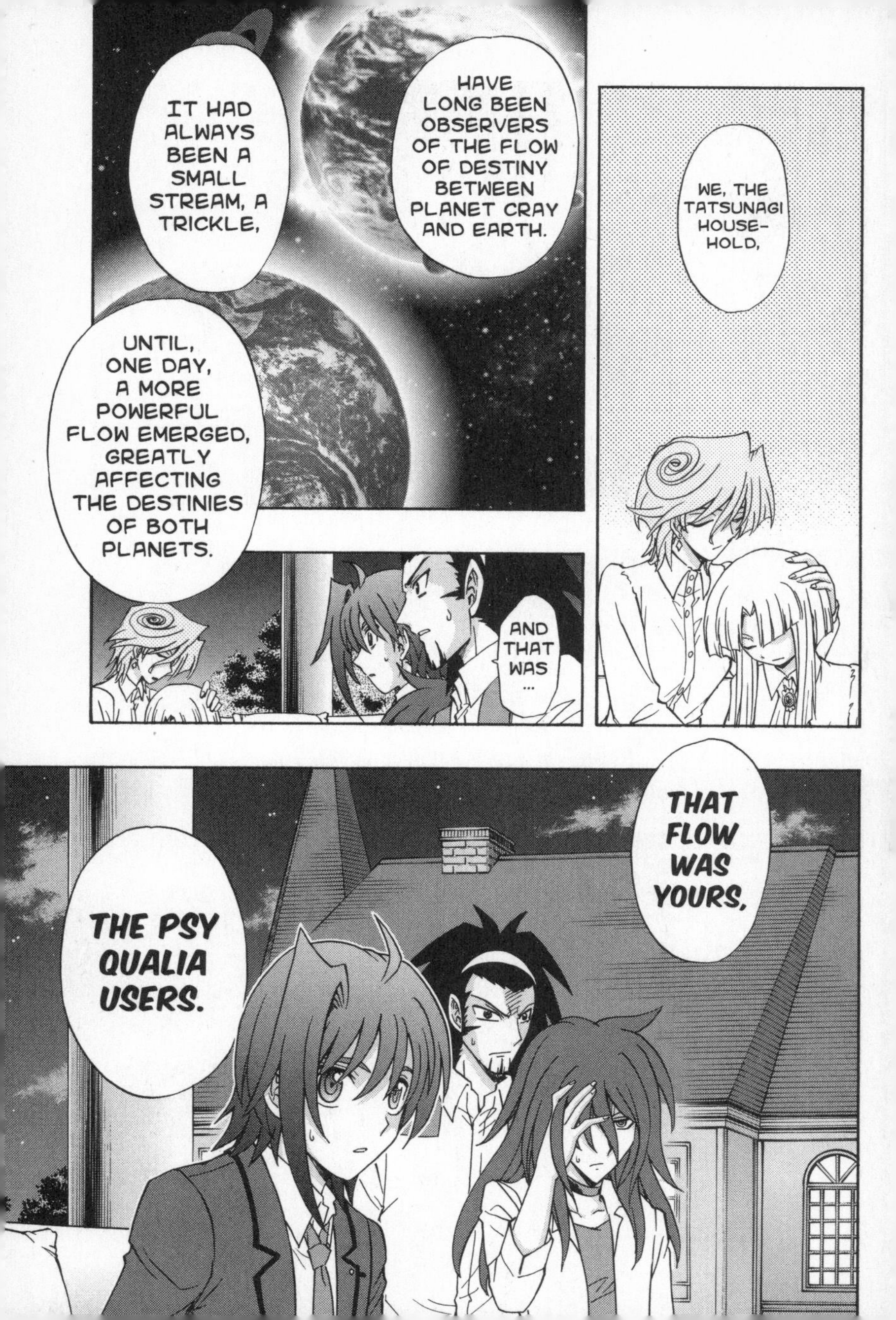
WE, THE TATSUNAGI HOUSE-HOLD,
HAVE LONG BEEN OBSERVERS OF THE FLOW OF DESTINY BETWEEN PLANET CRAY AND EARTH.
IT HAD ALWAYS BEEN A SMALL STREAM, A TRICKLE,
UNTIL, ONE DAY, A MORE POWERFUL FLOW EMERGED, GREATLY AFFECTING THE DESTINIES OF BOTH PLANETS.
AND THAT WAS ...
THAT FLOW WAS YOURS,
THE PSY QUALIA USERS.

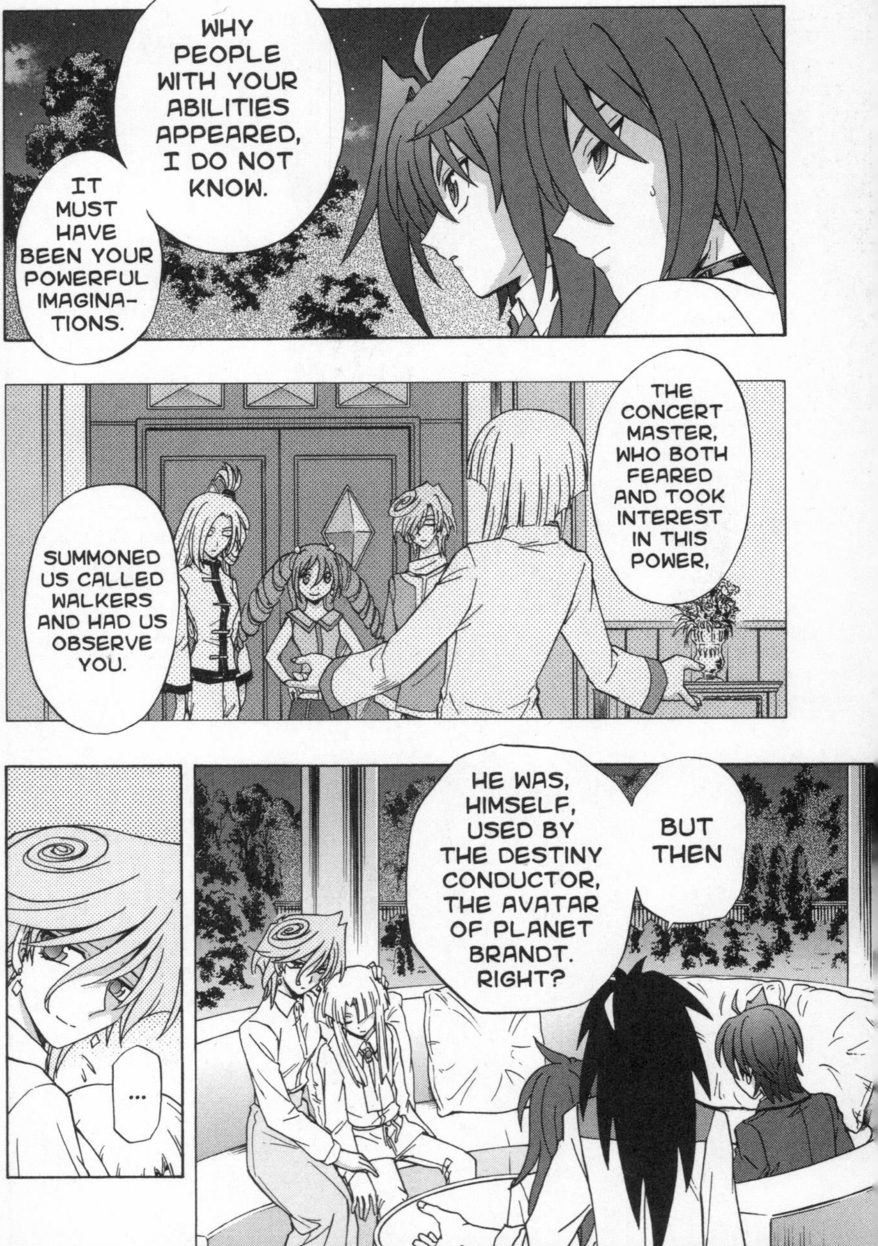
WHY PEOPLE WITH YOUR ABILITIES APPEARED, I DO NOT KNOW.
IT MUST HAVE BEEN YOUR POWERFUL IMAGINA-TIONS.
THE CONCERT MASTER, WHO BOTH FEARED AND TOOK INTEREST IN THIS POWER,
SUMMONED US CALLED WALKERS AND HAD US OBSERVE YOU.
BUT THEN
HE WAS, HIMSELF, USED BY THE DESTINY CONDUCTOR, THE AVATAR OF PLANET BRANDT. RIGHT?
...

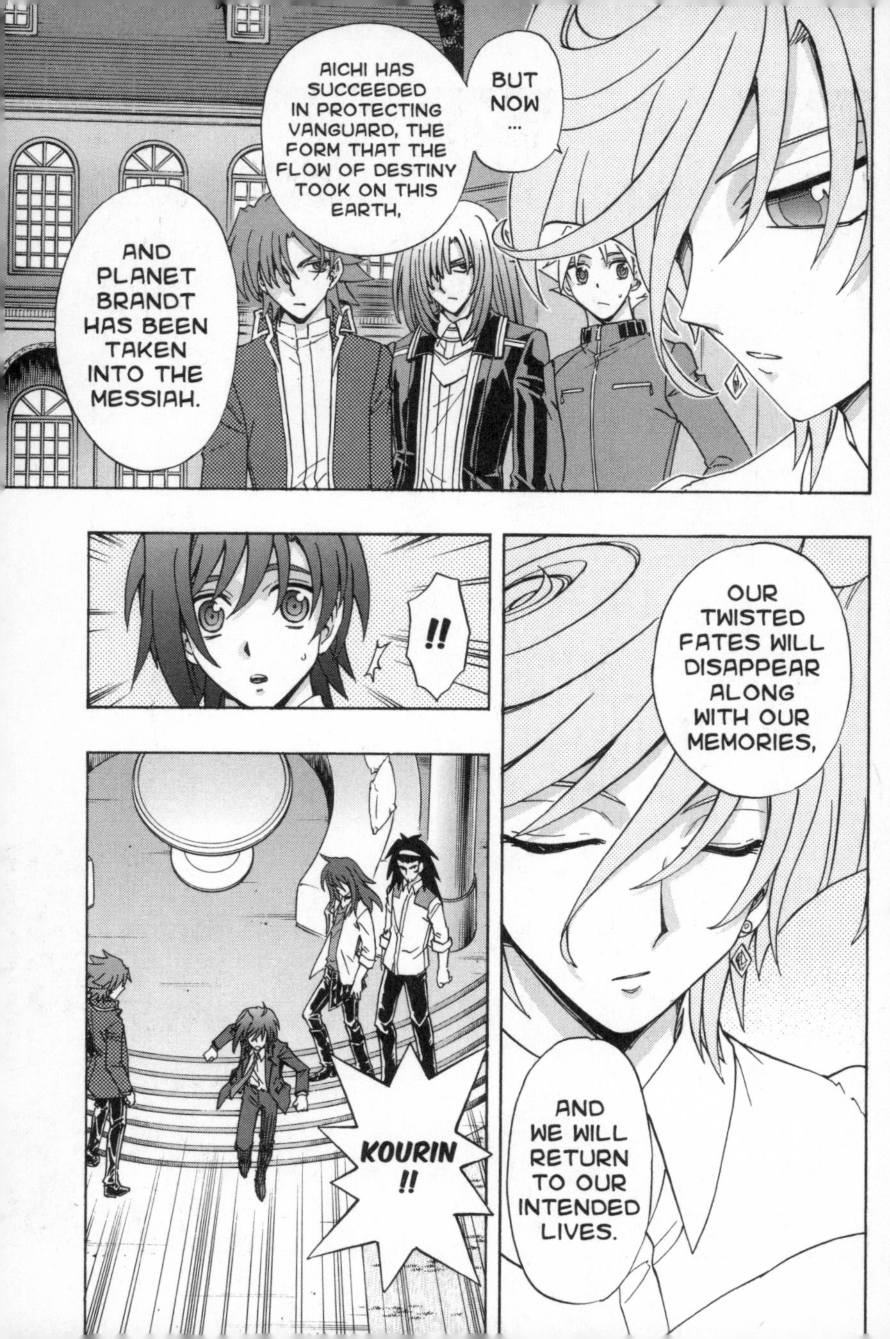
BUT NOW ...
AICHI HAS SUCCEEDED IN PROTECTING VANGUARD, THE FORM THAT THE FLOW OF DESTINY TOOK ON THIS EARTH,
AND PLANET BRANDT HAS BEEN TAKEN INTO THE MESSIAH.
OUR TWISTED FATES WILL DISAPPEAR ALONG WITH OUR MEMORIES,
AND WE WILL RETURN TO OUR INTENDED LIVES.
!!
KOURIN !!

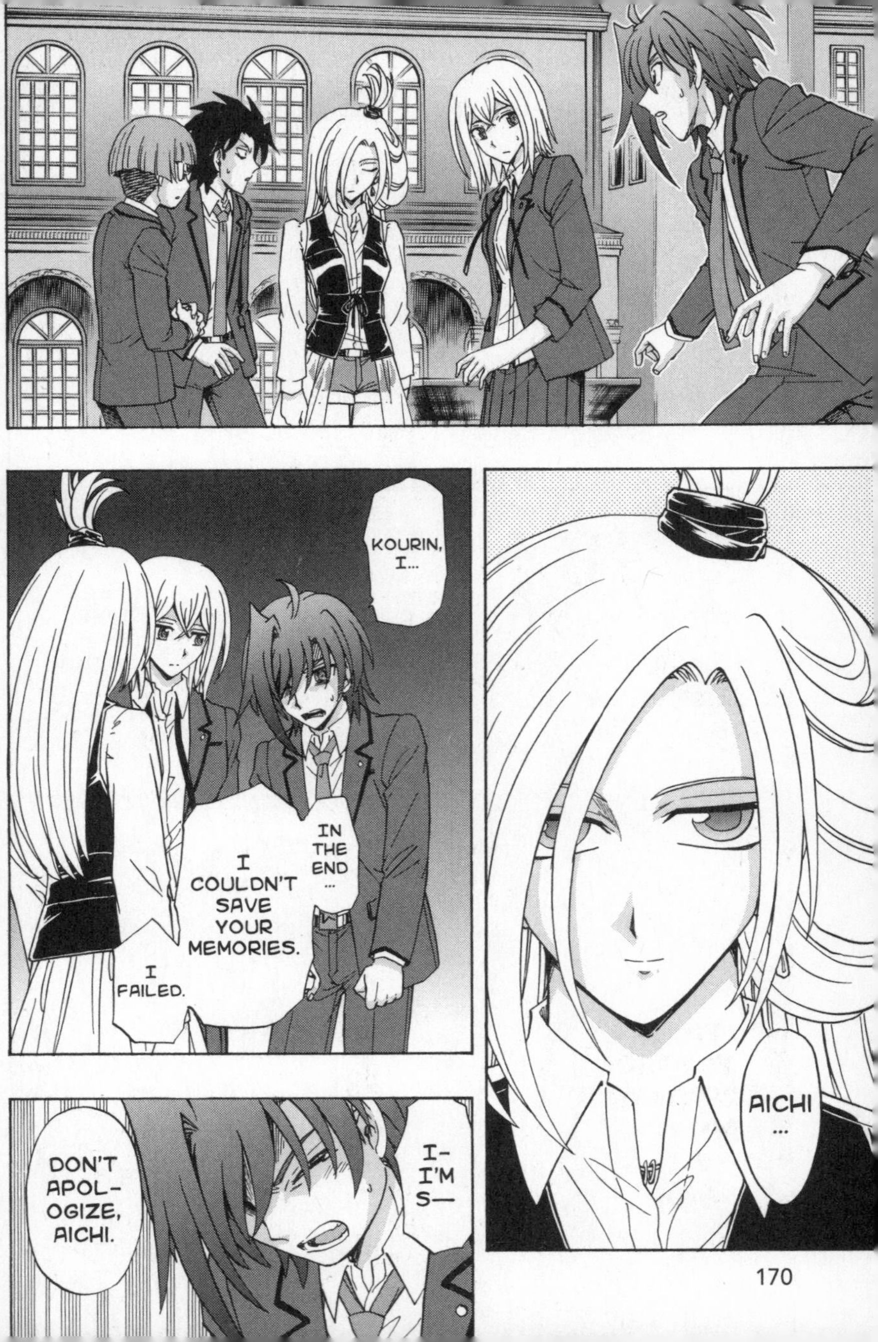
AICHI …
KOURIN, I…
IN THE END …
I COULDN'T SAVE YOUR MEMORIES.
I FAILED.
I- I'M S—
DON'T APOL-OGIZE, AICHI.

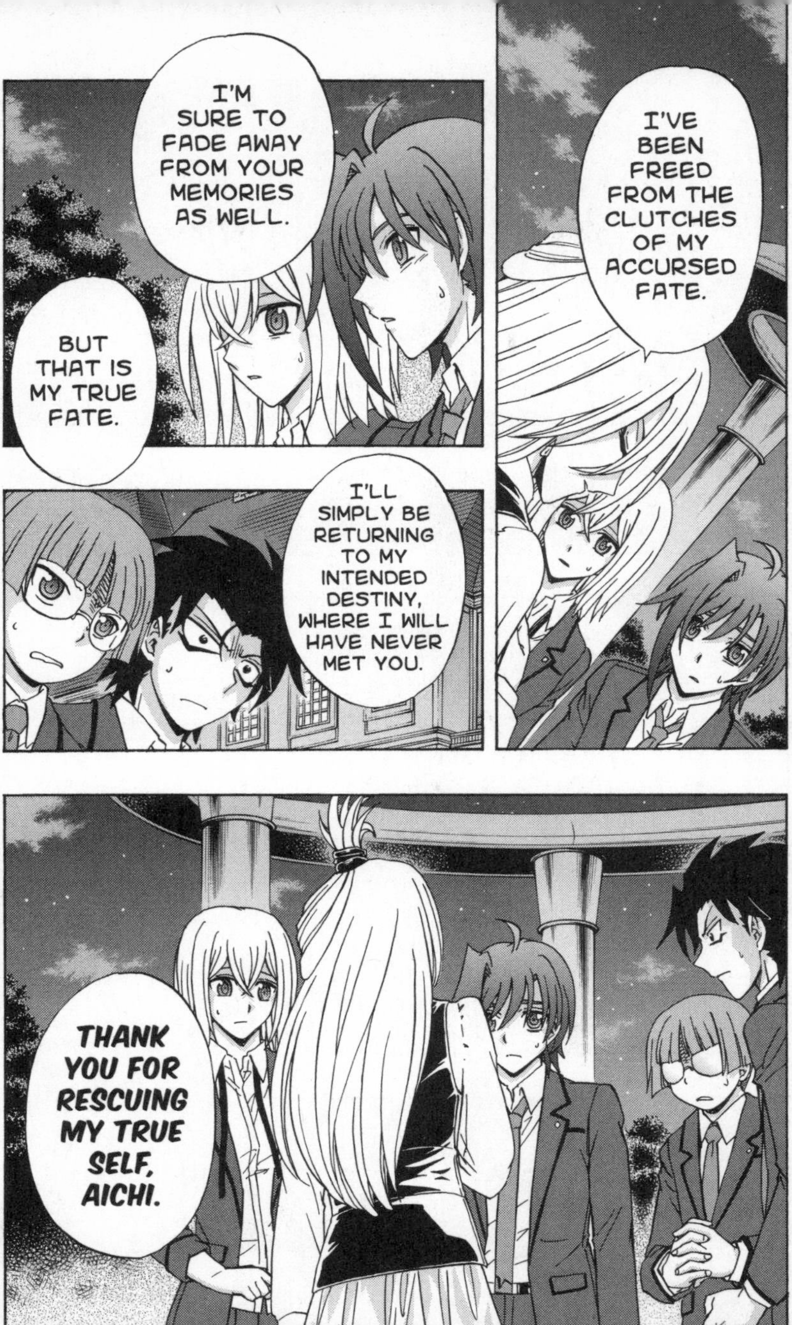
I'VE BEEN FREED FROM THE CLUTCHES OF MY ACCURSED FATE.
I'M SURE TO FADE AWAY FROM YOUR MEMORIES AS WELL.
BUT THAT IS MY TRUE FATE.
I'LL SIMPLY BE RETURNING TO MY INTENDED DESTINY, WHERE I WILL HAVE NEVER MET YOU.
THANK YOU FOR RESCUING MY TRUE SELF, AICHI.

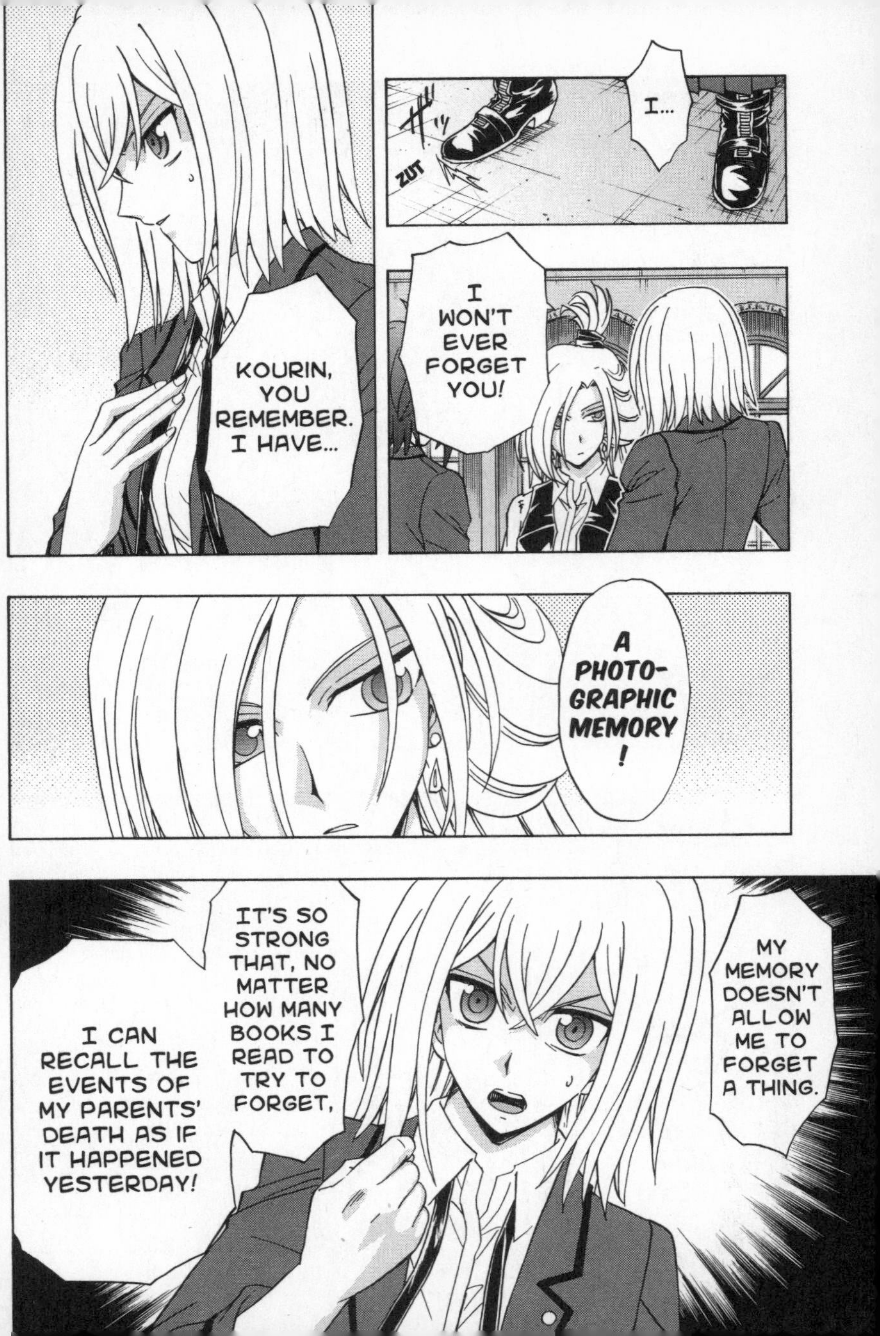
I...
ZUT
I WON'T EVER FORGET YOU!
KOURIN, YOU REMEMBER. I HAVE...
A PHOTOGRAPHIC MEMORY!
MY MEMORY DOESN'T ALLOW ME TO FORGET A THING.
IT'S SO STRONG THAT, NO MATTER HOW MANY BOOKS I READ TO TRY TO FORGET,
I CAN RECALL THE EVENTS OF MY PARENTS' DEATH AS IF IT HAPPENED YESTERDAY!

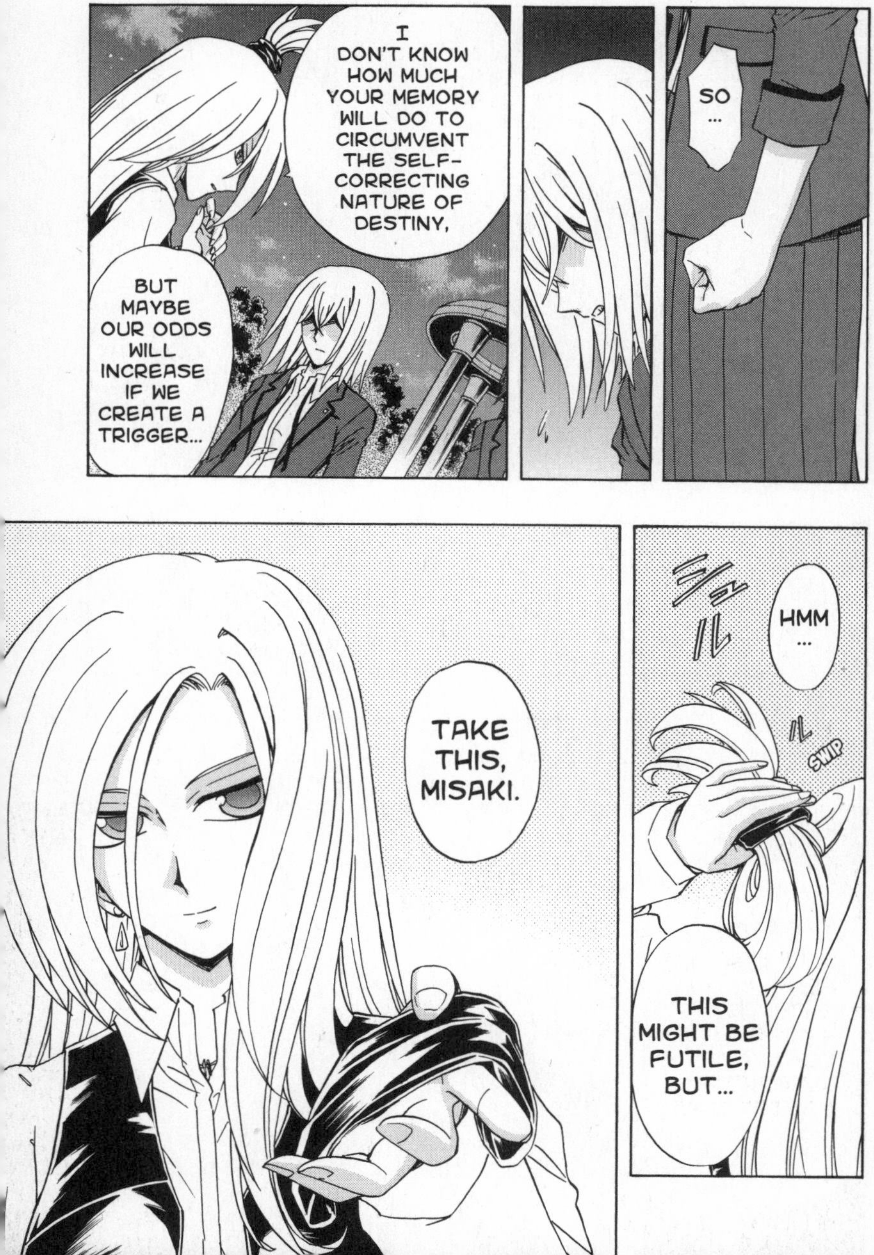
SO ...
I DON'T KNOW HOW MUCH YOUR MEMORY WILL DO TO CIRCUMVENT THE SELF-CORRECTING NATURE OF DESTINY,
BUT MAYBE OUR ODDS WILL INCREASE IF WE CREATE A TRIGGER...
HMM ...
シュル
ル
SWIP
THIS MIGHT BE FUTILE, BUT...
TAKE THIS, MISAKI.

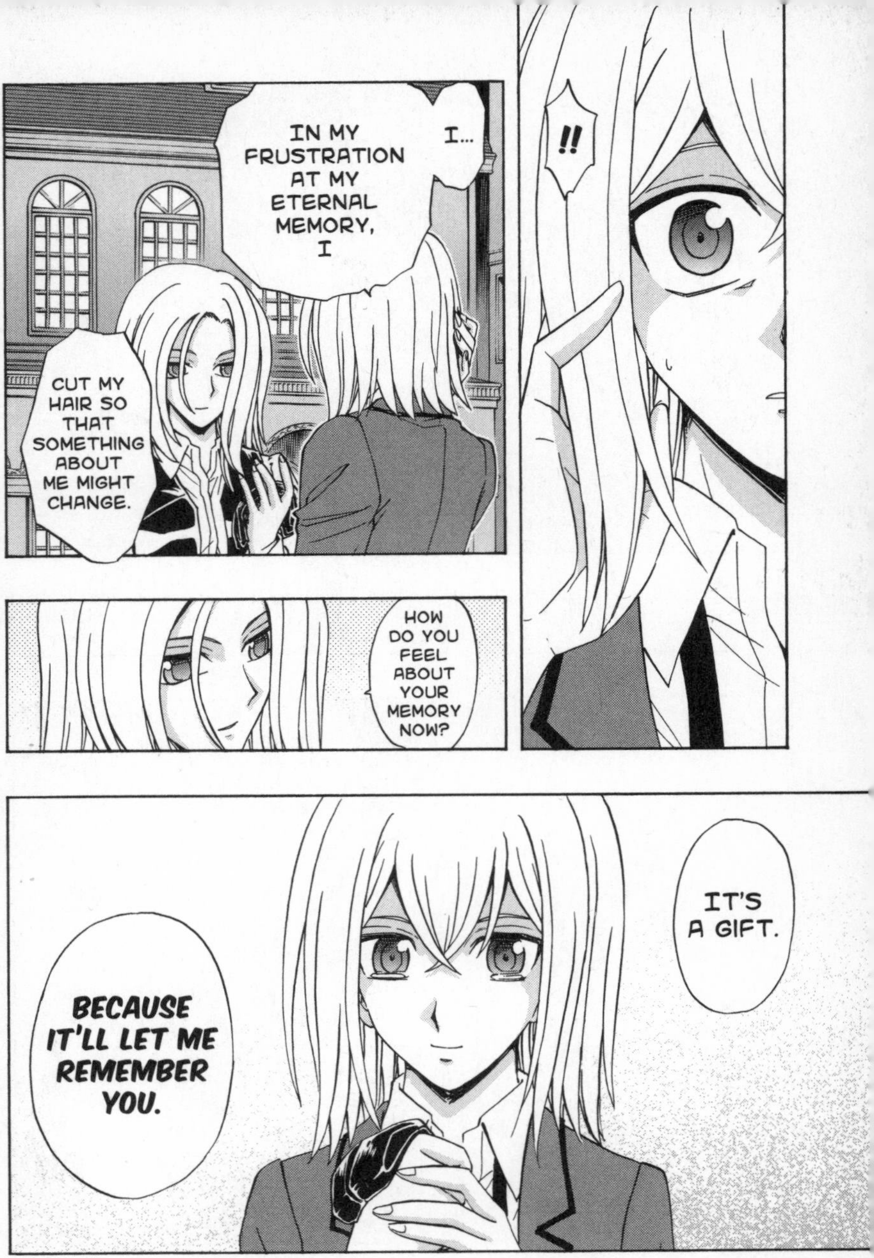
!!
I...
IN MY FRUSTRATION AT MY ETERNAL MEMORY, I
CUT MY HAIR SO THAT SOMETHING ABOUT ME MIGHT CHANGE.
HOW DO YOU FEEL ABOUT YOUR MEMORY NOW?
IT'S A GIFT.
BECAUSE IT'LL LET ME REMEMBER YOU.

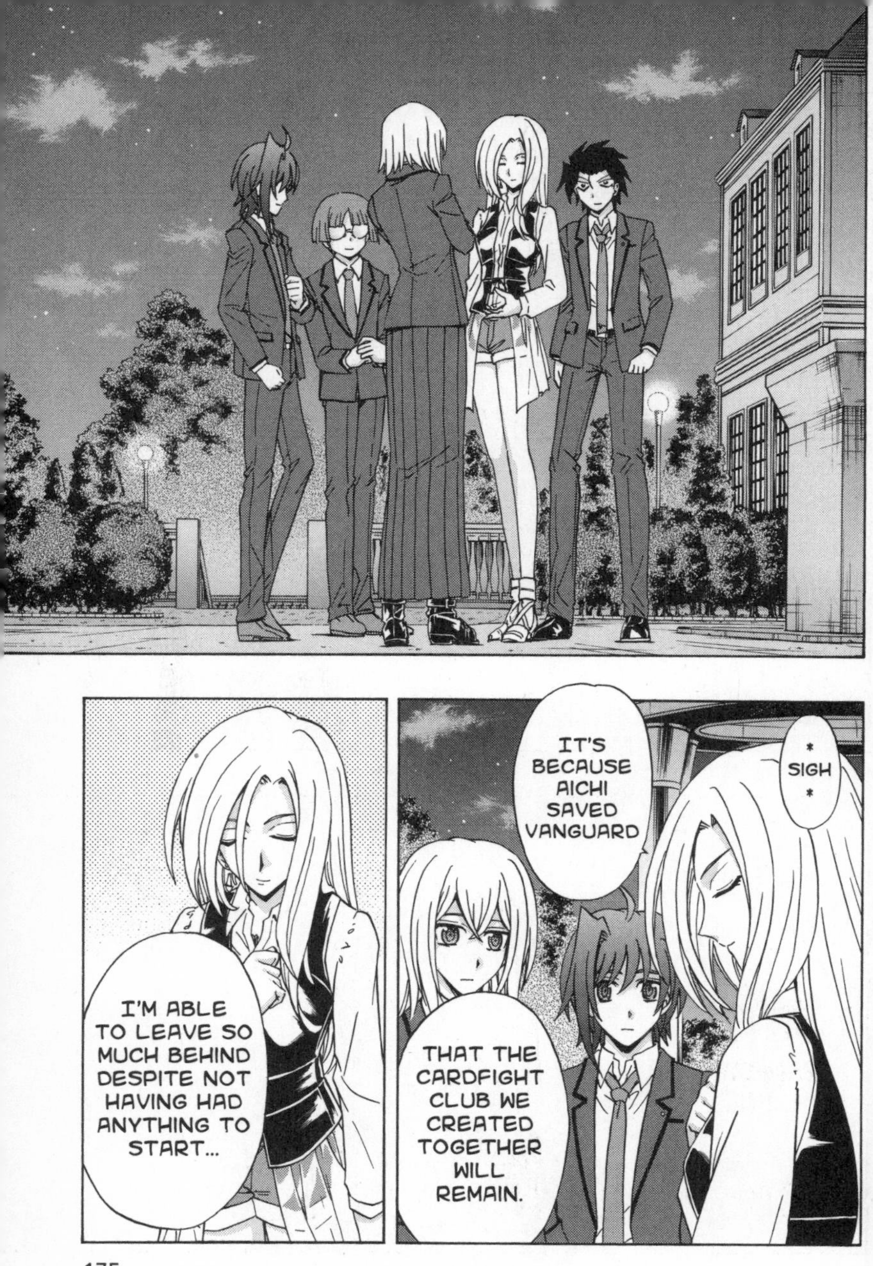
* SIGH *
IT'S BECAUSE AICHI SAVED VANGUARD
THAT THE CARDFIGHT CLUB WE CREATED TOGETHER WILL REMAIN.
I'M ABLE TO LEAVE SO MUCH BEHIND DESPITE NOT HAVING HAD ANYTHING TO START...

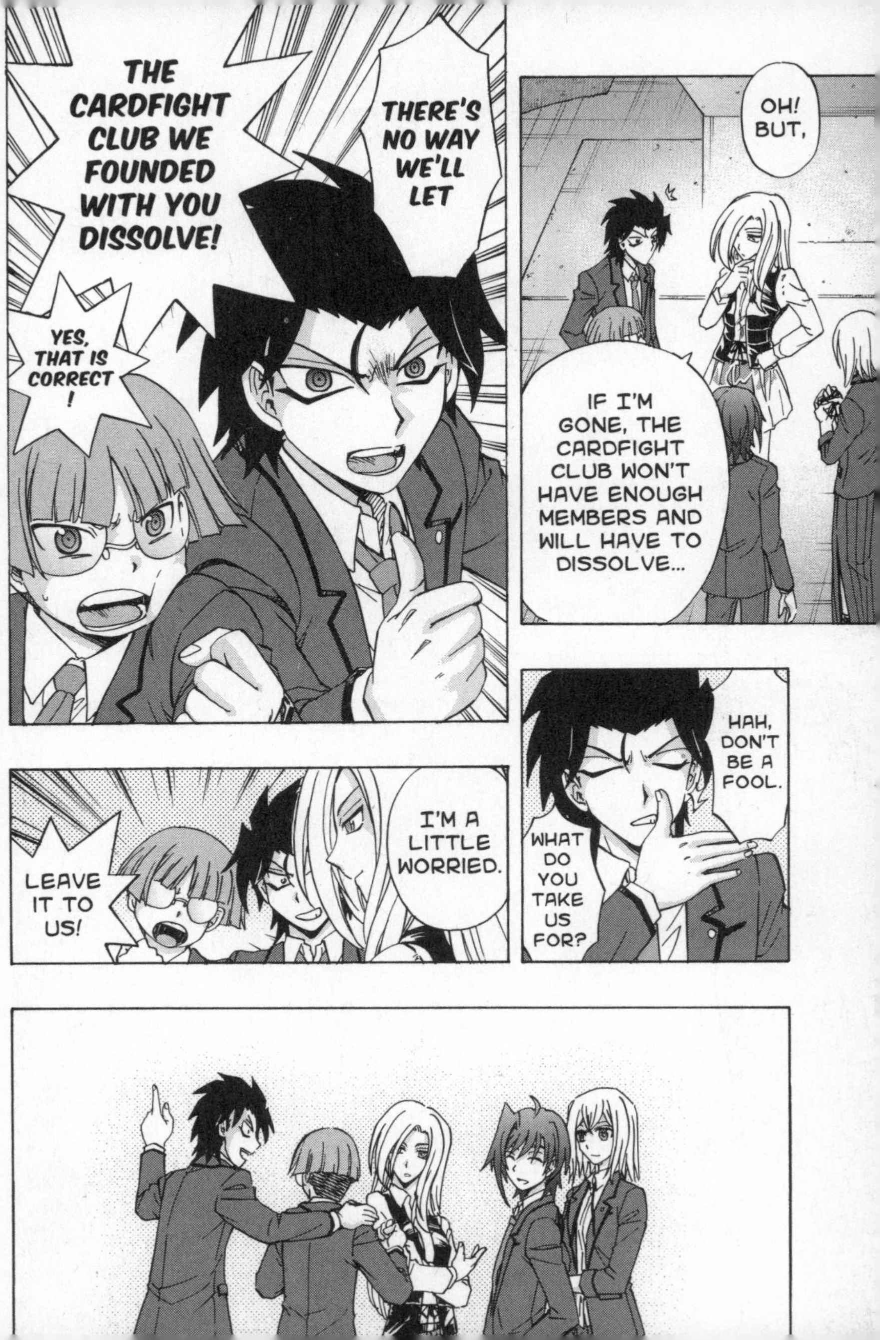
OH! BUT,
IF I'M GONE, THE CARDFIGHT CLUB WON'T HAVE ENOUGH MEMBERS AND WILL HAVE TO DISSOLVE...
THERE'S NO WAY WE'LL LET
THE CARDFIGHT CLUB WE FOUNDED WITH YOU DISSOLVE!
YES, THAT IS CORRECT!
HAH, DON'T BE A FOOL.
WHAT DO YOU TAKE US FOR?
I'M A LITTLE WORRIED.
LEAVE IT TO US!

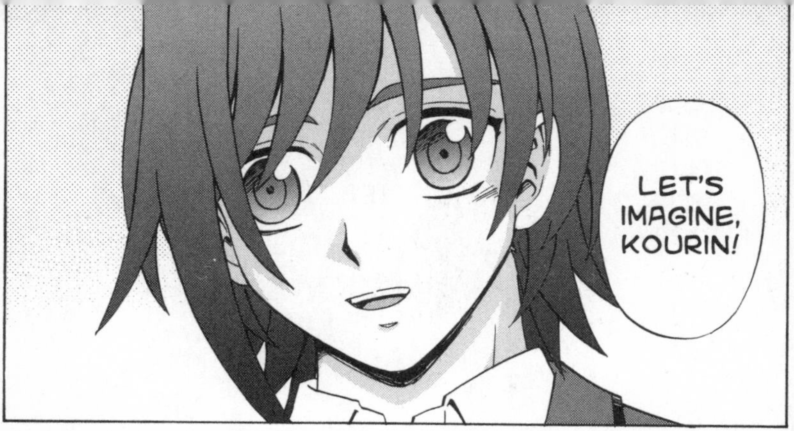
LET'S IMAGINE, KOURIN!

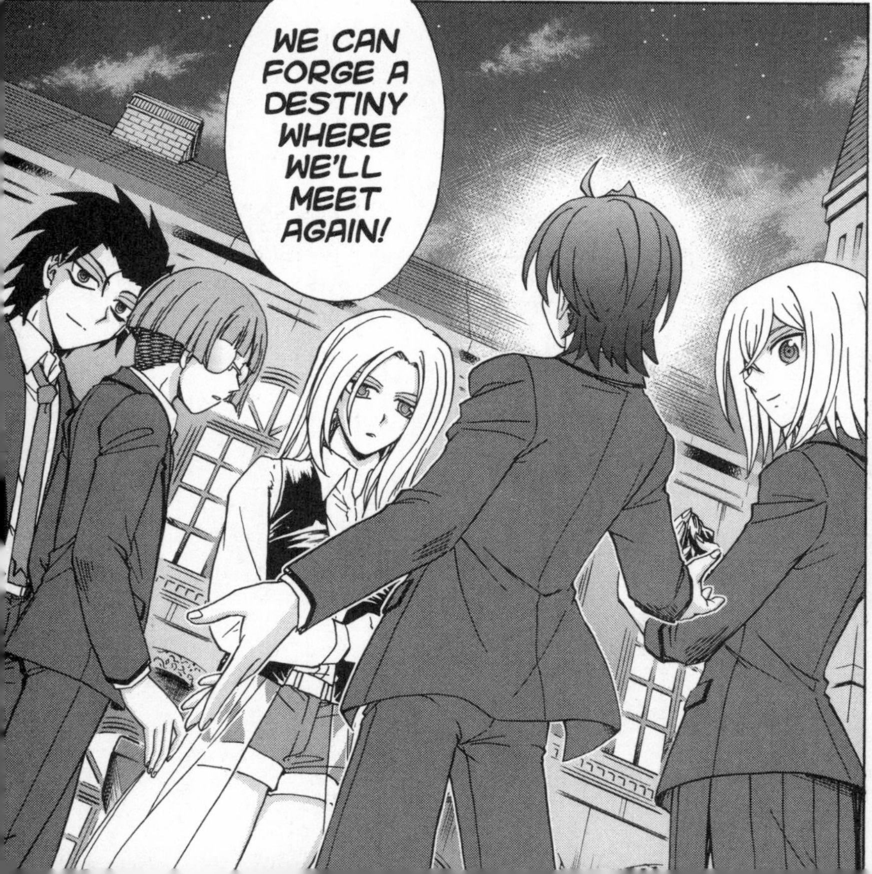
WE CAN FORGE A DESTINY WHERE WE'LL MEET AGAIN!

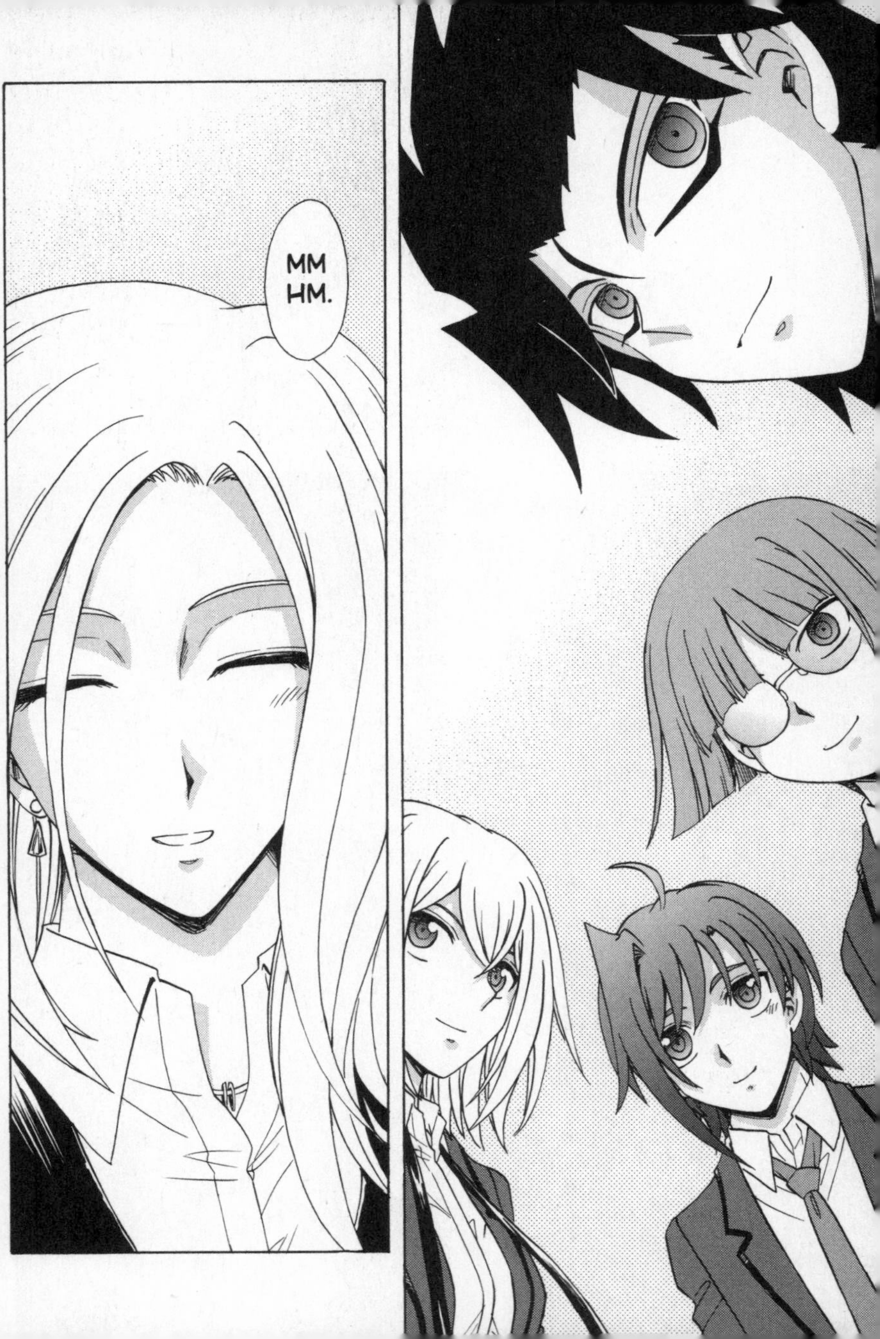
MM HM.

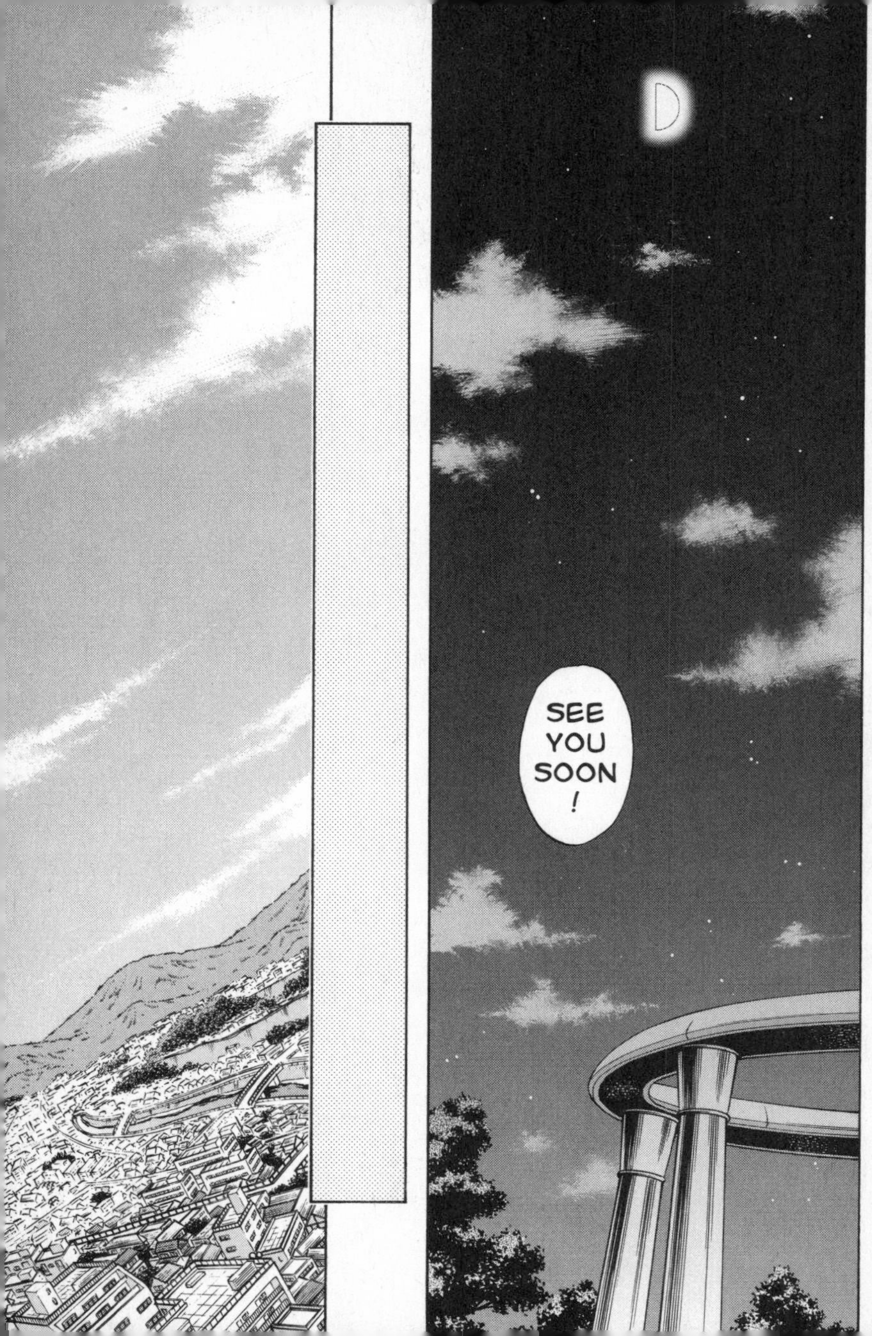
SEE YOU SOON !

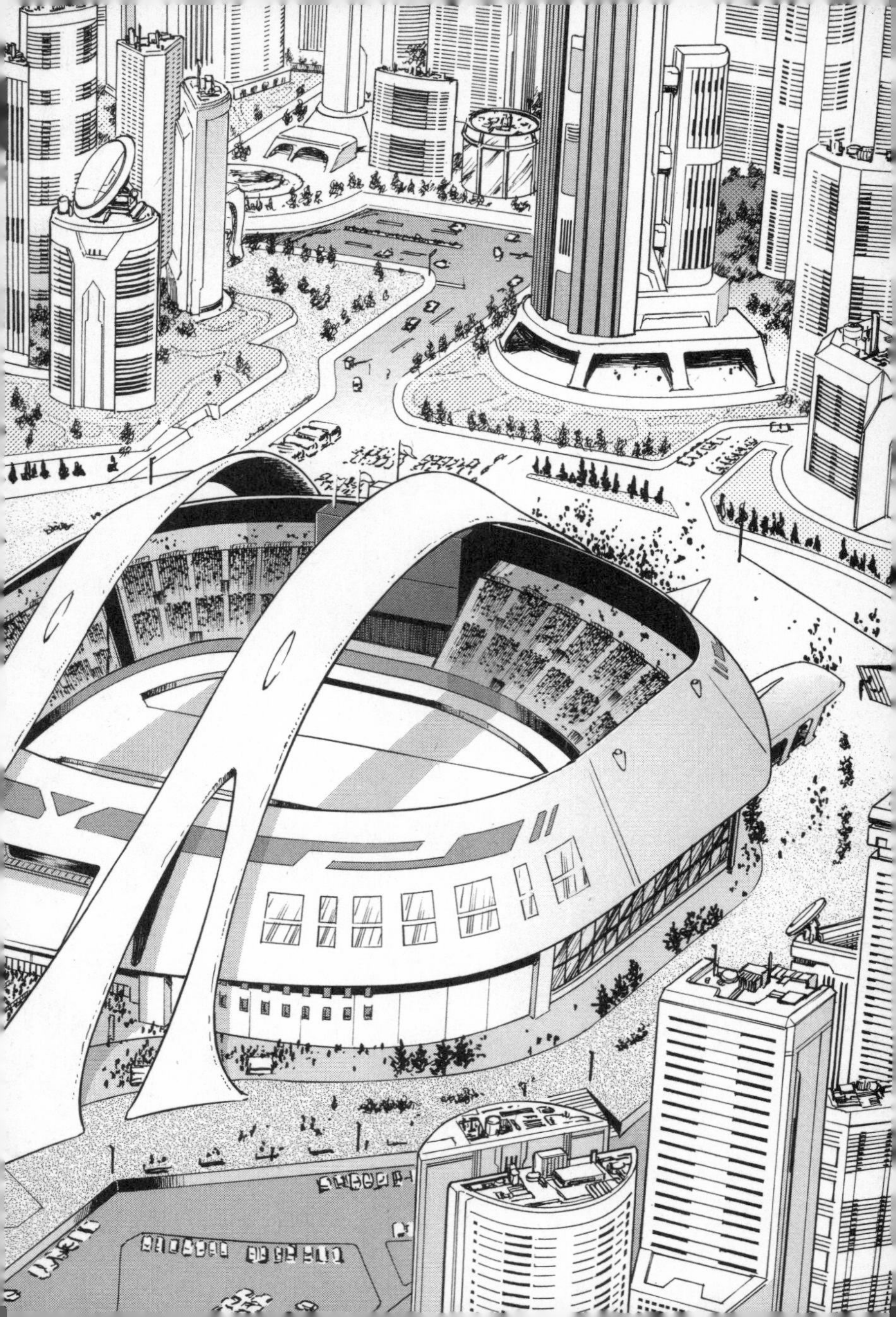

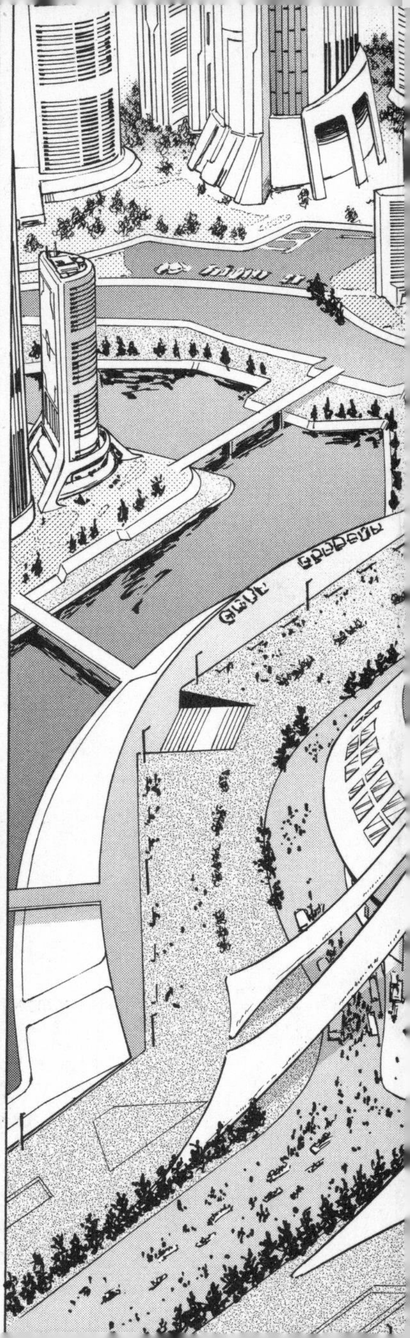
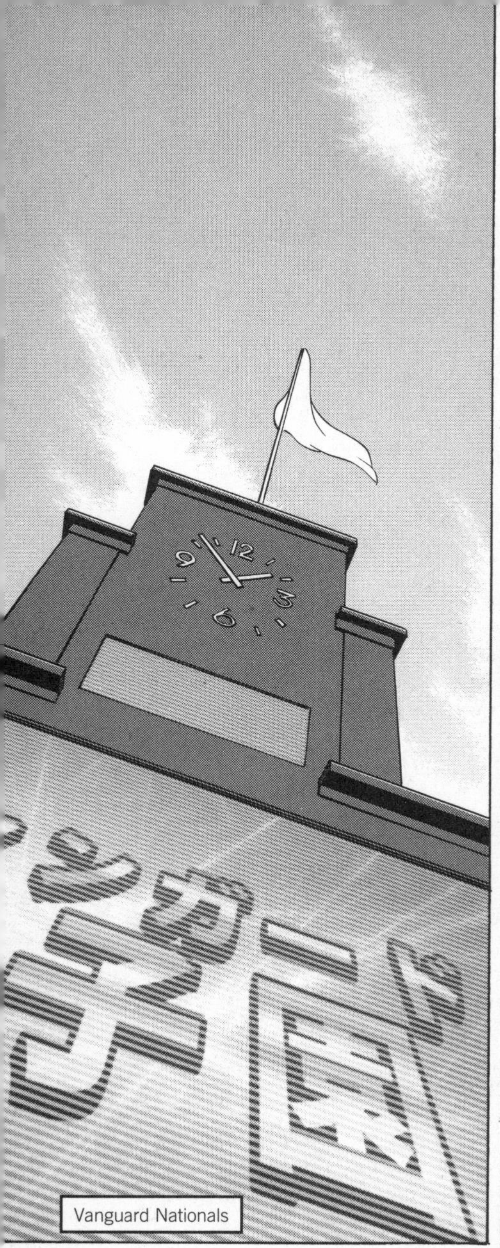
Vanguard Nationals

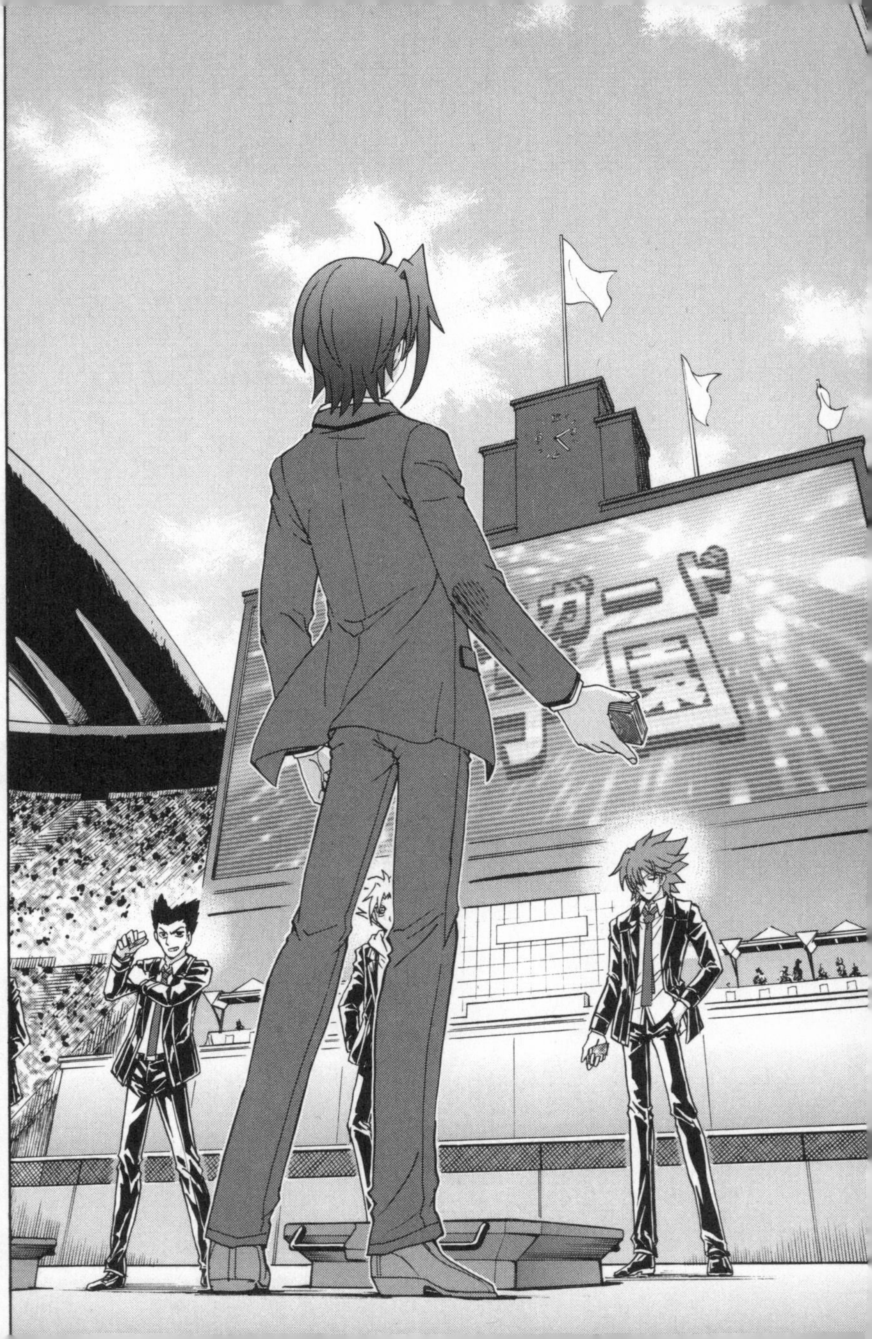
カード

CARDFIGHT!!
Vanguard

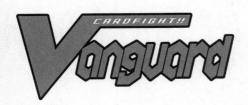

BONUS! CARDFIGHT!! Vanguard

NEVER-BEFORE-SEEN IMAGE BOARDS

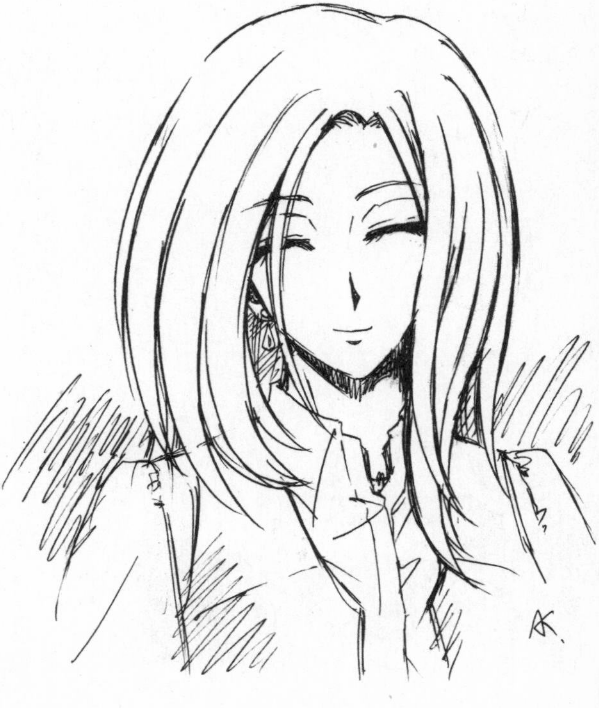

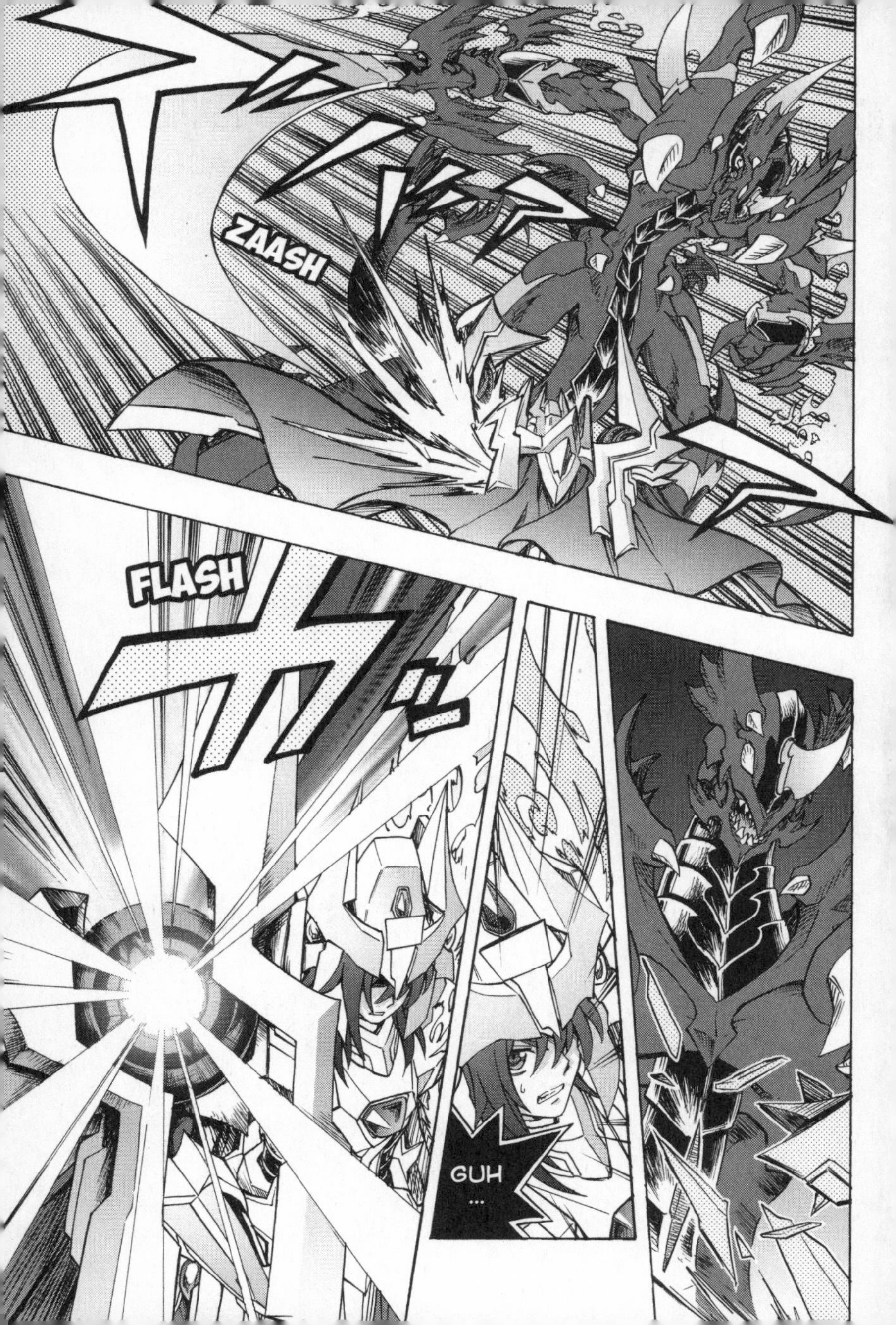
ZAASH
GUH ...
FLASH
カッ

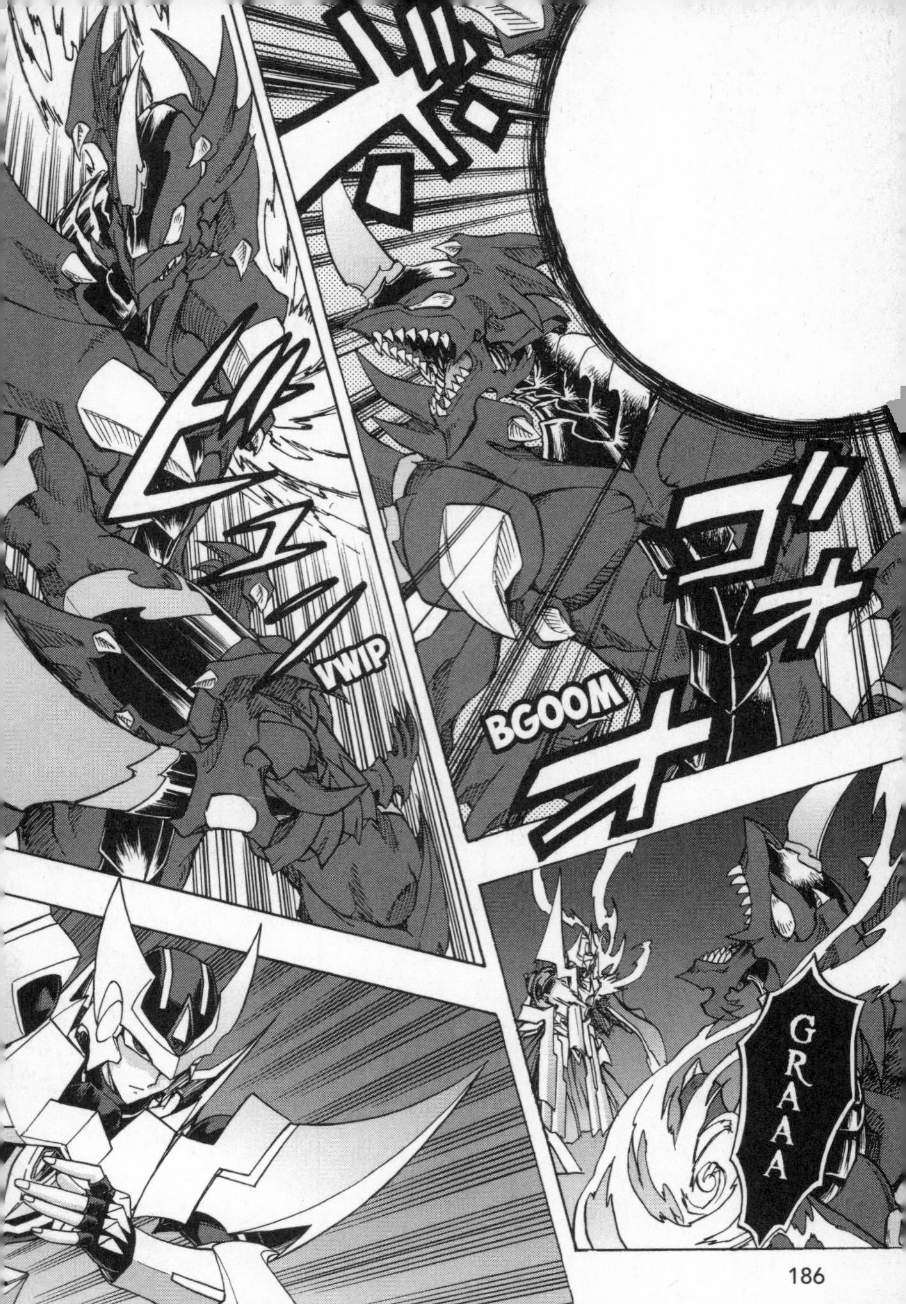
BGOOM
VWIP
GRAAA

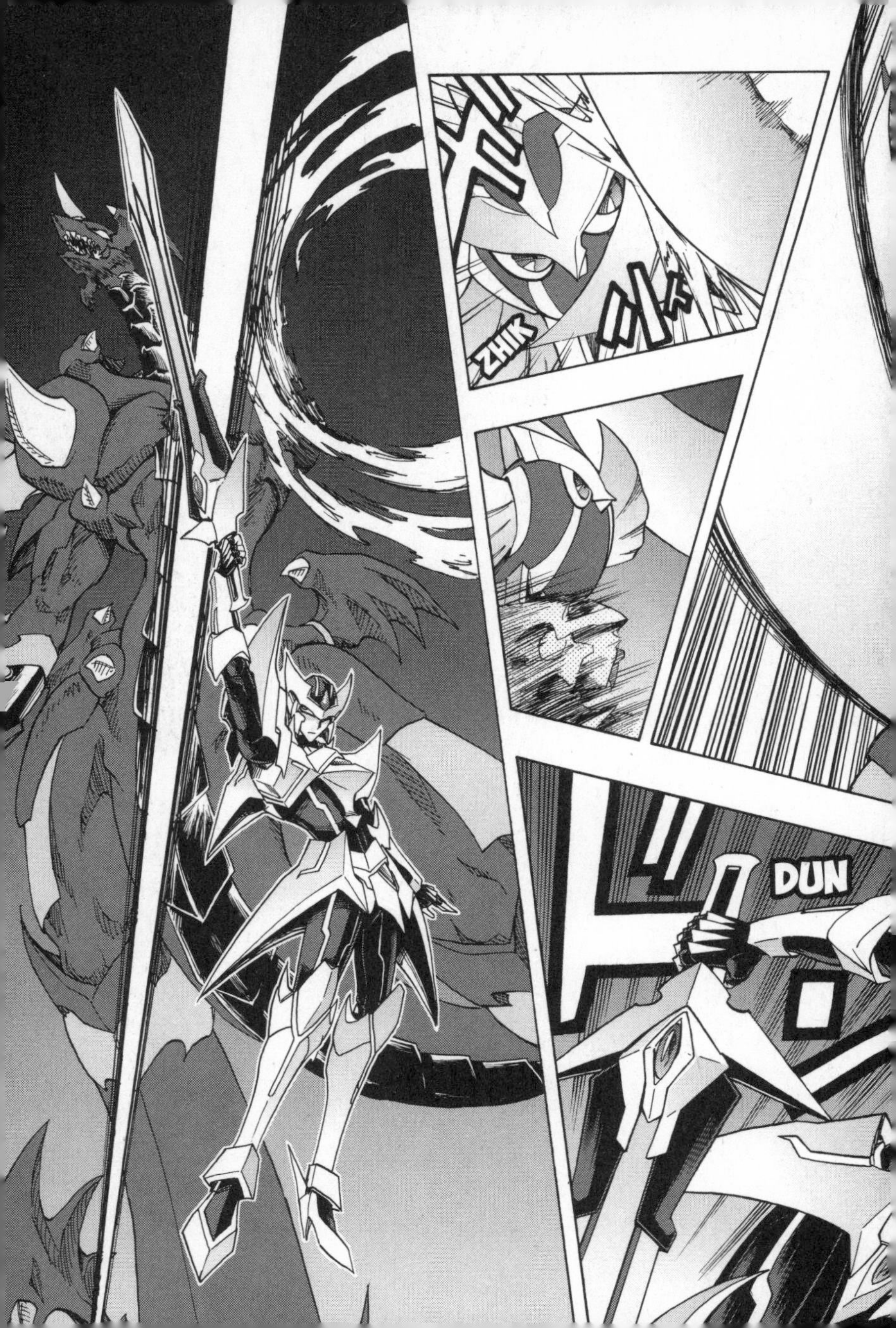
ZHIK
DUN

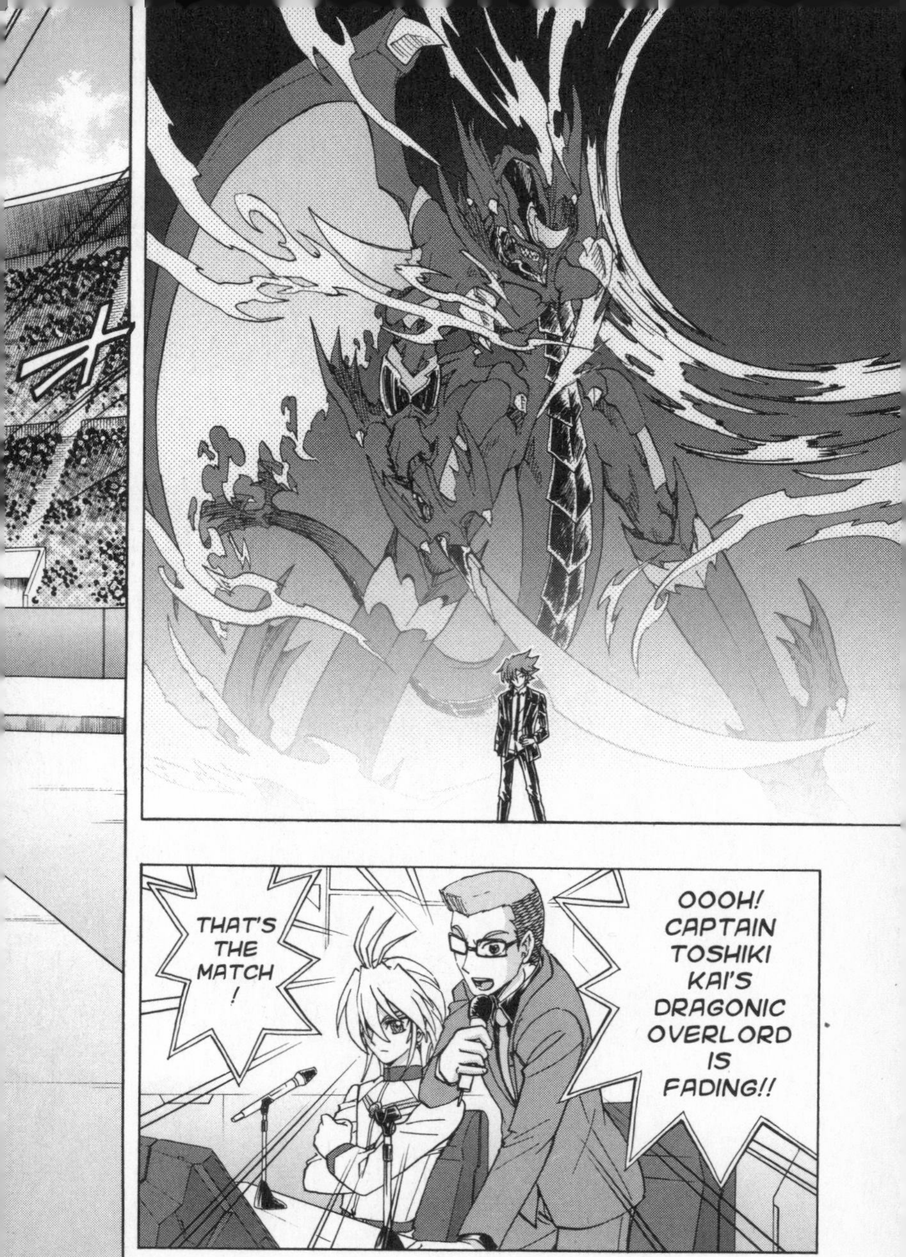
OOOH! CAPTAIN TOSHIKI KAI'S DRAGONIC OVERLORD IS FADING!!
THAT'S THE MATCH!

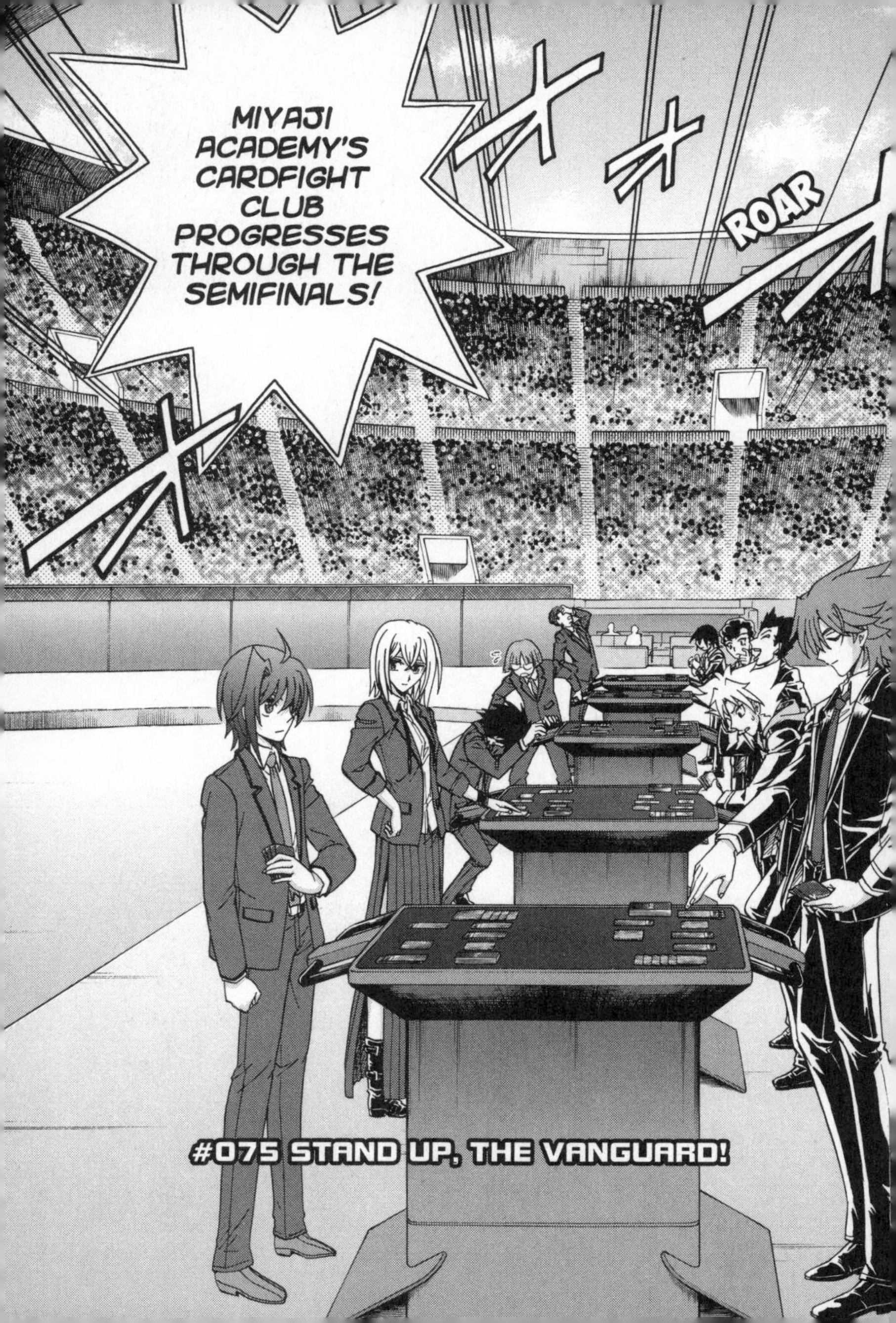
MIYAJI ACADEMY'S CARDFIGHT CLUB PROGRESSES THROUGH THE SEMIFINALS!
ROAR
#075 STAND UP, THE VANGUARD!

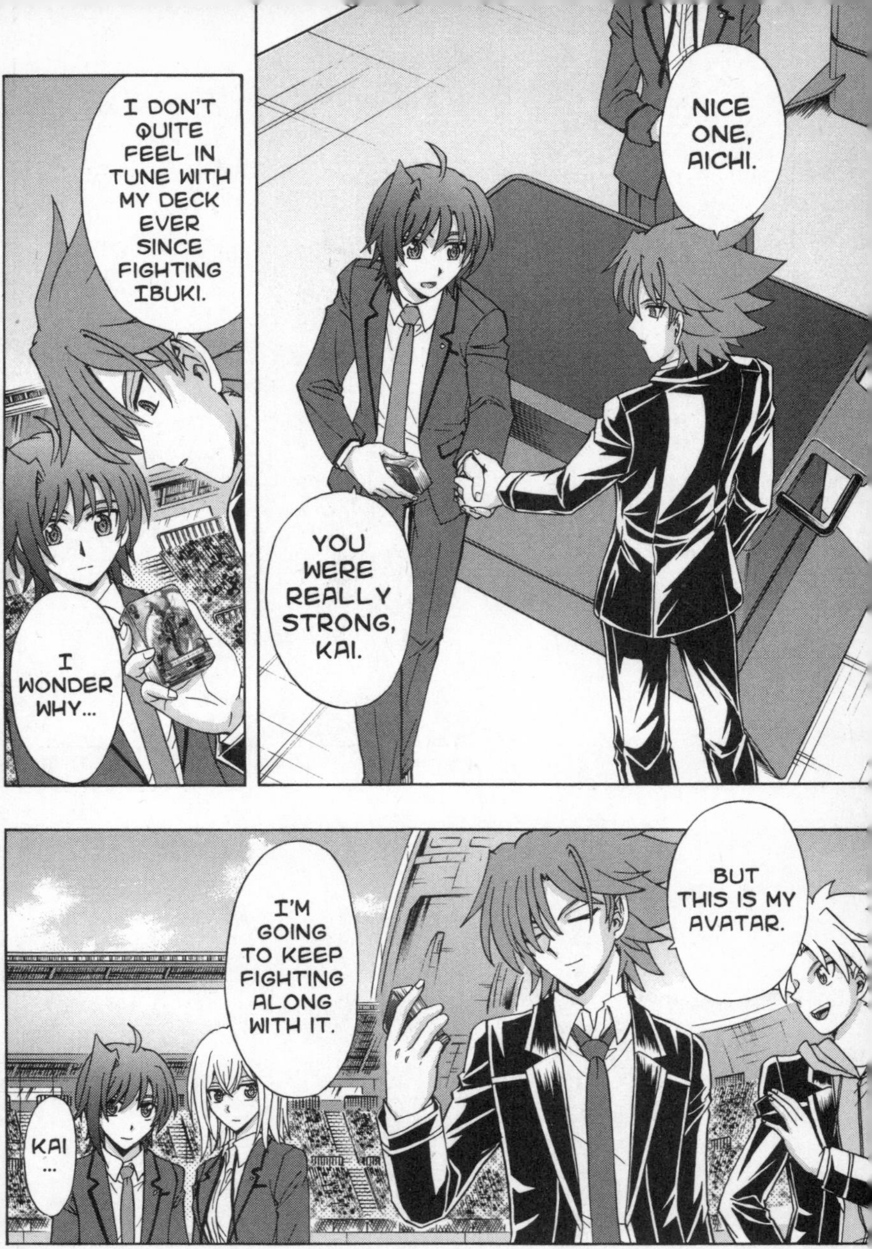
NICE ONE, AICHI.
YOU WERE REALLY STRONG, KAI.
I DON'T QUITE FEEL IN TUNE WITH MY DECK EVER SINCE FIGHTING IBUKI.
I WONDER WHY...
BUT THIS IS MY AVATAR.
I'M GOING TO KEEP FIGHTING ALONG WITH IT.
KAI ...

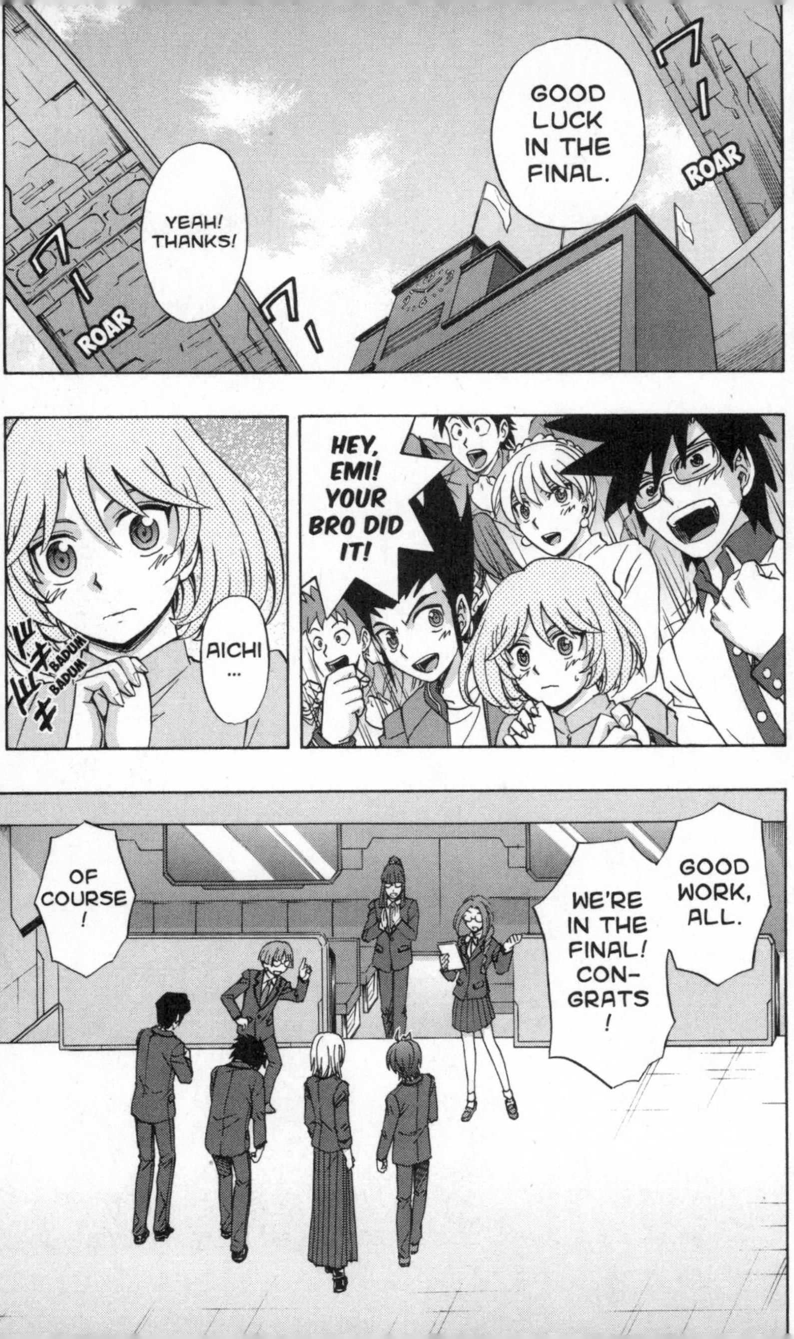
GOOD LUCK IN THE FINAL.
ROAR
YEAH! THANKS!
ROAR
HEY, EMI! YOUR BRO DID IT!
AICHI ...
BADUM BADUM
GOOD WORK, ALL.
WE'RE IN THE FINAL! CON-GRATS!
OF COURSE!

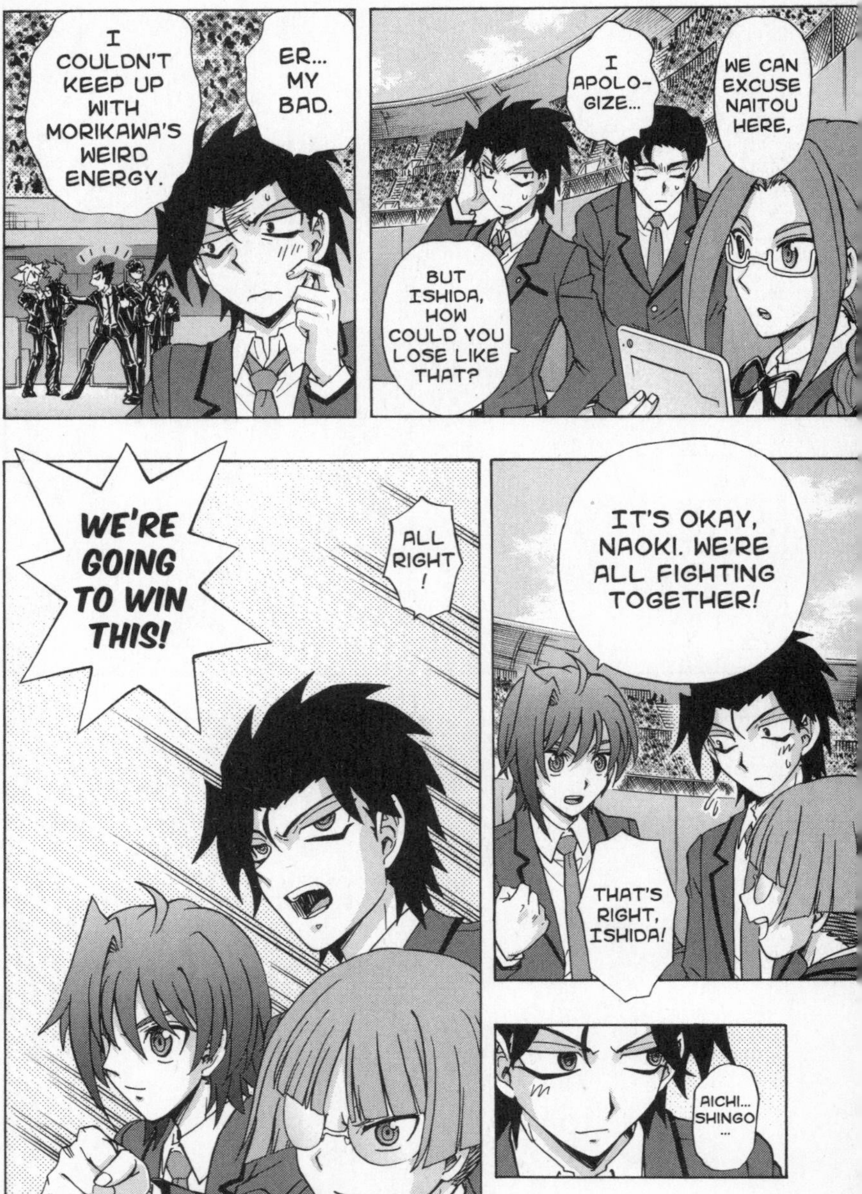
WE CAN EXCUSE NAITOU HERE,
I APOLOGIZE...
BUT ISHIDA, HOW COULD YOU LOSE LIKE THAT?
ER... MY BAD.
I COULDN'T KEEP UP WITH MORIKAWA'S WEIRD ENERGY.
IT'S OKAY, NAOKI. WE'RE ALL FIGHTING TOGETHER!
THAT'S RIGHT, ISHIDA!
AICHI... SHINGO...
ALL RIGHT!
WE'RE GOING TO WIN THIS!

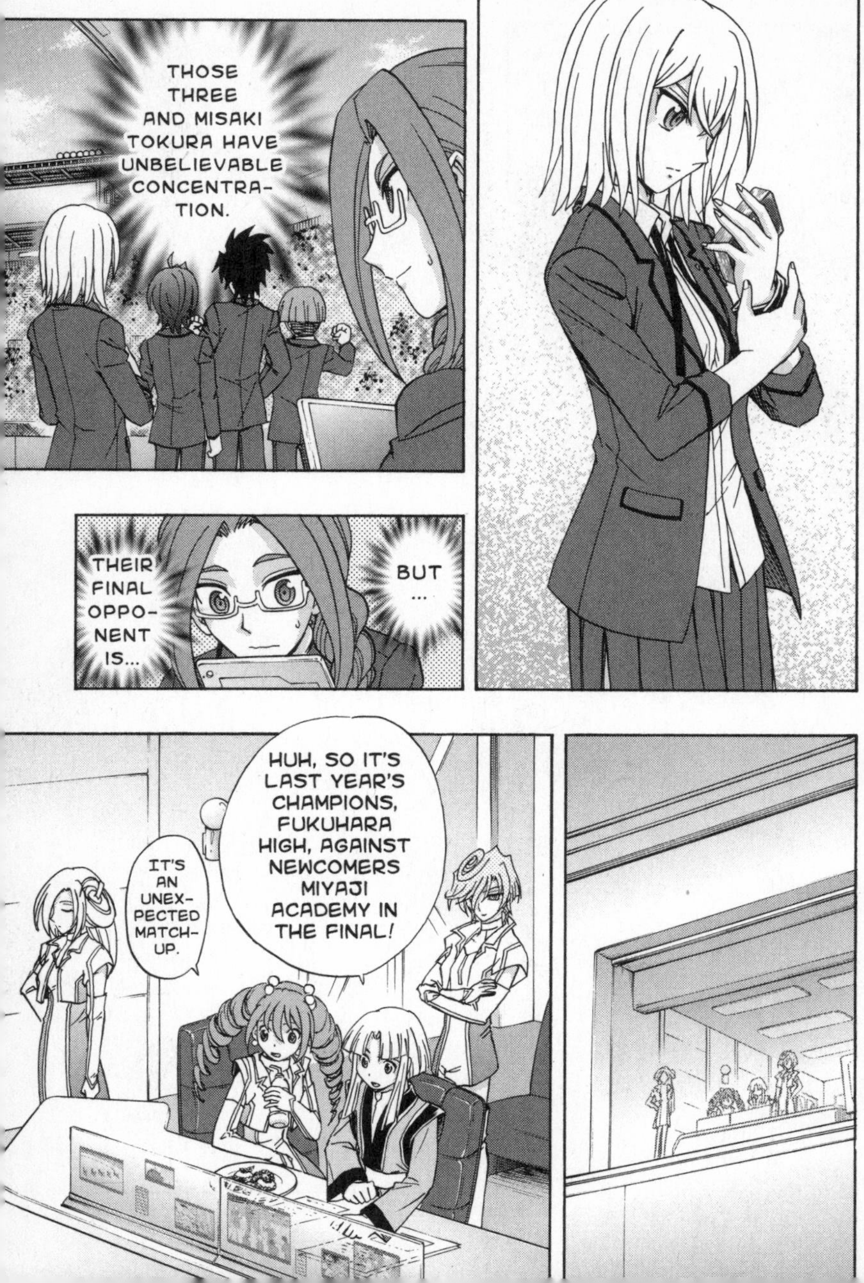
THOSE THREE AND MISAKI TOKURA HAVE UNBELIEVABLE CONCENTRA-TION.
BUT ...
THEIR FINAL OPPO-NENT IS...
HUH, SO IT'S LAST YEAR'S CHAMPIONS, FUKUHARA HIGH, AGAINST NEWCOMERS MIYAJI ACADEMY IN THE FINAL!
IT'S AN UNEX-PECTED MATCH-UP.

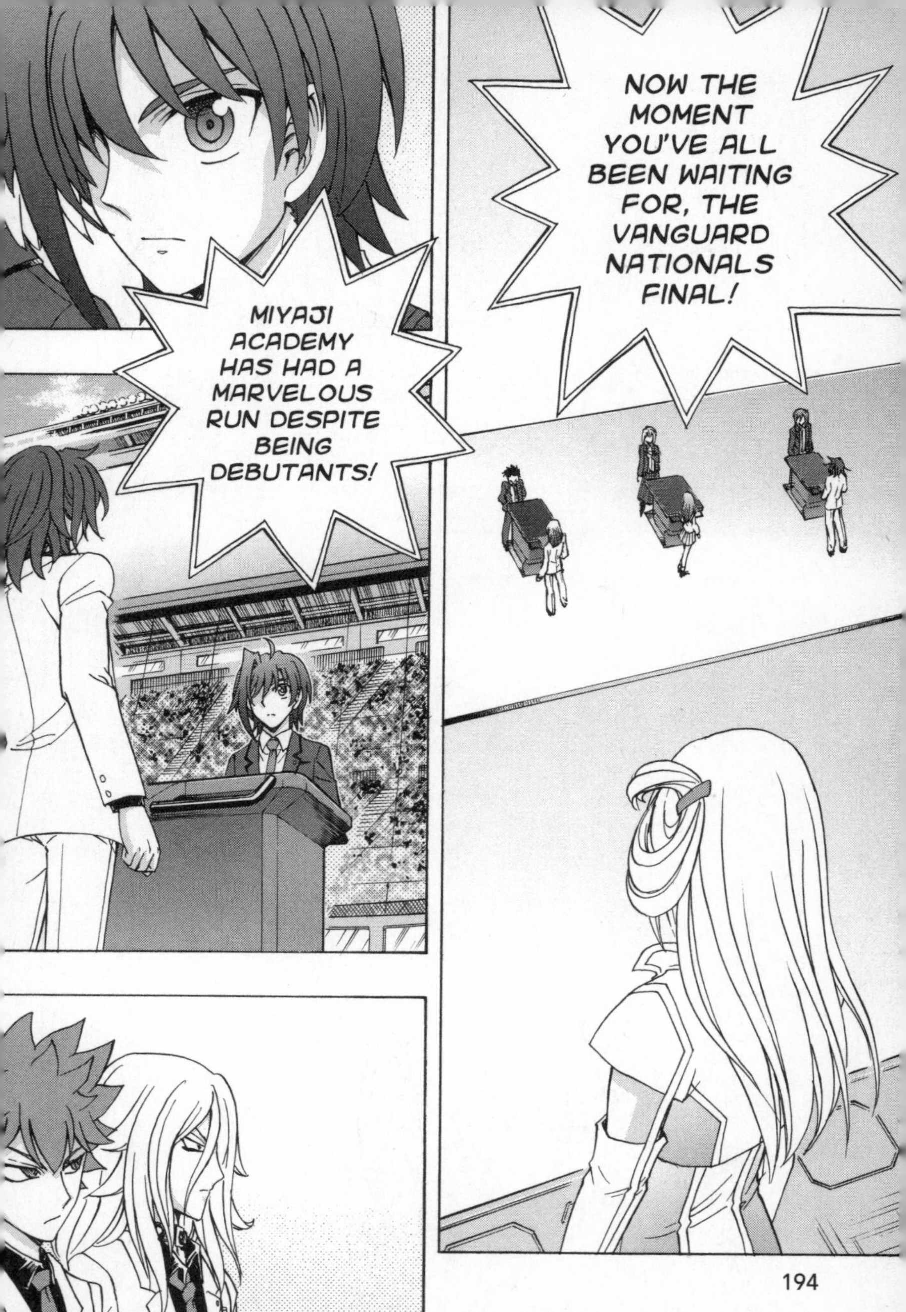
NOW THE MOMENT YOU'VE ALL BEEN WAITING FOR, THE VANGUARD NATIONALS FINAL!
MIYAJI ACADEMY HAS HAD A MARVELOUS RUN DESPITE BEING DEBUTANTS!

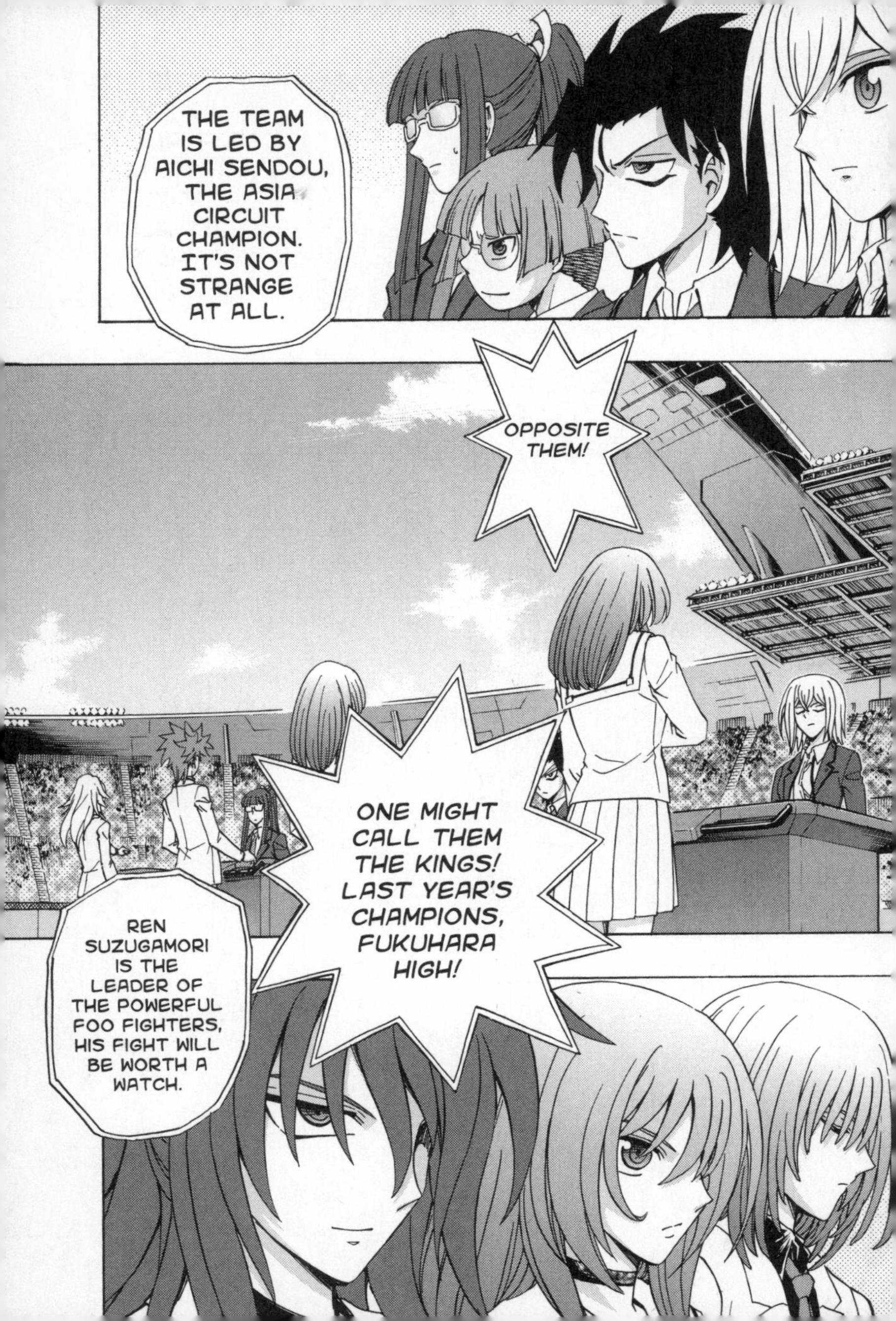
THE TEAM IS LED BY AICHI SENDOU, THE ASIA CIRCUIT CHAMPION. IT'S NOT STRANGE AT ALL.
OPPOSITE THEM!
ONE MIGHT CALL THEM THE KINGS! LAST YEAR'S CHAMPIONS, FUKUHARA HIGH!
REN SUZUGAMORI IS THE LEADER OF THE POWERFUL FOO FIGHTERS, HIS FIGHT WILL BE WORTH A WATCH.

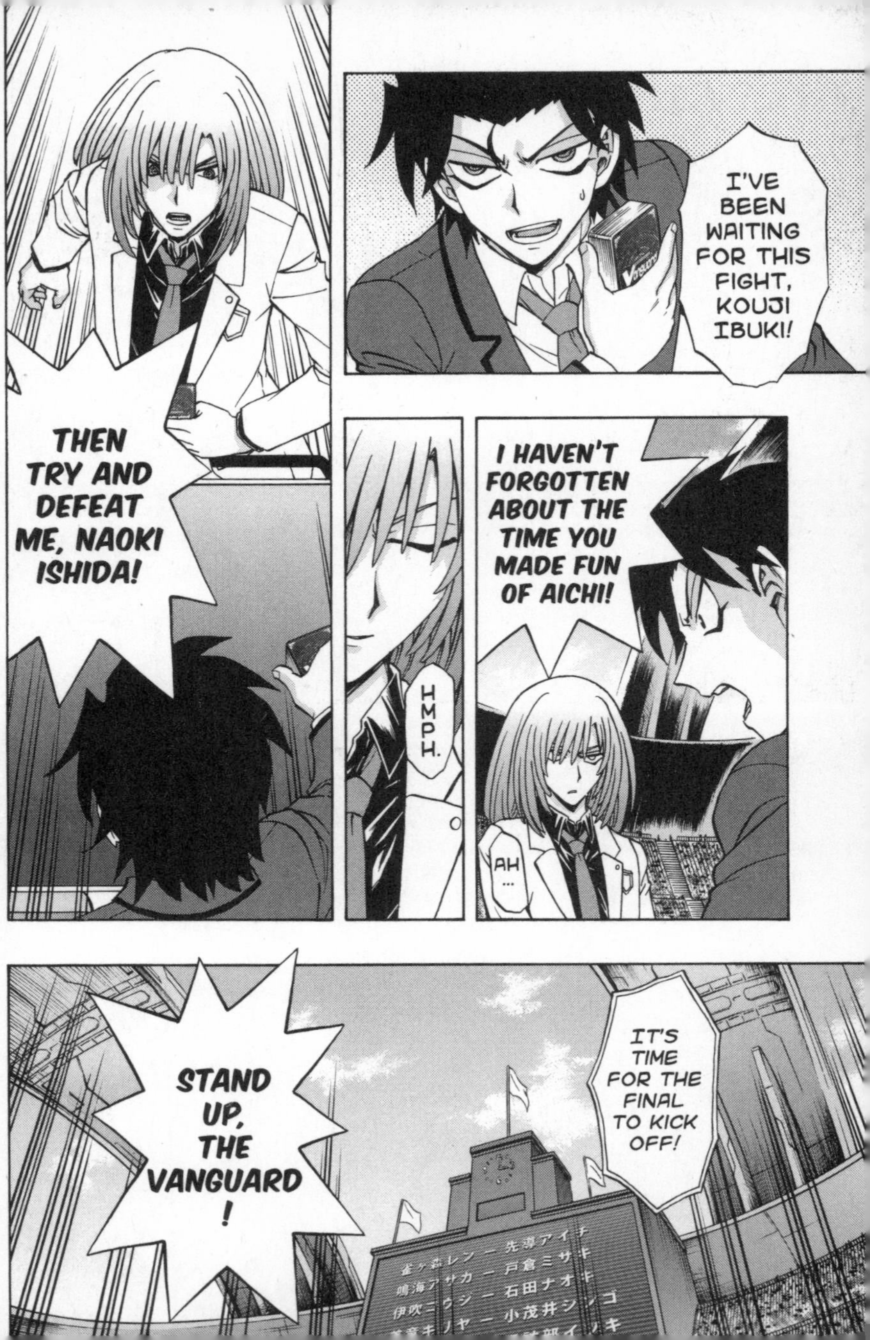
I'VE BEEN WAITING FOR THIS FIGHT, KOUJI IBUKI!
I HAVEN'T FORGOTTEN ABOUT THE TIME YOU MADE FUN OF AICHI!
AH...
HMPH.
THEN TRY AND DEFEAT ME, NAOKI ISHIDA!
IT'S TIME FOR THE FINAL TO KICK OFF!
STAND UP, THE VANGUARD!
雀ヶ森レン ー 先導アイチ
鳴海アサカ ー 戸倉ミサキ
伊吹コウジ ー 石田ナオキ

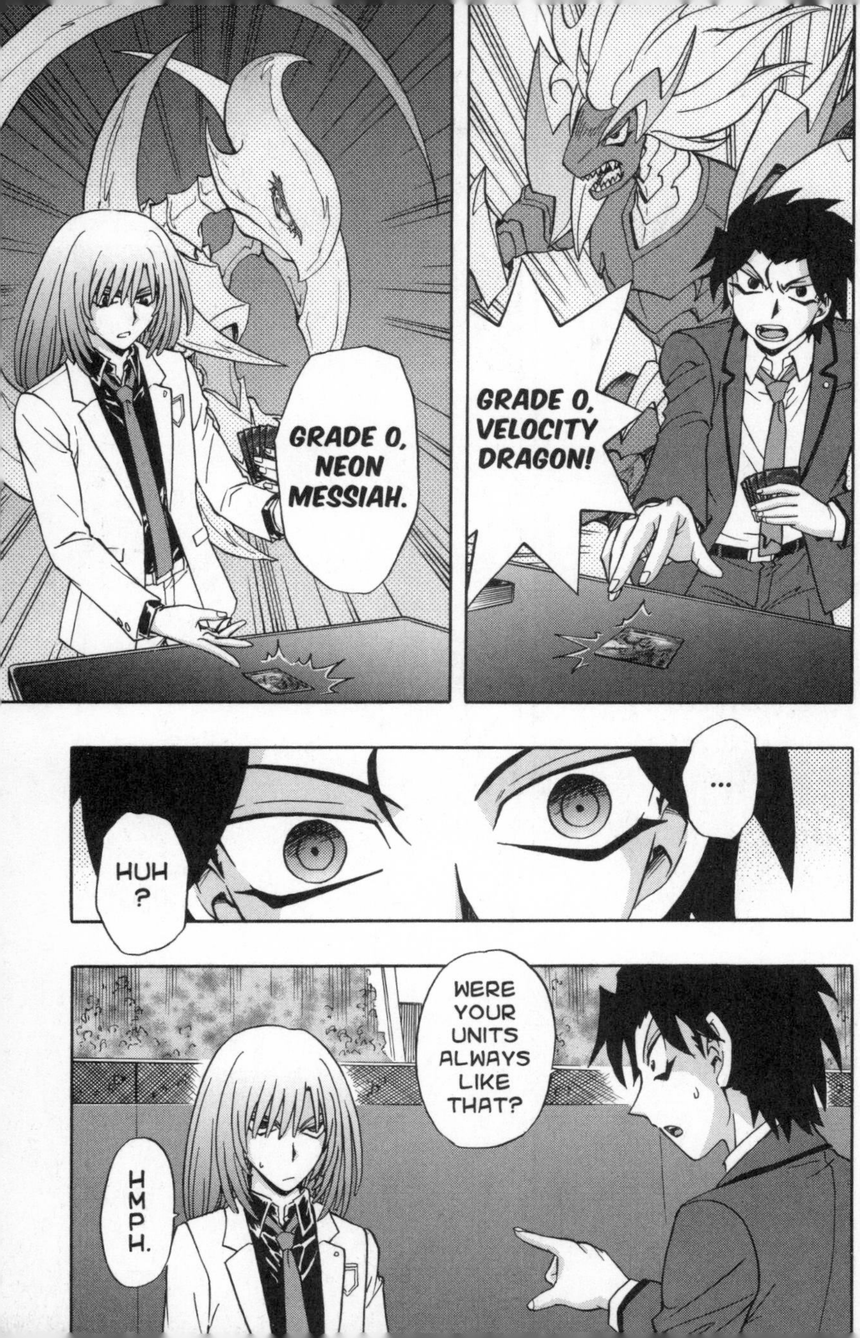
GRADE 0, VELOCITY DRAGON!
GRADE 0, NEON MESSIAH.
...
HUH?
WERE YOUR UNITS ALWAYS LIKE THAT?
HMPH.

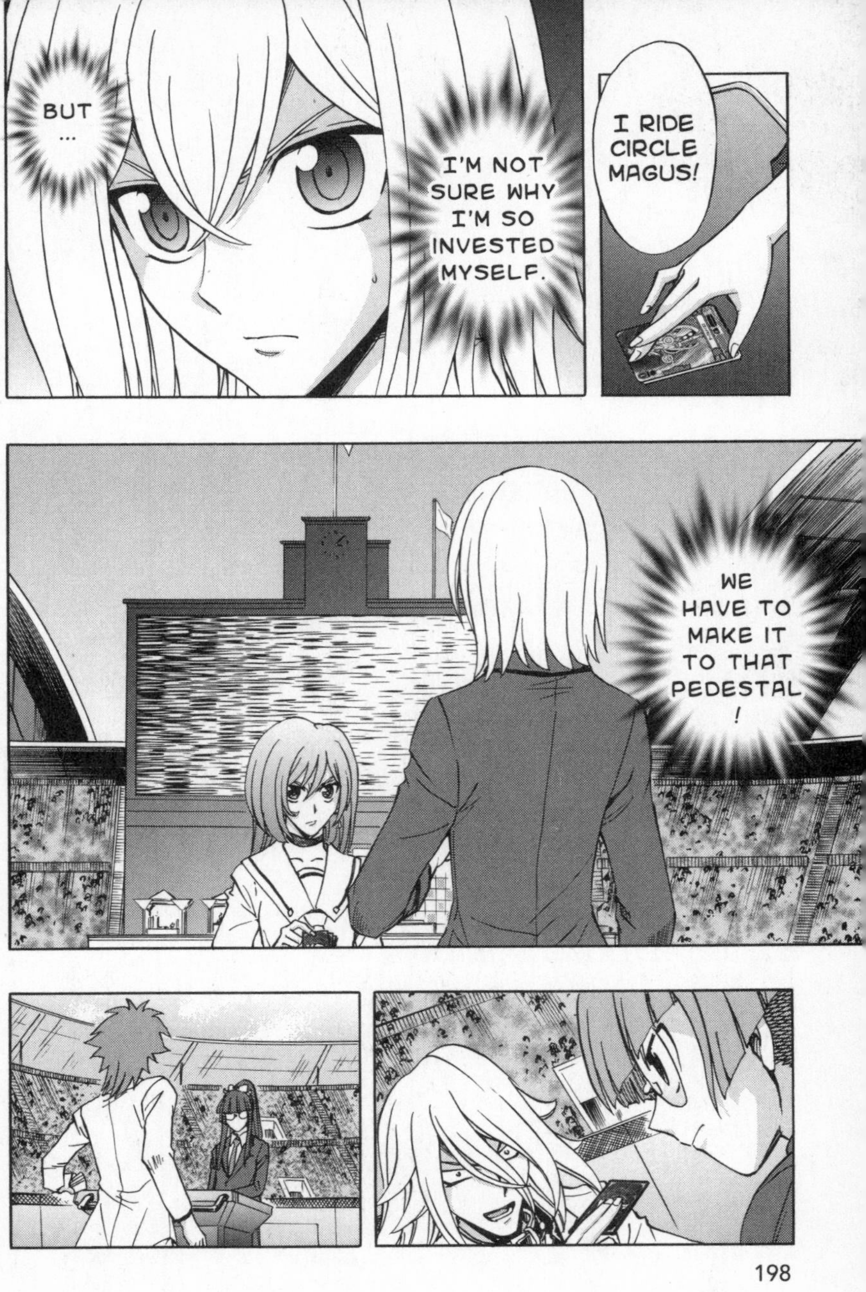
I RIDE CIRCLE MAGUS!
I'M NOT SURE WHY I'M SO INVESTED MYSELF.
BUT ...
WE HAVE TO MAKE IT TO THAT PEDESTAL!

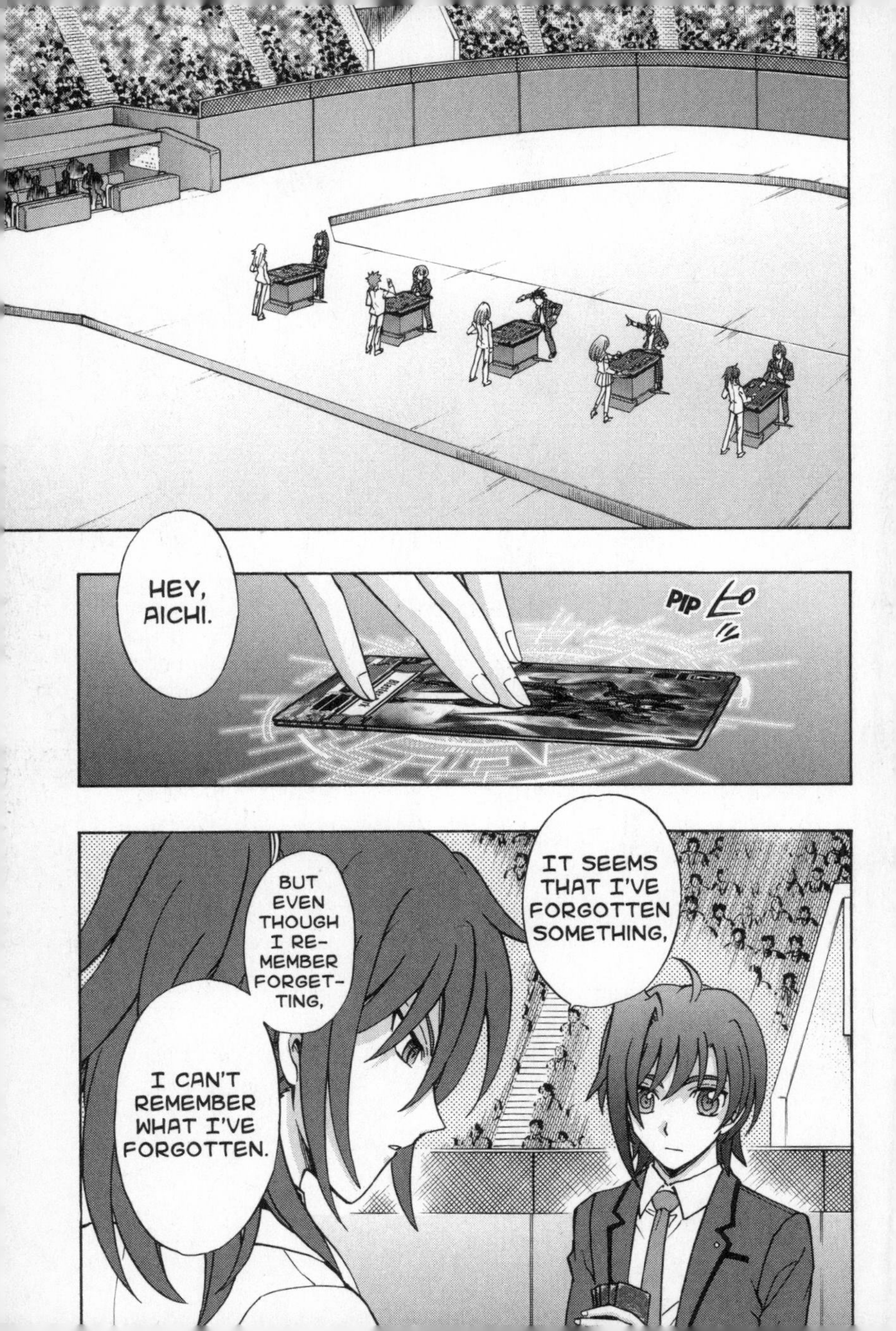
PIP
HEY, AICHI.
IT SEEMS THAT I'VE FORGOTTEN SOMETHING,
BUT EVEN THOUGH I RE-MEMBER FORGET-TING,
I CAN'T REMEMBER WHAT I'VE FORGOTTEN.

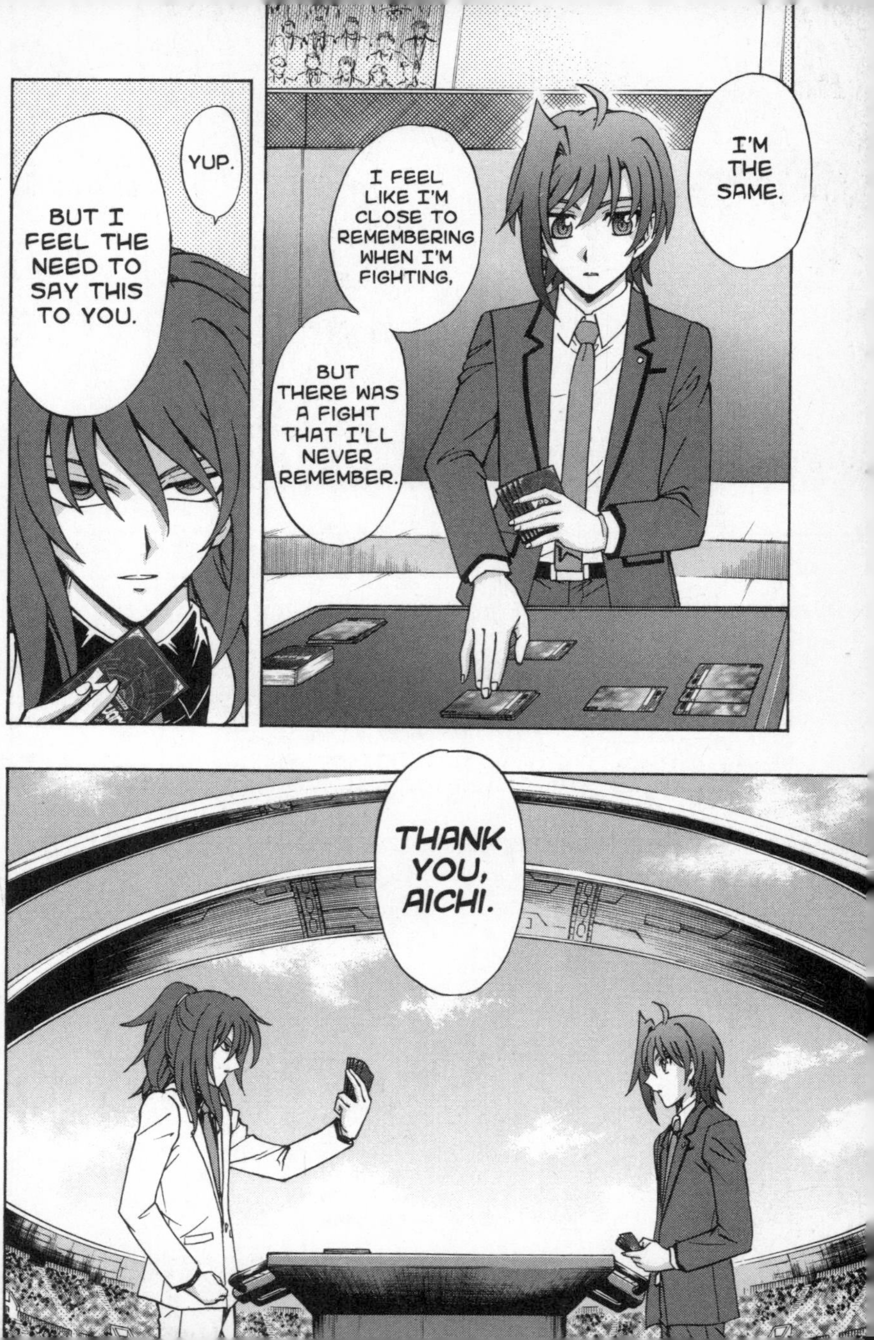
I'M THE SAME.
I FEEL LIKE I'M CLOSE TO REMEMBERING WHEN I'M FIGHTING,
BUT THERE WAS A FIGHT THAT I'LL NEVER REMEMBER.
YUP.
BUT I FEEL THE NEED TO SAY THIS TO YOU.
THANK YOU, AICHI.

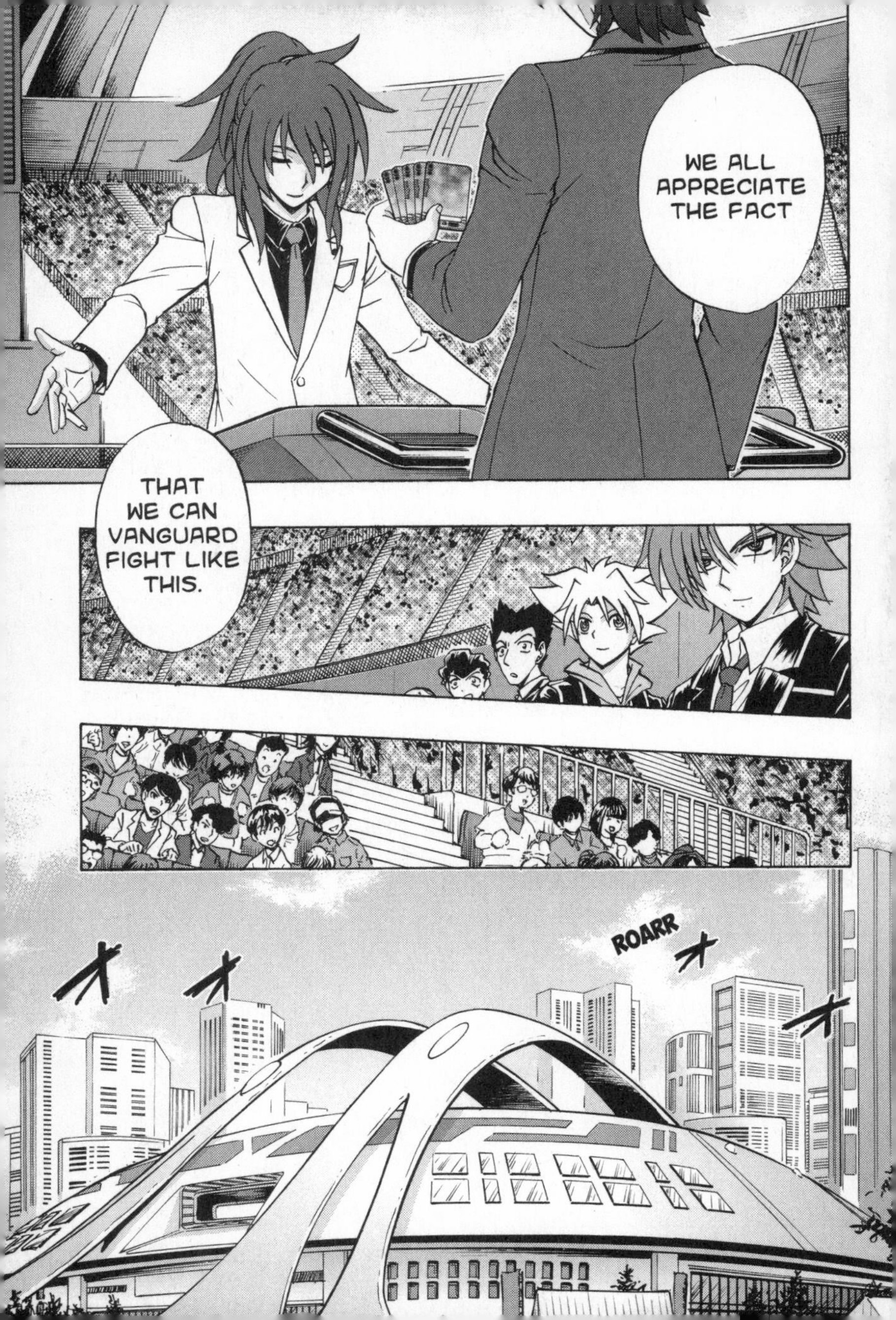
WE ALL APPRECIATE THE FACT
THAT WE CAN VANGUARD FIGHT LIKE THIS.
ROARR

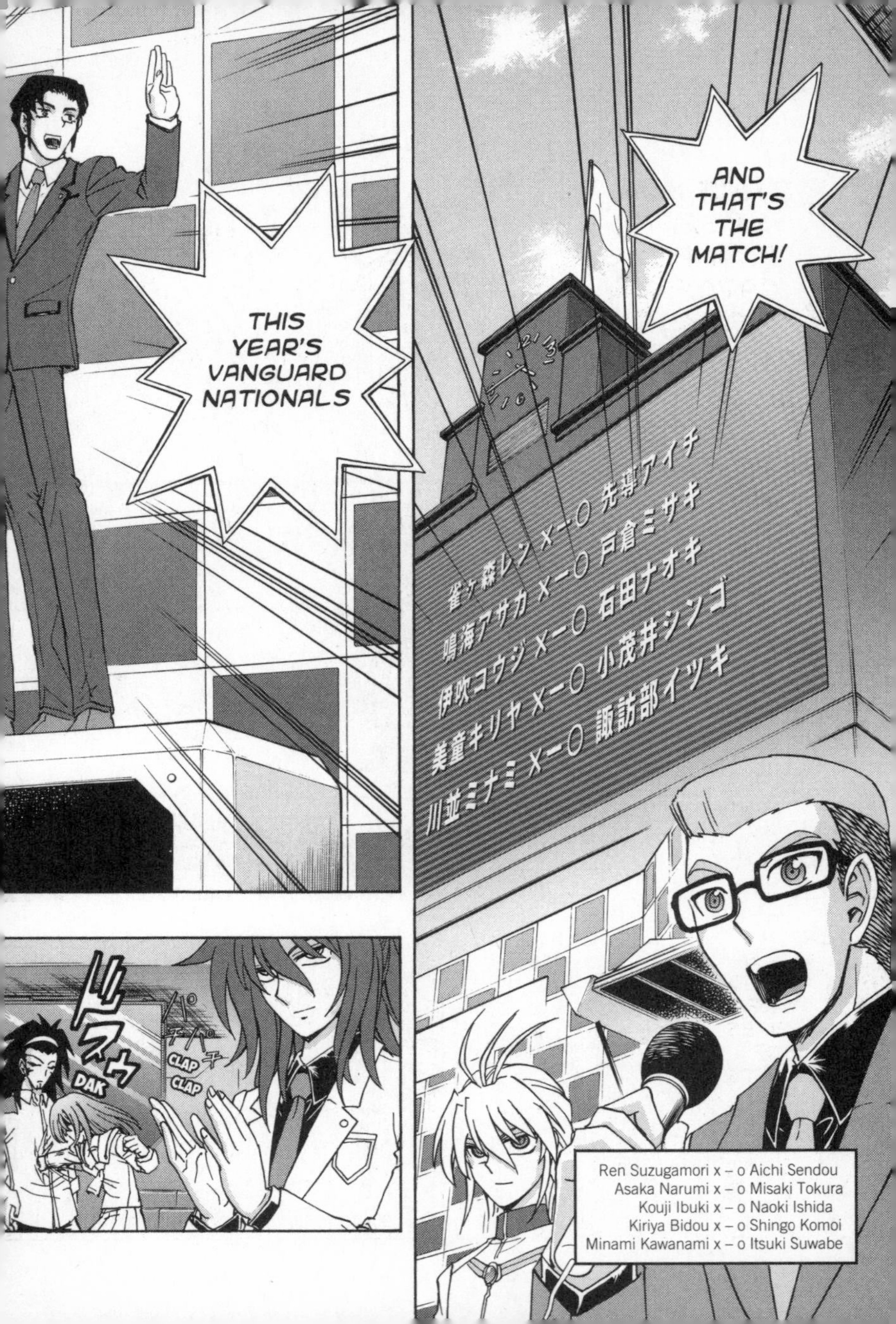
AND THAT'S THE MATCH!
雀ヶ森レン ×−○ 先導アイチ
鳴海アサカ ×−○ 戸倉ミサキ
伊吹コウジ ×−○ 石田ナオキ
美童キリヤ ×−○ 小茂井シンゴ
川並ミナミ ×−○ 諏訪部イツキ
Ren Suzugamori x – o Aichi Sendou
Asaka Narumi x – o Misaki Tokura
Kouji Ibuki x – o Naoki Ishida
Kiriya Bidou x – o Shingo Komoi
Minami Kawanami x – o Itsuki Suwabe
THIS YEAR'S VANGUARD NATIONALS
DAK
CLAP
CLAP

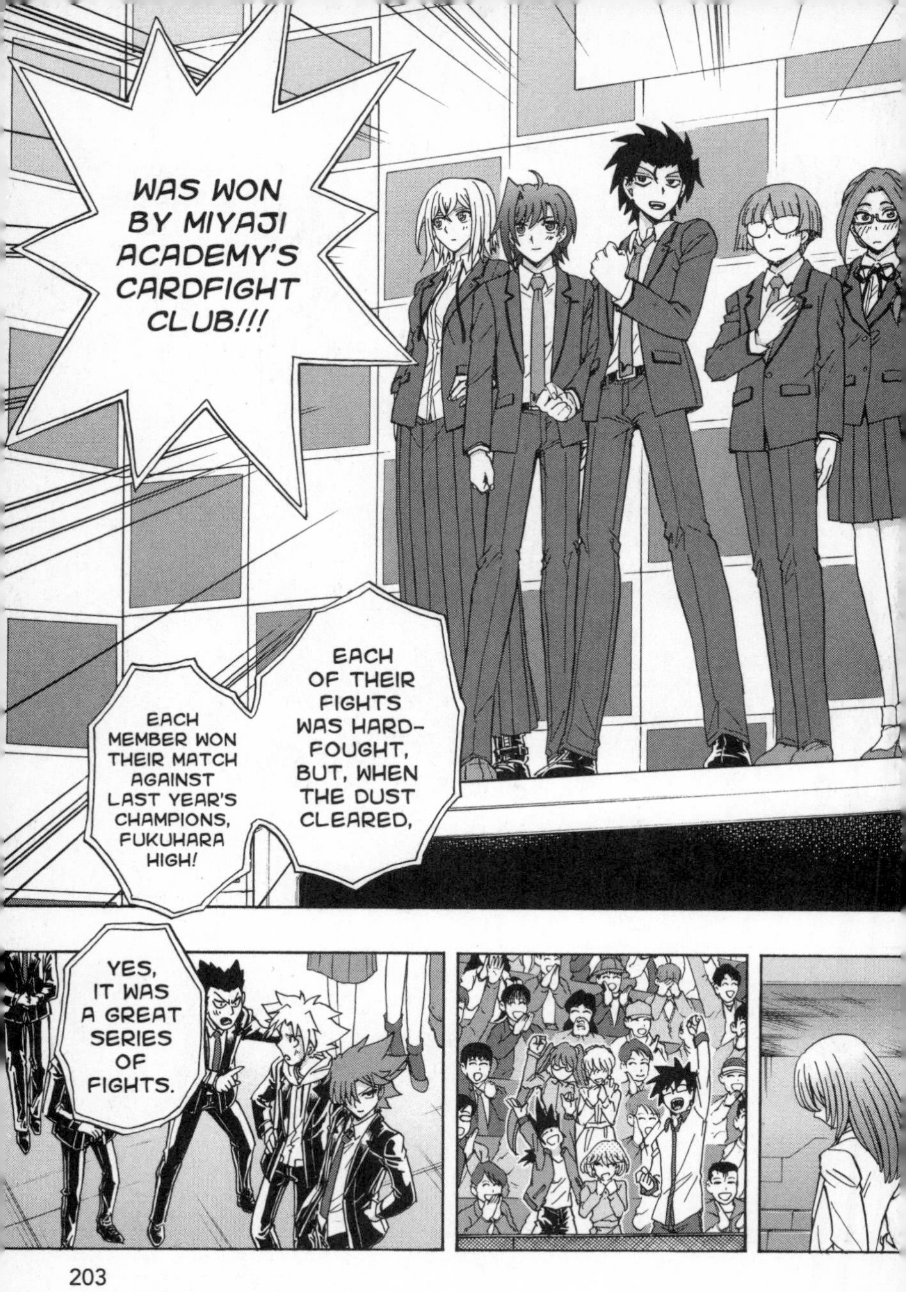
WAS WON BY MIYAJI ACADEMY'S CARDFIGHT CLUB!!!
EACH OF THEIR FIGHTS WAS HARD-FOUGHT, BUT, WHEN THE DUST CLEARED,
EACH MEMBER WON THEIR MATCH AGAINST LAST YEAR'S CHAMPIONS, FUKUHARA HIGH!
YES, IT WAS A GREAT SERIES OF FIGHTS.

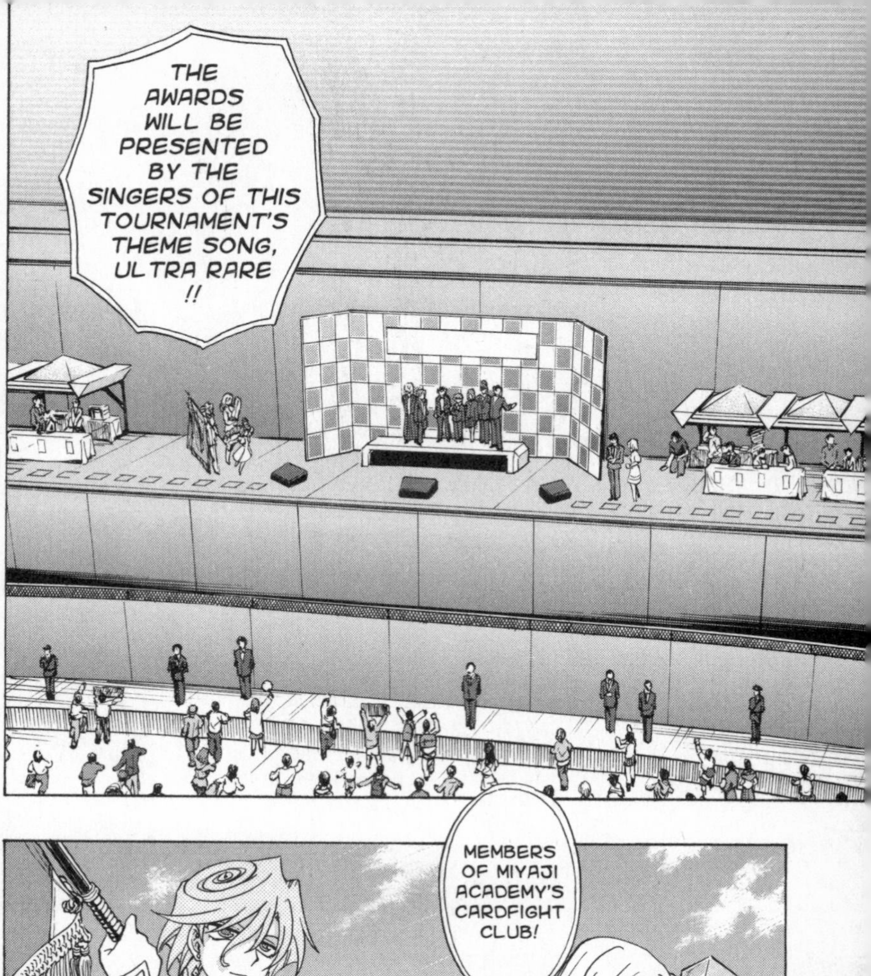
THE AWARDS WILL BE PRESENTED BY THE SINGERS OF THIS TOURNAMENT'S THEME SONG, ULTRA RARE !!
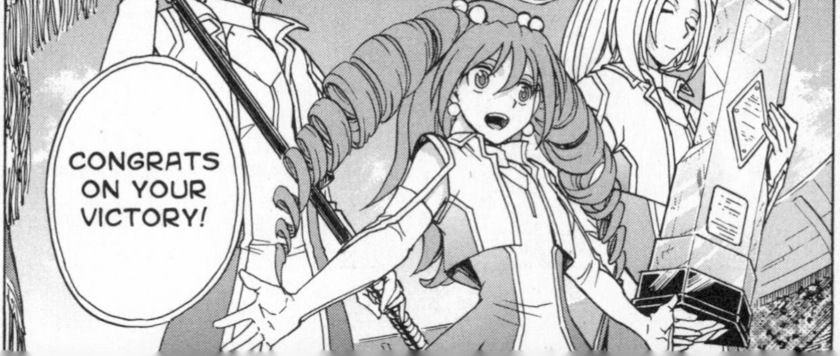
MEMBERS OF MIYAJI ACADEMY'S CARDFIGHT CLUB!
CONGRATS ON YOUR VICTORY!

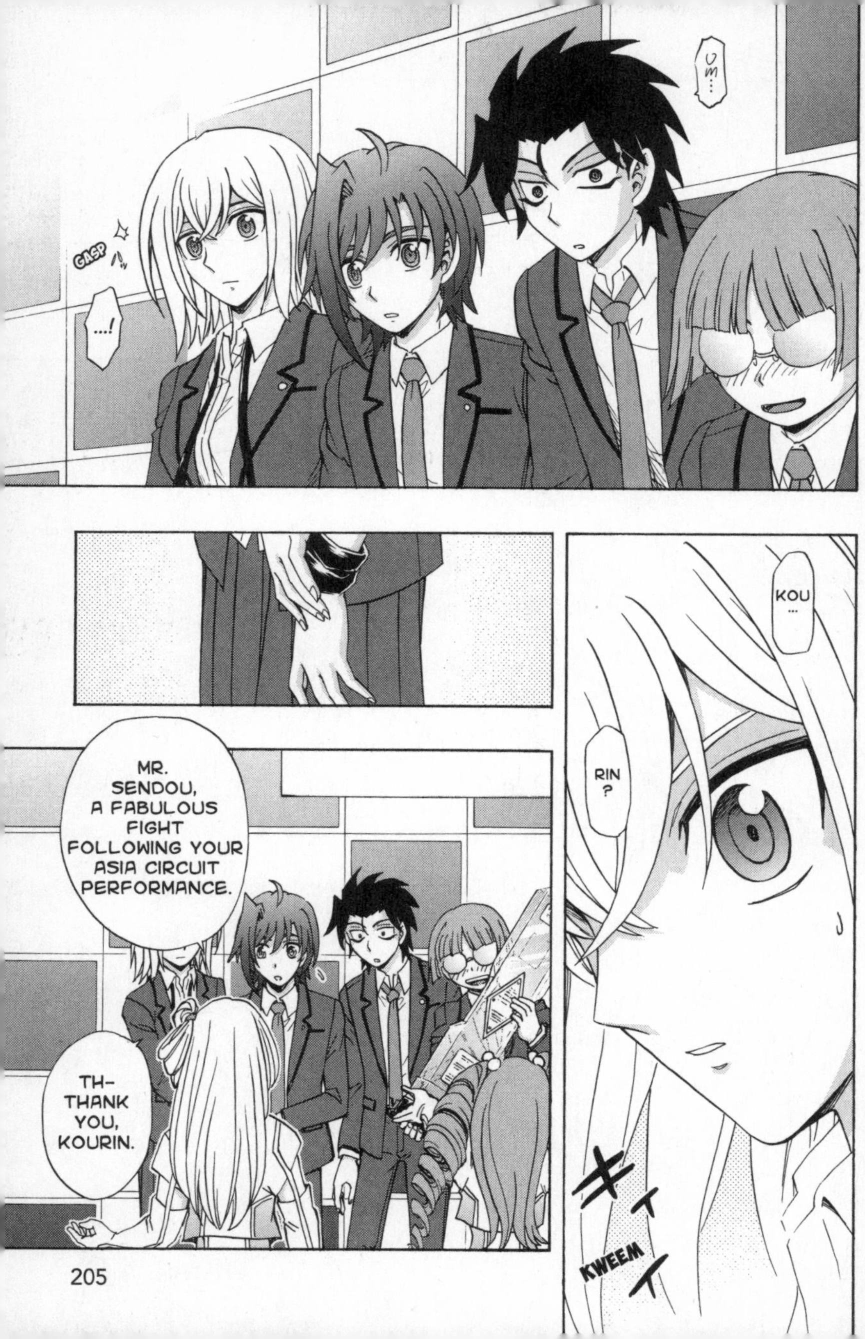
UM...
GASP
...!
KOU...
RIN?
KWEEM
MR. SENDOU, A FABULOUS FIGHT FOLLOWING YOUR ASIA CIRCUIT PERFORMANCE.
TH-THANK YOU, KOURIN.

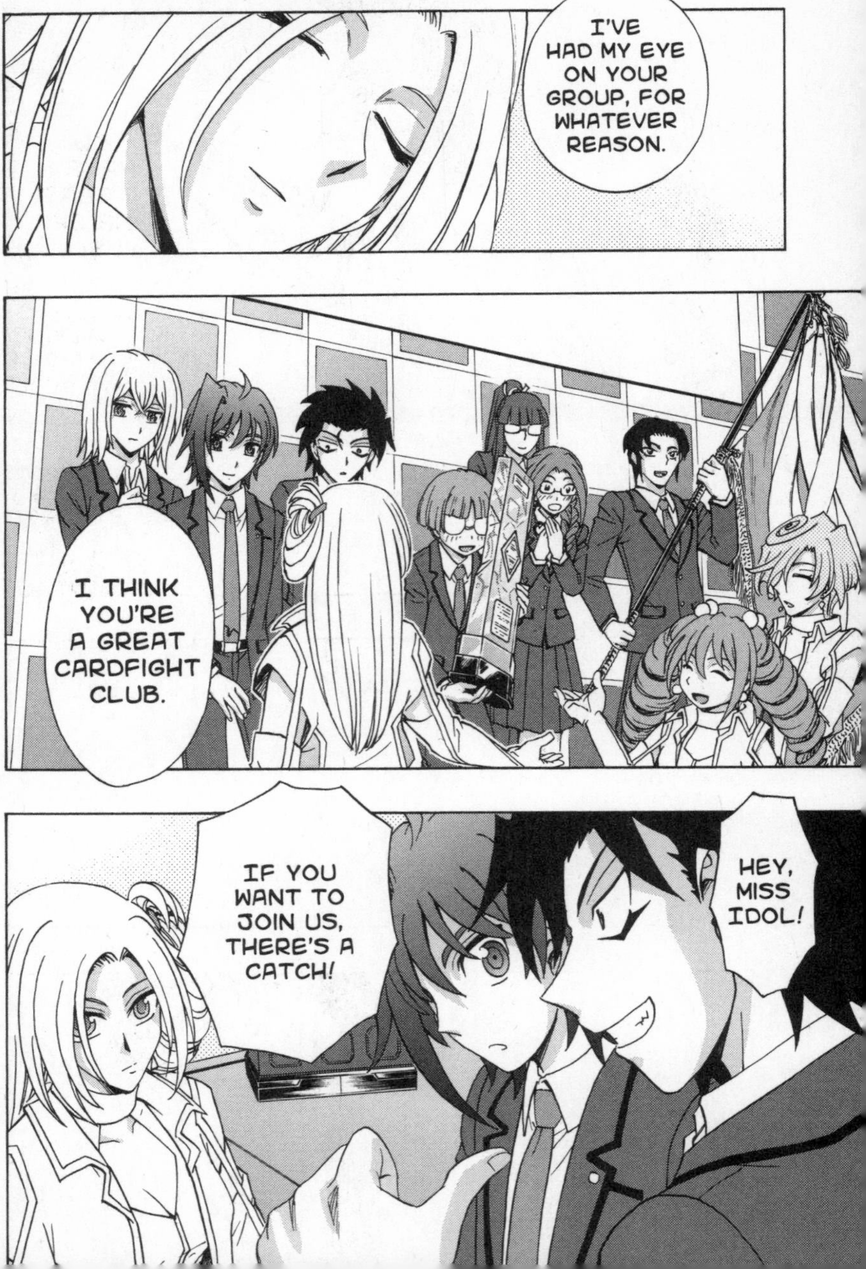
I'VE HAD MY EYE ON YOUR GROUP, FOR WHATEVER REASON.
I THINK YOU'RE A GREAT CARDFIGHT CLUB.
HEY, MISS IDOL!
IF YOU WANT TO JOIN US, THERE'S A CATCH!

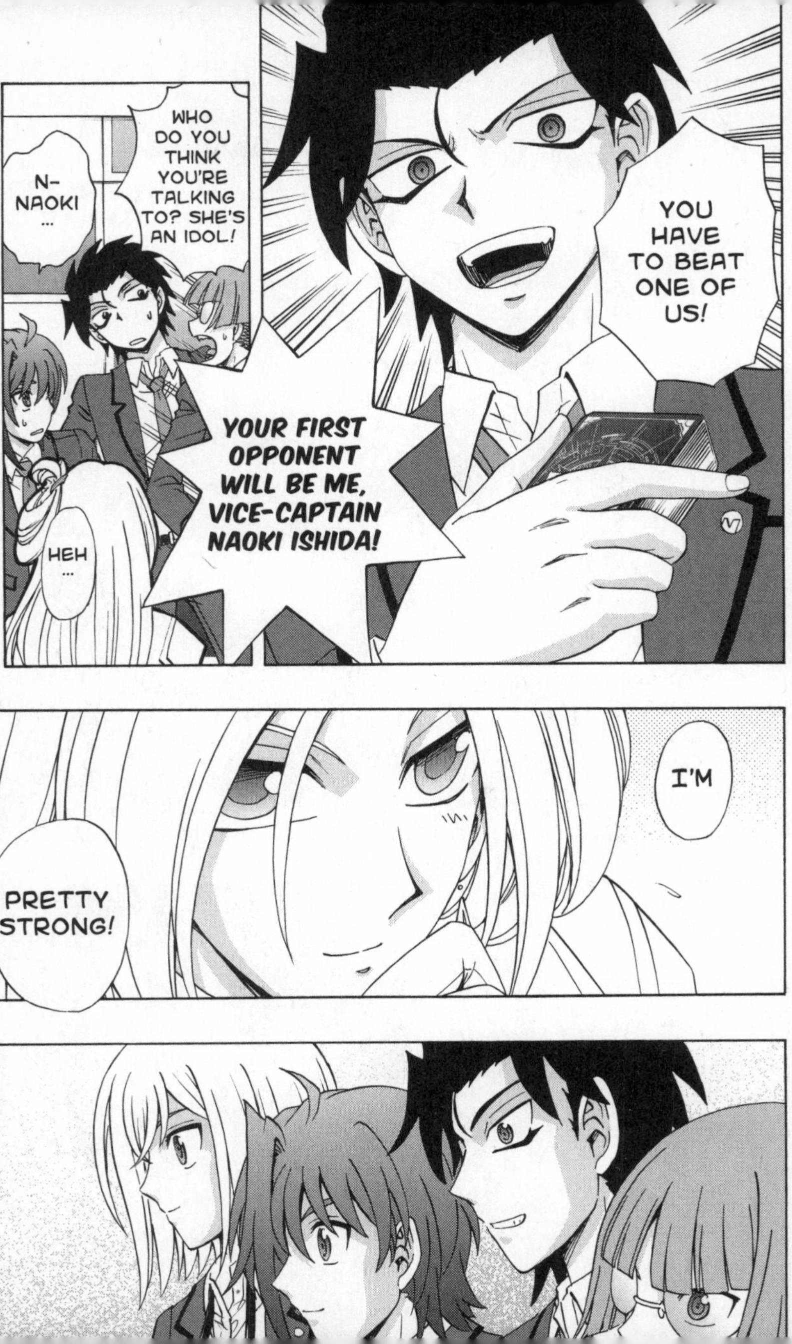
YOU HAVE TO BEAT ONE OF US!
YOUR FIRST OPPONENT WILL BE ME, VICE-CAPTAIN NAOKI ISHIDA!
WHO DO YOU THINK YOU'RE TALKING TO? SHE'S AN IDOL!
N-NAOKI ...
HEH ...
I'M
PRETTY STRONG!

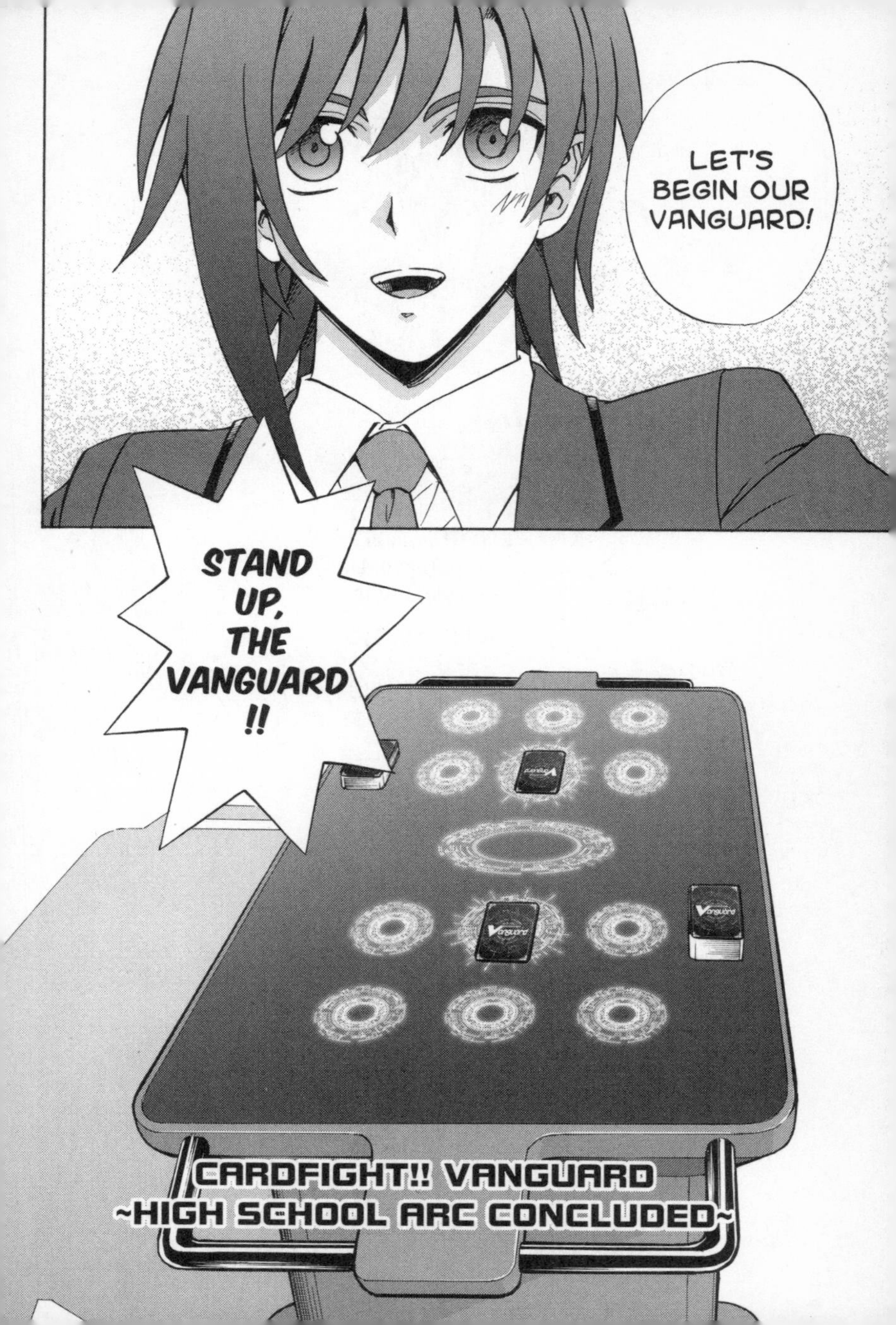
LET'S BEGIN OUR VANGUARD!
STAND UP, THE VANGUARD!!
CARDFIGHT!! VANGUARD
~HIGH SCHOOL ARC CONCLUDED~

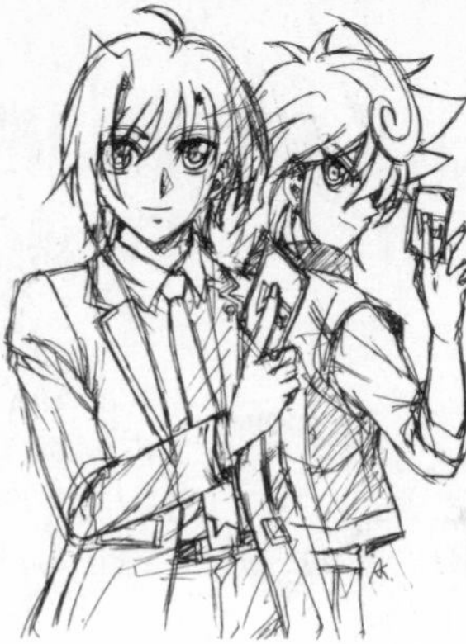

CARDFIGHT!! VANGUARD VOL. 12
ORIGINAL DESIGNS OF THE FEATURED UNITS

CHAPTER 67
Dark Vanquishing Dragon, Leadbronner /
高橋智也 (Tomoya Takahashi, Original Unit Contest 2015)

CHAPTER 69
Wingal / トムス・エンタテインメント (TMS Entertainment)
Bringer of Good Luck, Epona / 安達洋介 (Yousuke Adachi)
Alabaster Owl / パトリシア (Patricia)

CHAPTER 70
Yggdrasil Maiden, Elaine / トムス・エンタテインメント (TMS Entertainment)
Little Sage, Marron / 山崎奈苗 (Nanae Yamazaki)
Knight of Silence, Gallatin / トムス・エンタテインメント (TMS Entertainment)

CHAPTER 71
Flash Shield, Iseult / タイキ (Taiki)
Arc Saver Dragon / コシミズマコト (Makoto Koshimizu)

CHAPTER 72
Weapons Dealer, Govannon / Hirokorin

CHAPTER 73
Harmonics Messiah / 百瀬寿 (Hisashi Momose)

CHAPTER 75
Neon Messiah / 百瀬寿 (Hisashi Momose)

All Other Units / 伊藤彰 (Akira Itou)

Mobile Suit GUNDAM WING
Endless Waltz
Glory of the Losers

Story: Katsuyuki Sumizawa
Art: Tomofumi Ogasawara
Original Concept: Hajime Yatate and Yoshiyuki Tomino

One of the biggest anime properties of all time returns with the release of *Mobile Suit GUNDAM WING*. Following the actions of five fighters and their mobile suits, *GUNDAM WING* is a heavily political, dramatic action work that is centered around a war between Earth and its surrounding colonies in space.

In the year A.C. (After Colony) 195, mankind had flown its nest, the Earth, to search for new hope while living in space colonies. However, the United Earth Sphere Alliance has used its military might under the guise of "justice and peace" to seize control of some colonies, and those colonies have lost their autonomy and have been forced into silence. But the seeds of resistance have not been entirely crushed. "Operation Meteor" is about to take flight...

Volumes 1-7 On Sale Now!

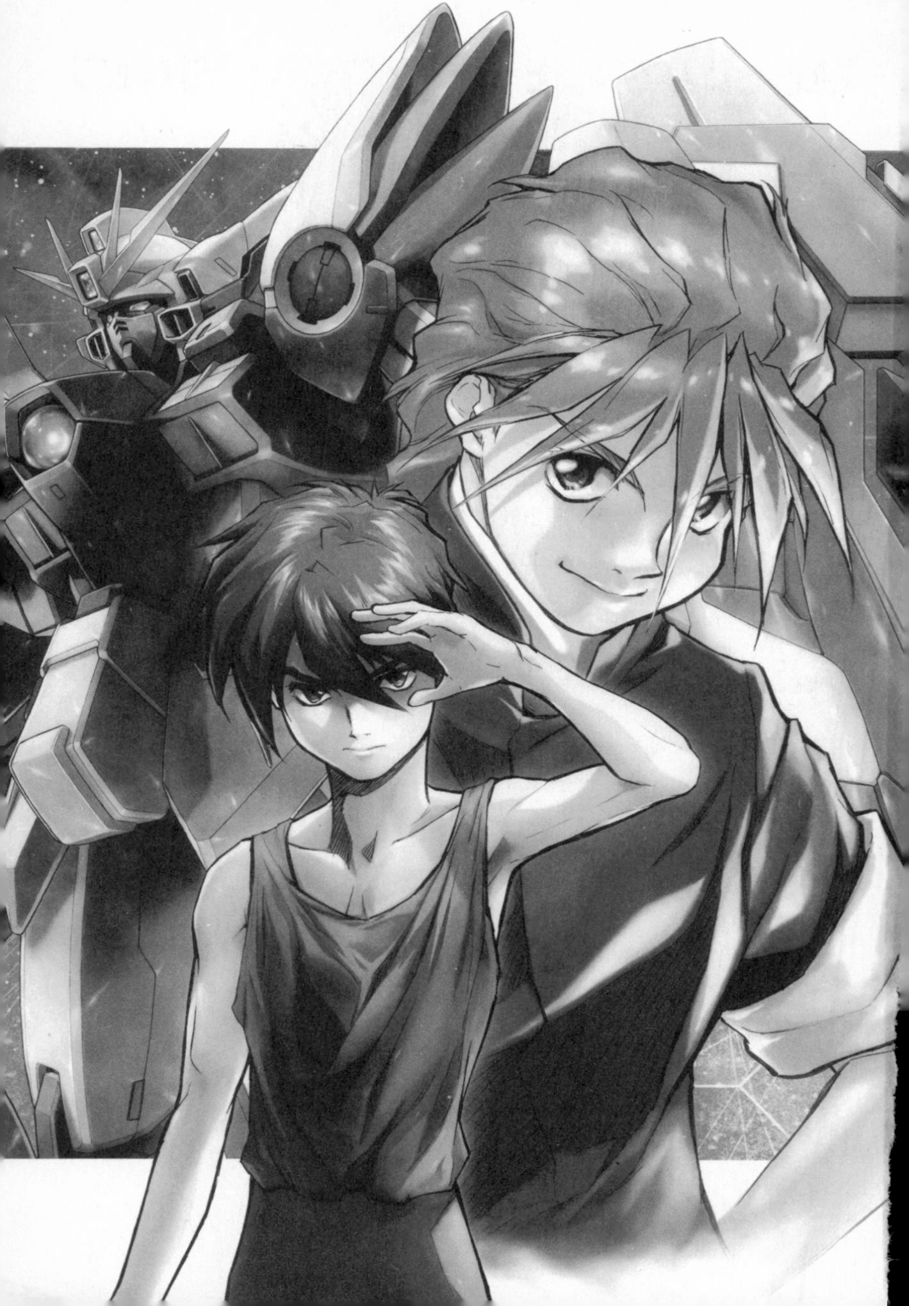

CARDFIGHT! VANGUARD
VOLUME 12

Translation: Yota Okutani
Production: Grace Lu
         Anthony Quintessenza

Copyright © Akira ITOU 2017
         © bushiroad All Rights Reserved.
First published in Japan in 2017 by KADOKAWA CORPORATION, Tokyo.
English translation rights arranged with KADOKAWA CORPORATION, Tokyo
through TUTTLE-MORI AGENCY, INC., Tokyo.
English language version produced by Vertical, Inc.

Translation provided by Vertical, Inc., 2018
Published by Vertical, Inc., New York

Originally published in Japanese as *Kaadofaito!! Vangaado 12* by KADOKAWA
CORPORATION
Kaadofaito!! Vangaado first serialized in *Young Ace*, 2011-2017

This is a work of fiction.

ISBN: 978-1-947194-08-3

Manufactured in Canada

First Edition

Vertical, Inc.
451 Park Avenue South
7th Floor
New York, NY 10016
www.vertical-inc.com